D0931365

THE GOLDEN AGE OF SPAIN

THE HISTORY OF SPAIN
Edited by John Parry and Hugh Thomas

THE GOLDEN
AGE OF SPAIN
1516-1659

Antonio Domínguez Ortiz

TRANSLATED BY JAMES CASEY

WEIDENFELD and NICOLSON
5 WINSLEY STREET LONDON WI

ISBN 0 297 00405 0

Printed in Great Britain by
Cox & Wyman Limited
London, Fakenham and Reading

CONTENTS

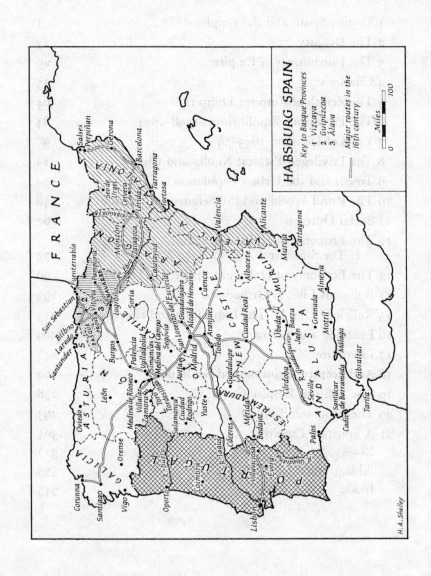

HABSBURG SPAIN

Key to Basque Provinces
1 Vizcaya
2 Guipúzcoa
3 Álava

Major routes in the
16th century

Miles
0   100

H. A. Shelley

CASTILE, SPAIN
AND THE EMPIRE

The first difficulty facing any historian of Habsburg Spain is the problem of defining what he means by 'Spain'. Nowadays the term has a precise political significance, but in those days it was a rather vague concept consecrated by popular usage while having no foundation in law. Administration and internal politics varied from one to another of the kingdoms comprising the monarchy of the Catholic Kings, a variety which was even more characteristic of the complex empire of Charles v. On the other hand there was unity of action in foreign policy. The notion of Spain, therefore, while too broad to be applied to Castile alone, is too narrow for the monarchy of the Habsburgs whose horizons stretched far beyond it. The international politics of those monarchs would in no way be characterized as Spanish today. To speak of a history of Spain in this period is to be guilty of an anachronism. The same problem of course confronts a historian of Italy, Belgium, Germany or the United Kingdom.

People then associated Spain with the territory comprised in the Roman *Hispania*; that is, the Iberian peninsula. It was a geographical term, reinforced by a degree of ethnic and cultural identity. In this sense not only Castilians, Aragonese, Catalans and Navarrese called themselves Spaniards, but the Portuguese as well,[1] until the growing political significance of the name Spain and its identification with Castile gradually came to exclude them and mean something different from Portugal. As a state structure Spain did not exist until the eighteenth century. Official terminology used the term only sparingly and it echoes popular usage. The Habsburgs never called themselves kings of Spain, but kings of Castile, Aragon, Navarre, Sicily, etc. Only towards the end of the seventeenth century did there emerge the formula 'Catholic King of the Spains, of the two Sicilies,

Jerusalem, the Indies . . .', partly in order to shorten the long and tedious list of their titles, but also because the popular, modern notion of Spain was making its way into the ossified chancellery formulas, although it still had not become a reality in law. Spain existed in the mind of classicists; artists depicted it as an armed matron, with a crown on her head; it also existed in the consciousness of the peoples of the peninsula who even before they were ruled by the same sovereign felt a sense of belonging and of distinctness from the rest of Europe; in addition, the terms 'Spain' and 'Spaniards' were popularized by foreigners who were not well informed about the autonomous regimes of its various kingdoms, and saw only that they presented a common front abroad under a common authority.

But despite these elements of unity Spaniards were not ready to abandon their differences at home, nor did the government, respectful of tradition, think of abolishing them. The union brought about by the Catholic Kings was a simple, personal union, which left the individuality of the old kingdoms untouched. The only institution which extended its jurisdiction over the whole present-day territory of Spain was the Supreme Tribunal of the Holy Inquisition. The rest were separate: the three kingdoms of the Crown of Aragon each had its Cortes separate from those of Castile and Navarre and there were also separate currency and tax systems. A tariff barrier intervened between Castile and her neighbours. Castilians were legally foreigners in Aragon and Aragonese in Castile, and were therefore incapable of holding civil or ecclesiastical office.

Within the huge conglomerate formed by the monarchy of the Habsburgs Castile had from the legal point of view no special position. If she came by it later in practice this was because she pulled more weight and identified herself more completely with the dynasty than the other kingdoms. Both these facts are connected. The Castilians at first had no special leanings towards the Habsburgs; on the contrary, they were the first to agitate against incorporation in the universal monarchy of Charles v, in which they sensed a deadly threat to their traditional way of life and their autonomous political character. The failure of the *Comuneros* put an end to this attempt at resistance and from then on the crown had no more loyal and obedient province in its empire than Castile. It was also the wealthiest and the most populous until the internal disasters of depopulation and economic decline which marked the end of the sixteenth century. For both reasons the kings fixed their residence in Castile and became more and more castilianized. Philip II knew that his authority would not have been so easily accepted in Lisbon, Barcelona, Naples or Brussels as it was in Madrid; there was in the choice of Madrid as capital an element of calculation, later mingled with habit and affection.

From the time of Philip II the kings not only fixed their residence in Madrid but rarely left it, since unlike Charles v they had no great love for travel. It has been said that this growing remoteness of the king diminished the loyalty of the non-Castilian provinces; the Catalan nobles in particular, we are told, were annoyed at not getting the lucrative posts which attendance at court brought with it. There is some truth in this, but after all Zaragoza and Barcelona were not more distant from Madrid than Seville or Corunna. There was no prejudice at court against non-Castilians and some of them did get high office.

The ordinary people had less reason to complain of the absence of the king, since his presence brought more hardship than gain: 'Kings are all right, out of sight' (*Reyes tengamos y no los veamos*), so ran a Castilian proverb. Castile alone bore the burden of a sumptuous court and of the general apparatus of the monarchy. Distant lands which never saw their sovereign, like Sardinia, Franche Comté, and the Indies, were completely and utterly loyal: distance hid from them the failings of the king and allowed them to lay all the blame on his ministers. Pressure from the centre was not so noticeable in the more remote areas; local franchises maintained themselves better, as did the self-government of their own oligarchies. Castile by contrast was exploited to the limits of her possibilities and her free institutions were done away with, or at least systematically undermined. If some individual courtiers grew rich, the mass of the population suffered rather than benefited by the presence of its kings. What Castile gained from royal favouritism was a wealth of symbolic and artistic values: fine buildings, rich archives, the Prado museum, the costly honour of the leading part in world history in an era of profound change.

In its narrowest sense Castile includes merely the inland provinces of Spain, the Meseta, divided into Old and New

Castile by the formations of the central mountain chain. In terms of jurisdiction Castile covered most of the peninsula; the people of Galicia, Andalusia, Extremadura, Asturias, and Murcia also formed part of Castile, being subject to the same laws and tribunals and represented in the same Cortes or parliament. True, it included some 'kingdoms', as they were called – Toledo, Seville, Granada, Córdoba, Jaén, León, Murcia, and Galicia. But these kingdoms were memories of the past; the only administrative relic was that their capitals sent two deputies to the Cortes. Only the Basque provinces (Vizcaya, Guipúzcoa, and Alava) had a special position within the Crown of Castile, allowing them great autonomy, though subjecting them to the authority of the Council of Castile and to the system of *corregimientos*. The *corregimiento* was an administrative division ruled by a *corregidor* who was appointed and dismissed by the Council of Castile. The *corregidor* was the eyes and right arm of the crown at the local level throughout Castile; endowed with extensive political, administrative, and judicial competence, he had his seat in a big town where he presided over the *ayuntamiento* or town council, and from there kept an eye on the area under his jurisdiction. At the end of the sixteenth century there were sixty-eight *corregimientos*, which rose to eighty-six in the course of the following century.

The internal regime of the Crown of Aragon was very different. The various kingdoms which composed it each had an individual character and they formed a confederation of equals. The kingdoms of Aragon and Valencia and the principality of Catalonia had their own Cortes and separate administration. So too had the Balearic Isles, though they had no Cortes. This whole complex came under the jurisdiction of the Council of Aragon. In addition the little kingdom of Navarre had its own currency, laws, Cortes, and special Council, though in some matters it was subject to the Council of Castile.

The Catholic Kings had already carried through a policy of European expansion – even world expansion, if one thinks of the exploration of the Indies which had begun. Even without the dynastic fortunes which joined Spain's destiny to that of the House of Habsburg there would probably have been a Spanish imperialism in the sixteenth century, like that which followed the separation of the two branches of the House of Habsburg in 1555. Aragonese expansion had lost its drive owing to the growing internal weakness of the eastern provinces of Spain, but its markers were still solidly anchored throughout the Mediterranean: Sicily, Sardinia, Naples, and fortified points in North Africa. The expansionism of Castile was stimulated by its own internal dynamism which the political genius of Ferdinand the Catholic had channelled towards foreign enterprises, soon to be underpinned by the inexhaustible treasures of the New World.

The empire of Charles v was a construction of a very special nature, with no possible comparison with anything which has existed before or since. Beneath the old dreams of universal monarchy, potent nationalist forces were at work; within the idealistic and out-of-date concept of his empire there was a move towards a solidly structured state on modern lines. Its own internal contradictions caused it to collapse from within. But Charles, in his desire to give his son Philip most of his inheritance, assigned to him two key territories, a baleful gift which meant that the more simplified and more Spanish state that might have come from the division of the Empire was never realized. Consequently the empire of the Spanish Habsburgs was almost as mixed a bag as that of Charles v. The two territories in question were Milan and Flanders. The first, an Italian land and an imperial fief as well, had never had close relations with Spain. But Flanders was different. Flanders meant much for Castile, not in the political but in the economic sphere, since the Flemish woollen industry absorbed large quantities of the Castilian raw product, and this economic link was reinforced by a considerable cultural influence, evident in the presence of Flemish artists in Castile. Of course this was no basis for a close political connection between Spain and Flanders; but the exceptional situation of Flanders between Germany, England and France made it a first-class base for action in the whole northwest of Europe. The link between this northern outpost and Spanish Italy was not clear as yet, but it was beginning to take shape in the enclave of Franche Comté, in the policy of friendship pursued towards the fickle Dukes of Savoy, and in the hope, never abandoned by Charles v, that he could check the advance of the French towards the Rhine. In fact, one of his last campaigns was the costly siege of Metz, which was meant to be a link in the chain joining the two parts of his empire. The whole of the later policy of the Spanish Habsburgs, with its difficult problems, was implicit in the legacy of Charles v. Essentially the so-called Spanish Empire was Spain, Italy and Flanders, with a staunch, though remote, rearguard in the Indies, while in the middle there was France, half surrounded, with an instinctive tendency to fight free of that mortal embrace. For two centuries the rivalry of France and Spain was to be the *leitmotiv* of European politics, dragging a divided Germany within its range, while England, more her own mistress but no match for either of the two great powers, was able to tip the balance at a given moment.

Since the term empire was reserved for the rulers of the German empire, the nexus of kingdoms and lordships subject to the Spanish Habsburgs was called the 'Monarchy', a word that came to acquire something of its etymological meaning: sole rule. This was not a claim to universal monarchy, but it was a claim to exercise a certain hegemony which was only surrendered when Louis xiv, at the height of his strength and arrogance, forced the decadent Spanish government to recognize the precedence of his ambassador in Rome. Until then the Spaniards could feel that if the German empire had fame and tradition behind it, the greatest effective power belonged to the king who sat in Madrid.

And yet this vast empire was too heterogeneous ever to develop as a modern state. Some of its parts were individually in a position to make the step, especially Castile, where we find traces of a modernity surprising for the sixteenth century – an early nationalism, a strong royal authority, a sense of the community, and a respected and capable bureaucracy. One of the clear symptoms of the maturity of the Castilian state in the second half of the sixteenth century was the scope and thoroughness, unsurpassed for the time, of the statistical enquiries ordered by Philip ii.[2] By contrast, in other parts traditional institutions remained very strong, the structures had ossified, and no development seemed possible. If the crown, driven on by the needs of war, tried to find out what they could pay or tried to streamline their administration, the result, so far from being a step forward, was to spread corruption, to cripple them financially, and undermine their old forms of government without putting anything new in their place. It led in some cases to an outburst of discontent which succeeded in frightening the crown into allowing things to go on as before, with the traditional authorities continuing to rule the country.

It is this final surrender on the part of the monarchy which has come to be known in some circles as 'neo-foralism', a phenomenon of the second half of the seventeenth century. It appears very clearly in the case of Catalonia, which even after the failure of the revolution of 1640 retained its oligarchic form of government.[3] But it is to be found in the rest of the monarchy as well, and can be explained by the final collapse of a movement which had had its point of origin in Castile. For Castile, after being in advance of most other European nations in laying the basis for a truly national state, fell behind, its traditional institutions in ruins, leaving as a poor substitute a bureaucratic framework which under the last Habsburgs became more and more incompetent and oppressive.

If in the institutional aspect the various parts of the monarchy developed only slowly where they did not decay, we need not be surprised that the whole never became united. The so-called Spanish empire had no institutions in common. There was no imperial bureaucracy; the king, counselled by his secretaries and the Council of State, was alone in his power to consider general questions. There was nothing remotely approaching an imperial budget, since it was Castile that bore the burden of expenditure while the contribution from the other parts was confined to occasional demands for aid. Nor was there any economic unity. Needless to say, there was no concept of a Commonwealth or a Common Market in those days, only the beginnings of a sort of imperial preference which consisted in giving to the other kingdoms the same terms enjoyed by friendly or allied countries in the Spanish market. But the Italian states traded more among themselves than with Spain, and the Flemings never gave up trading with the enemies of the monarchy. In the maritime sphere there was no greater unity, although the sea was the most important element of union among the different parts of the Empire. Here too the preponderant role of Castile is evident; its communications with the Indies were safeguarded by fleets of a calibre that was usually proof against defeat. By contrast Flanders contributed little more than privateers, and the Italian naval forces did not extend beyond a small number of galleys which were barely enough to defend the coasts from pirates or safeguard what were perilous communications with Spain.

This empire was never a Spanish empire, properly speaking,

though the preponderant role of Castile and the identification of its monarchs with Spain gave it something of that character in fact if not in law.[4] From the point of view of day-to-day life the Spanish element developed in direct proportion to the activity of colonizers and inversely with the capacity for resistance of the pre-existing culture; it was a complete triumph in the Indies (which were indeed the Spanish empire); it had a fairly important role in the south of Italy through ethnic similarity, the immigration of numerous Spanish families, and an intensive cultural contact; Spanish influence is much less evident in Milan, very small indeed in Flanders, and almost non-existent in Franche Comté, which was nevertheless a model of loyalty to the empire.

Though the king was the only element of union among the different parts of the empire his authority as such is difficult to estimate since each of its members saw him exclusively as its own ruler. There were considerable differences between the restricted authority allowed him as count of Barcelona or lord of Vizcaya and the wide power he enjoyed as king of Castile. In every case there was the notion of a pact, formal or implied, between the king and the kingdom, an arrangement that was already out of date in the sixteenth century and incompatible with the modern idea of a state. The concept of a pact or social contract existed, of course, long before Rousseau and was open to differing interpretations. Jurists formed in the school of Roman law had revived the theory of a voluntary and irrevocable abdication by the Roman people of its original sovereignty in favour of the emperors, and with a total lack of historical, even common sense, applied it to the monarchies of the Renaissance. The Scholastics had reworked this theory, giving it a philo-sophical-cum-theological basis: sovereignty originally lay in the community which had handed it over to the king (or the magistrates of the commonwealth) because it did not believe itself fit for collective self-government. How broad and irrevoc-able this delegation of power had been, authors did not agree.

Without going into such speculation, the people saw in the king the supreme and remote authority from which they could expect redress of the grievances caused by their immediate rulers; the supreme judge, immune to favour or corruption; the visible head of the nation, the symbol of its unity, the father of all his vassals. The literature of the age is full of these sentiments of respect, love and veneration. For the noble class there counted as well a tradition of loyalty and personal fealty which turned to meek, often self-seeking attendance at court once the days of the baronial revolts were past. The clergy in addition looked on the king as the defender of the church and the leader of the crusade against the infidel. The Spanish kings were not so sacrosanct as the French; they were not anointed with holy oil; they were not invested with the power of curing certain diseases; but their subjects never doubted that their authority was more than human.

Only rarely was the epithet 'absolute' applied to the Spanish kings in this period, nor did the word mean arbitrary or despotic, as it later did. The phrase *rex legibus solutus* implied that the kings, as authors of the laws, were independent and above them, but only as regards the laws of the state, not as regards divine law or the precepts of the natural law which were binding on them as on all men.[5] Even in the sphere of positive law they were obliged to observe the laws, privileges and liberties of their kingdoms in accordance with the oath they took at the beginning of their reign when their vassals swore allegiance and recognized them as king. This double oath was the symbol of the pact which bound king and kingdom, kingdom signifying the body of the vassals not in a formless group but in a hierarchy of classes, orders, regions and towns whose most authentic voice was the Cortes or parliament. In time the oath-taking became a mere ceremony which was frequently postponed and sometimes even dropped altogether. Not through any deliberate desire to violate the liberties of its vassals but rather spurred on by the needs of its foreign policy the crown began extending its authority, in piecemeal fashion depending on the degree of opposition it encountered. The result was that by the end of the seventeenth century the extent of royal authority no longer depended so much on archaic legislative texts as on the balance of power between both contestants. Only the Bourbons however drew the final conclusions from this and did away with that distinction between the king and the kingdom by which each had an inherent sovereignty, with interests which were different and even opposed. The identification of king and state was something the Spanish Habsburgs could never quite achieve because they always looked on the network of their dominions as a family patrimony, an entail which had to be preserved in its entirety at all costs. This is obvious in the case of Charles v who was so concerned about the interests of his House, but it also emerges in the will of Philip iv who ordered his successor under no circumstances to give up the Low Countries. There is also the case of Carlos ii who finally decided to hand over his inheritance to his enemy Louis xiv rather than have it dispersed.

The men of the Renaissance not only distinguished between the royal administration and the competence of corporate and local bodies, they also differentiated between the person of the king and his ministers, even when they acted in his name. This sentiment emerged in the cry 'Long live the king and down with bad government!' which was heard in riots and disturbances. In a way the crown approved this attitude, with its permission to 'obey but not put into effect' (*obedecer y no cumplir*) certain orders.[6] This meant that while everything was done in the name of the king most of the orders came really from his secretaries or ministers, who might make a mistake or abuse their power. Royal absolutism was a reality under Philip ii; under his successors it was the ministers who were absolute, greater enemies to the privileges of the vassal, wrote Bisaccioni, than the prince.[7]

The idea that the sovereign handled every piece of government business however small was never more than a legal fiction. Though all complaints, claims and reports were submitted to him, it will be readily appreciated that he was not able to read and arrange everything for himself; he had to have the help of royal secretaries and Councils. The amount of work delegated depended on how hard-working the king was: Philip ii was immensely energetic, Philip iii immensely lazy. Even where one monarch was concerned there might be a lot of confusion as to how much power his colleagues had. A secretary could be a second-rate figure or a real minister if he enjoyed the royal favour, like Don Francisco de los Cobos under Charles v. Even the watchful and suspicious Philip ii fell victim to his complex and mysterious secretary Antonio Pérez, the man who for reasons which have never been cleared up abused the royal confidence to have the envoy of Don John of Austria put to death. When Philip ii realized that his secretary was playing a double game he had him put in prison, but Pérez escaped and fled to his native province of Aragon where he put himself under the protection of the local laws and the jurisdiction of the

Justicia Mayor. The king sent an army into Aragon and had the *Justicia* Lanuza beheaded for attempting an absurd resistance. But Antonio Pérez fled to France and from there to England, where he wrote and intrigued against his former master.

If a man like Philip II could not keep abreast of the vast volume of government business and had to rely on men who were not always worthy of his confidence it is no wonder that less energetic monarchs tried to shift most of their responsibility on to favourites, *privados* or *validos* as they were called. The best known, Lerma and Olivares, both of whom operated in the seventeenth century, acquired such power that a whole literature sprang into being justifying their office, with obvious intent to flatter. However the nation as a whole never approved of such delegation of authority: the nobles through jealousy and envy of those who achieved eminence; the common people from an idea that direct government by the king was best, perhaps because they thought him more disinterested, or perhaps believed him guided by a special divine protection, however little basis the idea had in practice. The *valido* was a combination of the old concept of the king's friend with the modern one of prime minister. He was compounded of a traditional, personal element and a modern, institutional one. Sometimes he gave good results, as France found with Richelieu. Spain was less fortunate in this respect.

To some extent the present-day ministry corresponds to what was then the Council, but there were important differences. The Council had its president but it was a collegiate body, in accordance with the 'conciliar' concept of administration, which was not only Spanish but European. Since the division of powers was unknown it had responsibility equally in the legislative, executive and judicial spheres. It was not obligatory for the king to follow the opinion of the Councils, but he did not usually oppose it without good reason. To the Councils set up by the Catholic Kings (State, Castile, Aragon, Inquisition, Indies, Military Orders) there were added under the first two Habsburgs those of Italy, with the territories of that peninsula under its authority, Portugal, created at the time of the incorporation of that kingdom, Flanders, more short-lived, Finance, which was the old *Contaduría Mayor* transformed, and finally *Cámara*, which was really a committee of the Council of Castile with responsibility for appointments to office and the distribution of favours. The Council of Castile, pre-eminent in its administrative and judicial competence, was the most important element in domestic affairs, just as the Council of State was in foreign policy.

The chief instrument of collaboration between the nation and its sovereigns was the Cortes, analogous to the English parliament. Despite the unity achieved under the Catholic Kings, the Cortes of Castile and Navarre and those of the Crown of Aragon (Aragon, Catalonia and Valencia) remained separate during the Habsburg period. The effective power of these assemblies was limited; they could not make laws, but only present petitions to the king who might or might not heed them. In line with the traditional custom they took the oath to the new kings, and the kings bound themselves to observe the *fueros* and liberties of the kingdom. But this was little more than a ritual; at that time no one would have dared maintain that without prior recognition by the Cortes the power of the king was unlawful.

The principal weapon of the Cortes was that they alone could authorize the imposition of new taxes. Faced with a growing need of funds the kings tried to get round this limitation in two ways: multiplying the taxes which by their nature did not need the sanction of the Cortes since they pertained to the royal rights (*regalías*), as for example customs duties or the minting of money; or else, bringing pressure to bear on the Cortes. The Castilian Cortes showed themselves too compliant in this respect, and this made them unpopular.

Another factor which discredited the Cortes was their largely unrepresentative nature. In the non-Castilian kingdoms there still existed the three traditional *brazos*: nobility, clergy and people. The nobility was represented both by great lords and by lesser *infanzones* or *cavallers* analogous to the Castilian *hidalgos*. In Navarre too there was a plentiful representation of the middle and lower nobility. In the ranks of the clerical estate sat bishops, abbots and delegates of ecclesiastical chapters. The popular *brazo* was represented by the towns; in little Navarre there were thirty-four, which was a fairly complete representation. In the lands of the crown of Aragon they were also fairly numerous. By contrast, in Castile the number of towns with the right to send two *procuradores* had been reduced to eighteen. Of these, half were in the Duero basin, four in New Castile, another four in

Andalusia, and last but not least there was the town of Murcia. Whole regions were left without representation: Galicia, the Cantabrian coast, Extremadura. Each town spoke in the name of a province or kingdom, but the two *procuradores* were elected or drawn by lot from among the members of the municipal corporation who held their offices in freehold; therefore they lacked any democratic character.

Despite these limitations the Castilian Cortes were responsible for an interesting job of work as allies of the crown in the later Middle Ages and during the reign of the Catholic Kings. But with the Habsburgs they declined rapidly. The Cortes of Toledo in 1538 refused Charles v a new tax which he wanted on articles of basic necessity; the three *brazos* of the Cortes stood firm in their opposition, with the noble estate particularly resolute. Irritated, Charles v never called the noble or the ecclesiastical arm again, so that the Cortes were reduced to the representatives of the towns. This fact was decisive for their subsequent development; henceforth the kings had no difficulty in imposing their will on an assembly of only thirty-six members, from which the most respected figures of the nation were missing.

Philip II did not pay much attention to the Cortes; sometimes he listened to their petitions, but more frequently he replied evasively, when he did not openly retort: 'There is no need for any change here'. And yet there were still deputies of worth, sound men who saw that the voice of the nation reached the monarch.

Under Philip III and Philip IV the decay of the Castilian Cortes was complete; the master stroke was to give the deputies a share in the sums they voted (usually around 1·5 per cent). In addition they received *ayudas de costa* or subsidies for their upkeep in Madrid during the long years which the sessions lasted. When they ended the more docile *procuradores* received offices, habits of the Military Orders and other favours, while those who had shown any independence were left out in the cold.

The right to send a deputy to the Cortes came to be so sought after that some towns which did not have it proved willing to buy it. Despite the resistance of the other towns which did not want to share their privilege, Philip IV sold a vote in the Cortes to seven towns of Galicia which paid jointly and took turns to use it, another to Palencia, and another to six towns of Extremadura. Philip IV obtained whatever he wanted from the Cortes but at the price of discrediting them so completely that they never recovered their former prestige. In the reign of Charles II they were not called again, on the quite correct assumption that it was cheaper to ask the towns directly for their consent to continuing grants of taxes, since this was the only function left to the Cortes.

In the non-Castilian lands the Cortes kept their three *brazos* and their independence; and for this reason the kings summoned them rarely. The Cortes of Catalonia stood out by their resistance to the great subsidies or *servicios* which were asked of them. Philip IV convoked them in 1626 and had to prorogue the session without obtaining the desired sums; and the same thing happened at the second summons in 1632. These events are seen as steps on the road to the rising of 1640. The Cortes of Aragon and Valencia granted some subsidies after much haggling and in return for rewards for their deputies. As for the Cortes of Navarre, they were of purely local interest. The very poverty of the country sheltered it to some extent against the king's demands.

Much more important as organs of the community were the townships, although their representative and autonomous character also suffered great changes under the Habsburgs. The great vitality they enjoyed in the Middle Ages was much reduced as the modern age began. The enemies of the independent townships were the king on the one hand and the nobility on the other. The crown had used them as allies against the nobles, but as it consolidated its own power it set out to reduce what seemed to it the excessive authority of the towns, putting the most important under *corregidors* who presided over the town councils. With the Habsburgs this policy of intervention became more marked; municipal property and municipal rents were subjected to close inspection and many of their old offices, though not suppressed, were left with no real function. This happened with the *alcaides* in charge of fortresses which were usually in a tottering state, the *alfereces* of a local militia which no longer went out on campaign, and the *alcaldes* who dispensed justice, but only in cases of first instance since appeals went to the royal *Audiencias* and *Chancillerías*.

For its part the nobility contributed to the decline of the townships by getting control of their principal offices which, from being annual and elective, came to be for life and even hereditary. This put an end to their democratic character. It was in Andalusia that this abuse became most widespread, to the benefit of the big landowning aristocracy, but it was also to be found in greater or lesser degree in the other regions. The Habsburgs made it worse by putting a large number of municipal posts up for sale. Towns which were poor and small were better able to keep their old form of government intact. In some, especially in the northern provinces, there were still meetings of the *cabildo abierto*, that is, the general assembly of the heads of households; but more frequently it was the *ayuntamiento*, an offshoot of the assembly, which was responsible for administration. Some towns had succeeded in excluding nobles from the government, but most often it was a case of 'half the offices', that is, the equal division of jobs between nobles and commoners.

Since office was not remunerated it was more feared than coveted by those who did their work properly, since there fell to them the inspection of inns, taverns, weights and measures, the care of keeping the population fed, repair of roads, preservation of woods, public order, assessing taxes, and many other obligations. If office kept its charms it was because it also had notable advantages and afforded opportunities to further one's own interests and even grow rich. And yet self-interest was not the whole story behind municipal office-holding. For those who had a political vocation, qualities of leadership and the desire to participate in public life, there was virtually no other field of action but that of local government; and what a wide field it was! Local feeling was very well developed and showed itself in a thousand ways: in the residence of many rich, noble families in the poor neighbourhoods where they had their ancestral homes; in the endowment of innumerable foundations of a religious, charitable, or teaching nature; in the development of a vast local historiography where love for the *patria chica* showed itself in myth and hyperbole. The men of those days looked on themselves, first and foremost, as members of the local community which gave them birth; next, of the district or region, and only in a vaguer sense of that political body, as yet not clearly defined, which today we call Spain. As for a sense of belonging to the empire, it existed if at all only in small degree; Castilians, Portuguese, Neapolitans, Latin Americans and Flemings were too diverse, too cut off one from the other to feel themselves members of the same community. There existed certainly a loyalty to the sovereign, more for what he stood for in his own person than as the embodiment of a common destiny; and this sentiment was reinforced by a common faith in the era of the religious struggles. This today seems to us an inadequate basis on which to found such a vast and far-reaching political edifice, yet it held out for centuries against the internal and external forces undermining it.

THE DYNASTY

Under the Ancien Régime the role of the monarch was so important that his own character had an often decisive influence on the course of events. It does not explain everything, as the old school of history believed, but it does provide the key to a great deal; especially in the case of the Spanish Empire which was a product of dynastic combinations whose underlying logic to a large extent determined the actions of its kings.

Beneath certain common family traits the five Spanish Habsburgs proved to have very marked individual characteristics. Charles V was psychologically a late developer, as can be seen by comparing the youthful portraits, that painted by Orley for example, with the magnificent Titians depicting the mature man. The prominent jaw of that family was so marked in his case as to be almost a caricature. His health, which was never very strong, succumbed early to stress, continual travelling, lack of sleep, and a horrible diet; when he abdicated at the age of fifty-five he was old and worn-out and had only another three years of life ahead of him. But even in his monastic retreat at Yuste, heedless of gout he weakly gave way to a pathological appetite for food which undoubtedly hastened his death. Sexual pleasures he indulged in more sparingly. He married only once, in 1526, his bride being his cousin Isabel of Portugal. Financial considerations, which dogged him continually, seem to have been uppermost in this match. At first he had thought of Mary Tudor, daughter of his aunt Catherine; but apart from the fact that she was a child the English court could not make him the dowry he needed. Instead Isabel brought him the promise of a million ducats, though the sum actually collected by Charles was scarcely half that. Marriage of convenience though it was, it was no less a love-match and from it were born Philip II (1527), Maria, wife of the emperor Maximilian, and

Juana, who ruled Castile for a time during the absence of her father and brother before marrying prince Juan of Portugal.

When the Empress Isabel died in 1540 Charles, though still young, did not make a new match, but his sensual temperament led him into a series of amorous escapades. These bore fruit with two individuals of major importance for the following reign: Margaret and Don John of Austria. The first, daughter of a Portuguese lady, was subsequently governor of the Netherlands and mother of Alexander Farnese. Don John had very little Spanish blood in his veins; he was born of a German woman, Barbara Blomberg, whose character was as vulgar as her origins. But he rose to become viceroy of Naples, the victor of Lepanto, and governor of Flanders in a short but brilliant and heroic career. If his brother Philip looked on his ambition with misgiving, he cannot be reproached with having denied him the opportunity to live as befitted the son of an emperor.

Charles v had too bustling a nature to get down to the routine job of governing, and this he left to his secretaries. In the first years of his reign the chancellor Gattinara was the most influential person. Subsequently the burden of affairs as regards Spain fell to Don Francisco de los Cobos, an uninspiring figure too fond of making money, but steady and hard-working. Outside the peninsula it was the Burgundian, Nicolas Perrenot de Granvelle, who was in charge. He was the father of Antoine, Cardinal Granvelle, later famous as minister of Philip ii. In private matters the emperor's confidant was Don Luis de Ávila who followed him even to his retreat at Yuste. Charles had first-rate helpers as well in his two daughters, Juana and Maria, and in his son Philip, for whom he left 'Instructions' in government which are a model of prudence and foresight.

Attention has often been drawn to the contrast between the fortunes of Charles and his younger brother Ferdinand. The latter, born and reared in Spain, appealed more to the Spaniards as their future king and Ferdinand the Catholic, in great annoyance at the Flemish clique which surrounded Charles, was once on the point of altering the law of succession in his favour. As a result Ferdinand was packed off to Germany as soon as Charles arrived in Spain, as a threat which had to be kept at arm's length. This virtual exile was the cause of his triumph. Spaniard though he was, he adopted fully the character and customs of the Germans who accepted him as one of them. King of Hungary and Bohemia, Emperor of Germany, Ferdinand left to his descendants the Austrian half of the Habsburg inheritance, while Charles, originally rejected in Spain as a foreigner, became more and more Spanish and eventually chose a remote corner of Castile for his retirement.

Philip II is one of the most controversial characters in history, not only because his rather secretive personality does have something enigmatic about it, but also because he embodied a movement in history which has had the most enthusiastic panegyrists and the most bitter detractors. Today the extremes have drawn much closer together, and he is judged more objectively. We look beneath the decisions of the politician for the secret of the man, though this remains elusive. The contrast between Philip and his father is obvious, and perhaps derives from his mother, who reinforced the Trastámara strain with its pathological traits. He was a typical introvert behind his mask of haughty dignity. In his youth he travelled widely, yet the varied nature of his experiences and contacts did not succeed in making his character more open. Instead, on his return to Spain he fixed his residence in Madrid, choosing a permanent capital as much because of his own sedentary inclinations as because of the increasing sophistication of the machinery of state. Growing more rooted with time, he withdrew to the isolation of the Escorial, and there was a general complaint in his last years that the king was unapproachable.

This trend towards a growing remoteness was allied, as so often in such temperaments, with a love for nature and a jovial warmth in the company of his intimates. We can see this in the letters he sent from Lisbon to his daughters, or in the anecdotes collected (or invented) by Porreño.[1] It is said that the cold impassiveness which unnerved those who met him was a mask he assumed to hide his shyness and insecurity. But it is more probable that it was a basic trait in his character, inspired by the high idea he had of the dignity of a king. Tradition has it that Charles V mourned the death of Atahualpa because he was a fellow monarch. Philip II went much further, reproaching Don Francisco de Toledo with the execution of the last member of the Inca royal family on suspicion of conspiracy; one of the best viceroys he had in Peru, his successes were forgotten and the rebuke was so stern that it hastened his death.[2]

Another unfortunate trait in his character was the hopeless

slowness with which he worked, which led to a great backlog of business piling up. This stemmed from an innate indecisiveness which sometimes, as in the preparations for the great Armada, changed to bursts of frenzied haste, and also from an instinctive sense of mistrust that made him want to examine and decide all questions for himself. He was, as has been truly said, a bureaucratic, desk-loving monarch. The way he was let down by Antonio Pérez must have increased his innate caution and led him to reduce the number of those who worked with him to a handful of intimates. In the second half of his reign his favourite secretary was Mateo Vázquez de Leca. Between them they got through a staggering amount of business until, worn out with work and the gout, the king entrusted the affairs of state to Don Juan de Idiáquez, those of Aragon and Italy to the Count of Chinchón, and those of Portugal to Don Cristóbal de Moura. The three took decisions with Mateo Vázquez and the latter brought their *consultas* to the king for him to scrawl his comments in the margins and the spaces between the lines.[3] This was how the administrative part functioned, but in international politics the most influential voice was that of Cardinal Granvelle once he left the Low Countries.

One of the most surprising things about this monarch (as with Napoleon) was the way he combined vast, world-wide projects with a care for the smallest practical detail. Philip II was not above giving over part of his precious time to correcting a badly written word or weighing the merits of a candidate for a vacant chaplaincy. He was a stickler for accuracy, and sent back a budget of millions because he spotted an error of a few *maravedís*. But this did not cause him to forget the general European situation, or what was happening in the Indies, or discoveries in the Pacific. But if his range of vision was vast it can hardly be called inspired. His greatness lies in the fact that he had an unparalleled instrument at his disposal which, with obstinate determination, he turned to the service of throne and altar in a period crucial for the future of Europe. It is futile to argue whether he harnessed politics to religion or the other way round, because that sort of distinction did not occur to the men of an age in which heresy was a crime punishable by the civil law and resistance to the legitimate ruler a sin that merited hell fire. Philip II never fought a purely religious war, but religious factors were hardly ever absent from those he did fight.

Philip II is not known to have had any illegitimate children. If he did have one in his youth he would have taken great care not to promote him publicly as his father had done. The abnormal mortality of those days, which was no respecter of royalty, and political motives led him to contract four marriages. The first was with Maria of Portugal, who died on giving birth to the prince, Don Carlos. Out of obedience to his father he married his aunt, Mary Tudor, who was older than he was and gave him no heir. The third match, with Elizabeth de Valois, was the happiest, but that delightful queen died young, leaving two little princesses, Isabel Clara and Catalina. With no male heir he was obliged to contract a fourth marriage with his niece, Anne of Austria, who gave birth to the future Philip III.

The death of Don Carlos, blamed on his father's jealousy, became one of the most widespread of slanders from the time of William of Orange's 'Apology'. It is hardly worth refuting any more, but there is still a lingering doubt whether Philip was not too severe with his son, treating him as a state criminal rather than the poor invalid he was. All the symptoms suggest Don Carlos became insane early on, and this showed itself in a growing irritability, a hatred of his father and an urge to break away, which took shape in the hare-brained scheme of going to Flanders to join the rebels. Philip realized his son was incapable of governing and that he must be locked away. Ideally, one would have thought, he should have been treated as gently as possible; but subjected as he was to a prison regime the prince sank rapidly and died. On the king's side it can be argued that madness was then treated as a crime or a sin rather than as an illness; but it is probable that if the patient had been one of his daughters his reaction would have been different.

Philip II was respected and feared rather than loved by his people. He was too remote from the tastes and aspirations of the common man ever to be popular.[4] And yet he is taken as a typical representative of the Spanish character; if, that is, one believes in the theory of 'national characters' which has now deservedly fallen into disrepute. At most one can allow that he identified with a particular current of Catholic–royalist zeal among the upper classes of Castile. But one could argue whether the latter moulded the character of the king, or whether the king, with his reserve, his natural dignity and his stiff etiquette, set the tone for the higher echelons and eventually coloured the attitudes of the middle and lower orders.

'A saintly king, unfortunate in his ministers', so a contemporary described Philip III. The phrase is scarcely accurate, inasmuch as if he lacked good ministers it was because he did not try to pick better ones; and saintliness is hardly the word for a minute and superficial piety which left long hours free for hunting and gaming. Where his father had been inherently cautious, eager for work, high-principled, concerned to find the best man for each job, the son was frivolous, incompetent, capable of giving the key positions in the administration to unprincipled men who were only interested in their own advantage. The new king (1598–1621) assumed power with a minimal knowledge of public business, of which his father had kept him in almost total ignorance, and always showed very little interest in it. The strange thing is that the elder Philip, who had realized this weakness in his son[5] and the excessive hold which Don Francisco de Sandoval had over him, did nothing to prevent it. The favourite got rid of the personnel surviving from the previous reign and governed with the aid of unscrupulous men like the count of Villalonga, later brought to trial for the embezzlement of public funds, and Don Rodrigo de Calderón, beheaded at the beginning of the next reign. Sandoval, elevated to the title of duke of Lerma, was later made a cardinal at his own request in order to save him from the vengeance of his enemies. He amassed an immense fortune, of which he was stripped only afterwards.

Philip III was a disaster as king, but as a person he had no great vice – just the opposite of his contemporary, Henry IV of France, who was a great statesman and an incorrigible libertine. Philip had only one wife, Margaret of Austria, who died early, leaving him three sons and two daughters – Maria, whose hand was later sought in vain by Charles Stuart, and Anne, who became the wife of Louis XIII of France and mother of Louis XIV.

Philip IV was born in Valladolid in 1605 and reigned from 1621 to 1665. It was therefore one of the longest reigns in the history of Spain and also one of the most unfortunate, because it was then that the decline of the Monarchy, which had started under his predecessor, set in irreversibly: lands were lost, the economy ruined, the nation forfeited its glory, art and letters suffered an eclipse. But it should not be forgotten that this sombre picture is only really true of the second half of the reign, for in the first half there were still flashes of brilliance and some positive features. Philip iv is taken as the symbol of Spain's decline, saddled with failings which are his own and those of others. Clearly he can be blamed for the choice of Don Gaspar de Guzmán, Conde Duque of Olivares, as first minister. Olivares arrogated a wide-reaching authority to himself, and with the best of intentions drove the monarchy down the road to ruin, partly from a failure to view the situation realistically, partly also through neglect of the true interests of Spain which were sacrificed to a policy of prestige abroad. In this case the responsibility of the king, who kept his minister in office longer than should have been necessary for his failure to become evident, is beyond all doubt. In the turn taken by the economy his responsibility is less, since this was a product partly of Spanish policy itself, partly of factors outside his control. Finally in the unfavourable turn of events abroad (the collapse of Germany, the rise of France) little or no blame can be laid at his door unless it be his failure to realize the changes taking place.

The personality of Philip iv is much more distinctive than that of his father or his son. His physical features are exceptionally well-known, thanks to Velázquez, in whom we can follow the premature ageing of the handsome, sporting young man of the earlier period. The reports of the Venetian ambassadors, which are usually reliable, are another valuable guide to his life history. Cornaro, who was in Spain from 1631 to 1634, says that he rose at eight and spent his time partly in attending to business, partly with the queen or in reading Italian history books, of which he was very fond. Good-natured and devout, he gave the impression that he would govern well if he were on his own. He had by now left behind the hot passion of early youth. He was not lavish in his favours, nor was he extravagant nor addicted to gaming. He went to church more often, and it was thought that in time he would be as devout as his father and grandfather. Years later, Contarini called him an 'excellent prince', but too much under the thumb of the Conde Duque who even told him what to wear. His health was in decline; he ate too much, and in summer he had fevers. Girolamo Giustini-ani tells us in 1649 that he indulged his appetite to excess and ate almost nothing but meat – fish only on days of abstinence; by contrast he only drank cinnamon water. He was very diligent, devout, and compassionate; he hated war, and would have liked to make peace but was held back by his irresolution, and this was costing him the love of his people. In his final years, according to Domenico Zane, he had become more temperate but his illness was now past cure: his left arm trembled continually and sometimes his head as well. In these circumstances the ambassador thought that marital life with the new young queen would do him no good at all.[6]

His physical decay had no doubt something to do with the horrible way he ate, but there was also the stress of such a turbulent reign and family misfortunes, which made their mark on a man of his affectionate nature. He does not seem to have shown any special fondness for his brothers, Carlos and Ferdinand. The first died young without having done anything worthy of note. The second, appointed to the archbishopric of Toledo while still a mere child and subsequently made cardinal (the *Cardenal Infante*), lacked a religious vocation, but had considerable gifts in the political and military spheres instead. He also died young, as governor of Flanders. Philip was more fond of his sister Maria, whom he never saw again after she took ship in 1630 to be crowned Queen of Hungary and afterwards Empress of Austria.

While he was still a prince he married Elizabeth, daughter of Henri IV of France. This marriage brought him no political advantages, but instead long years of conjugal bliss. The death of Elizabeth filled him with acute sorrow, comparable only to that which he felt at the death of Prince Baltasar Carlos, his son, who had barely reached the age of puberty. In these reverses, Philip saw a sign of God's anger for his sins and those of his people. He tried to make amends and ordered the civil and ecclesiastical authorities to take steps against public sin. There were years in which he, a man so fond of the stage, closed all the theatres in Spain. But his will was weak and his relapses frequent. Despite the love he professed for his wife, his conjugal infidelities were numerous and he left several bastards. Only one was legitimized – Don Juan José of Austria, who was given considerable rents, held high office in Naples and Flanders, and subsequently played an important role in the reign of Carlos II. Spurred on by the need for a male heir, he arranged a second marriage in 1647 with his niece Mariana of Austria, daughter of his sister Maria. The fruits of this almost incestuous union were not biologically sound: Prince Felipe Próspero, despite his promising name and the optimistic forecasts of the astrologers, died at an early age, and the future Carlos II was at the death of his father a rickety child of four years of age, retarded in mind and body.

Philip IV was a king of excellent parts, humane, intelligent, and neither as frivolous nor as lazy as legend paints him. If he handed over power, first to Olivares then to Don Luis de Haro, it was not only because he needed to share the immense load but also because his weak irresolute character led him to seek out someone on whom he could rest his tremendous responsibilities. But he always kept himself well informed of the business of government, and spent long hours taking decisions with his ministers and secretaries. His fault was in not having snatched the helm in time from a man who was bringing the ship of state to her doom. When he did so, things were already in too much turmoil for it to be possible to turn back.

The king of Spain was at once the richest and the poorest of men; he had belongings of inestimable wealth but no money which he could call his own. Though the distinction between the king's public and private treasury was not clear (the very title *Real Hacienda* – royal property – is indicative of this confusion), there was a royal patrimony made up of palaces, hunting reserves and other properties, administered by the *Junta de Obras y Bosques*. Its yield was spent on the expenses of upkeep and repair, and far from there being anything left over, it sometimes had to be subsidized from the public Treasury. This patrimony was considered to be an entail and inalienable. The vast quantity of jewels, arms, books, pictures and other articles which the kings amassed added up to an inestimable wealth, but one which was unproductive. The Habsburgs contributed to its growth, whether by commissions to famous artists or purchases abroad (Velázquez was sent twice to Italy by Philip IV to obtain pictures), or by the costly presents they received. In addition the crown collected the *quinto*, a fifth of the pearls of America, some of which were given as presents to shrines or individuals, others going to swell the royal collection of precious stones. The Spanish court was never wanting in splendour, even when times were hardest: when Philip IV went to the French frontier in 1660 to hand over his daughter, Maria Teresa, to Louis xiv, the gifts he bestowed were far more valuable than those received from the French.

The upkeep of the court depended on an annual budgetary allowance which kept getting bigger, to the intense annoyance of the subject who remembered the modest way of life of the Catholic Kings. Under Charles v the Burgundian etiquette was introduced, with its complex ceremonial and its hordes of servants. At the head of it all was the *mayordomo mayor* or chamberlain, whose salary and emoluments were very considerable. The office, much sought after, was held by a member of the higher nobility. Next came the ordinary mayordomos, the *gentileshombres de la casa* or gentlemen of the household, the others who waited at the royal table (*de la boca*) and other lesser offices. Lastly there were the pages, guards, porters, and an incalculable number of servants. All of these, in addition to their salary, had a right to rations of food, firewood, candles, ice and so forth, according to their rank. The stables, with hundreds of horses, the Royal Chapel and the dispensary were a few of the other pieces which went to make up that city in its own right, the royal household.

Though it is not possible to give exact figures, Carande calculates that the emperor at the end of his reign had some 600 persons in his service who cost some 200,000 ducats annually, a figure which would have to be at least doubled if we added in the allowance for the empress and the princes, alms, and other expenses. By strict economy Philip ii kept himself down to 400,000 ducats which, taking into account the loss in the purchasing power of money, was a considerable reduction. But Philip iii let his palace be overrun by greedy, spendthrift nobles, and despite the protests of the Cortes expenditure rose to 1,300,000 ducats. Philip iv began his reign with a policy of retrenchment. Many palace offices were suppressed and there was some cutting-back of services. But the total expenditure continued to be in excess of a million, since as well as the annual *asiento* or contract with the royal bankers for 600,000 ducats there were other expenses, both recurring and incidental. Thus each of the queen's ladies had to have one million *maravedís* in dowry when she got married. The cost of the palace of the Buen Retiro was met by the sale of privileges and offices, and by a charge on the export of raisins from Málaga.

Amid so much wealth the king had scarcely any ready cash, with the result that he was often forced to sell an office or two to get his hands on the proceeds, or to write a note to the president of the Council of Finance ordering him to pay the bearer a sum 'for a business I have at hand' (*para un efecto de mi servicio*). To regularize this situation Philip IV created the *bolsillo del rey* or royal purse, which eventually disposed of some 50,000 ducats a year, which it got from the *señoreaje*, a small duty levied on the coinage of money. There was also a fund for 'secret expenses', replenished with a levy of one per cent on imports. With this the king gave alms and rewarded services which could be considered just as valuable if done for him as for the state, since there was no clear boundary separating the two.

The figure of a million ducats is exorbitant in a budget where discounting consignments to the public debt net income was usually not more than six or seven millions. But with the net national product over 150 millions in the case of Castile alone its weight was hardly likely to be much felt. The thesis which attributes the decline of the seventeenth century state to the expenses of the court does not seem defensible to the present author, though it may have been a contributory factor. Anyway, excessive luxury and the custom of maintaining a vast servant body was not exclusive to the court.

The setting for this sumptuous court was the old *alcázar* of Madrid, once Philip II had fixed his capital there in 1560. Before that the kings changed residence frequently. Charles V was married in the *alcázar* of Seville, and made a lengthy stay in the Alhambra at Granada; he witnessed the birth of his son Philip in Valladolid, and he also lodged in the *alcázar* of Toledo. Philip II, who was sedentary in his tastes, made only three long trips within the peninsula, one to Aragon, another to Córdoba and Seville, and another to Portugal, when that kingdom was taken over. Instead he restored and enlarged the *alcázar* of Madrid, making it capable of holding not only the court but the councils as well, in other words the central administration of the monarchy. In addition he built the Escorial, a monastery, museum, pantheon and royal residence all in one. His successors also travelled little. Philip III, who visited Portugal, was never in the south of Spain. Conversely Philip IV, who at the beginning of his reign made a pleasure trip to Andalusia, was never in Portugal. Who knows whether, if he had got in touch directly with its problems, the secession might have been avoided! The growing immobility of the monarch is to be explained in part by the trouble and expense of shifting about. Where Charles v was light of foot and had little baggage, the royal journeys of the seventeenth century became the terror of the towns which lay along their route thanks to the trouble and expense of putting up hundreds of persons and their trains.

More and more attached to Madrid, the Habsburgs acquired another palace there, which was conceived as a pleasure garden with fine big buildings, gardens, lake, theatre and zoo. This was the palace of the Buen Retiro, built for Philip IV by his favourite, the Conde Duque. They also enlarged and embellished some palaces in the neighbourhood which before were mere rustic retreats or hunting lodges, like Aranjeuz, the Pardo and the Zarzuela. Of these buildings little now remains. The Madrid *alcázar* was destroyed by fire in 1734 and replaced by the present-day palace. Most of the Buen Retiro disappeared in the War of Independence, and of the residences in the neighbourhood only the Escorial has been kept as it was in the days of the Habsburgs, for the others were completely renovated by the Bourbons.

The emotional life of these kings, with its ups and downs and its problems, was like that of any middle-class family. It is said that the education of royalty as it was practised under the Ancien Régime, with its rigorous etiquette and its marriages of state convenience, weakened family ties. In support of this argument one can point to the inhuman treatment meted out to the unhappy Juana la Loca. Most of her long life was spent in the confinement of Tordesillas, while the royal family forgot all about her. Another strange case was that of Juana, sister of Philip II and wife of John of Portugal. In 1554, twenty days after her husband died, the future king Sebastian was born; his mother left him in Portugal to take up the regency of Castile and never saw him again. But these are the exceptions. The Habsburgs, apart from occasional lapses, were model husbands and loving fathers. As persons they are above serious reproach. As rulers, no overall judgement can be made on them since their characters and circumstances varied greatly.

3
THE INSTRUMENTS
OF EMPIRE

The Habsburg empire was a weakly structured one with virtually no bureaucracy in common, resting mainly on the three pillars of material resources, armed might and diplomacy. These three aspects will be dealt with in relation to Spain, which is not to distort the picture overmuch since most of these resources were Spanish in origin.

This was particularly true of finance. Each of the states of the monarchy had its own treasury and there was never any attempt to centralize resources. Their ordinary revenues were just about enough to cover running costs. So when the monarch turned to the lands beyond Castile to help him in his wars he had to be content with selling offices, titles, or bits of the royal demesne, or being voted an extraordinary *servicio* by the Cortes or other representative assembly. This is not to say that the contribution of the non-Castilian territories was negligible. Far from it: at certain times and in certain places it was to cause movements of rebellion. But Castile was the cornerstone, for two reasons. First, because with America in train it was the wealthiest part of the empire; second, because of the continual presence of the king in Castile and traditions of loyalty and a submissiveness which went back to the failure of the movement of the *Cumuneros*. All this enabled the treasury to turn the screws harder there than anywhere else.

Nowadays quite a lot is known about the Castilian finances thanks to the classic work of Carande on Charles v and his bankers, and the more schematic studies which Modesto Ulloa and the present author have made of the finances of Philip II and Philip IV respectively. The conclusion to emerge from these studies is a decisive one: Castile was weakened by the ruthless exploitation to which the global policy of the Habsburgs gave rise. This policy in turn failed once the resources of Castile began to falter.

In 1517 the backbone of Castilian public finance was, first, the *alcabala*, a tax of medieval origin on sales and purchases, high in theory (ten per cent on each transaction) but subject to numerous exemptions and latterly commuted for a fixed sum; and second, a triennial *servicio* granted by the Cortes, whose real worth, like that of the *alcabala*, was tending to fall in that age of inflation. There were other revenues as well of varying yield: customs on land and sea, rents from certain royal properties like mines or the *maestrazgos* of the Military Orders, the bull of the *cruzada* which the pope had granted for the crusade against the infidel, returns from the Indies, and a few other items of smaller value.

In 1523 Charles v set up a Council of Finance whose chief function was to administer the royal revenues, in some cases directly, or more often by farming them out to private individuals or entrusting their collection to the towns themselves since the administrative apparatus at the disposal of the Council was very rudimentary. It was clear that such resources were too meagre for a policy of grandeur. They were just enough for ordinary expenditure – little more than the cost of running the royal household, the councils, the high courts of justice, an embryonic fleet and a standing army, as well as servicing the public debt (the *juros*). When expenses occurred beyond the ordinary, generally in connection with war, special revenues had to be created, and when these failed the government got itself deeper and deeper into debt – a *leitmotiv* of all Habsburg policy.

Not only were the revenues themselves inadequate but their collection was slow and irregular. The king's treasury had no efficient administration which could ensure the payment of the troops and the servants of the royal household at fixed intervals, or meet unforeseen contingencies. Much less could it make loans against future revenue. These functions might have been carried out by a state bank, but plans of this kind came up against insuperable obstacles. Instead it was left to private bankers, also called *asentistas*, to channel their own fortunes and those of their clients towards a hungry royal treasury. They saw to the transfer of money, whether in coin or by means of letters or bills of exchange through the fairs. And it was up to them to change the money they collected in Castile (usually copper coin which had no currency elsewhere) into the gold or silver currency required for settlements in Italy, Germany or Flanders. These financial operations, whose nucleus was the contract known as the *asiento*, surpassed in scope anything which had gone before and made Castile a pivot of international high finance and a rendezvous for the great bankers. This was a game where the winnings were sometimes huge, but the losses just as huge on occasion. The crown would have liked to reserve the business to Castilian bankers, and in fact some of these, like Rodrigo Dueñas or Simón Ruiz, achieved a certain eminence in the sixteenth century. But the big names were foreigners, Germans (Fugger or Welser) and above all Genoese (Spínola, Centurión, Balbi, Lomellini, etc.).

Charles v did not manage to get new taxes of any great value and had to be content with selling offices or church property and other *ad hoc* expedients which were not worth much. So it was that despite the large quantities of gold and silver he received from America in the later years of his reign his indebtedness grew to such proportions that as his daughter Juana, governor of Castile, wrote in 1554, every revenue was pledged in advance up to and including the year 1560. These circumstances played a big part in his final undoing. When he abdicated in 1556 the treasury debt to the *asentistas* was 6,761,276 ducats, and the *juros* or state bonds in private hands came to an even larger sum.

The first task facing Philip II was to declare the double bankruptcy of 1557–60, the first of a long series. The term 'bankruptcy', generally used to describe these operations, is too strong. The king of Spain did not break his word or fail to acknowledge his obligations, but since he could not make ends meet he thought it best to take a high moral tone about the usurious interests the bankers were charging him. That was fair enough: the bankers were collecting from fourteen to twenty per cent as well as other additional benefits, not counting their speculative exchanges – though of course one must remember that the risks attached to these operations were also enormous.

The operation had two parts. There was a reduction in the rate of interest which had fallen in arrears, which meant a reduction in the total backlog of debts; and the floating debt was consolidated by paying the *asentistas* in *juros* which generally yielded from five to seven per cent. The bankers in their turn paid their own creditors with these *juros*; however their own losses in cash and credit were still sizeable. The relief for the state was only temporary. The revenues assigned to satisfy the bankers were taken out of pawn, but at the price of a rise in the public debt, which involved the treasury in an annual outlay of 1,600,000 ducats at the beginning of the reign and some 4,600,000 towards the end. Philip II repeated the operation in 1575, with destructive effects on the European economy as a whole, as seen in the bankruptcy of numerous commercial and banking houses, and again in 1596.

The increase in the debt was not due merely to the *juros* which were given to the bankers in compensation for their credits. There was also a public market for these bonds, whose high yields made them very popular. The bankruptcy of 1575 frightened the general public away from the *asientos* which were deemed too risky. But the credit of the *juros* remained intact, and if perhaps there were some ten million ducats' worth sold in the first twenty years of the reign the figure for the last quarter of the sixteenth century may have reached forty millions, a fabulous sum for the period.[1]

In this reign there was a substantial increase in revenue. The *alcabala*, which it had been settled the kingdom would pay as a fixed sum and which had been gradually eaten away by inflation, was now more than doubled. Permission was obtained from the pope to impose two substantial taxes on the clergy as a contribution to the struggle against the infidel: the *subsidio* and the *excusado*. Salt mines in private hands were taken over by the crown. But all this was not enough, and after the disaster of the Armada against England the Cortes authorized a duty on articles of basic necessity (meat, wine, oil and vinegar) which everyone had to pay without exception of class. It was called the *millones*, and though it was introduced as a temporary measure it had come to stay. It soon became the most unpopular of any tax, and much of the responsibility for Castile's decline was attributed to it. Philip II enjoyed in addition a wide market for his *juros*, not only in Spain but abroad as well, and was particularly fortunate with the Indies where shipments of precious metals reached their peak in his reign. Despite the combination of circumstances in his favour, the enormity of the foreign burden is revealed in the fact that his reign closed with a debt of sixty-eight million ducats, with half the total budget of 9,731,407 ducats going to service it.[2]

Philip III, heir to this unhappy situation, was a peace-loving king as much from necessity as from temperament. He succeeded in avoiding any new taxes and met his obligations by increasing the amount of copper money in circulation and reducing its fineness. This remedy proved inadequate, for between 1598 when the reign opened and 1609 when the truce was concluded with the Dutch, expenditure abroad rose to 37,488,565 ducats, not counting four and a half millions interest on letters of change and *asientos*. As a result – and in no small measure also because of the increase in court expenses – there had to be a new suspension of payments to the bankers in 1607, though the bankers, mainly Genoese, secured relatively favourable conditions.

Under Philip IV the Castilian treasury had to come to terms with a permanent state of war and rocketing expenditure. It was then that public finance took on the shape it was to retain until the last years of the Ancien Régime. As well as existing taxes, new ones were introduced, including a stamp duty, a tax in commutation of the old military obligation of the nobility (the *lanzas*), a duty on sugar and monopolies of tobacco and playing-cards. The *millones* and the *alcabala* were increased as well. Among the extraordinary devices of which most use – and abuse – was made were; manipulation of the currency, aids and forced loans, and sale of office, land and lordships. When the yield from most of the old or new taxes began to dry up because they were pledged to the *juros*, a fifty per cent discount was introduced on these. This was originally a temporary measure, but it subsequently became permanent and dealt a severe blow to state credit.

The insolvency of Philip IV brought about the ruin of his bankers. There was an initial bankruptcy in 1627. The monopoly which the Genoese bankers had hitherto enjoyed was broken and they were forced to share their financial dealings with the Portuguese *marranos* (Jews converted to Christianity). For twenty years this strange coalition provided the funds needed to finance the foreign policy of the monarchy, until a fresh bankruptcy in 1647 drove many of them out of business. The relief which this afforded the royal treasury was of very short duration, since by 1650 revenue was already being anticipated as far ahead as 1655. New bankruptcies of 1652 and 1662 succeeded in undermining the whole system of *asientos*. The few bankers who still kept on terms with the crown confined themselves to furnishing small sums at high rates of interest.

Thus the vast financial network which the Genoese had woven across Europe was no longer at the disposal of the kings of Spain.

The nine million ducats which were needed every year to service the public debt at the death of Philip IV consisted to a large extent of *juros* which had been assigned to the *asentistas* in part-payment of their credits. But since the revenues of Castile were barely equivalent to that sum and a basic minimum had to be set aside to prevent the machinery of state grinding to a halt, many of these *juros* were not paid at all, or only in part. The deflation which characterized the later seventeenth century economy aggravated still further the burden of this debt – a direct reversal of the situation a century before. Thus arose the Spanish paradox: crushing taxation, a monstrous debt ill-paid, and a state living from hand to mouth on what it could snatch from its creditors. Only the tax farmer and the tax collector did well out of this disastrous situation, compared with which the financial difficulties of the first two Habsburgs were almost a Golden Age.

At first sight it would appear that there must be some exaggeration behind the complaints of contemporaries about the depopulation and ruin of Castile. After all, the revenue to the treasury was never more than ten per cent of the national income, a percentage greatly exceeded in the modern state.[3] But the modern state assumes responsibilities which were then left to a variety of institutions, and these must be reckoned an additional heavy charge. Tithe alone was as heavy a burden as all the royal taxes put together, and then there were the profits made by the tax farmers as well, not to mention those of the local town oligarchies. The latter took over the administration of revenues, the pickings from which constituted a major source of income for this parasitic class. A by-product of the excessive fiscal pressure of the Habsburgs was the fact that the mounting public debt fostered the growth of an idle class of rentiers.

In the seventeenth century the profitability of the *juros* fell considerably. One of the chief resorts of Philip III in his attempt to reduce the debt and pay his bankers was to convert from five to three per cent. Philip IV went further, seizing half the liquid assets. The *juros* declined in popularity, but the state had begun to force people to take them. One of the more profitable pickings for those with influence at court was to buy up devalued *juros* and get them paid in full. In this and similar instances it is apparent how economic ruin went hand in hand with the moral decadence occasioned by favour and corruption.

The Hispanic empire owed its origin to matrimonial alliances, but it was defended and expanded by a military machine as many-sided as the many territories in which it was recruited. Few campaigns were complete without the presence of Spaniards, Germans and Italians, and often too there were contingents of Walloons, Lorrainers, Irish, Croats and other nationalities. In the sixteenth century they were all volunteers, mercenaries attracted by the prospect of pay or booty or the lure of an independent and adventurous existence. A heterogeneous body, they were few in number. A major army on campaign could rarely muster more than twenty to thirty thousand men, and even these small numbers proved difficult to hold together for more than a few months at a time. This was because the money to pay them would fail to come through or supply services would break down. The army lived on the countryside, being almost as much of a pest to its friends as to its enemies.

The Spaniards had no numerical superiority in the army, but they did constitute its backbone.[4] Towards the end of the sixteenth century a soldier wrote that 'though the Spanish contingent does not have such numbers as any of the others, their valour points them out as the sinews and strength of the army and as those who in matters of weight and importance must bear the brunt'.[5] The superiority of the Spaniards came from their recruitment. They were often drawn from the middling and lower nobility who had not yet forgotten the martial traditions inherited from centuries of fighting the Moslems. That tradition, which made it dishonourable to flee from an enemy though he be superior in number, gave rise to an *esprit de corps* even among the ordinary soldiers. Those who lacked the distinction of nobility could aspire to win it by feats of arms. So for a century and a half the Spanish infantry kept Europe in awe through its zeal in attack and its dogged resistance, and when it fell at Rocroi its claim to the respect and admiration of the victors was established.

The core of the army was its infantry. The artillery units were

few, and the cavalry only became important in the seventeenth
century just when the infantry was in decline. The foot soldiers
were still organized by *tercios*, as established in the days of the
Catholic Kings. At full strength a *tercio* had three to four
thousand men, divided into twelve to fifteen companies. A full
muster would show some four hundred musketeers, two and a
half thousand arquebusiers and a thousand pikemen, but these
figures were rarely reached. Generally the *tercio* was not more
than one and a half thousand strong, and could fall below that
through the officers' putting down fictitious names in the lists in
order to draw more pay.

The tactical efficiency of the *tercio* lay in its clever combination
of steel and fire-power in an age when the slow and heavy gun
was not yet master of the battlefield. Long pikes were an excellent defence against enemy cavalry, and the use of serried ranks
of arquebusiers carried the day at Pavia and elsewhere. Another
advantage of the *tercio* was that it was not a static mass. Itself a
separate and complete unit commanded by a *maestre de campo*,
it was further divided into companies led by captains, and into
groups under subalterns and sergeants. The multiplicity of
officers kept costs high but it made the army more manœuvrable,
and with the initiative left to small groups a premium was put
on individual enterprise, at which the Spaniards excelled.

The psychology of the Spanish soldier of the sixteenth century,
as studied by van der Essen, was a complex mixture of chivalry,
idealism, loyalty, greed, and indiscipline. They called themselves the 'Catholic Army', and ill-clad and hungry they more
than once stormed the breach when other nationalities refused
to fight because they had not been paid. But it is true also that
they committed terrible atrocities, while the mutinies of the
army of Flanders came to be something of an institution with
rules of its own. When pay fell too far in arrears obedience was
refused to the leaders and a chief was elected from the ranks who
imposed an iron discipline. According to the circumstances,
they would either stay inactive (a sit-down strike, as we would
say today) or try to make good the pay owed to them by looting.[6]
The most notorious of these affairs was the sack of Antwerp in
1576, a direct consequence of the bankruptcy decreed by Philip
II in the previous year, upsetting the system of *asientos*. In the
reign of Philip IV the privations suffered by the Spanish troops
in Flanders had not lessened, yet few mutinies are recorded.

This is perhaps because the troops were from different back-grounds, the nobility and the freebooters having declined in number and been replaced by conscripts who had not the same unruly character as their predecessors and were more respectful of military discipline.

This change in the recruiting base was one of the causes of the military decline of Spain. In the later years of the sixteenth century there were complaints of the neglect into which the profession of arms had fallen; rich rewards awaited those who followed civil careers, a fact which was causing the nobility to forsake the army. Even in other sectors of society a more *bourgeois* spirit was evident – there was less sense of adventure and little inclination to fight for the sake, as like as not, of leaving one's bones behind in foreign lands or coming back mutilated to live off public charity. The government paid little heed to old soldiers and only a few privileged individuals were nominated to be wardens of castles or given some other minor office to live off. Towards the middle of the seventeenth century the Marquis of Aytona described the sad fate of those who had no luck with their petitions:

Some return indignant to their lands, trusting to a relative, resolved to put up with the most abject poverty rather than re-enlist. Others go back in despair to the army, and not only do they become trouble-makers in the ranks since they have so little inclination to serve, but I have been assured that this caused more than one and a half thousand veterans and two hundred men relieved of duty to go off to serve in Venice and in Florence, and elsewhere in the years 1644, 1645 and 1646; and many take sides with our enemies. Others fall by the wayside and take menial jobs to live. Many have recourse to vice. Others seek alms in the convents, even in the streets, and others perish of want.[7]

Already during the rebellion of the *Moriscos* of Granada (1568–70) a dangerous shortage of troops had become evident. The core of the army was either garrisoned in Italy or on campaign in Flanders, and within Spain itself there was no more than a purely decorative royal guard and small contingents in frontier fortresses. It was necessary to call on the nobility and the town councils to come with the forces they could muster. The quality of these improvised troops was deplorable and they won more renown for their excesses than for their valour. Again in 1580 for the campaign to occupy Portugal, it became apparent that the only trained units were outside Spain, and they had to be called in as on the previous occasion.

To remedy this situation Philip II ordered a militia of sixty thousand men to be set up to look after internal security and defence. It was to be recruited if possible from among volunteers who were to be offered exemptions from the local courts of justice and other benefits. If this was not sufficient to fill the quota conscription would be brought in. The soldiers would be given officers and would drill on the outskirts of the towns on holidays. Though renewed in 1609 these orders had little practical effect. The militiamen looked on the training as a waste of time, and, equally, the state and the town councils failed to supply them with proper equipment. At the demand of the Cortes the militia was dissolved, except in places situated less than twenty leagues from the coast.

The great international projects which heralded the beginning of the reign of Philip IV involved a total reorganization of the military machine, whose weight was no longer to fall exclusively on Castile. Regarding the empire as a single whole, the Conde Duque of Olivares drew up a plan for the 'Union of Arms' which involved the formation of a standing army of one hundred and forty thousand men, of which Castile with the Indies would provide forty-four thousand, Portugal, Catalonia and Naples sixteen thousand each, Flanders twelve thousand, Aragon ten thousand, Milan eight thousand, Valencia six thousand, Sicily six thousand, and the Balearic and Canary Isles another six thousand. The plan was coldly received, not just from a spirit of local separatism, but because the assignment of the quotas demonstrated a total ignorance of the most elementary facts: it was absurd, for example, to claim that Catalonia with barely half a million inhabitants should supply sixteen thousand soldiers, while Sicily, with over one million was only asked for six thousand. The plan came to nothing and Castile continued, with Italy, to provide the bulk of the military forces, while Portugal, Flanders, the Crown of Aragon and Navarre refused to send soldiers much beyond their own frontiers.

Unfortunately the Castilians were showing less and less enthusiasm for war, in contrast to the continuing military vocation of the French nobility. Olivares pointed bitterly to the contrast and attempted a reorganization which would remedy some of the most glaring defects. By the ordinance of 1632 eleven regiments were created with 1,375 posts. Rates of pay were fixed, so were rewards for distinguished service, while pensions were offered to the disabled. Three years later the outbreak of hostilities with France made it necessary to keep an army in the peninsula. The Basques and the Catalans fought bravely on their own soil and the fighting was fairly even up to 1640. Indeed the resounding victory of Fuenterrabía was won in 1638. But Portugal was upset at troops being taken out of that kingdom, and Catalonia indignant at the depredations perpetrated by foreign *tercios*, and this led to uprisings in both countries. This was the real cause of the final *débâcle*, which can be traced back therefore to problems arising out of a faulty system of recruitment.

These very grave events made it necessary after 1640 to change the whole deployment of the military. In the preceding decade there had been a continual shuttle service of troops between Spain and Flanders; recruits had been sent to Flanders for their training and Walloons had been taken in exchange. The growing difficulty of communications made it necessary to suspend this interchange; henceforth, in order to defend the frontiers of Catalonia and Portugal, Castile would only be able to rely on the Italian contingents and her own forces, and this forced her to intensify recruiting by every means at her disposal. In the towns recruiting agents set up their standards and offered bounties; the great lords were ordered to organize regiments in their estates. Since these methods were not enough, recourse was had to the forced levy of vagabonds and to *quintas* among the working population, measures accompanied by great brutality and injustice. The recruiting officers, eager to reach the target they had set themselves so as to draw their pay, seized the defenceless and dragged them off in chains to the front, where those who could ran away at the first opportunity. Summonses were sent out as well to the *hidalgos* and *caballeros* who were threatened with loss of privilege if they failed to show up; some came in person and others sent substitutes. Thanks to such methods the fronts were held and Catalonia was actually retaken in 1652. But Castile was so short of men and those that were left had such little heart for the fight that the campaigns of 1661-5 to reconquer Portugal rang down the curtain on the glorious era of the Spanish army.

While the peninsula was starved of troops, there were still
enough of them in the Low Countries to face up to the combined
forces of France and Holland, and even take the offensive, as in
1636 against Paris. This preference for the defence of outlying
provinces before Spain itself demonstrates that Spanish interests
were not the essential factor in Habsburg policy. Nor was the
army there particularly Spanish, being as heterogeneous as those
of Charles v.[8] In addition to the Spanish *tercios*, which were still
the *corps d'élite*, and the Walloons, there was a mixed bag of
Germans, Italians, Irish, English Catholics, French partisans of
Condé, together with the private army of the Duke of Lorraine.
The latter had taken refuge in the Low Countries after his
expulsion from his duchy by Richelieu, with his six thousand
men at arms and a picturesque caravan of sutlers, courtesans,
and herds of cattle in train. This spectacle, common enough in
earlier days, was beginning to be an anachronism from around
1650. Louis xiv, with his great national army, heralded the
coming of a new era, that of the great homogeneous arrays,
uniformed, disciplined, well-provisioned, wanting nothing in the
way of material, and superior in numbers to anything seen
previously in Europe.

The conduct of war in those days was a strange mixture of
barbarism and chivalry. In principle there were rules which the
generals made an effort to abide by, but great atrocities were
committed whether from a desire to terrorize the enemy or
because the licentious soldiery got out of hand. In the war
against Islam no quarter was given, which meant that the
defeated were put to death or taken into slavery; but on the
whole the fighting among Christians was conducted on more
humane lines. The wars fought by Spain were free from the sort
of atrocity which turned large tracts of Germany into a semi-
waste land during the Thirty Years' War. There were deplorable incidents during the first phase of the struggle in Flanders,
but a correct bearing was maintained in the subsequent fighting
with the French and Dutch. It was the Spaniards who introduced the custom of freeing prisoners upon their word of honour
not to take up arms again. The two thousand French prisoners
taken at Lérida in 1644 were hired as labourers by craftsmen
who needed a helping hand; others of them went in for agricultural work. There were many prisoners, too, who came back
after Rocroi, still carrying their weapons. At the height of the

war the mail between Spain and Flanders continued to traverse France, and when the Cardenal Infante died, his funeral cortege was permitted to follow the same route. Francisco de Melo, who was at the Battle of the Downs, tells us that before the final combat courtesies were exchanged between the Spanish admiral, Oquendo, and the Dutch, Tromp. Many of the Spanish casualties were afterwards taken to Holland and cared for there.

Though it means going a bit beyond our period, it is interesting to look at the reply of the Council of the Indies to the proposal of the Englishman Samuel Corinton, who suggested attacking foreign possessions in America by burning their towns and crops with a machine of his own invention, and poisoning the water and food supply. Shortly before this, there had occurred the terrible storming and sack of Panama. And yet the Council rejected his proposals, 'because they are highly contrary to the Christian polity and go beyond what is allowed by common law and natural law concerning the way in which war should be fought, however bitter the enemy'.[9]

The fleet, like the army, reflected the heterogeneous character of this vast political structure. At the risk of oversimplifying we could divide Habsburg naval strength into two main groupings: the oar-propelled vessels (galleys) of the Mediterranean and the sailing ships (galleons and smaller boats) of the Atlantic. The heavily-armed galleon was better suited to fighting at a distance, whereas the galley with its cargo of infantry came in close for boarding. The chief task of the galleys was to give protection against the Turkish and Berber pirates and secondly to safeguard official transports between Spain and Italy. The galleys of Spain, paid for out of the ecclesiastical *subsidio* granted by Pope Pius v, were based on Cartagena and Puerto de Santa María, and lay there for most of every year. The growing scarcity of money left them ill-equipped and their crews badly fed, thus greatly reducing their efficiency. The galleys of Italy, incorporating the autonomous squadrons of Naples and Sicily, suffered from similar defects. There was also a contract with the Genoese family of the Dukes of Tursi for the hire of their small but efficient private fleet to the Spanish crown. In all, the kings of Spain in their heyday had about one hundred galleys at their disposal, a number which fell considerably in the seventeenth century.

As for the Atlantic, it was a long time before the kings of Spain got round to keeping a permanent fleet there. It was the need to escort the vessels plying the route to America that led to the formation of the *Escuadra de la Guarda*, made up of heavy galleons which were rulers of the waves in their day. The outbreak of hostilities with France and England forced Philip II to create the nucleus of a permanent fleet, the *Armada del Océano*, which was assigned an annual sum of 500,000 ducats on the *millones* tax after 1590. It was to consist of forty ships of between 250 and 500 tons, to be obtained either from private citizens by hire or purchase, or from a government building programme. When the need arose, one device was to embargo merchant ships of whatever nationality – this happened in connection with the preparations for the Great Armada against England. The explanation is simple enough if we bear in mind the basic similarity between merchant shipping and men-of-war. The fighting ship only gradually took on a different form.

The ambitions of the Conde Duque extended to the navy as well. His idea was to have one great fleet amalgamating those of Portugal and Flanders. The kingdom of Galicia, in return for the grant of a vote in the Cortes, undertook to launch and maintain a squadron of six boats. At the same time there occurred the creation of the *Almirantazgo del Norte* (Admiralty of the North), with its base in Dunkirk and its mission to harry Dutch trade. Its units claimed a large number of prizes on the same basis as the privateers fitted out by ordinary citizens. The widely held belief that Spain ceased to be a great naval power after 1588 is contradicted by the fact that it retained a numerical superiority for a long time to come. The effective decline began around 1638, with the raids of the archbishop of Bordeaux on the Cantabrian ports and the burning of the principal dockyards, and 1639, date of the disastrous defeat of Oquendo's fleet by Tromp in the English Channel. The financial strain of later years prevented these losses from being made good, so that the final cause of naval decline was economic in character. But even in its heyday the Spanish navy was never fully able to cope, thanks to the number of its independent subdivisions, the variety of its tasks, and the range of enemies it had to face in every sea on the world's surface. It was quite an achievement in itself to have safeguarded the communications of a vast empire whose links were essentially maritime.

As in the case of the army the problem of recruiting men for the navy became more difficult as time wore on. There was no shortage of volunteers for the *Armada de la Guarda de Indias*, where there were various pickings to be had. There was less enthusiasm however, for manning the vessels of the *Armada del Mar Océano*, and less still for joining the ill-paid infantry on board the galleys. But with the galleys the basic problem was to find men to pull the oars, for this was a job whose harshness became proverbial. In view of the scarcity of oarsmen recourse was had to slaves and to those condemned for common-law crimes. Judges were frequently instructed to sentence offenders to the galleys. Since the conditions of service were so severe the sentence was limited to ten years; but the difficulty of finding replacements led to the limit being extended, though the victims were now treated as volunteers, which meant that they got a very small wage and their food and conditions improved.

Diplomacy on a continuous basis was one of the political novelties of the Renaissance. The resident, or ambassador, was not just the personal representative of the king who sent him, but an active agent for gathering information and weaving intrigue, a 'privileged spy', as Mousnier calls him. The diplomatic service of Charles v was mainly recruited in Castile and Flanders. In subsequent reigns there was a marked predominance of Castilians, though not to the exclusion of the other nationalities of the empire. Appointments to the key embassies (Rome, Paris, London, Vienna) were matters of the highest importance. In line with the ideas of the time the ambassador had to be a member of the aristocracy. Happily the Castilian nobility was able to furnish men of the highest ability who knew what they were about and had a real sense of dedication. Missions of this kind made heavy inroads on a man's fortune. Although the state budget included items for ambassadorial expenses, the sort of life they led and the suite of followers they had to attend to meant that they usually finished their term with impressive debts for which the royal treasury did not always indemnify them. A case in point is that of Don Antonio Pimentel, ambassador at the court of Queen Christina of Sweden and a skilful negotiator of the Peace of the Pyrenees, appointed by the government as governor of Cadiz to help him recoup his battered fortunes: he had to be relieved of the post for the haste with which he tried to make good.

Perhaps the most important embassy was that of Rome, not just for the delicate negotiations it involved but for its incomparable value as an international listening-post. One of the basic duties of the ambassador was to dole out pensions and prebends with the aim of keeping as large a party of cardinals as possible favourably disposed to the House of Habsburg, in the hope that they would support the general policy of the monarchy and when a Conclave occurred would ensure the triumph of a pro-Habsburg candidate. Not all the Spanish representatives in Rome had the necessary tact. Don Enrique de Guzmán, Count of Olivares and father of the Conde Duque, was at loggerheads with Pope Sixtus v because of his haughty temperament. Likewise in 1632 Cardinal Borja envenomed relations with Urban viii by his clumsy method of making a protest which was in itself justified. Disputes over precedence, brawls between page-boys and the native population, or between the retinues of different ambassadors, were then a common occurrence in embassies, but particularly so in Rome.

The embassy at Vienna was another key post in view of the close relationship between the two branches of the House of Habsburg. The financial dependence of the Habsburg emperors on the king of Spain gave his representatives an outstanding influence. They were respected, even feared counsellors of the imperial government, as well as embodying in the eyes of Viennese society an ideal to be imitated in point of dress, manners, and style of living. The count of Oñate held a special place in this regard during the first phase of the Thirty Years' War. The embassy at London could also boast some skilful diplomats, the outstanding name here being Don Diego Sarmiento de Acuña, count of Gondomar, who succeeded in gaining the favour of James i. The great politico-military school founded in the reign of Philip ii yielded its finest results in the reign of Philip iii, just as the reality of decline was becoming visible elsewhere. Philip iv could still count on a few skilful diplomats, like Pimentel mentioned above; but the golden age of Castilian diplomacy was by then at an end.

4

CHARLES V

Charles V is a figure on a world scale and therefore very difficult to write about from any purely national angle. With him, the history of Spain merges with the general history of Europe. The nebulous *weltanschauung* of his empire went beyond the framework of inter-state relations; and as an added complication there is the separate and vast story of the formation of Spain's overseas empire. The Spanish empire and the empire of Charles V are two different things, one as gigantic as the other, and they only partially overlap. For that reason the brief summary of the reign given here, which while attempting not to omit anything vital seeks to stay largely within the geographical limits of the Iberian peninsula, must leave something to be desired.

The development of Charles V's idea of empire has been examined by numerous authors, especially by Peter Rassow. Rassow defines it as a policy inspired by the general interests of Christianity, for with Charles religious motives were more important than political. He harboured no territorial ambitions, his wars were purely in self-defence, and of Francis I he demanded only what he thought belonged to him. Deeply grieved as he was by the split in the unity of Christendom, he yet delayed taking up arms against the Protestants for as long as he was able and placed all his trust in the General Council which was to restore Catholicism. This fundamentally religious concept of his power found expression in the ceremonies at his coronation, omitted by his predecessor. This mystic act of imperial baptism would allow him to speak and act in the name of the Church. Karl Brandi, another eminent biographer of the emperor, agrees with Rassow on many points, seeing the formulation of the idea of empire as a later growth in the mind of Charles V and one which owed much to the thought of his Italian chancellor, Mercurio Gattinara.

On the other hand, Menéndez Pidal in a short work pointed out the Spanish origins of the imperial idea. Before Gattinara it had been formulated by three Spaniards: Ruiz de la Mota, bishop of Badajoz, in the Cortes of Corunna; Guevara, author of the *Reloj de Príncipes*; and Alfonso de Valdés, Secretary of Latin Letters to the emperor. Another Spanish historian, J. A. Maravall, distinguishes three periods in the life and thought of Charles v. The first, up to 1530, is set against a Spanish background and strongly coloured by Erasmus, at that time the most widely read author in Spain. The second, from 1530 to 1542, represents a retreat from the somewhat utopian idea of universal monarchy towards more practical problems, with the focus on Germany, Italy and France. In the third phase Spain returns to the foreground, enriched now with America and undeniably the centre of imperial power.

Since Charles v in the later years of his reign wrote, or rather was the inspiration behind, some 'memoirs', it would seem logical to look there for his own idea of his mission and his views on the empire. But here the reader will get no satisfaction. His memoirs are a fairly dry narrative of events, unenlivened by any concepts of a general nature. Charles refers in them so frequently to his House as to give the impression that purely dynastic interests came before everything else. This is an argument in favour of those who argue that his political ideas were an anachronism. If he were purely and simply someone with a vision transcending national boundaries then he would have to be acknowledged as a forerunner of modern developments, for our emerging Europe is just the ghost of old medieval Christendom. But in his concern with his dynasty and his House, he seems out of step with an age which was moving visibly in the direction of the depersonalized state.

Born in Flanders of a Spanish mother and given a Franco-burgundian education, by upbringing and character Charles was the sovereign most suited to embodying the idea of universal monarchy. This idea had not triumphed in the Middle Ages; it could not be expected to triumph now at the height of the Renaissance, despite the unconditional support it was given in Spain. For this Holy, Roman and Germanic Empire met its greatest resistance in Germany and Rome. The conflict between universalism and nationalism was not the cause of its final lack of success. Despite his ideological heritage Charles was sufficiently realistic to appreciate that he lived in a Europe based on the plurality of sovereignty. There is no doubt – though on this point he never expressed himself clearly – that he conceived his imperial role as a mere hegemony of the West, compatible with the full independence of the individual states. If he clashed with the French king it was because the Burgundian legacy drove him to recapture territories held by France, while the Aragonese inheritance obliged him to defend Italian territories on which France had her eyes. If France seemed to embody the voice of the future in her claim to those regions where the French tongue was spoken, the same could not be said of her aspirations to Italy or Navarre.

On the other side there was Francis I's own desire to be emperor, motivated by fear of so great a triumph on the part of his rival or by his reluctance as sovereign of the most wealthy and populous nation in the West to acknowledge a superior. On the death of the Emperor Maximilian a struggle developed, its aim to purchase the conscience of the seven Electors. It ended in Charles' favour with his election as emperor in 1519. But the triumph cost him dear. To match the gold of Francis I and the Medici who supported his candidature, Charles had to negotiate a loan of half a million florins with Jacob Fugger, the Augsburg banker. The total cost of the election must have been near a million. Thus, at the bare outset of his reign, he found himself a prey to those financial difficulties which were to grow with time until they proved the greatest stumbling block to his political ambitions.

The diplomatic chessboard of Europe was then very straightforward. There was no Russia, England was still in an early stage of development, Italy and Germany were mere geographical expressions, leaving only three great powers – France, the Turkish empire, and the empire of Charles V. However upsetting it seemed at first, the chances of an alliance between the first two were clearly growing, and the alliance was indeed eventually concluded. Meanwhile Charles' resources, unmatched on paper, were undermined by the fact that his domains were so scattered, his enemies so numerous, and Germany in the throes of domestic turmoil. This is why he prized the English alliance so highly. Though England was not yet a great power, her situation off the coasts of France and Flanders enabled her to intervene and turn the balance in favour of one or other of the contestants. Hence arose the meetings between Charles and Henry VIII at Dover and Gravelines shortly before he was crowned emperor, his second and lengthy visit to England in the spring of 1522, and the projected match between Charles and Mary, the woman who was later to be his daughter-in-law. It will be appreciated what a disastrous blow it was to Charles' policy when he broke with Henry over the divorce of Catherine of Aragon, and why, to restore the precious English alliance, he forced his son Philip to marry his aunt and blood relation, Mary.

But the wavering friendship of England was of less consequence in the last resort than a strengthened hold on Spain. From his arrival in that country in 1517 the beardless youth with his rather ungainly presence and ignorance of the Castilian language had created an unfavourable impression, reinforced by the fact that he let himself be ruled by rapacious foreign advisers. His first act was the dismissal of the veteran regent, Cardinal Cisneros, who died providentially before receiving the royal letter. When the Cortes gathered in Valladolid to take the oath to the new monarch they demanded that he first of all swear to uphold the liberties of Castile. He did so, much to the annoyance of his Flemish councillors, Sauvage and Chièvres. But he gave no undertaking about not giving official appointments to foreigners, though there was discontent at his blatant favouritism – for example appointing a nephew of Chièvres as archbishop of Toledo. With a view to receiving the oath of loyalty and obtaining subsidies he visited Zaragoza and Barcelona. On hearing the news of his election as emperor he left to take ship at Corunna – but not before holding a Cortes which he cajoled and browbeat into giving him the money he needed for his journey and coronation. His Spanish subjects had now further cause for discontent: the monarch clearly would be absent for some time, while Spain would be incorporated into a supra-national structure in which its own separate interests would be lost to sight.

These complex sentiments and obscure fears led to the revolt of the *Comuneros* of Castile, which has become a subject of much interest in our own day. It is indeed a crucial episode in the history of Spain. The defeat of the *Comuneros* meant that a monarchy which had been contractual became absolute. From that date forward the ceremony of swearing the *fueros*, liberties and privileges, which each king had gone through at the beginning of his reign, became a mere formality in Castile, whatever significance it retained in the Crown of Aragon. There is no shortage of studies devoted to the *Comuneros*, yet their significance is still open to a variety of interpretations, which usually reflect the political preoccupations of the particular author or his age. For three centuries after the suppression of the movement there was an attempt to cast a veil of oblivion over an episode which was deemed disgraceful. Histories, whether of a general or a local character, passed over it in haste, laying the blame on a momentary aberration of the ordinary people, while documents and papers were abstracted from municipal archives lest they show the role played by the nobility. With the coming of the nineteenth century the outlook changed. The liberals turned to the *Comuneros* as their forerunners, and the names of the leaders were inscribed in the assembly hall of the Congress and in the streets of many Spanish towns.

In this century the interpretation of the *Comuneros* as a liberal, almost democratic movement, has come under fire for being too simplistic or, indeed, anachronistic. Marañón maintained that it was not a case of popular elements reacting against a tyrannical king who menaced their liberties, but instead a defensive move on the part of what today would be called the right: ecclesiastics who believed Catholicism threatened by foreigners, nobles who clung to their feudal privileges and their authority over the towns and sought to resist more modern and more liberal trends embodied by the emperor. Both points of view are dogmatic and overstate the case. The more recent study, by J. A. Maravall,[1] takes a more balanced view and on the whole comes out on the side of earlier writers. According to him, if the *Comuneros* were not liberals in the modern sense of the term they did represent the urban bourgeoisie of Castile, whose stand was anti-feudal and whose claim to speak for national, even democratic feeling was backed up by ample popular support.

To some extent the variety of interpretations stems from the fact that the *Comunero* movement was fairly complicated since it grouped separate social classes with separate aims. Its form changed too under the pressure of events. The genesis of

Castilian discontent can be found between 1518 and 1520 in the sermons preached by certain clerics and friars denouncing the rapacious foreigner and urging the 'middling sort' to be the first to take a stand, since the nobility would not.[2] The spark which set things alight was the action of Toledo, where a *hidalgo*, Juan de Padilla, took the lead. Almost simultaneously there was a rising in Segovia, the biggest industrial town in Castile. It was actually a section of the proletariat which put the deputy Tordesillas to death for voting the subsidies to the emperor, but the local nobility in the person of Juan Bravo took over control. In Salamanca the lead was taken by the noble family of the Maldonado, in Léon by the Guzmán, in Zamora by the bishop, Acuña. The movement was joined by Madrid, Cuenca, Ávila, Soria; that is, by almost the entire Castilian Meseta, and even by Valladolid, though it was the residence of Adrian of Utrecht the regent left by Charles v.

On the other hand the movement evoked virtually no response in the north where there were few big towns, or in Galicia which lacked an influential bourgeoisie. It received very faint support in a few towns of Andalusia and Extremadura, where the towns were in the hands of the greater nobility. No grandee joined the *Comuneros*; several took sides openly against them. The duke of Infantado kept Guadalajara in the heart of his estates quiet; the Constable and the Admiral of Castile collaborated with the regent. At the other end of the social scale there was, with rare exceptions, no trouble from the peasant masses. The movement therefore had as its leaders the bourgeoisie and the intermediate nobility of the towns (*hidalgos* and *caballeros*) and as its supporters the urban proletariat. The nobility drifted away eventually, as demagogic elements appeared and the impending collapse of the movement prompted them to seek an alibi. They actually managed to distort the meaning of what had taken place, claiming that it had been a revolt of the populace against the nobility. This was not in general the case, though there were local incidents where vassals took the chance to indulge their animosity against their lords.

Another debated question is the share taken by *conversos* of Jewish origin.[3] Most of them belonged to the urban bourgeoisie whose aims they therefore shared. There were hopes too of getting the activities of the Inquisition curbed or suppressed, which explains why many took part, though purely as individuals. As it happens their hopes were unfounded since the majority of the *Comuneros* believed in the strictest orthodoxy.

In 1520 representatives of the rebel towns met in Ávila and formed a Holy Junta. This government formulated a programme which had already been outlined in the instructions delivered by some towns to their representatives. The procedure recalls the *cahiers* of the French Revolution. The main emphasis was laid on the exclusion of foreigners from all functions of government, prohibiting the export of coin, limiting royal taxes, and respecting local franchises. If this programme had been carried out Castile would have been turned into a federation of autonomous towns presided over by a monarch with limited powers. There was no question of a return to feudalism, for towns had no place in a feudal system. It would have meant a situation akin to that in the maritime provinces of the Crown of Aragon where the towns were ruled by an urban patriciate including nobles as well as bourgeois; nobles who, it should be noted, were not above dabbling in trade. The ambition corresponded to the particular stage reached by the Castilian economy which was experiencing a pre-capitalist boom and struggling for an appropriate political outlet.

However great the influence of the rebel towns they were like islands in the middle of a rural sea which paid them no heed. Time was against them, for they kept losing rather than winning supporters. Burgos, a commercial centre of the first importance, followed the loyal path thanks to the influence of the Constable. The towns of Andalusia formed an anti-*Comunero* league. The lords who had initially given their support to the movement tacitly withdrew. The regent and his councillors by skilful manœuvring gradually isolated the rebels and got together a royal army to meet their ill-disciplined host. The clash between the two sides at Villalar ended in decisive victory for the royalists. The following day Padilla, Bravo and Maldonado were beheaded (1521). There was no further resistance except briefly on the part of Toledo where the staunch widow of Padilla was in command. On his return from Germany the emperor granted an amnesty to which there were numerous exceptions. One of these was the brave bishop of Zamora, who was put in prison at Simancas and when he tried to escape by killing the warder was hanged from one of the battlements.

At almost the same moment as the rising of the *Comuneros* in Castile the Valencian region was the scene of the *Germanías*. This was a social rather than a political movement, a product of the traditional hostility of the people towards the semi-feudal nobility and its harsh rule. The strength of the movement lay in a popularly based militia which existed to defend the coasts against pirates. Royal power was anyway at a low ebb. A junta of thirteen members under the leadership of a woollen worker was set up in Valencia, while all over the kingdom there occurred frequent incidents, attacks and clashes between a mainly urban militia and the nobility which was arming its Christian and Moslem vassals. A mistaken reaction on the part of the *Agermanados* was to attack the Moslems and force them to receive baptism, when the obvious course would have been to win them over with a view to forming a united front against the nobility. Discredited by their demagogic excesses the *Agermanados* succumbed in 1522 to the combined royal and seigneurial forces, and the seigneurial regime re-emerged stronger than ever.

The *Germanía* of the island of Majorca had very similar features. It began in the city of Palma with a rising of workers and artisans against the wealthy and high-born, and subsequently against the landed nobility of the island. The wildest excesses were committed on both sides. In 1522, with order re-established in the peninsula, a fleet arrived and the royal forces subjected the *Agermanados* to a harsh repression.

The rivalry of Charles v and Francis i is a classic theme and one frequently discussed in modern history. It was not a confrontation of two nations in the modern sense of the term. There were more than a few medieval overtones to the struggle; for example the way in which the ransom of Francis i was handled, according to the custom that made the capture of an enemy a subject for barter, or the completely feudal attitude of the French Constable, Bourbon, who considered that the grievances he had suffered at the hands of his sovereign entitled him to break the bond of vassalage and ally with the enemy. But a critical reception was accorded to both attitudes; so apparently they were out of date as far as European opinion was concerned. The fact that these struggles coincided with the religious split was disastrous for European unity and for any chance it had of resisting the advance of the Turk, who now expanded to his farthest limits along the Danube basin and in the Mediterranean.

France had emerged from the Hundred Years' War, like Spain after the *Reconquista*, with a tradition of fighting and a fever for expansion, directed in this instance against Italy. The rich and glorious civilization of that peninsula was quite incapable of defending itself, which made it an irresistible temptation. Its inability to make the transition from city to nation state caused a power vacuum in Italy. Like a cyclone it drew into itself everything around – Spaniards, French, Germans, and Turks. The skilful diplomacy of Ferdinand the Catholic aided by the military genius of the Great Captain (Gonzalo Fernández de Córdoba) had succeeded in maintaining Spanish supremacy in the south of Italy and checking the initiatives of Charles VIII and Louis XII. But Francis I, a young and spirited king at the head of a nation which was then the most populous in Europe, with a nobility dedicated to war and ample opportunities of recruiting an excellent infantry in Switzerland, could not resist the temptation to try his luck again. There were other problems too arising out of the division of the Burgundian state. Charles was upset at the annexation of Burgundy, the ancestral possession of his dynasty, by France, and Francis that Franche Comté and the county of Flanders, an old fief of the French crown, still lay outside his domain and left Paris dangerously close to the frontier. The question of Navarre was another irritant, its incorporation by Castille not having been recognized by France. Francis was also resentful of Charles' claims to the imperial crown. And, above and beyond all this, there was the conviction that it was feats of arms that brought lustre to a reign. Both sovereigns, then, would don their armour and take up their weapons – swords of course, not guns, another medieval touch.

In 1515 Francis I took the duchy of Milan. Shortly afterwards, taking advantage of the disturbances caused by the *Comuneros*, he invaded Navarre with the aim of re-establishing there the old dynasty of French origin. Navarre in the hands of the French was a deadly threat to Castile; so the victorious troops of the Emperor and the vanquished *Comuneros* forgot their differences and united to drive out the invader. At the same time the forces of Charles and of Pope Leo X re-established Francis Sforza as

duke of Milan. Imperial diplomacy had succeeded in winning
the alliance of the pope, who was at first hostile, and of Henry
VIII of England, who had been courted simultaneously by
Charles and Francis.

Francis I did not lose heart at these reverses. He knew that the
aid given to his adversary by England and the pope was not to
be relied on. A safer ally for Charles was the French Constable,
who had been stripped of his goods and threatened with death
and who now joined his private army to the emperor's, laying
waste Provence. These were no more than preliminary skirmishes.
The main confrontation occurred when Francis I crossed the
Alps in person and occupied Milan, forcing the small Spanish
garrison to take refuge in Pavia. While the French were
besieging this stronghold the emperor's men rounded up a
motley force of Spaniards, Germans and Italians. The French
king accepted battle on most unfavourable terms. The garrison
of Pavia made a spirited sortie and he found himself caught in a
crossfire. The Spanish arquebusiers carried the day, mowing
down the French cavalry, which suffered enormous casualties.
Among the prisoners was the French king himself.

The royal captive was taken to Madrid and became the
object of long deliberations on the part of Charles and his
councillors as to the procedure to be followed. Harsh terms
could be imposed, or he could be allowed to leave freely in the
hope of winning his friendship. Charles opted for the first
alternative. The French offered to give up all their claims to
Italy and Flanders. The chancellor, Gattinara, was in favour of
accepting this offer. Charles, harking back to family tradition,
demanded Burgundy as well, and his resolution was stiffened by
the arrival of another influential councillor, Nicholas Perrenot
de Granvelle, a native of the Franche Comté, that is, of that
part of the old Burgundy which had remained in the hands of
the House of Habsburg.

Francis signed everything that was demanded of him by the
Treaty of Madrid of 1526. But once he was set free he refused to
give it effect, pretending by a very modern argument that the
Burgundians were, and wanted to remain, French. The truth is
that his renunciation of Italy and Flanders involved no more
than a renunciation of hypothetical claims, whereas giving up
Burgundy would have meant handing over a territory already
in his hands. It is doubtful whether Francis would have kept his

word even had the terms been favourable. In fact the only tangible gains which Charles derived from the treaty were the two million *escudos* which Francis had to deliver in order to ransom his two sons whom he had left behind as hostages.

Not only did the French king break the treaty, but within a few months he joined the anti-imperial League of Cognac, skilfully prepared during his absence by the Queen Regent, Louise of Savoy. Taking part were Milan, Genoa, Venice, Florence and the pope, in other words the same parties who had helped Charles against Francis. What the small Italian states wanted was to play the two colossi off against each other, banding together each time against the stronger. It was a typical device of the weak, an over-subtle policy which could have no long-term success. What must have incensed Charles most was the attitude of the pope. On the death of Leo x the emperor had procured the election of his tutor, Adrian of Utrecht (Adrian vi). The latter arrived with his reforming programme which was not at all to the liking of the Curia, and to the great satisfaction of the Romans, he died within a couple of years. The new pope, Clement vii, was a Medici, more concerned with his family interests than those of the Church. He demonstrated this by taking sides against the emperor, regardless of the great efforts Charles was making to resolve the religious crisis in Germany and defend Christianity against the Turk, while Francis i was actually seeking the support of Suleiman the Magnificent. Meanwhile at Mohacs the Turks smashed the army of Louis ii of Hungary, brother-in-law of the emperor, and established themselves on the Hungarian plain where for a century and a half they were to be a mortal threat to the House of Habsburg and indeed to the West as a whole.

However the avenging thunderbolt was to fall on Rome without any action by the emperor – he was actually in Spain, having recently married the beautiful Isabel of Portugal. He had left his army in the north of Italy in an intolerable position for lack of pay. The force was made up to a large extent of Lutheran mercenaries from Germany under the command of the French Constable, Bourbon. When they had exhausted their supplies in the duchy of Milan the Constable offered to lead them against Rome. The attack on the Eternal City began and though Bourbon perished in the assault the defences were breached and a fearful sack ensued. It is futile to argue whether

Spaniards or Germans were responsible for the greater atrocities; both, with no leader to restrain them, behaved as might be expected of a greedy and brutal mercenary band. The sack of Rome (1527) created a profound impression everywhere, and the enemies of Charles v exploited it by means of pamphlets and broadsheets. In defence of his master Alfonso de Valdés composed the 'Dialogue between Lactancio and an archdeacon' in which he interpreted the catastrophe as a judgement of God on a city which had failed in its mission to lead and set an example to Christendom. Charles v showed signs of regret, suspending the festivities prepared in celebration of the birth of his son Philip; but he did not neglect to take advantage of the situation. Clement vii had to buy his freedom by giving up Parma, Plasencia, and Modena, and paying a ransom of 400,000 *escudos*.

All in all the emperor had no grounds for complacency at the beginning of 1528. The north of Italy was in the hands of the French and their allies. Henry viii had joined them by the treaties of Westminster and Amiens. Francis i undertook the conquest of Naples, which was besieged on land by the army of Lautrec and on sea by the fleet of Andrea Doria. Then suddenly the tables were turned. Doria, irritated with the king of France, went over to Charles' side. The French army, deprived of support at sea and decimated by plague, beat a retreat. The pope changed his mind since he needed the support of Charles to re-establish the government of the Medici in Florence. To crown it all both contestants were severely short of funds. The Peace of Cambrai, or the 'Ladies' Peace' (because of the role played by Louise of Savoy and Margaret of Austria) restored the situation as it was after Pavia. Charles gave up Burgundy, Francis gave up Italy and Flanders (1529). Francis Sforza, his earlier turncoat activities forgiven, was restored to the duchy of Milan, an imperial fief. The Medici recovered Florence as well, after a fierce siege in which they were assisted by the emperor; and this time they had come back to stay. These years mark the climax of Charles' reign. After a lengthy sojourn in Spain he arranged a meeting with Clement vii at Bologna and was crowned emperor by him.

The seven years' peace with France was a time of feverish activity. During this period Charles travelled continually from one end to the other of his empire. Now with the Italian question settled Germany became his chief concern. His first act after his coronation as emperor was to summon Luther to the Diet of Worms to get him to recant. In contrast to the apathy of the papacy Charles became tireless in his efforts to preserve the unity of the Church, for he saw himself as its temporal protector. Luther's obstinacy met with the backing of the duke of Saxony and the ban published against him was not put into effect. Temporal and spiritual questions now become hopelessly entangled in this dispute. To say that Charles was hostile to the Protestants does not reveal the full complexity of the conflict, for he kept postponing the formal breach while there were Protestant princes loyal to him and Catholics opposed to him. Beneath the confessional struggle and interwoven with it there was the old opposition of the German princes to any loss of independence or to becoming mere subjects of a tightly centralized Habsburg state. The danger seemed to them more imminent than ever: could the Emperor not draw on the vast power of Spain, Italy and Flanders, and, at a distance, of the Indies as well? It is probable therefore that without Luther the rebellion of the German princes would still have taken place under other forms, with other pretexts, but still of course with the backing of France.

The unity of the West, then, was an unattainable ideal, even in the modified form envisaged by Charles, even making full allowance for national separatism and established rights. Castile proved the mainstay of Charles' dream, Castile subdued by force of arms in the first instance, then captivated by the grandeur of the ideal which was set before her. Yet even she hesitated timorously on the edge of an undertaking in which she could sense tremendous dangers for herself. The hostility of France was a foregone conclusion. In Italy only the old Aragonese provinces could be relied upon; all the other Italian alliances, even that of the pope, were built on shifting sands. Nor was the English alliance any more secure. Henry VIII's initial inclination to carry on the tradition of war with France changed after Pavia, in part because the French king was no longer a menace to him, but also as a result of the personal factor involved in his divorce from Catherine of Aragon. Even in the Low Countries disturbing events were taking place like the rebellion of Ghent, suppressed with a harshness which shows the little affection Charles had for his native city.

Even after this brief survey we can see why Charles never came within reach of his lifelong goal of peace. Peace demanded unity, or at very least what was later called the European Balance. The former was unattainable while the latter, given the disproportionate power of Charles, could only be achieved by a combination among those who lay outside his orbit. In fact after each of his triumphs such a combination instinctively emerged. Beyond question the religious crisis deepened European differences; but these were bound to erupt in bitter conflict sooner or later.

The religious affairs of Germany and the efforts of Charles with regard to the summoning of the General Council can only be touched on briefly here, in so far as they affect the history of Spain. There is a difference which must be brought out between the influence of religion on the foreign policy of Charles v and on that of Philip ii. Both shared the idea that their duty was to defend Catholic unity. But while Charles saw it in terms of a domestic problem which would settle itself sooner or later, Philip came to it as an outsider from Catholic Spain, and started with the idea that the rupture was definitive. Hence Charles was always striving after a compromise, which to his son would appear out of the question. Following the Diets of Speyer and Augsburg there emerged in 1531 the politico-military grouping of the Protestant princes known as the Schmalkaldic League. In itself the league was not very strong, but it could rely on the backing of France and even on the Duke of Bavaria, who though a Catholic was jealous of the preponderance of the Habsburgs, whose territories surrounded his own. The clash which seemed imminent was delayed by the Turkish assault on Vienna which threatened all alike. At the head of troops from all over Germany Charles marched to the relief of the city, and the Turks, without waiting for him to arrive, beat a retreat (1532).

Francis i had never been sincere in his promise not to intervene in the affairs of Italy. On the death of Francis Sforza he revived his claims to Milan, which led to a new war of two years (1536–8). The king of France could no longer rely on the German Protestants, having alienated them by the harsh religious repression for which he was responsible in his own country. But no scruple of this kind could weigh in the balance against the ruthless logic of *raison d'état*. Turkey, wooed for some time, now became a formal ally, and to the amazement of Christendom the Turkish fleet was welcomed in the port of Toulon, a fleet whose aim it was to carry destruction into the western Mediterranean. Charles v retorted by invading Provence with an army led by his best generals, the marquis of Vasto, the duke of Alba and Don Antonio de Leiva. The French withdrew, razing the country systematically as they went, and this combined with the destruction caused by the imperial troops left whole areas waste. But the invaders were short of supplies and proved unable to take Marseilles, and so had to return to Italy. Thanks to the mediation of Pope Paul III the two sovereigns arranged the Truce of Nice. Several years of peace, even amity, ensued, to all appearances sincere. It was at this time that Charles passed through France on his way to punish Ghent and received cordial hospitality from Francis, who chivalrously refused to listen to advisers who urged him to take revenge for his captivity in Madrid.

There was yet another war, however, the fourth of the series, from 1542 to 1545. For at bottom the old discord had not disappeared, notably over Milan which Francis hoped his rival would hand over to one of his sons. When he learned that Charles had given the investiture to his own son Philip he made renewed preparations for war, preceded by secret treaties with the German Protestants and the Turks. Two envoys from the king of France to the Sultan were assassinated as they crossed Italy, probably on the orders of the Spanish authorities, and this incident furnished the pretext for a declaration of war. The French showed great energy at the outset, attacking the frontiers of Spain, Flanders and Savoy, and they gained some initial successes. But Charles had assured himself of the support of Henry VIII, who had his eyes on Boulogne. Faced with the threat of a combined attack on Paris, Francis I signed the Treaty of Crépy. This added nothing substantial to earlier treaties, except that the emperor promised to hand Milan or the Low Countries over to the duke of Orleans, younger son of Francis, as a dowry for his projected marriage with a daughter of Charles. But the arrangement came to nothing since the duke died.

Francis I died in 1547, almost at the same time as Henry VIII. Only Charles remained on the scene, now resolved to decide the German question by force of arms. For years he had trusted that he would find a peaceful settlement by means of a

Council; but this idea had aroused no enthusiasm either among the Protestants or in Rome itself. With the accession of Paul III there was at long last a pontiff ready to issue the summons, if he could be sure of keeping it under his own control. Charles tried unsuccessfully to have it meet in Germany; but a compromise was reached by which it would be summoned to Trent, a town situated on the borders of Germany and Italy. The Protestants did not turn up and the Council, dominated by its majority of Italian and Spanish bishops, took a course which was not the one the emperor had anticipated.

The emperor in any case had gradually lost many of his ecumenical illusions and had reached the conclusion that only a resort to arms could unravel the tangled political and religious situation in Germany. In 1547 the international scene seemed to favour a coup. Charles sought to avoid taking his stand on purely religious issues: Philip of Hesse and John Frederick of Saxony, heads of the Schmalkaldic League, were stripped of their titles at the Diet of Ratisbon on charges of disobedience and rebellion. Maurice of Saxony and other Protestant princes fought on the emperor's side, though the chief credit for the victory at Mühlberg goes to the Spanish arquebusiers. The outcome was the disintegration of the Schmalkaldic League. Maurice of Saxony received the electorate of which his cousin had been dispossessed. And in the Diet of Augsburg the emperor published a resolution, the controversial *Interim*, by virtue of which the Catholic faith was restored in Germany until the Council of Trent made its final decision. There were two concessions to the Protestants: communion under both species and marriage of the clergy.

Spain seems at first sight to be outside this complex web of wars and treaties; but in fact her importance as the mainstay of imperial policy was growing all the time. Without the wealth of Castile, without her soldiers as well as those of the Italian territories of Spain, imperial politics would have had no material foundation. It was from the 1530s that the river of gold and silver coming from the Indies began to swell spectacularly: from 518,833 ducats which went to the king in the years 1531–5, to 1,621,062 in the next five years, to 4,354,208 in the last five years of the reign. But this could supply only part of the capital drained abroad. Foreign enterprises had led to confiscation of private silver from America, to sales of land and office, and to many other extraordinary measures. In 1546, for the German campaign, the bishops, nobles and rich merchants of Castile were asked for a loan of 432,000 ducats.[4]

Paradoxically, the more Charles V depended on Spain the less time he spent there. His longest stay was the seven years from 1522 to 1529, as though to satisfy the clamours which had arisen over his absence. Subsequently he came to stay for shorter periods, and after 1543 he did not return until his abdication. It is true that he kept up an active correspondence with Don Francisco de los Cobos and with his son, Philip; but the recurring theme in his letters was the need for sending more subsidies. Castilian fears, as expressed in the demands of the *Comuneros*, were confirmed, while the complaints of the deputies in the Cortes show that only a very small minority were willing to make the sacrifices demanded by imperial policy.

From a strictly Spanish point of view the most interesting aspect of the many-sided activity of Charles was the struggle against the Turks and Berbers in the Mediterranean. It was no longer a question of following up the *Reconquista* of the Iberian peninsula by conquering North Africa along the lines laid down by Isabella the Catholic in her will. The expeditions had more limited objectives: they were basically defensive, despite their aggressive appearance, being aimed at destroying the pirate bases, widening the chain of garrison enclaves (*presidios*), and installing friendly princes who would accept a protectorate independent of the sultan of Constantinople. Settling people there would have been a more radical solution, but it was impossible because the surplus population of Spain was drained off in other directions, and the surplus itself dwindling fast. Charles took personal charge of two expeditions. In 1535 he captured Tunis, restoring Muley Hassan who had been dethroned by Barbarossa; twenty thousand Christian captives recovered their freedom. Six years later he made another attempt, this time against Algiers, but it ended in failure because of raging storms. This failure, allied to the loss of Bugia and Tripoli, was a decisive setback. The menace to navigation and even to coastal dwellings in the Mediterranean was to get worse from year to year.

In 1547 Charles V was at the height of his power and glory. His kingdoms were at peace; he had regulated the affairs of

Germany; he was beset by no imminent peril. For half a decade he was the undisputed arbiter of Europe. But after 1552 the situation deteriorated rapidly. The new king of France, Henry ii, was no less impatient than his father of Charles' pre-eminence. In Germany there was a veneer of calm but dis-content was seething beneath, for the *Interim* had satisfied neither Catholics nor Protestants. The German princes were as suspicious as ever of any strengthening of authority which might convert the empire into a monarchy. If the Catholics hesitated to adopt an attitude of open defiance, the Protestants had not the same scruples. By the Treaty of Chambord they purchased the alliance of France, thanks to the cession of Metz, Toul and Verdun. Henry ii took possession of these fortresses and then invaded Alsace; Maurice of Saxony, in an unexpected change of sides, led an army towards the Alpine retreat where Charles was resting. The emperor only avoided captivity by a hasty flight in a litter, where he lay afflicted by gout, across the snow-bound passes of the Tyrol towards Carinthia. Realizing that his whole life's work in Germany was on the point of collapse, he left his brother Ferdinand to reach an agreement with the Protestants, even at the price of granting them religious freedom. But he did not abandon the hope of punishing the French. Even here he had no success, for the large army he had assembled for an attack on Metz was dispersed by plague and by the rigours of an exceptionally cold winter.

To these political reverses was added the increasingly precarious state of his health. Gout tormented him cruelly, making an invalid of him, for he could no longer ride a horse. From the time he raised the siege of Metz until his embarkation for Spain he made only one short excursion from Brussels. The state of his finances was deplorable; it was only with great difficulty that he could find money, and then at very high interest. He made up his mind that he would not carry on with duties which were too much for him. But first there were two questions he wanted to settle. England was one, a country which had never ceased to interest him. The death of Edward vi gave the throne to Mary and held out the promise of a restoration of Catholicism with the prospect of a permanent relationship with the Habsburgs. No one can say how things might have gone had the marriage of Philip and Mary produced heirs to rule over both England and the Low Countries. France had reason to congratulate herself that the scheme came to nothing.

The other question preoccupying Charles was the division of his inheritance. Since the time his brother Ferdinand had taken charge of the patrimonial states of the Habsburgs and received the title of King of the Romans, thus giving him a right to succeed to the imperial crown, the division of the House of Habsburg into two branches was a foregone conclusion. But paternal affection or perhaps a reluctance to allow his vast domains to be split up prompted Charles in his later years to press hard for the title King of the Romans for his son Philip. This meant that he might then succeed to the imperial dignity after the death of his uncle Ferdinand. The plan was frustrated by the opposition of Ferdinand and his son Maximilian, and by the hostility of the German princes to the idea of having a Spanish emperor. Balked on this point, Charles assigned to Philip two states which, at least in theory, belonged to the empire and which were very important strategically in international politics – Milan and Flanders. In doing so he tipped the balance heavily in favour of the Spanish Habsburgs, who would from now on be the mainstay of the Austrian branch.

After the abdications at Brussels (October 1555–January 1556) father and son bade each other farewell in Ghent. During the two years Charles lived in Yuste he kept up an active correspondence with Philip and took an interest in political developments. Tradition has it that he lamented that his son did not march directly on Paris after the victory of Saint Quentin. He grew indignant at the light terms imposed on the aggressor pope, Paul iv; and was deeply upset at the news of the fall of Calais into French hands. He was worried too by the appearance of the first offshoots of Protestantism in Castile. Still sound in mind, he died in his monastic retreat on 21 September 1558.

5

THE ZENITH OF
EMPIRE: PHILIP II

Philip II belongs to that group of rulers for whom foreign policy comes first. It could hardly have been otherwise, in view of the fact that he was master of the greatest empire yet seen. For a while it appeared that the division of the legacy of Charles V would simplify his son's task; but instead Philip's policy was even more global in scale and the Austrian Habsburgs played only a subordinate role. The pattern is complex, and does not admit of easy exposition. But leaving American topics to one side we can divide it into two principal parts: the Mediterranean and the Atlantic. In the early years of his reign the Mediterranean had an importance which it gradually lost to northern Europe, with the Atlantic eventually absorbing all the king's time and material resources.

When he came into possession of his father's legacy Philip II was King Consort of England. English support helped to bring about the victory of his forces in the north of France. Here the Truce of Vaucelles had only effected a few months' armistice, and when Henry II broke the truce Philip obtained a decisive victory at Saint Quentin (1 August 1557). Instead of exploiting his advantage by marching triumphantly on Paris, as he was advised by Philibert of Savoy who was in command of his troops, he judged it more prudent to carry on with the siege of the fortress of Saint Quentin which held out for another few days. The French were given time to reorganize their forces and they achieved a notable success in the capture of Calais, news of which caused deep gloom in England. The following year Philip recovered the initiative once more with his victory at Gravelines, where he was helped by the English fleet. But even this was not decisive in view of the exhaustion of both parties. Henry II and his councillors were worried at the progress made by the Huguenot faction, while Philip was beset by economic difficulties which forced him to suspend payments to his bankers. These circumstances induced both sides to sign the Treaty of Cateau-Cambrésis.

Taken as a whole the treaty was very favourable to Philip, since though France kept Calais she gave up her conquests in Italy. In that peninsula the French had found an ally in Pope Paul IV whose family, the Caraffa of Naples, were pro-French. On learning of the tactics to which Philip had resorted during the Conclave to prevent his election the pope developed a frantic hatred of him and indeed of the Spanish people as a whole. The latter he called a medley of Moors, Jews and heretics, words which prompt questions about the pontiff's mental health. It was Paul IV who urged Henry II to break the Truce of Vaucelles. For his own part he declared war on Philip on the flimsiest excuse, in the expectation that the duke of Guise would bring him aid. But the duke of Alba who was viceroy of Naples drove back the French and advanced to the gates of Rome, arousing fears of a repetition of the terrible scenes of 1527. But the fears proved groundless, for the Spanish troops maintained perfect discipline and the peace terms imposed on the pope were moderate. He was to break off the French alliance and hand back what he had confiscated from the supporters of Spain (1557).

The Peace of Cateau-Cambrésis, rounded off by the marriage of Philip, who had just lost his wife Mary, to Elizabeth of Valois, left Italy firmly in Spanish hands for years to come and initiated a period of peace and collaboration between France and Spain. The important factor was the weakness of the French monarchy as a result of the Huguenot menace. It served to offset the loss of the armed assistance of England. Philip's position in England had never been a very strong one because of lack of popular support, but it was swept away completely on the death of Mary. He subsequently did his best to preserve something of the old relationship, but he was powerless to avert a collision in the end. He had no wish now to stay on in Flanders where he did not feel at home. He returned to Spain, sensing intuitively that this was the real centre of his power, the Spain he was never again to leave. Almost at the very moment he was on his road home his father lay dying in Yuste; meanwhile the peace with France marked the final outcome of forty years of imperial policy. The reign of Philip II began to some extent on a totally different footing.

The return of the sovereign to Spain might be expected to have produced a greater attentiveness to the problems of the Mediterranean where the Turkish threat still loomed large. The state of Europe did not justify hopes of organizing a general crusade. So Philip II intended to keep essentially on the defensive, whether passively (as by fortification of the coasts and galley patrols) or actively (seizing strategic points without intending to occupy the hinterland). The second type of operation was to be seen in the capture of the Isle of Djerba in 1560, which was soon lost again, and the Peñón de Vélez de la Gomera on the Moroccan coast. Defensive too was the brilliant victory won by the viceroy of Naples, Don García de Toledo, over the Turks who were besieging the island of Malta (1565).

Two acts of aggression by Islam provoked the Christians into taking the offensive for a time. The bey of Algiers had seized Tunis, expelling a dependant of Philip II (1570); at the same time the Turks were laying hands on the island of Cyprus. The Republic of Venice, which had always preferred trade to war, had now no alternative but to take up arms. While this was taking place in the centre and east of the Mediterranean, towards the west, in Spain itself, the *Moriscos* of Granada erupted in dangerous rebellion, seeking and obtaining aid from their co-religionists, though in very limited quantities. The potential threat was serious, because there were no trained troops in Spain and the rising might well have spread to the coastal region of Valencia. The Spanish government could feel that it was under an all-out attack from Islam in these years; taking advantage of the temporary willingness of the Venetians to cooperate, it negotiated the formation of a league of Catholic nations.

The Holy League was given life by Pope Pius v who backed it with subsidies. But no other great power gave its support, so that the undertaking was limited to Spain and Italy. The allied fleet assembled in Messina and set sail eastwards, though too late to prevent the fall of Famagusta, the last Venetian stronghold in Cyprus. It met the Turkish fleet at Lepanto, near Corinth. The forces were evenly matched: the Ottomans had nearly 300 ships; the Christians could muster 79 Spanish galleys (including those of Naples, Sicily, and of Genoa which were on hire), 105 Venetian (and five big galeasses as well), 12 belonging to the pope, 3 to Savoy, and 3 more to Malta, manned by a total of fifty thousand soldiers and sailors. Don John of Austria, who held the supreme command, placed himself in the centre, with the Venetians on his right and the Genoese and papal ships on his left. In the rear was the Spanish admiral, the marquis of Santa Cruz, in charge of the reserve. The lines drew nearer, and after a furious exchange of fire the vessels grappled. At this point the fighting came to resemble a land battle rather than a naval engagement. On the wings the Turks carried the day; but Don John broke through the enemy in the centre, killing their admiral, Ali Pasha. This clinched the victory. The Turks suffered very extensive though undetermined casualties and left 117 galleys in Christian hands, not counting the many others which were sunk. The victors paid dearly for their triumph: eight thousand dead and fifteen thousand wounded (7 October 1571).

Lepanto did not settle the Mediterranean question. The Holy League disintegrated, since the Venetians preferred to negotiate rather than go on fighting. Tunis, retaken for a while by the Spanish fleet, was soon lost again. The coasts continued a prey to pirates and shipping was just as unsafe as ever. It is symbolic that Cervantes, who fought at Lepanto and was wounded in 'the most glorious action which the ages have witnessed', was taken captive to Algiers in the following year on his return from Italy to Spain. And yet the menace of Islam would never be quite so great again. Piracy was a nuisance but it had no influence on major political decisions. Big Turkish fleets were never seen again in the western Mediterranean. The invasion of Italy, which had been a very real risk before, was now out of the question. It is very possible that in addition to its material effects Lepanto had a salutary influence as well, imbuing the Turks with a healthy respect for Spanish naval power. More decisive, perhaps, as a factor in their loss of interest in the West were their growing difficulties in the East, namely the conflict with the Persian empire. But more than anything there was a loss of vigour and a technical stagnation within the Ottoman state which would create an ever-widening gulf between its resources and those of the western world.

If Islam was showing signs of weakness, Philip II, champion of Christendom, seemed for his part to be losing interest in the struggle. He had no intention of concentrating on the Mediterranean since he was aware that the European centre of gravity was shifting north and that it was there that the major issues would be resolved. It is curious too that the popes after Sixtus v, as Braudel pointed out, relegated the fight against the Mohammedans to the background and concentrated on the northern heretics: the English schism, the Protestants of Holland, the Huguenots of France. Their attitude is comprehensible. If Europe returned to the Catholic fold the Turkish threat would be a secondary consideration; whereas if heresy triumphed in the north it would be scant compensation to rule over the impoverished lands of Islam, inhabited as they were by populations which would resist conversion. The change of attitude explains why a kind of unwritten peace was observed on both sides. But for Lepanto the great Armada against England would have been an impossibility. There were even diplomatic contacts between Philip ii and the Ottomans in the later years of the century, though little is known as to how far they went.

The fact that the Mediterranean was in less danger now and that France was effectively neutralized by domestic strife meant that Philip ii could turn north with renewed energy. But there were other pieces on the chessboard of world politics and these did not escape his vigilant eye. In 1578 when the affairs of Flanders were at their most entangled, his nephew, the young King Sebastian of Portugal, undertook a foolhardy expedition to Morocco and perished at Alcázarquivir with a large part of his army. Those who were not killed were taken prisoner by the Moroccans who demanded large sums for their ransom. As Sebastian had no direct heir the succession to the Portuguese crown was left open, since the aged Cardinal Henry, uncle to Sebastian, had only a short time to live. Philip, as the grandson of Manuel the Fortunate, was the legitimate heir. The tenacious policy of Iberian marriages initiated by the Catholic Kings and pursued by Charles v was about to yield its fruit. The mass of the Portuguese people were not pleased at the idea of having a Castilian king. Strong but futile demands were made that the Cardinal contract marriage under licence from the Holy See; Henry died at the beginning of 1580 leaving to a Council of Regency the task of settling the succession problem.

In addition to having a better right than anyone else, Philip could count on some sections of the community being well-disposed to him, people who made up in influence what they lacked in numbers. Some of the nobility, for example, needed financial assistance in order to ransom their relatives imprisoned in Africa. The overwhelming majority of the business world wanted to share in the trade to the West Indies which was then at its height. Most of these merchants and financiers were *marranos*, that is, forcibly converted Jews who were constantly harassed by the Portuguese Inquisition and who hoped, thanks to the change of king, to escape from a country which had virtually become their prison. Lastly there were the Jesuits who had acted from the beginning as loyal servants of the House of Habsburg.

However, a section of the population had proclaimed as king Dom Antonio, prior of the monastery of Crato, an illegitimate son of a Portuguese Prince of the Blood. Philip II was determined to stand up for his rights. Since the representatives of the Portuguese people seemed in no hurry, to put it mildly, to recognize him, he laid his plans with an unusual briskness. Veteran troops were summoned from Italy and Flanders in order to stiffen the inexperienced militia of Castile; the command was given to the fearsome duke of Alba who was just then in disgrace, confined to his house in Uceda because his son had married without licence of the sovereign. The punishment did nothing to weaken his loyalty. He set out from Badajoz in the direction of Lisbon, making his entry after brushing aside the partisans of Dom Antonio who tried to block his path. At the same time the fleet of Don Alvaro de Bazán made its entry into the harbour of the Portuguese capital. Dom Antonio, after an attempt at resistance at Oporto, took refuge in France and afterwards, with the help of French shipping, in the Azores where the population was on his side. When he was driven from there as well he laid down his arms. Philip II took the oath as King of Portugal at the Cortes of Tomar (1581), and promised to respect the liberties of Portugal, a promise which he scrupulously fulfilled. Portugal continued to be a kingdom independent of Castile in every respect, in its laws, its finances, its army too. The Castilians were legally foreigners there and therefore incapable of obtaining office. The kingdom would have to be governed by a Portuguese viceroy, unless he was a Prince of the Blood. Further, it was to be administered by a Council of Portugal which was instituted for the purpose.

For Philip II the annexation of Portugal represented a great increase in his power, not only through the incorporation of

Portugal herself, whose capital was still the centre of the spice trade, but through that of her vast colonial empire stretching from the Moluccas to Brazil. Philip remained in his new dominions until 1583, when after seeing his son sworn as his heir he returned to Castile. He left mixed feelings behind him in Portugal. The commercial middle class, the higher clergy, and the nobility who had received many favours at Tomar, showed themselves well-disposed to the Iberian union; but the populace did not hide its dislike of Castilians and cultivated the myth of *sebastianismo*, the belief that King Sebastian was still alive and would return some day to take over his kingdom.

If on the whole the Mediterranean policy of Philip II was a success and the incorporation of Portugal a great triumph, the panorama in northern Europe was more gloomy. The year 1568 is a turning-point in the king's life: as a family man he was confronted with the imprisonment and death of the prince Don Carlos; as regards the affairs of Castile there was the rebellion of the *Moriscos* of Granada; and abroad the Huguenot menace on the Pyrenean frontier and the rising of the Low Countries marked a new departure.

Despite his Burgundian blood and the time he had spent in Flanders Philip was the man least suited to understanding the Flemish people. His passionate religious convictions and his authoritarian temperament jarred with the turbulent religious situation and the traditions of autonomy of those provinces. The problem which arose in Flanders was perhaps ultimately insoluble; the answer was certainly not, as some councillors proposed, that the king should go there himself. There were various points of friction, but the basic one was religious dissidence and on this no concession could be expected from Philip.

From 1520 a decree of Charles V made heresy punishable by death, and in fact several Reformers perished at the stake. Nevertheless Calvinism made great strides in the Low Countries. It was the only part of Philip II's domains where Protestantism did spread and take firm hold, perhaps because it was outside the Latin orbit, at the meeting-point of several different highways and trends. Religion alone did not bring about the revolt. There was also discontent at various infractions of provincial immunities, as for example the presence of foreign troops.

Questions of an economic character eventually attained crucial importance, even overshadowing those of religion, but it was religion which gave the dispute its intractable nature.

On his return to Spain Philip had entrusted the government of the region to Margaret of Parma, illegitimate daughter of Charles v. She was assisted by a Council of State whose leading figures were William of Nassau, prince of Orange, and Cardinal Granvelle. William of Orange is an enigmatic figure. Officially a Catholic, subsequently a Lutheran, and eventually a Calvinist, his inner convictions remain open to question. He could well have been a means of conciliation if he had taken a middle-of-the-road stand; but when the opposition between the two sides grew he took sides openly against Philip ii's regime, probably more for political than religious reasons. As for Antoine Perrenot de Granvelle, scion of a distinguished Franche Comté family noted for its support of the Habsburgs, he never separated his loyalty to Philip ii from his devotion to the Catholic Church. The hostility of the two men was inevitable. It ended for the time being with the withdrawal of Granvelle. The Spanish troops also left the country, thus satisfying one of the most urgent demands of the Flemish malcontents (1564).

These concessions by Philip were major ones and show that his attitudes were not inflexible. But they were deemed insufficient, since he was at the same time urging Margaret to enforce the decrees of the Council of Trent and set up the new bishoprics which were to supervise religious conduct. The people for their part were at fever-pitch, with the Calvinists preaching incessantly against the Catholic clergy and their government backers, and evoking a response not only among the populace but among some of the nobility as well. On 5 April 1566 two hundred nobles, not all Calvinists, came to see the Princess with a bundle of petitions in their hands. It was then that a councillor gave them the epithet *gueux* (beggars), which they adopted and made famous.

In August of the same year the Calvinist agitation came to a head with the attacks on churches in Antwerp, Ghent, Amsterdam, and other towns. Images and other objects of devotion, many of them of great artistic value, were smashed in a senseless iconoclastic fury. It was no organized movement, just an anarchic explosion combining religious resentment with the long-standing hate of the mob and fringe elements of society for the authorities and the established order. The argument which assigns a large part of the blame for this explosion of fury to passing economic difficulties, like the harshness of the previous winter or the temporary shortage of grain, does not really carry much conviction.

The news of these events caused Philip acute indignation. Though Antonio Pérez and the prince of Eboli and other councillors advised moderation, he leaned towards the views of the intransigents, making up his mind to send their leading spokesman to Flanders – Don Fernando Alvárez de Toledo, third duke of Alba. His route was the one many other expeditions were to take in the future: the first stage was by sea as far as Italy, then followed the overland journey through Piedmont and on to Luxemburg via the Franche Comté. When he reached Brussels at the head of seventeen thousand men the country was completely tranquil. Many of the culprits had fled abroad, including the Prince of Orange, who did not feel safe after the equivocal attitude he had adopted. Margaret felt her authority undermined by the plenipotentiary powers of the recently arrived commander-in-chief, and preferred to leave (1567).

The duke of Alba had come first and foremost to punish rebellion; the defence of the outraged Faith came second. Good general though he was, he showed himself but a mediocre ruler, partly because he was ill-informed, partly because his inflexible spirit was not what was needed to resolve the very complex situation. It is doubtful whether any lasting pacification could have been achieved without concessions in the matter of religion, but these were out of the question given the inflamed state of sensibilities at the time. Alba was not the bloody monster depicted in enemy propaganda, but he was the agent of a clumsy and heavy-handed repression. The Council of Troubles of hateful memory, went too far in the number of sentences it issued, especially since the majority of those responsible for the disorders were no longer there. The exact number of its victims is not known: 12,302 people sentenced, of whom 1,105 were executed, between 1567 and 1573.[1] Among those beheaded were the counts of Egmont and Horn, leaders of the Dutch nobility, men whose conduct had been fairly equivocal but who might have acted as mediators in the conflict. The responsibility for these executions lies rather with the king than with the duke, who did not want to carry the repression too far.

To all appearances the country had been successfully reduced to obedience. The people remained cowed and quiet. An invasion conducted by Orange and his brother, Louis of Nassau, at the head of Flemish emigrés and some German contingents ended as a fiasco. With the cannons taken from the enemy a statue of the duke of Alba was cast and erected in the citadel at Antwerp. It is possible that this gesture was part of the duke's policy of setting himself up as a scapegoat in order to divert hostility from the king, who bore the real responsibility for the policy of harshness. A general pardon was decreed and great masses of the population who had been involved in the troubles flocked into the churches demanding to be reconciled with the Faith. Their sincerity is at very least problematical. Trusting too much to appearances and unaware of the deep discontent which was welling up under the surface calm, the duke of Alba sought to finish his task as ruler by the introduction of certain tariffs on commercial transactions. These were based on the Castilian *alcabala* and would not only relieve the embarrassed situation of the treasury but serve as a symbol of the submission of those stiff-necked provinces.

His decision marks a turning-point, yet one whose significance is difficult to assess. For Pirenne, 'Spain could not have left the Low Countries with an autonomy which confined her to the soul-destroying task of defending them from their enemies. . . . Essentially the duke of Alba did not come to punish rebels but to impose new taxes.'[2] The counterpart to this argument is that it was the new taxes above all rather than the imposition of orthodoxy which provoked resistance. From the the time history stopped being a mere chronicle of events, historians have seen their task essentially as one of probing the motives of men's actions. These actions are infinitely complex, variable, and frequently irrational, which is why it is so rash to indicate causes, especially main or unique causes. The idea that religion was at the heart of the conflict is now in the process of being replaced by another school of thought which sees the economic factor as all-important. In this early stage of the struggle in Flanders it is difficult to show that it was, although later it did become so. But for the indignation of Philip II at the excesses of the Calvinists the established order might have been maintained indefinitely in the Netherlands; it was the Calvinists, albeit a minority, who succeeded in giving coherence to the resistance of those who were initially lukewarm. The wars in Flanders were not exclusively religious, but it is unlikely that they would have broken out if there had not been religious disaffection. Catholics and Protestants were at one in their indignation at the new taxes and the presence of foreign troops, but it was the Protestants who first resorted to arms.

The focal point of the new uprising was in the maritime provinces of the north. Flushing, dominating the Antwerp estuary, and Rotterdam proclaimed Orange as their *Stadhouder*, and they were followed by the rest of Holland, Friesland, Zealand and Gelderland. At first sight the struggle of a small country against the vast empire of Philip II seemed a lost cause. The imbalance is less evident if one remembers that the Dutch were fighting on their own soil, with the aid of powerful neighbours, English, Germans and French, while Philip II, with other fronts requiring his attention, could not concentrate his power in those parts. The supremacy of the Dutch at sea was not absolute. But either on their own or with the help of the English fleet from time to time they managed to mount a sufficient threat to maritime communications between Spain and Flanders for an alternative to be sought in the long overland route which ran from the north of Italy. This land route was to be a continual source of friction with the countries through which the *tercios* had to pass.

Chaunu has emphasized that the war in Flanders was an expensive conflict, fought with mercenaries who in addition to being paid had to be transported from distant lands.[3] It was hardly ever a war of campaigns, and pitched battles were rare. Hostilities, limited anyway to the months of good weather, were confined to sieges. The task of taking towns one by one, in a well-populated country part of which was liable to flooding, was costly in terms of men, time and material. The best of captains, the bravest of soldiers were sacrificed to a struggle which dragged on endlessly and indecisively. When in 1648 the king of Spain agreed to recognize the independence of Holland the respective positions had hardly changed in eighty years of war.

The advance of the Sea Beggars in the northern provinces had been helped by Alba's fear of an invasion proceeding from the French frontier, which obliged him to concentrate his troops in that quarter. Saint Bartholomew's Day removed the danger. The struggle in the north now began in earnest. Malines was taken and sacked by the royal troops. In 1573 Haarlem fell, after an epic siege disgraced by the atrocities committed on both sides; most of the defeated garrison was put to the sword and the civil population had to ransom its life with a fine of 100,000 ducats. These cruel acts did not have the effect of daunting the rebels. If such had been the calculation of the duke of Alba he was a poor psychologist in this as in other respects. His offer of pardon was turned down. Crestfallen and weary of the horror of it all, aware too that he had failed, he insisted on resigning.

The substitute for Alba was the mediocre Don Luis de Requesens, who arrived with a programme of pacification: a general pardon, suppression of the new duties, but no mention of religious liberty. The only concession Philip II was prepared to grant the Protestants was permission to leave the country with all their possessions. This proved the stumbling block to the talks held at Breda between Requesens and the representatives of Holland and Zealand. Requesens died at the beginning of 1576, having achieved nothing except to make the conflict less ferocious and implacable than it had been at the outset. Don John of Austria arrived to succeed him at the end of the same year. In the intervening months there were very grave occurrences. The state bankruptcy had disorganized the system of *asientos*. The efforts of Philip II to replace the Genoese bankers by Castilians failed and the Spanish troops, left for some time without pay, refused to obey their leaders and began a sort of military strike. The southern provinces, fearing the worst from the soldiery, entered into negotiations with the north. Orange tried to take advantage of the opportunity to achieve the unity of the Low Countries on the basis of toleration by uniting Catholics and Protestants in a common sentiment of patriotism. A terrible disaster now strengthened the move towards solidarity. The Spaniards enclosed within the citadel of Antwerp made an impetuous sortie, seized the town after street fighting in which thousands of people died, and sacked it so thoroughly that it was assured their booty ran into some eight millions of *escudos*. These sorry events did not prevent Antwerp making a fairly speedy recovery; its definitive decline came with the blockade which the Dutch later imposed on its port.

Don John had as his first mission to satisfy the arrears of pay due to the troops, amounting to a million and a half ducats. Since the funds at his disposal were not enough he sold his own jewels. Meanwhile he was faced with the united opposition of the whole Flemish people which, surmounting its religious differences, was demanding the withdrawal of foreign troops. By signing the Perpetual Edict (also known as the Pacification of Ghent, 1577) Don John agreed not only to this condition but to the restoration of the old liberties and to the recognition of Orange as governor of Holland as well. The reason behind this obliging attitude, so out of keeping with Don John's character, was that he hoped Philip would authorize him to invade England. Such an undertaking appealed to his ambitious nature, but it was also vital to any definitive settlement in the Low Countries. The opponents of royal authority were getting the occasional subsidy from Germany or France, but their principal foreign backer was England.

Don John could count on papal support for his enterprise against England, but it was his brother who would have to furnish the means. To this end he sent his secretary, Don Juan de Escobedo, to Madrid. The latter not only failed in his mission of obtaining men and money, but got himself mixed up in a shady intrigue and was assassinated. Meanwhile Don John was finding himself increasingly isolated in Brussels; he was actually in danger, since the withdrawal of Spanish troops was far from having quietened men's spirits. He made a dash for Ghent and from there issued a summons to the Italian *tercios* who arrived at the beginning of 1578 under the command of Alexander Farnese. At Gembloux they routed a force of Flemings, Germans and Scots. But despite their great military prowess this small contingent of fourteen thousand men was incapable of holding the country. Only a part of the centre and south was in Don John's hands when he died a few months later, heavy-hearted at the failure of his grand designs.

The Spanish occupation of Flanders was so precarious that each new governor had to begin the job almost from scratch. Farnese found by far the greater part of the country in revolt, yet he was the one who came nearest to total victory. Perhaps he would have achieved such a victory had the king not forced him to divide his forces and direct them to other commitments. Alexander was the son of Margaret of Parma, and thus a grandson of Charles v as well as of Pope Paul iii, father of Pietro Luigi

Farnese. He was the first governor of Flanders to combine political talent with a military vocation. He was helped by the intransigence of the Calvinists, whose excesses alienated the greater part of the Catholic Walloons and led them to think that an accommodation with the king of Spain might have something to be said for it. There was also an element of fear on the part of the nobility and the middle class at the appearance of socialist demagogy among the Protestant masses. This sentiment found expression in the Catholic Union of Arras, to which the north replied with the Calvinist Union of Utrecht. Thus was foreshadowed the present-day division of the Low Countries into the states of Holland and Belgium. Farnese received the submission of the Catholic provinces, granting them the political concessions for which they had been fighting, including the withdrawal of foreign troops. On the other hand the hope of reuniting the country by peaceful means was fading away. The issues at stake became more clearly defined; tenaciously defended quibbles gave place to a stark sense of reality. Orange had to abandon the fiction he had been maintaining for some time that he was not making war on the king but on his evil ministers. The decree placing a price on his head was countered by his *Apology*, which besides being a fine and skilful piece of self-defence is one of the sources of the 'Black Legend' surrounding Philip's name.

Philip II wanted to have Margaret of Parma as governor, but her son Alexander refused to hold the military command just by itself, since he viewed the problem as much in political as in military terms. His demands were met, and his mother had to return to Italy. With equal firmness he convinced the Walloons that their own forces alone, even if they were assisted by German mercenaries, were no match for the enemy, and he won their consent to a recall of the Spanish and Italian troops. Even with this mighty military machine at his disposal he made but slow progress. It was a war of long sieges skilfully conducted in a country traversed by rivers and canals; the enemy was stubborn and very much at home in this amphibian milieu. Nevertheless the Spanish advance was a steady one: Dunkirk, Ypres, Bruges, Ghent, Ostend, fell into his hands, and finally Antwerp as well after a siege in which the utmost valour was displayed on both sides. The assassination of the prince of Orange had no appreciable effect on the course of the struggle.

More helpful to Farnese's cause was the humane way he treated the enemy, in contrast to the harsh fate which usually awaited captured towns.

Only the provinces of Holland, Zealand and Utrecht still remained in revolt, a small belt of territory surrounded on land but enjoying unlimited access to the sea. Despite their energetic resistance their fall could not long have been delayed had it not been for the growing involvement of the chessboard of European diplomacy in the later years of the century. For the king of Spain, his possessions in the Low Countries were of interest not so much for their own sake as for the fact that they provided an unrivalled base for surveying or if necessary intervening in the affairs of northern and western Europe. From his retreat in the Escorial Philip enjoyed a wider panorama of events than did Farnese who was absorbed in the problems of Flanders. The general strategy of the monarch in the final years of his reign assigned a pre-eminent place to France, for the situation there was reaching a crisis. The deterioration of relations with England would soon lead to open confrontation. Nor could Germany be quietly ignored: under a surface calm there occurred incidents from time to time which pointed to the brewing storm. The conversion of the archbishop of Cologne to Protestantism and the aid which the Dutch obtained from the territories situated beyond the Rhine obliged Farnese to divide his forces.

The open breach between Spain and England was preceded by a quarter century of tension and incidents of an increasingly grave character. At first Philip II's intention had been to maintain the English alliance and even the Anglo-Spanish union – he was one of the many suitors for the hand of the Virgin Queen. In subsequent years his more modest aim was to keep on peaceful terms, despite the promptings of Pope Pius V and Pope Gregory XVIII who realized that only by an act of force could there be any hope of Catholicism being restored in the island, and despite too the provocative acts of English seamen. The naval engagement at Vera Cruz between John Hawkins and the *flota* of the viceroy of Mexico (1568) was followed by the confiscation of Spanish ships which had taken refuge on the English coasts carrying valuable cargoes of money and wool. This led to reprisals and to the bankruptcy of several commercial houses. Taken in conjunction with the activities of the Sea Beggars, it meant the breakdown of the maritime route between Spain and Flanders, a route which had such import-ance in the economic as well as the political sphere.

For his part Philip could count on two potential allies against Elizabeth: the restless Irish Catholics and Mary, Queen of Scots, who though a prisoner could be made the basis of a plot aimed at overthrowing Elizabeth. It is an established fact that the Spanish ambassadors in London, Guzmán de Silva and Bernardino de Mendoza, had a hand in these intrigues. In 1574 there was created at Douai in Flanders the first of the English Colleges, run by Jesuits, whose prime aim of legitimate proselyt-ism was not easily distinguishable from the political activity associated with them. The increase in Philip's power as a result of the Portuguese inheritance was not calculated to please a nation like the English which was launched on a career of maritime expansion. In 1580 Drake was on his way home after the astounding voyage in which he had surprised the Spanish ports of the Pacific. It was no secret that the queen had a hand in these acts of war against an officially friendly country. The proximity of the Low Countries was another source of tension, stemming from religious strife, economic interest and the presence of enormous military resources at only a few miles' remove by sea from England. The fall of Antwerp to the troops of Farnese caused anxiety. In the following year (1585) an English army under the earl of Leicester disembarked in Flanders. It was the first official intervention by English forces in the conflict, and it proved not to be a very happy one.

Though the two countries were now really at war, both sovereigns tried to postpone the final rupture. Philip even with-held approval of the excommunication launched by Pius v against Elizabeth, in the belief, which proved justified, that the effect would be the opposite of that intended. If the execution of Mary, Queen of Scots, made him decide on military intervention it was from no sentimental consideration but simply because her disappearance destroyed the last chance of England becoming a power friendly to Spain and the Catholics.

Plans for the invasion of the island had been drawn up in advance and they were now finalized. There were thirty thousand excellent soldiers available, under the command of

Alexander Farnese, in addition to a few contingents of English exiles. The point of embarkation presented some difficulties, since Dunkirk and Ostend were too shallow for an operation on this scale. Farnese proposed taking Flushing, which would have had the added advantage of freeing Antwerp from blockade; but Philip was in a hurry and decided that the port of embarkation would be Sluys. Some three hundred flat-bottomed boats were made ready for the crossing; all that was needed was the arrival of a Great Armada which would establish sea supremacy.

This Great Armada (the Spanish government never called it Invincible) was being assembled in Lisbon drawing on every vessel which could be mustered, including a fair number of embargoed neutrals. Drake's surprise attack on Cadiz (1587) did no great material damage though it did help to raise English morale and set back Spain's naval preparations. The admiral, Don Alvaro de Bazán, died from the strain of work, from dismay too perhaps at a reprimand he had received from his impatient sovereign. He was replaced by the duke of Medina Sidonia, inferior in qualities to his predecessor though no mere aristocratic numbskull, as Mattingly makes plain. The Armada at last put to sea, not in such strength as had been forecast but enough to make an imposing array. It comprised 130 men-of-war and numerous auxiliary ships, with a total of 2,431 cannons and 22,000 men. The English fleet under Howard and Drake had equivalent numbers combined with greater mobility. Their cannons, though of lesser calibre, had a greater range. Their great advantage was that, fighting within reach of their base, they were able to replenish their munitions, for heavy demands were made on existing stocks.

From 31 July to 8 August 1588 there was fighting in the Channel, but no conclusion was reached. When the Spanish Armada exhausted its quota of fifty shots per piece its position became critical. Disorganized by the attacks of fire-ships but still substantially intact it got as far as Gravelines, where the last combat took place. Here too the fighting was indecisive, though the Spanish losses were heavier. Supremacy at sea had not been achieved and the army of Farnese did not dare attempt to embark. The Armada made its way back to Spain by circling round the north of the British Isles, and it was there, especially on the rocky coasts of Ireland, that it suffered its heaviest losses through storms. Nevertheless more than half the ships returned to the Cantabrian ports.

It was a serious defeat, but not a decisive one. The fighting continued on both sides. Philip II was obdurate. Closing his ears to the demands of the Cortes of Castile for peace, he put pressure on them for extra subsidies. He was the recipient as well of the greatest volume of treasure ever to arrive from the Indies: the fleets of 1595 alone brought 4,698,000 ducats for the king. A chronicler of Seville records that there was not enough room in the *Casa de Contratación* and the silver spilled out on to the patios. But the expenses of war were so great that in the following year not only was there nothing left of this treasure but payments to the bankers had to be suspended. This year 1596 also witnessed the attack on Cadiz by the fleet of the earl of Essex. The alarm throughout Andalusia was great because no preparations had been made for such an incursion. Seville sent off in haste to buy arms in Milan since only four hundred musty arquebuses had been found in the city armoury.[4] The last effort made by Philip against England was the sending of another fleet which was dispersed by storms before reaching its destination.

However grave these reverses appear it should be borne in mind that for the recluse of the Escorial they were only incidents in a vast global strategy. In the closing years of the century, in fact, he was more interested in the affairs of France than those of England. The policy of the king of Spain, following the interview at Bayonne between Elizabeth of Valois, wife of Philip II, and her mother Catherine de Medici (1565), was to give assistance to the Catholic party headed by the Guise without intervening directly in the struggle against the Protestants. He had no responsibility for the massacre of Huguenots carried out on Saint Bartholomew's Day, though it came at a very opportune moment, preventing an invasion of the Spanish Netherlands. However the affairs of France came to the fore once again in 1589 on the assassination of Henry III. If his heir, Henry IV of Navarre, came to the throne it would be a great setback to Philip's policy, because Henry was a Huguenot and anti-Spanish. It is easy to understand Philip's impatience with Pope Sixtus V, who instead of thundering excommunications against Henry IV patiently awaited the return of the strayed sheep to the fold. Pope and king justified their respective attitudes with arguments drawn from religion, but behind these there were others, unavowed, of a political character. Philip wanted to maintain France as a Catholic power and at the same time bring it into the Spanish orbit, giving it his daughter, Isabel Clara Eugenia, for its queen. Sixtus v, by contrast, hoped for a France which while Catholic would serve to offset the overwhelming Spanish supremacy in Italy.

Unable to intervene in England Farnese received the order to intervene in France. In effect he forced Henry to raise the siege of Paris, and left behind a garrison of four thousand men in the capital (1590). Two years later he returned to France in order to defend Rouen. These successes were purchased with the loss of Breda, Deventer and other Flemish towns, since his forces were not in a position to carry on a war on two fronts. Alexander Farnese died disheartened, though he was the man who came closest to reconquering the Netherlands for the Habsburgs. Ultimately Spanish intervention in France was neutralized by the skilful political manœuvre of Henry in becoming a Catholic. A brief war ensued between France and Spain along the Belgian frontier, in which neither Henry iv nor Albert of Austria, the new governor of the Netherlands, could achieve a clear-cut victory. Mutual weariness led to the Peace of Vervins (1598), ratifying the principal clauses of the Peace of Cateau-Cambrésis.

A few months before he died Philip ii deceived himself into thinking that he was leaving the affairs of Flanders in order by ceding the territory to his daughter, Isabel Clara, and her husband, the Archduke Albert. But there were so many conditions attached to the cession that in practice everything stayed the way it was. Antwerp, Ghent and other key points must have governors appointed by the king of Spain. The provinces must revert to Spain if, as happened, their new princes had no issue. In any case it was very doubtful if they could have maintained their independence without the military and financial backing of Spain. In place of a regime based on direct rule they came under a sort of protectorate.

When Philip ii died in the Escorial after a painful illness stoically borne (1598), it could not be said that he had achieved the grandiose objectives of his policy. But neither could he be considered a failure. Not only had he kept his realms together but he had enormously increased them. He checked the all-conquering march of Islam in the Mediterranean. He assigned

Protestantism the limits of its furthest advance. He brought about the union of the Iberian peninsula, the great ambition of the Catholic Kings. He continued Spanish expansion in the Pacific where a great archipelago bears his name. In truth, and for the first time in history, here was an empire on which the sun never set.

6

THE PRECARIOUS
EQUILIBRIUM 1598—1634

Rarely has the start of a new reign marked such a new departure
in politics as when Philip III, in 1598, succeeded the recluse of
the Escorial. The change was greeted with relief by the majority
of Castilians, weary and exhausted as they were with the
military enterprises of the previous reign. They also hoped for a
change in policy at home, with a more human, more approach-
able king – even though the approach had to be made through
ministers or favourites. So at first there was no opposition to the
privanza or favoured position of Don Francisco de Sandoval y
Rojas, marquis of Denia, soon raised to the title of duke of
Lerma, which is the name by which he is known in history. The
changes at ministerial level were complete. Don Rodrigo
Vázquez de Arce, President of the Council of Castile, was
replaced by the count of Miranda; the Portuguese aristocrat,
Don Cristóbal de Moura, confidant of Philip II, was sent away
from court and given the viceroyalty of Portugal. And when the
primatial see of Toledo fell vacant, the favourite succeeded in
having one of his uncles appointed. Soon the favouritism and
self-interest apparent in high places spread to every level of
government and Philip II's prophecies about his son's in-
capacity to rule were amply fulfilled.

Despite everything, he cannot be said to have been an
unpopular king. In Aragon, where he held a Cortes, he
granted a general pardon for past events, and the family of
Antonio Pérez was reinstated. The nobility were pleased to see
the gates of the royal palace open to them, being given the high
posts which the late king had usually reserved to *hidalgos* of
modest estate. The clergy could find nothing to reproach in a
king whose piety was matched only by that of his wife, Margaret
of Austria; a king who by the expulsion of 300,000 *Moriscos*
agreed to the loss of considerable revenues in order to maintain

the unity of the faith. The general citizen body was given a rest from demands for new taxes. This involved a less ambitious foreign policy. Madrid sought peace, though not at any price. Philip III and the duke of Lerma were pacific by temperament and by design; but they had inherited wars which could not be settled all at once. It so happened that the monarchy had never had better or more loyal servants than at this time. In the councils, in embassies abroad, in viceroyalties and in military commands there was a galaxy of men, formed in the traditions of the previous reign, identified with the ideals of empire, and at times disposed to seize the initiative without paying too much heed to orders emanating from what appeared a spineless court. This led, especially in the case of Italy, to some friction.

There were other motives too which prompted the rulers in Madrid to be prudent; the weariness of Castile was evident. The Indies continued sending treasure at the same rate, but there were increasing signs of a downward trend here as well. A killer epidemic had ravaged almost the whole of Spain, coinciding with the beginning of the reign. After 1609 the consequences of the expulsion of the *Moriscos* made themselves felt, particularly in Valencia and in varying degrees in other regions. Fate took a helping hand in Philip III's desire for peace. The death of Elizabeth of England and Henry IV of France freed him from two dangerous enemies. A short-lived triumph of the peace party in Holland enabled a truce to be arranged after forty years of hostilities. If at the close of his reign he found himself caught up in the Thirty Years' War, his early death spared him more than the easy and triumphant overture.

The hostilities which the English and the Dutch mounted against the Atlantic ports of Spain, Madrid answered by fomenting rebellion in Ireland. In 1601 a Spanish fleet landed at the Isle of Wight, but was scattered by a storm. The following year another very powerful fleet left Lisbon and landed a contingent of 3,000 men in Ireland. It is hard to see why the maritime preparations were so extensive when the help given was so small. Perhaps the forces of the Irish were believed to be larger than they actually were. Tyrone's Irish were beaten, the handful of Spanish were left divided and besieged, and their leader, Don Juan de Águila, had no choice but to sign an honourable surrender. The death of Queen Elizabeth (1603) put a stop to a struggle which was absorbing vast sums of money to no apparent purpose. There were those in Madrid who sought to revive the old tradition of attaching England to the Spanish crown; a plan was devised of uniting England and Flanders (as Charles v had already dreamed of doing) in the person of Isabel Clara Eugenia and her husband, the Archduke Albert. But since there was no strong Catholic party in England this scheme was utopian. Fortunately James I was also moved by ideas of peace, and a treaty was concluded and ratified at Valladolid by Admiral Howard (1605). For the Spanish this meant that the Atlantic was cleared of a dangerous enemy; for the English it meant two big concessions: freedom of trade with peninsular Spain and religious liberty (in the realm of conscience) for English residents in Spanish territories. In the years which followed James I's attitude continued friendly, thanks in part to the Spanish Ambassador, the count of Gondomar, who won the friendship of the English monarch.

France had tried to put obstacles in the way of the Spanish–English peace. Without any open declaration of war Spain aided and abetted French malcontents, while Henry IV made things difficult for Spain by encouraging the Dutch and preparing himself for battle. His assassination by Ravaillac in 1610 was an indirect service to Spanish diplomacy. The Dowager Queen, Marie de Medici, who had always been pro-Spanish, gave a new direction to French policy. The change was made formal in the usual manner by a double marriage, that of Elizabeth de Bourbon to the prince of Asturias, Philip, and of Anne of Austria to Louis XIII. Both women renounced in advance any claim to their country of origin so as to prevent a possible union of the two crowns.

The most serious problem in Spanish foreign policy was the war in Flanders. For some time now the Spanish government had given up the idea of conquering Holland. Its influence in the north and centre of Europe would be safe enough if it could keep the Catholic half of the Low Countries. If the war continued it was because of the needs to neutralize the attacks of the Dutch by sea. There was also a matter of principle involved: could the Catholic King negotiate with rebellious subjects as equals? The marriage of Isabel Clara with Albert of Austria seemed to be an effort to remove the heavy responsibility from Spain's shoulders. But the government in Madrid had no intention of dropping its interest in Catholic Flanders by granting it any real independence, nor had the archdukes the means to carry on the war on their own. There was no substantial change in the situation, therefore, and the fighting continued to claim Spain's treasure and the flower of her armies.

News arrived that the archduke's army had been defeated by Maurice of Nassau in the dunes of Nieuwport near Ostend. A great effort was made including the sending of veteran *tercios* from Italy. With the *tercios* went two brothers of the Genoese family of the Spínola, one of those patrician families whose links with the Spanish monarchy were so close. Federico Spínola died in naval combat. Ambrogio, a wealthy banker, laid siege to Ostend with the idea of widening the narrow coastline of Catholic Flanders. It was a long siege and a bloody one, a sort of seventeenth-century Sebastopol. A coalition of Dutch, English and French held the city against the attacks of Spanish, Italians and Walloons. Religion was a fine dressing for a fierce conflict of material interests and political rivalries. The town, half in ruins, gave itself up in 1604. Maastricht also surrendered to Spínola. These brilliant triumphs solved nothing and had to be offset against the naval success of the Dutch. Madrid's desire for peace met with an echo among an influential section of the Dutch *bourgeoisie* led by Oldenbarneveldt. The military party by Maurice of Nassau preferred to carry on the war. In Madrid there was also a division of opinion. Lerma wanted peace and he had his way over the head of the military, who deplored the loss of prestige, and of those, few in number perhaps but influential, like Saint Juan de Ribera, viceroy of Valencia, who protested against making peace with heretics. A peace with so many reservations and so much opposition could not be a lasting one. It was limited to a twelve-year truce, beginning in 1609. In the empire overseas it was never strictly observed.

Italy with its numerous little states and its constantly shifting alliances, was from the Renaissance onwards the great headache for European politicians. Despite her supremacy Spain was confronted by serious problems. If in the south her power was solidly established, in the centre she had to take account of the attitudes of the popes and of the Medici dukes: in those earlier years of the seventeenth century they showed themselves pro-Spanish. On the other hand, in the north, she had to deal with the pro-French tendencies of Venice, sometimes aided and abetted by the fickle dukes of Savoy, on whom no reliance could ever be placed. Charles Emmanuel, though the son-in-law of Philip II, resented the fact that the Spaniards would not allow him to enlarge his boundaries. He could count on the possible help of Henry IV. The assassination of the latter put his plans into abeyance for a while; but shortly afterwards he took advantage of the death of the duke of Mantua to invade his states, and when Spain ordered him back he dared to invade Milan as well. He was defeated by the governor of Milan, but not punished or humiliated as the supporters of the policy of the mailed fist would have liked. Madrid preferred to lose face rather than spend money on war, and the White Peace of Asti was signed (1617).

Three supporters of the policy of the mailed fist held important positions in Italy at that time: the duke of Osuna, viceroy of Naples, the marquis of Villafranca, governor of Milan, and the ambassador in Venice, the marquis of Bedmar. The duke of Osuna was a legendary character, extravagant, spendthrift and ambitious, but no traitor as his enemies claimed. He made himself popular with the ordinary people while earning the hatred of the Neapolitan aristocracy. He governed Naples as he saw fit without paying too much heed to the instructions he received from Madrid. He kept up a sort of private war against Venice, which had some justification inasmuch as the Republic claimed the monopoly of the Adriatic. For this purpose he patronized the Uscoques, those bandit patriots who had their hide-outs on the coast of what is now Yugoslavia.

The Venetians laid the chief blame on Osuna for the so-called 'Conspiracy of Venice', an affair which has not as yet been fully brought to light. Most Italian writers assert that there was a conspiracy; the Spaniards deny this. Was there a plot by foreign mercenaries to destroy the shipyard and ruin the naval power of Venice, in conjunction with Osuna and Bedmar? It has never been proved; but Venice believed in its existence – or pretended to, so as to get rid of some undesirable elements. She demanded the withdrawal of the Spanish ambassador. The court in Madrid while not admitting his guilt did not stand on its dignity. Instead its forbearance extended to recognizing the supremacy of the Adriatic claimed by the Venetians, including the obligation of foreign vessels to ask for permission and pay an entry due. As Pérez Bustamente reminds us, 'when in 1630 Maria, daughter of Philip III, travelled to Trieste to marry Ferdinand of Austria, she had to make the trip in Venetian ships, since the Republic refused to allow the passage of a Spanish fleet'.[1]

At the price of some feeble statesmanship there was general peace in the realms of Spain in 1618. But in the same year, almost at the very time the alleged culprits were hanged in Venice, there began the most terrible conflagration to ravage Europe until the Napoleonic Wars, the Thirty Years' War. The duke of Lerma had by now lost his place as favourite, being replaced by his son, the duke of Uceda. But if Spain intervened in this war it was not because the new ruling team had adopted a more bellicose outlook. It was because no Spanish monarch, however fond he was of peace, could watch unmoved the collapse of the Austrian branch of the Habsburgs, especially if this political disaster was accompanied by the collapse of Catholicism in central Europe. The first phase of the war, in any case, gave no hint of what serious trouble was to follow. The troops of the emperor, helped by others sent by Spain from Italy and Flanders, were victorious at the White Mountain and reconquered Bohemia (1620). At the same time the marquis of Spínola, setting out from the Low Countries, crossed the Rhine and seized the lands of the Elector Palatine, the unsuccessful candidate for the imperial crown. The Palatinate was turned into a useful stage on the route from Italy to Flanders.

When Philip III died in 1621 it cannot be said that he had added any lustre to the monarchy; but the inheritance he had received he passed on intact to his son Philip IV.

The alternation between peaceful reigns and those of war was as characteristic of the Habsburg monarchs as of the early Bourbons. It depended less on the personal inclinations of the monarch than on the absolute need to recoup depleted resources and also to follow a policy different from that pursued by the old ruling team. In this sense it was a great blow to Castile that the peaceful reign of Philip III was short, compared with the warlike ones before and after.

Philip IV was not by temperament a warlike king, any more than his chief minister, Olivares. But the latter pursued from the outset a policy of grandeur, and the young king played along with this. When he saw where it was leading and got rid of his favourite, it was too late. The spectre of a destructive and never-ending conflict haunted him until he drew his last breath.

The motives behind Olivares' foreign policy stem in part from his authoritarian character: the dictatorial type of person will tend to carry on his foreign policy with the same intransigence he displays at home. As well as this, there was the need to discredit the previous government. Lerma and Uceda were criticized as corrupt and also for the weakness they had shown in the face of foreign enemies, allowing even small powers like Savoy and Venice to defy the monarchy with impunity.

Olivares satisfied public opinion as well as indulging his personal animosity by punishing the old favourites and setting up a junta for the reformation of manners. Brothels were closed down, extravagant living was penalized and an effort was made to cut down on the number of idle persons thronging the court. An order was even issued requiring from public officials an inventory of personal possessions, the aim being to stop them making a profit. Some of these laws proved lasting, like that replacing the costly ruff by the simple *golilla*. But the majority of measures were dropped in view of the difficulties and opposition they encountered.

Abroad Olivares sought to inaugurate a policy not of aggression but of firmness, as befitted the greatest power in the world. In doing so he started with a number of false premises. He thought he could achieve by means of the Union of Arms a concentration of power similar to that enjoyed by the king of France, unaware of the difference between a nation state which was geographically compact and a scattered network of vastly dissimilar territories most of which had no intention of shouldering the burden weighing on Castile. He was equally blind to the gradual shift in the centre of gravity from southern to northern Europe. He failed to see that the grandiose policy of Philip II had been helped by the eclipse of France, that France was now on the road to recovery and about to become, under Richelieu and Mazarin, the greatest power in Europe, while the Austrian branch of the Habsburgs, paralysed by the Thirty Years' War, would be more of a burden than any real assistance. Nor could he foresee the fundamental long-term change which was taking place in the economy, beginning around 1600 and gathering momentum with disastrous results from 1621, that is from the beginning of the reign. By an irony of fate Spain began her last desperate attempt to maintain her hegemony and her status as a world power at the very time the state of the economy and the political situation would have dictated a course of prudence.

The Twelve-Year Truce with Holland expired just as the new reign began. The desire for a renewal of hostilities was comprehensible. The Dutch had only observed the truce half-heartedly, continuing to harass the Portuguese possessions in the Far East. From 1619 the intransigent Calvinist party led by Maurice of Nassau with the mercantile middle class behind him demanded war so as to permit a future West Indies Company to emulate the profitable activities of its East Indies cousin. For its part Madrid was not loath to clamp down on this aggressive nest of sea pirates. The war in Flanders which broke out in 1621 was not much in common with the one of 1568. The religious motive was not totally absent – it explains the loyalty of Belgium, maintained in such adverse conditions. But it had faded into the background, as had the question of Dutch freedom which was hardly any longer an issue. What was at stake now was maritime and colonial supremacy, for which the little republic dared to throw down its challenge to Spain. The creation of the West Indies Company, with ample resources and strong military backing, was accompanied by licence from the States General to operate in any land or sea in the western hemisphere as far as New Guinea. Allied to the previous creation of the East Indies Company it was, in the words of Boxer, 'a reply to Pope Alexander vi's famous Bull which divided the non-European world between Spain and Portugal in 1493'.[2]

The death of the archduke Albert without heirs (1621) put an end to the fiction that Spanish Flanders was an autonomous state. The rich if dangerous legacy reverted to the king of Spain as of right, though his aunt, Isabel Clara, was left there as governor, with Spínola in charge of the army. The land war with Holland followed the traditional pattern: a costly and slow affair of sieges, conducted by heterogeneous armies of mercenaries who fought only in the good season. The victory of Fleurus and the taking of Breda (1625), immortalized by Velázquez, made a promising beginning. But then came the rupture with England, hostilities in Italy, and an intensification of the conflict in Germany. Spain could not concentrate her strength, and though she tried to deliver 300,000 *escudos* promptly every month in Flanders the decisive victory still eluded her. A new thrust north in 1627 was checked by the arrival of four hundred pieces of artillery from Sweden.[3] The war at sea had reached stalemate too. Spain had set up the *Almirantazgo del Norte*, which, using vessels from Dunkirk, organized an effective privateering campaign. Meanwhile Don Fadrique de Toledo destroyed a Dutch fleet in the Straits of Gibraltar and retook the town of Bahia in Brazil. But a new Dutch admiral, Piet Heyn, captured a Spanish fleet laden with silver at Matanzas (Cuba). Dutch reinforcements were rushed to the Brazilian coast where a bloody and ruinous guerrilla warfare began which had no decisive result.

In 1625 James I of England died, faithful to the last to the Spanish friendship despite the failure of his efforts to have the Palatinate restored to his son-in-law, Frederick. The seal of this friendship was to have been the marriage of his son Charles to the Infanta Maria, sister of Philip IV. But the Spanish government showed no enthusiasm for a match which it could see would bring political and religious problems in its wake. The romantic journey of the Prince of Wales to Madrid ended in failure. Despite the sweet words and presents which were meant to sugar the pill, the Prince took offence. As soon as he came to the throne his first step was to dispatch an expedition against Cadiz, which however came to nothing. This was no more than a passing incident. War was not in the interests of either party, and following some insignificant hostilities a new treaty of peace and commerce was negotiated in 1630. It was to last for a quarter of a century.

In this first phase of the reign relations with France were fluctuating. Richelieu's power was not yet firmly established. The first clash came over the occupation of the Valtelline by the Spaniards. The Valtelline is the upper valley of the Adda river, a superb natural pass between the north of Italy and the south of Germany. Its Catholic inhabitants were under the rule of Swiss Protestants, a fact which furnished the count of Fuentes, governor of Milan, with a pretext for intervening in the valley and erecting a fort to dominate the approaches. This meant that the transit north of Spanish and Neapolitan troops would no longer depend on the good will of Savoy. The Venetians however took fright at finding themselves cut off from France and surrounded by the Habsburgs. In answer to their request

France sent troops to the valley. An open conflict was avoided through the preoccupation of Louis XIII and his chief minister with the Huguenots and turbulent nobility. Consequently the Treaty of Monzón (1626) was favourable to Spain, allowing her to keep the right of passing through the Valtelline.

To sum up, then, at the beginning of 1628 none of the great issues had been decided but no losses had been incurred, and the Spanish monarchy could continue to look on itself as the greatest political power in the world. But from that date things began to change, slowly at first and then with rapidly gathering momentum. Essentially there were two factors involved: the steady deterioration in Spain's economy and the recovery of France, brought about by Louis XIII and Richelieu with implacable zeal and total disregard for anything but *raison d'état*. Ties of kinship, the interests of Catholicism, neither sufficed to divert them from what they took to be the interests of France.

An early confrontation took place in Italy. There was a dispute over the succession to the duchy of Mantua between the prince of Guastalla, a protégé of the emperor, and Charles de Rethel, duke of Nevers, who seemed to have the better claim but was distrusted by the Habsburgs because of his French background. The duchy was invaded by the governor of Milan, Don Gonzalo Fernández de Córdoba, in collaboration with Charles Emmanuel, duke of Savoy, who had been promised part of the spoils. Richelieu, having now overcome the Huguenot resistance at la Rochelle, reacted by leading an army across the Alps; Pinerolo fell, a place of immense strategic value dominating the approaches to the Po valley. The hostile attitude of the Venetians threatened to catch Milan in a cross fire. The danger was averted by the arrival of German contingents which took Mantua and sacked it brutally. In view of the gravity of the situation the aged Spínola was summoned from Flanders; but his failure to take Casale in Montferrat was followed by his death soon after. Another death was that of Charles Emmanuel, a perpetual turncoat who had dreamed of greatness for his country but now saw it invaded on all sides.

The stage was set for a pitched battle between the French and the Germans and Spaniards, the latter being now superior in number, when Pope Urban VIII sent Mazarin as his legate to negotiate a truce. Mazarin did not neglect the opportunity of making a name for himself as a skilful negotiator and of helping

France into the bargain. The Spaniards raised the siege of Casale. The French were supposed to pull out at the same time, but they stayed on. This led to a clamour among Spaniards that they had been tricked by the pope and Mazarin. But they ratified the truce, and by the Peace of Ratisbon (1631) Charles de Rethel kept Mantua, France kept Pinerolo and Casale, while Spain was left out in the cold.

With the end of the Mantuan War Italy passed into the background and attention was now focused on the bloody fields of Germany and the increasingly menacing attitude of France in those parts. Both problems in fact were two sides of a single question. The Emperor Ferdinand II after his victory over Christian IV of Denmark might have been able to restore peace if he had observed the moderation counselled by Madrid. Instead he insisted on his Edict of Restitution which forced the Protestant princes to hand back the lands they had secularized in the last seventy years. This led them to take refuge in the arms of Gustavus Adolphus of Sweden, for whom at the outset they had no particular affection. From that date forward the war deteriorated on the emperor's side. The Madrid government was influential at Vienna, but could not control events. It could see that the open intervention of France would not be long delayed after her diplomatic success at Ratisbon, and with all the friends she had in Germany. But the Spanish government was a prisoner of its own ideals: it could not abandon Austria to her fate nor leave Catholic Flanders isolated.

In a recent study,[4] Ródenas Villar has shown the enormous complexity of Habsburg policy in these years. Vienna demanded subsidies from Spain while giving only a feeble and equivocal support in return. The emperor intervened in Mantua all right, but then he made peace without consulting Madrid, leaving his ally out in the cold. No greater enthusiasm was shown for the Spanish project of establishing a naval base in the Baltic with a view to harrying Dutch trade. Government papers make little mention of religion; they make it plain that Spain intervened in Germany because of Flanders. She sought to keep Bavaria in her camp by dangling before her the prospect of the Palatinate, and tried to get the emperor to intervene actively against Holland. The solidarity between the two branches of the House of Habsburg was more apparent than real. Each tried to obtain from the other the maximum advantage while giving as little as possible in return: it was a game in which the Spanish Habsburgs can hardly be said to have come off best.

One of the most surprising aspects of the war is the insistence of Philip IV and his chief minister on the principle of sovereignty over the rebel provinces. It was this insistence which caused the breakdown of the talks held at Rosendaal with the Prince of Orange, who was inclined towards peace. Contrary to general opinion it was not Olivares who was most stubborn on this point but Philip IV, who opposed any peace which was not honourable.[5] At most he was ready to negotiate another truce, for he found it hard to agree to the definitive abandonment of Holland. But any impartial observer could see that it was now out of the question to recover the lost provinces and that it was enough to hold on to those which were still loyal.

The defence of these Flemish provinces was central to every-thing else. Cut off from Holland they no longer enjoyed the prosperity of former days. For Madrid they were little more than a military vantage point, useful for keeping a check on the activities of France, England or Germany. The troops fighting there were only partly Spanish, but the money which paid them continued to come from Spain and the Indies. The contribution of the people of Flanders was also heavy; but the influence of the clergy and the danger of falling into the clutches of France or Holland nerved them to bear the burden of that interminable conflict. Only in 1632 was Spanish authority under any challenge. The threads of this particular intrigue were woven by Richelieu who was annoyed that the Queen Mother, the king's brother Gaston d'Orléans, and other malcontents had found refuge in Brussels. Some disaffected nobles joined the revolt. One of them, the duke of Bergh, issued a manifesto, while Hol-land urged the Flemish Catholics to rebel, promising to safeguard their privileges and religion. These appeals fell on deaf ears; the loyalty of the Belgians to their distant monarch was unequivocal to the last. For their part the Dutch, while pocketing subsidies from Richelieu, kept their hostilities by land to a minimum. Years later, when the breach with France made the struggle more bitter, a Spanish soldier in Flanders recalled with nostalgia 'that happy time when the army went out on campaign in August, when it could almost be said to have reaped its way along, for once the grain was done it withdrew into winter quarters'.[6]

For France in her stronger condition the Spanish presence in Flanders was a source of profound irritation. Flanders then was larger than present-day Belgium, extending as it did almost to the Paris basin: it could be used, as experience had shown, to mount a direct offensive against the French capital. This was not the only factor involved. The Dutch fleet had made communications by sea dangerous, so that military reinforcements were sent to Flanders overland from the north of Italy along a route which, though liable to change, always meant following the frontiers of France and Germany. The operation was calculated to give the French the impression that they were being encircled by the Habsburgs. As van der Essen has shown,[7] Spain's central European policy was determined in large measure by the need to keep this route, or bunch of routes, open. It was a difficult and costly task, and its highest cost was one not anticipated by Spanish statesmen – eventual conflict with France.

On the long road from Italy to Flanders there was one safe stage: the Spanish Franche Comté. The others changed according to circumstances. While the dukes of Savoy showed themselves friendly, men and money passed through their territories from Milan and Genoa, for it was the shortest route north. When Savoy moved into the French orbit the route had to be shifted east, to cross the Alps via the Valtelline or the Saint Gothard and then follow the Rhine valley. As early as the reign of Philip III Spanish troops had occupied Bonn, Neuss, Rheinberg, and other points along the Rhine. They even held Strasbourg for a while. The fortress of Breisach dominating the river proved to be a key position during the Thirty Years' War. The archbishoprics of Mainz and Trier formed part of an itinerary which had its destination in Luxemburg, while Cologne lay along a direct route to Brussels through Liège. The Duchy of Lorraine would have been another magnificent route had Richelieu not expelled its duke and taken it over. The duke became an ally, if not a very reliable one, of the Spaniards to whom he hired out his private army like any Renaissance *condottiere*.

This was the complicated state of affairs in 1632. Meanwhile Gustavus Adolphus was making his spectacular advance through northern Germany and the Rhineland. Communications with Flanders were severed and the ruin of the Austrian

Habsburgs seemed imminent, to the great satisfaction of France. Nor did the news upset particularly that appalling pontiff Urban VIII, 'more Italian than Catholic, more of a temporal prince than Head of the Church'.[8] Despite the urgent requests of Spain for moral and material support he preferred to employ the treasure and armament he had amassed in a private war of interest to no one outside the members of his own family. Strange though it may seem, Rome was not praying for a Habsburg victory. Its ambition was a compromise which would not forfeit French sympathy.

The death of Gustavus Adolphus on the battlefield solved nothing since the Swedes remained firmly entrenched in the heart of Europe. The decision was now taken to send the Cardenal Infante, Ferdinand, brother of Philip IV, to Flanders. He was adequately supplied with funds, arrived in Milan, and after lengthy preparations crossed the Alps. At Nordlingen he inflicted a crushing defeat on the Swedes (1634). Southern Germany and the Rhine valley were cleared of the enemy. France now became convinced that it was not enough to raise up enemies against the House of Habsburg and back them with subsidies: she herself must throw her full weight into the balance. In February, 1635 Richelieu signed an alliance with the Dutch, and in May declared war on Spain and the Empire.

7
YEARS OF DISASTER
1635—59

From the time the French declared war the balance was to swing against the Habsburgs, but not all at once. Until 1640 it seemed that the situation might develop in any direction. Indeed even after the outbreak of civil war within Spain the Spanish monarchy was able to mobilize its huge resources in order to stave off defeat and, after a lengthy struggle, in the end obtain an honourable peace. Spain's prestige did not plummet immediately. It was only later that both Spaniards and foreigners became aware of the price which Spain had paid for waging these interminable wars. The middle decades of the seventeenth century were years of total war, affecting almost the whole of Europe, the oceans, and the colonies. It was a literary struggle as well, a propaganda war, with the French being blamed for a nationalism which could only split Europe for good, so dismayed were the Spaniards by a hostility which they had neither expected nor desired.[1]

France had no veteran troops at her disposal, so the opening campaign went in Spain's favour, with an army from Flanders reaching Corbie, a short distance from Paris (1636). The imminent peril roused patriotic feeling in France and Corbie was retaken. Hard fighting took place too in Mantua and Savoy, and along the Pyrenean frontier. In 1638 a French invasion of Catalonia was beaten back, their siege of Salses had to be raised, and in the Basque country their attack on Fuenterrabía was foiled. Fuenterrabía in particular was a cause for great rejoicing in Spain, and the Conde Duque was rewarded with numerous favours. But meanwhile the French took the fortress of Breisach, thus cutting the route from Milan to Flanders. This was a grave development in view of the perilous state of communications by sea: in May 1638 public prayers had been offered in thanks to the Almighty for the safe arrival of a fleet bearing five thousand soldiers and a million and a half ducats in silver. The following year an expedition was planned on a grander scale. Seventy ships were assembled at Corunna under the command of Admiral Oquendo, with 25,000 soldiers and sailors. They reached the English Channel by September 1639 and engaged the Dutch fleet under Tromp on the sixteenth and seventeenth. Honours were even, and the fleets parted, Tromp anchoring at Calais and Oquendo at the Downs, seven miles from Dover. Since the English refused to send supplies he decided on a sortie; but it was too late. Tromp, violating English territorial waters, attacked him with fire-ships, destroying forty-three vessels and six thousand men. No further attempt was made to establish a sea link with Flanders.

However great the difficulties of the monarchy at the beginning of 1640 hopes could still be entertained of staying the pace of doom. Within Spain the greatest efforts were made to muster resources. The Indies fleets were still arriving regularly, though with decreasing quantities of silver aboard. New subsidies were demanded of the Cortes and money was also raised by means of aids, sales of office, and other extraordinary measures. Recruiting was stepped up, the shortage of volunteers being made good by *quintas* and forced levies. The *hidalgos* were obliged to take the field on pain of loss of privileges, and the knights of the Military Order were mobilized. The existence of a state of war prompted the monarchy to nerve every muscle and raised more sharply than before the problem of getting each region to pull its own weight. This had always been a favourite preoccupation of Olivares. He was drawing money from the Indies, men and money from Flanders and Italy, but within the peninsula the contribution of Portugal and the Crown of Aragon was, proportionately, greatly inferior to that of Castile.

The origins, course and outcome of the revolt of Catalonia are now well-known, thanks to the work of Elliott, Sanabre and Zudaire. Interpretations may vary but one thing is clear: the picture, popularized by some romantic historians, of a people driven to fight for their freedom by the excesses of a tyrannical government, is in need of revision. The Catalan question obsessed Olivares, in part because he overestimated the country's economic and demographic potential. The Catalan *Corts* had an independence which those of Castile had lost. Summoned in 1626, prorogued, and recalled in 1632, they were dissolved before agreeing on anything: the Principality was being asked for a contribution which was simply too great for it. Then there was the troublesome question of the *quintos* which was a legacy of the previous reign. These were a fifth of certain revenues owing to the king collected by the towns of Catalonia; but the towns had failed to hand them over, alleging expenditure on armaments and suchlike.

Catalonia was internally unstable and its relations with the central government ill-defined. Its chief representatives met in the *Diputació de la Generalitat*, a sort of committee of the *Corts*. Though an oligarchic body and lacking a popular base it could pose as the guardian of the ancient liberties of the Principality against the viceroy. In 1638 there came to join the *Diputació* a certain canon from Urgel by the name of Pau Claris, who was to play a decisive role in the coming political events. The bishops, royal nominees to a man, and the higher nobility, influential if few in number, together with the Jesuits and some of the middle classes were unhesitatingly loyal. But the poorer nobility of the mountain areas, to whom the bandits looked for protection, and the lower clergy were the ready-made leaders of a popular protest movement.

Olivares asked the Catalans for a contribution to the war with France and they did in fact fight bravely in Roussillon. But he failed to see that the effort could not be kept up indefinitely; nor did he appreciate, since he knew nothing of local conditions, the violence of the reaction in the countryside against the outrages committed by the Italian and Castilian *tercios*, whose abominable conduct was typical of the age. The Catalan rebellion began as a rising of peasants and then moved to Barcelona. If there had been a calm and energetic viceroy order might have been preserved. Instead, the count of Santa Coloma panicked and was cut down as he fled to the harbour to take ship. In the 'Corpus of Blood' part of the populace of Barcelona joined the reapers (*segadors*) who had come into the city and assassinated several royal functionaries and sacked their houses (7 June 1640). At the same time clashes occurred between peasants and royal troops in different parts of the country.

Despite the gravity of what had happened relations between Madrid and Catalonia were not broken. The Catalan bourgeoisie was disturbed at the demagogic overtones of the movement. The new viceroy, the duke of Cardona, was a greatly respected figure and might perhaps have remedied the situation, but he died almost immediately. The chief point of friction between the *Diputació* and the authorities in Madrid was the withdrawal of troops, a step which Olivares would not consent to for fear of exposing the Principality to a French invasion. At court the advocates of moderation wrangled with the party of repression. It was on receiving news of the rebel seizure of the port of Tortosa that the decision was taken to send an army to restore royal authority. Meanwhile Pau Claris persuaded the *Diputació* of the need to proclaim Louis XIII of France as their sovereign. Richelieu's triumph was complete, and he hastened to send troops into Catalonia. The marquis of Los Vélez reached Barcelona at the head of the royal army and attacked the fort of Monjuich overlooking the city; but Catalans and French combined inflicted a bloody defeat on his men (January 1641).

The Catalan example proved contagious in that other disaffected part of the peninsula, Portugal. A large part of the Portuguese people had never been happy with the union with Castile, although it left the separate character of the kingdom untouched. As long as things were going well dissatisfaction was confined to a feeling of nostalgia, which was particularly prevalent among the lower classes. But as the state of the monarchy deteriorated hostility in Portugal grew. The war with the Dutch had caused her serious losses: a large part of the East Indies was gone and Brazil was torn by bitter fighting. The accusation that the Madrid government accepted these losses with indifference is totally unjust. As we saw above, Don Fadrique de Toledo recovered Bahia with a fleet fitted out in Spain. In 1630 the Dutch took Pernambuco. Attempts to recover it were in vain, partly because the Portuguese would not furnish the means. Their attitude is all the more astonishing because their contribution to the general running costs of the monarchy was minimal: even the salary of the viceroy, Margaret of Savoy, was paid by the Castilian treasury.

The reasons for the Portuguese revolt are not to be looked for in fiscal pressure, which was actually less than that suffered by other nations then at war, nor indeed in any plan of the royal government to do away with the separate character of the kingdom, for such a plan would have involved a military presence and of this there was no trace, except for an ineffectual and symbolic force of Castilian soldiers in Lisbon. What it came down to, in the end, was that the population was dissatisfied, and this dissatisfaction, as in Catalonia, could crystallize through institutions which the Habsburgs had allowed to continue. It was a discontent which sprang from general economic malaise. Businessmen, almost all of them crypto-Jews, were being driven into emigrating with their capital to Spain, the Indies, or ultimately Holland, both to escape the Inquisition and to find a more suitable field for their activities. The Portuguese protested at the shelter given to crypto-Jews. They used arguments of a religious nature, but at bottom they were concerned to prevent the impoverishment of the country by the withdrawal of capital and the flight abroad of the most active elements.

This poor, discontented people was in no mood to listen to demands for subsidies, no matter how small. In 1637 an insurrection broke out which was focused on Évora. It was quickly stamped out, but it ought to have warned Madrid of the latent peril. Either through an oversight or an act of generosity the duke of Braganza was left in complete freedom. This was a man who owned immense fiefs and who as a descendant of the old national dynasty was to be central to the plans of those preparing a Restoration. The demand for soldiers for the Catalan campaign was the immediate occasion of the revolt, which broke out in Lisbon in December 1640. Margaret of Savoy, aunt of Philip IV, was treated chivalrously but her hated secretary, Vasconcellos, was put to death. There was almost no resistance. A few hundred conspirators seized the offices of government, the little garrison surrendered, and the whole country, virtually bare of troops, followed the example of the capital. So did the colonies which were still in Portuguese hands, except for Ceuta which preferred to continue in union with Castile. The duke of Braganza, who had had no hand in the conspiracy, was proclaimed king as John IV.

It appeared for a while as though the rot would spread and Spain be plunged back into the days of the medieval Taifa kingdoms. The duke of Medina Sidonia, one of the most powerful territorial magnates in Andalusia, whose sister was married to the new king of Portugal, tried to get the south of Spain to rise in rebellion. Some years before there had been disturbances in Vizcaya because of the imposition of a tax on salt. In Aragon some conspirators tried to proclaim the duke of

Híjar as king, possibly without his consent. All these attempts failed for lack of popular support. Andalusia, unlike Catalonia or Portugal, had no tradition of political self-expression. Aragon was very Castilianized. Vizcaya was too small. When it came to the test the internal unity of Castile proved fairly resistant; but the outlying kingdoms were still unsafe.

It was another of Olivares' strategic blunders to put the Catalan front first before the Portuguese. The war along the extensive Portuguese frontier was one of forays and skirmishes conducted by irregular troops. The small forces available were concentrated in Catalonia where, in view of the French presence, no early victory was to be expected. If some picked troops had been sent against Portugal in 1641 they would have found her virtually defenceless and with minimal chances of assistance from outside, and they would probably have won the day. When the attempt was eventually made twenty years later the circumstances had altered completely: Portugal had gained experience, and with the support of France and England was now a match for the utterly exhausted forces of Castile.

Philip IV believed that by placing himself in person at the head of an army he could rouse Castilian spirits and bring the Catalans back to their obedience. The royal campaign, to which all the nobility of the kingdom were summoned, proved a great fiasco. The king had no military talent and the army was not ready. The marquis of Leganés at long last reached Lérida, but was beaten back by the Franco-Catalan army, and his retreat became a disaster owing to lack of food and medical supplies (1642).

The king now gave way to the general clamour and ordered Olivares to resign office (1643). Shortly afterwards Louis XIII and Richelieu died. The chief actors were leaving the stage one by one, but their disappearance brought about no great changes in the overall situation. Those who had hoped for miracles from the departure of Olivares were disappointed: the war continued virtually as before. Every spring an army of fifteen to twenty thousand men was scraped together, some of them brought in from outside, others raised by the very unsatisfactory means of the forced levy. With such impoverished resources no victory could be expected on the Catalan front. The capture of Lérida in 1644 was a brilliant success, but it had no sequel. The next few years witnessed fierce fighting in the neighbourhood, with Condé making vain efforts to retake the town.

The main theatre of war continued to be the Low Countries, which claimed the pick of the king of Spain's troops – 80,000 men, including Spaniards, Germans, Walloons, Italians and Lorrainers. Despite every obstacle, three million *escudos* in pay was still being sent to them every year; the balance, as well as the nuisance of billeting was a charge on the Catholic provinces. If that army, enormous as it was for the time, had been in Castile, Portugal and Catalonia would have been reconquered with ease. This is a fact which should be borne in mind by those who accuse the Habsburgs of being too Castilian in their outlook.

On the death of the Cardenal Infante Ferdinand the governorship of Flanders was bestowed on Don Francisco de Melo. The latter laid siege to Rocroi, but had to face a relief force led by the duke of Enghien, the future *Grand Condé*. The Spaniards bungled their tactics; the veteran *tercios* crumbled under the fire of the French artillery, and the battle of Rocroi has gone down in history as a sort of equivalent on land of the Armada. It is a fact that like the latter it had no decisive results, and one may doubt whether it would have acquired such fame but for the eloquence of Bossuet. The loyalty of the Flemish provinces remained as unshakeable as ever, and the gains to France from her victory were few. Condé took another three years to capture Dunkirk; but this was an important prize, being an old-established privateering base. Another blow was the total exhaustion of Austria which had resolved on peace. Negotiations were proceeding with painful slowness, but eventually resulted in the Treaties of Münster and Osnabrück, popularly called the Peace of Westphalia (1648).

The Peace of Westphalia is generally held to be the starting point of a new European order. It signified the final collapse of Habsburg aspirations to supremacy, and confirmed the hegemony of France and the political eclipse of Germany. It also ushered in the new era of religious diversity and marked the end of the wars of religion. All these aspects have been commented upon and analysed time and time again. From a Spanish viewpoint Westphalia admits of another interpretation. In the first place it did not mean peace since Don Luis de Haro, successor to Olivares, did not accept the French proposals which involved their keeping Catalonia. The government in Madrid pinned its hopes on an outbreak of internal revolts against the Queen Mother and her favourite, Mazarin, and events proved it right. On the other hand peace was concluded with Holland, since it was in the interests of both parties. Feelers for peace had been put out many years before. Gradually the Spaniards had resigned themselves to treating with the Dutch on an equal-power basis. The religious question had ceased to be an insurmountable obstacle. There remained the colonial question. While Philip iv was king of Portugal he had the duty to defend her colonies and demand the restitution of those which had been seized. The rebellion of Portugal simplified matters. For their part the Dutch had great ambitions to be admitted to the important Spanish market to which they had hitherto had but an indirect and restricted entry. The conversion of the old enemy into a friend, even an ally, was in the logic of events.

Spain therefore could pursue her interminable struggle with France without worrying about the Dutch, though this gain had to be offset against the withdrawal of the emperor from the war. In Italy too changes had taken place, and it is worth while looking for a moment at how the king of Spain was able to restore the balance in a very critical situation. As in Flanders, the Spanish presence in Italy would not have survived long without the fundamental loyalty of the natives to the Habsburgs. The French, by contrast, failed to capture the sympathy of either the Catalans or the Italians. Even the malcontents who had called them in were soon trying to liberate themselves from their 'liberators' as quickly as possible.

The duchy of Savoy still played the role of a buffer state between the two great powers. The dukes, who had tried to turn their position to good account by expanding their dominions, had only succeeded in making their country a battlefield, and their continual changes of side had won them general distrust. The career of Thomas of Carignano, son of Duke Charles Emmanuel i, suggests the options open to Savoy on the eve of the Peace of Westphalia. Thomas fought in his youth against the Spaniards and got married in France. On his return to Savoy he became worried at the expansionist designs of Richelieu and went over to the Habsburg side. He held a command in Flanders and took part in the offensive of 1636 against Paris. Meanwhile his sister-in-law (widow of Duke

Victor Amadeus I) having negotiated an agreement with the French, Thomas took up arms against her and managed to take Turin. Then he broke with the Spaniards in 1640, patched things up with them the following year, but subsequently switched sides and served the French on campaign in various parts of Italy.

The prince of Monaco was more consistent. A traditional ally of Spain, when he saw that the tide was moving against the Habsburgs he signed an agreement with Louis XIII in 1641 replacing the small Spanish garrison by a French one and making his tiny state thenceforth a sort of French protectorate. It was a minor incident, but none the less symptomatic, and it deprived the galleys of a valuable anchorage on their coastal route from Barcelona to Genoa. The duke of Modena was another case in point. He had spent some time in Madrid hunting for favours and had allowed a *tercio* to be recruited in his lands. But once he saw which way the wind was blowing and noticed that subsidies were drying up, he became a client of France.

In 1646 Mazarin dispatched an expedition against the Spanish *presidios* in Tuscany. The object was to intimidate the new pope, Innocent X, who had just been elected to succeed the Barberini, Urban VIII, who had shown himself pro-French to the end. The object was attained: the Barberini were not persecuted and during the events of 1647 Rome became a centre of anti-Spanish intrigue.[2] The year 1647 seemed to sound the death-knell of Spanish supremacy in Italy, with insurrections in Naples and Sicily coinciding with attacks by the French. The Neapolitan rising, led in its initial stages by the fisherman Masaniello, was particularly serious. Its roots were manifold and deep. The tax on fruit introduced by the viceroy, the duke of Arcos, was but the signal for an outburst of the latent discontent which had spread to every sector of society. The discontent stemmed from a combination of two factors: the pressure of war, and the onset of a general economic depression and social malaise characteristic of the Mediterranean world as a whole. The lesser nobility were among those affected, and one of several symptoms was an alarming increase in banditry, as the analysis of Rosario Villari makes clear. The Neapolitans were threatened by the arrival of a fleet under Don Juan of Austria, natural son of Philip IV. They proclaimed a republic and sought the support of France. But the support which came was tardy and feeble, and after some indecisive fighting the French fleet withdrew (1648). What determined the collapse of the insurrection in Naples, as of the one the year before in Sicily, was that the nobility held fast to the royal cause. Though they had their grievances against the Spanish administration, they detected greater dangers in the democratic and anti-seigneurial overtones of the popular movements. At the same time the Spanish *presidios* in Tuscany were recaptured and the situation was restored on the borders of Milan with Savoy and Modena.

These successes were due in large measure to the outbreak of internal revolts in France. The Spanish Low Countries were the resort of the enemies of Mazarin, as of those of Richelieu earlier, and later of the English Royalists as well. Flanders swarmed with adventurers and emigrés, some of them useful to the king of Spain, others serving only to multiply his expenses with the pensions considered appropriate to their station. These illustrious personages lacked any nobility or disinterestedness; they were barren of feelings of patriotism, loyalty, or gratitude. Condé, after fighting against the Spaniards, joined them against his fellow countrymen, and then turned against them once more. The duke of Lorraine, a bizarre character if ever there was one, fought for the Spaniards until he was imprisoned in the *alcázar* of Toledo on suspicion of treason. As for the pretender Charles Stuart, he lived for a while with his court on Spanish subsidies, which admittedly were neither plentiful nor punctual. He was barely seated on his throne when he concluded an alliance with Portugal, to the shock of the simple-minded Philip IV. And to think that Spanish diplomacy had still the reputation of being machiavellian!

Spain's most tangible gain from the *Fronde* was the recovery of Catalonia. Philip IV had promised the Catalans that he would respect their liberties and forgive the past, and with demonstrable generosity he kept his word. Meanwhile the French yoke was growing increasingly burdensome in those areas still subject to it. Irritation at the excesses of the French and the conviction that Catalan liberties were safer under a Spanish regime aided the pro-Spanish faction. The temporary enfeeblement of the French army made possible the recovery of Barcelona (1652), and a knot of irreconcilables took refuge in Roussillon. The twelve years of French occupation left such a bad memory that

E

Catalonia was thenceforth to become the most anti-French of the Spanish regions.

The growing military and financial exhaustion of Spain prevented her turning the eclipse of France to better account. In order to pay for the campaign in Catalonia it had been necessary to decree a rise in the tale of *vellón*, a measure which allied to a poor grain harvest had caused serious riots in Seville, Córdoba, and other cities of Andalusia. Mazarin, meanwhile, had succeeded in restoring order and re-establishing royal authority. In 1654 Louis xiv was crowned king, though he was too young as yet to be able to dispense with his all-powerful minister. The sole ally of any importance left to Philip iv was the prince of Condé. Together with the Archduke Leopold, the new governor of Flanders, he had recovered Dunkirk and Rocroi. The war was entering a stalemate once more and both contestants were eager for peace, for the internal affairs of France were in no very satisfactory state either. In 1656 Hugues de Lionne arrived in Madrid on a secret mission. The negotiations broke down, partly through the insistence of the king of Spain that Condé be not only pardoned but restored to all his offices as well, a demand which was patently excessive. No agreement was possible on Portugal either. Philip iv would not hear of recognizing the Braganza as independent sovereigns.

At the stage of exhaustion which both parties had reached the intervention of a third would likely tip the balance. The third party was England, which after going through a period of internal upheaval was now once more united and strong under the iron hand of Cromwell. Cromwell had no fondness for either Spain or France; looking only to British interests he was ready to sell himself to the highest bidder. The assassination of the British Resident in Madrid by a group of Irish Catholics was an unfortunate incident, but it was not a decisive factor in the negotiations. Cromwell demanded that English residents in Spain be granted freedom to practise their religion and restrictions on the Indies trade removed. Both demands affronted the basic principles of Spanish policy. The Spanish ambassador in London, Don Alonso de Cárdenas, offered important subsidies instead, together with a right to the port of Calais which was to be taken from the French. Mazarin promised Dunkirk – after the Spaniards had been driven out. The offers seemed to balance each other; but the prize to which

Cromwell aspired was not a mere port in the English Channel. Without a prior declaration of war an English fleet took the defenceless island of Jamaica by surprise in 1655. The Anglo-French treaty was signed on 24 October that year and the official declaration of war on Spain followed in February 1656. An English fleet stationed off Cadiz forced the *flota* of the Indies to take shelter in Santa Cruz de Tenerife, where most of it was destroyed. The *flotas* of the following years were re-routed to the ports of northern Spain.

On the crucial Flanders front the landing of an English force was perhaps less decisive than the interruption of normal communications with the Indies. For it was this which aggravated the financial problems of the monarchy to such an extent that it became impossible to pay for the large army stationed there. Still, in 1658 Don Juan of Austria was sent 1,200,000 *escudos*, 'which is the greatest effort we can manage, since it has been necessary to spend such large sums on the fleet for the Indies'.[3] On 14 July 1658, at the Dunes, that sandy coastline where so much blood had already been spilled, the Anglo-French army under Turenne defeated Condé and Don Juan of Austria. The outcome of the battle was the loss of Dunkirk, Ypres, Gravelines and other vital strongholds. The risk of the French overrunning the whole country was now very real indeed.

Despite the gravity of his position Philip iv had one trump left to play – his daughter, Maria Teresa, whom Anne of Austria, sister of Philip iv, had set her heart on marrying to her son, Louis xiv. Queen Anne had had little influence with her husband, Louis xiii, and had been powerless to prevent the conflict between her former and her adoptive homeland. Her ambitions foundered on the rock of Richelieu's power. But now her ascendancy with Mazarin drove him towards a peace which seemed dictated more by family than political considerations. In order to achieve the Spanish match he had to moderate his demands in such fashion that, given the balance of forces in 1659, the Peace of the Pyrenees cannot be considered too disadvantageous to Spain.

True, she gave up Artois and several fortresses in Flanders, as well as the Catalan territories of Roussillon and Cerdagne on the French side of the Pyrénées: but these were territories already lost, and it is doubtful whether they could have been recovered.

The prince of Condé was restored to his honours and possessions. Mazarin attempted to mediate in the question of Portugal, but the Spanish negotiator, Don Luis de Haro, was adamant. France gained much by the commercial clauses of the treaty which would enable her products to conquer the Spanish market. Finally it was stipulated that Louis should marry Maria Teresa, after she had renounced for herself and her descendants any right to the throne of Spain. These were the principal clauses of the peace signed in the Isle of Pheasants, situated on the frontiers of both kingdoms. In the same spot a year later the two courts came together for the transfer of the Princess amid an impressively luxurious display.

The Peace of the Pyrenees was followed by the Peace of Oliva (1660), putting an end to a struggle among the Baltic powers which was linked with that between France and the Habsburgs. As late as 1658, when disaster was imminent and there was a shortage of funds for even the most pressing needs, the Spanish Council of State was debating whether to send supplies to the king of Denmark and the elector of Brandenburg to enable them to resist Charles x of Sweden.[4] There is something pathetic about this insistent imperial ambition at a time when the means were lacking for such grandiose designs.

While Europe attained a precarious peace and began a new era under the sign of the hegemony of France, the Spain of Philip IV had one last war to finish off, a war which was to demonstrate just how feeble militarily she had become. The kingdom of Portugal had consolidated its strength by now and its army had gained experience. In 1658 the Portuguese besieged Badajoz and though they could not capture the town they defeated the Castilian army at Elvas. Once peace had been concluded with France the Spanish government scraped together some foreign troops, since the soldiers left in Spain were few in number and of poor quality. Time and again, right through to the death of Philip IV, attempts were made to invade Portugal through the natural route of penetration, along the Tagus valley towards Lisbon. This was the way the duke of Alba had gone in 1580. To everyone's amazement these offensives were a total fiasco. It is true that – contrary to the stipulations of the Treaty of the Pyrenees – Portugal received aid from France, which had no wish to see Spain re-emerge as a great military power. Some English contingents also fought alongside the Portuguese – a bitter pill to swallow for the diplomats in Madrid who, if they had not contributed directly to Charles ii's restoration, had at least given him shelter in Brussels. Despite this assistance from abroad Portugal would hardly have been able to hold out had it not been for the fact that Castile's once mighty armies had been shattered by so many years of war and sacrifice. The few heterogeneous forces remaining – the militia, the Italians, and the German mercenaries – fought well but without conviction against an enemy which was fighting for national independence. The price had now to be paid for the obstinate attempt to maintain in north and central Europe a position which no longer corresponded to the balance of power. The weakness of a monarchy which but a short time before had held Europe in awe now lay exposed. Philip iv died in 1665, overwhelmed by the catastrophe but still making no concessions and insisting in his will that Flanders should not be abandoned. But he, if anyone, must have known that if Spain stayed on in Flanders it would not be through her own strength but because the other powers were interested in keeping those provinces as a barrier to French expansion!

8

THE PRIVILEGED ESTATES: NOBLES AND CLERGY

The difference between the hierarchical society of old and the class structure in which we now live has been pointed out often enough. Under the hierarchical system a class had privileges which were recognized by the law and frontiers which were, in theory, well defined and independent of wealth. Nowadays the law no longer distinguishes one citizen from another by reason of his origins, while such social distinctions as do exist are based on socio-economic and professional criteria and correspond to evaluations of a private nature. That, anyway, is the theory. In practice the differences between the two systems are not quite so rigid. Under the Ancien Régime economic criteria were not totally absent from the hierarchical division, any more than they enjoy a monopoly today when it comes to social classification. Similarly with social mobility: it existed in bygone days despite what the law had to say about it, nor can our modern theory of equal opportunity disguise the fact that many people totally lack the means of self-improvement. In both cases the way people live is governed by an inherent logic which is of more interest to the historian than written laws.

The nobility and the clergy were the two traditionally privileged estates. Whoever did not belong to them was lumped with the Third Estate, a vast category including artisans, merchants, peasant proprietors, labourers, vagabonds, physicians and lawyers of plebian origin. Taken together the nobility and the clergy made up something like an eighth of the Spanish population, but their wealth, culture and position made them the most dynamic and influential section of the community.

Ennoblement by act of royal power existed, but it was ill-received by the theorist. For him nobility was an inherent quality which flowed in the veins: it was not to be obtained in any other manner, nor was it possible to lose it. This crude racist theory made life difficult for many people who had been ennobled for their services and yet were never fully accepted by the rest of the nobility as equals. It was for this reason that the sales of *hidalguía* organized by certain monarchs had very little success, despite the material advantages they offered. The daily spectacle of nobles whose style of life was not up to the standard expected of them was not admitted as a countervailing argument: this mysterious quality which ran in the blood, so it was alleged, would emerge triumphant sooner or later, if not in the present generation then in their descendants.

Nobility was a unique and indivisible quality, but several categories of noble could be distinguished according to fortune. The *hidalgos* made up the proletariat of the nobility. They lived off small rents from modest rural domains, and sometimes even worked with their hands. More than one found himself reduced to the proud mendicancy satirized in the literature of the age. The *caballeros* were an intermediate class of urban dwellers. They were quite well-off, indeed sometimes fairly wealthy, with their fine houses emblazoned with coats of arms, their rural properties, and the income they derived from the government bonds (*juros*) and from the private loans (*censos*). Many also exploited their monopoly of municipal office. The distinction between the two categories was vague: a *caballero* from a small town might not be more highly regarded than a simple *hidalgo* in a big city.

From the point of view of social prestige or honour it was more important that the possession of nobility should date from time immemorial and never have been challenged. If the holder had to fight a lawsuit in order to obtain recognition, whether in his home town or in the *Chancillerías* of Valladolid or Granada, a certain stigma would attach to his name even though he obtained an *ejecutoria* certifying that his nobility had been proved. It was a fine thing to be able to point to an *ejecutoria* in a sumptuous binding, adorned with armorial bearings and a family tree, but even better never to have had one's nobility of blood called in doubt. The proof required was immemorial repute, as testified to by one's neighbours. Additionally, certificates could be exhibited to the effect that the ancestors of the suitor had been exempt from personal taxation as *pecheros*, or had belonged to noble fraternities. Supplementary proofs would include having a front seat in church, a family tomb, a chantry or two, a palace or an ancestral home with armorial bearings and servants, and, of course, not having worked as a merchant or artisan, or for hire in any capacity, even in the liberal professions of physician or clerk of a court.

The possession of a title into the bargain did not imply any intrinsic improvement but it did carry great social prestige. In order to maintain the dignity of the position the family was expected to have some property in entail, estimated at around six thousand ducats annual rent in 1600. The source of the income was also a matter of some importance. It had to be derived, at least in part, from real estate and seigneurial rents, for a title implied jurisdiction over towns or territories. Perhaps it is this semi-feudal partnership with the crown in the exercise of authority which is the outstanding feature of the titled nobility. This was particularly true of the Grandees Grandes) of Castile, who were an upper crust of the nobility and were called 'cousins' by the king himself. They usually had estates of enormous dimensions. Most of them were dukes, but more and more marquises and counts were appointed to their ranks. The twenty-five Grandees formally recognized by Charles v in 1520 grew to one hundred by the middle of the next century. The ordinary titled nobility rose in the same proportion: Philip III created twenty marquises and twenty-five counts, Philip IV sixty-seven and twenty-five respectively, while Carlos II broke all records in this respect.

The geographical distribution of the Castilian nobility followed the same ordering by zones to be seen in other aspects of the country's social history. This reflected the nature of the Reconquista, which started in the north and only very gradually moved south. Of the 1,300,000 or so families in Castile towards the end of the sixteenth century, 133,000 – about a tenth – were noble. The greatest concentration was in the Cantabrian provinces. In two of these, Guipúzcoa and Vizcaya, the whole population claimed to be nobles, so that it sufficed to prove that one came from there to enjoy all its privileges in any part of Spain. In Santander and Asturias half the population was noble. In Galicia and the Duero basin the proportion fell considerably but still remained quite high. The whole of this northern nobility were hidalgos; there were extremely few caballeros or titled nobility. Often they were driven by sheer necessity to work for their living, nor could all the explanations and subterfuges in the world justify this flagrant breach of conduct. It was fair enough if they turned their hand to the plough, for the theory, based on Cincinnatus and other classical precedents, held that agriculture was not degrading. But the same could not be said of swarms of coachmen, lackeys and drawers of water at court who were indisputably of noble birth. Facts like this ruffled the defenders of nobility by discrediting the class as a whole. Yet they were not prepared to see nobility as anything other than inalienable; so they had little choice but to say that it continued in force, though it fell into abeyance as long as the individuals in question lived in degrading circumstances.

In the south, especially in Andalusia, the proportion of nobles was very small (one per cent or less), but on the other hand they enjoyed an outstanding social and economic importance. There were few *hidalgos*, rather more *caballeros*, and a large number of wealthy Grandees and titled nobility owning extensive estates, handsome palaces and impressive retinues of servants. The populace ungrudgingly recognized their superior position based as it was on tangible distinctions. In the towns of Old Castile, though, the population was more homogeneous in composition, and the exemptions enjoyed by one sector under the title of *hidalgos* was a continual source of irritation and conflict.

In the lands of the Crown of Aragon the hierarchy of nobles had certain features peculiar to itself. The landed nobility of Valencia could be compared to the Andalusian, being few in number and fairly rich, though the expulsion of the *Moriscos* dealt its revenues a severe blow. In Catalonia and Aragon, as in northern Castile, the lower and intermediate nobility predominated, and are typified by the rough *infanzones* of the Pyrenean region. The Catalan mountain nobility, impoverished, aggressive and turbulent as it was, created a lot of trouble with its feuds and conflicts, which were often indistinguishable from banditry pure and simple.

The most original feature of this Catalan nobility was the existence of an influential class of *ciutadans honrats* (distinguished citizens), originally bourgeois but assimilated to the aristocracy since the close of the Middle Ages. They had abandoned their old trading interests, investing where possible in fixed rents and land so as to complete the process of ennoblement. They controlled the governments of the most powerful towns, not least Barcelona itself, where the *Consell de Cent* was largely directed by them. In some Valencian towns as well *ciutadans honrats* held sway, whereas in Aragon, which was more rural, they were important only in Zaragoza, the one big commercial centre in the kingdom.

There were various privileges of a legal nature enjoyed by the nobility. The most highly regarded was that of immunity from taxation. After the medieval idea, personal taxes were considered to constitute an intolerable grievance, turning those who paid them, and their descendants, into *pecheros*. When the needs of the monarchy obliged the nobility to contribute as well, recourse was had to expedients like indirect taxes or aids on a more or less voluntary basis. And it is true that many noble houses spent a large part of their fortune serving the king in the army or as ambassadors, or in other posts which brought more prestige than reward.

The exemption from taxation was usually justified on the grounds that if the commoner served the king with his money and the priest with his prayers, so the noble served with his sword. The actual state of affairs was rather different. In the sixteenth century the *hidalgos* were still the backbone of the *tercios*. But in the seventeenth century the nobility increasingly lost its military vocation, so that when Philip IV summoned the *hidalgos* to fight the French many of them made excuses or sent substitutes instead.

The privileges they enjoyed at law were also very substantial. They could not be seized for debt – and debts they certainly had in plenty. Nor could they be tortured except in cases of treason. Their prison was different from that of the common herd, being generally some castle or their own home. They could not be sentenced to lashes or the galleys or other degrading punishments, and if their crimes were grave enough to warrant capital punishment they were not hanged but decapitated, a distinction which had great importance in their eyes. These legal privileges were reinforced by an unwritten though no less effective law specifying that a noble should always be preferred before a commoner for any position, particularly if it were an important one. This was inevitable, the customs of the age being what they were. The general in command of an army had to be of the highest rank so that those who served under him did not feel themselves dishonoured. Viceroys and governors had to be Grandees, titled nobles, or sometimes of the blood royal itself in order to avoid giving offence to the individual provinces.

Only in the case of his intimate advisers could the king afford to be more flexible, though even here it would have caused a scandal had a royal secretary not been a *hidalgo* at very least.

Despite the considerable number of poor *hidalgos* the nobility as a whole owned a large part of the country's wealth. Some great houses like the Admirals of Castile, the Constables, the dukes of Medina Sidonia or Medinaceli, had over a hundred thousand ducats in rent. Other Grandees and titled nobility had between thirty and eighty thousand. These were fabulous sums for the time. And yet the economic circumstances of these great houses were far from being satisfactory. The majority, ill-administered as they were, staggered under a burden of debt. The extent of their obligations and commitments ruled out the possibility of mortgage. Constant petitions flowed in to the king, demanding permission to charge new *censos* on estates which were already mortgaged to the hilt. Many abandoned their ancestral homes and went to look for lucrative employment at court. But this was a double-edged remedy, since life at court was ridiculously extravagant and enormously expensive. The chief posts in the Household and the viceroyalties of Italy and the Indies were the most remunerative positions, but they were within reach of only a privileged few. Many had to be content with an *encomienda* of the Military Orders.

The Military Orders, created in the Middle Ages during the struggle against the Infidel, had become purely honorific bodies but they still held vast tracts of land divided into *encomiendas* which were in the king's gift. An *encomienda* consisted of a town with some land attached whose inhabitants depended on a *comendador* to whom they paid certain dues. It was a sort of fief, but limited to one life only. In principle the *comendador* was supposed to reside on the spot and rule his vassals, but being a courtier in practice he seldom put in an appearance. Some held more than one *encomienda* at a time; indeed they were even granted to women and children. Those who were not influential enough to obtain one made do with a *habit* of the Orders. To wear a habit with the red cross of Santiago, Alcántara or Calatrava conferred no economic advantage but considerable social prestige for it meant that the wearer was of pure noble blood. These distinctions had an indirect financial importance. For example, if someone obtained a habit for the man who would marry his daughter, he could be sure of having his choice of suitors without having to provide an enormous dowry.

The essence of the chivalric virtues was honour in arms and was not always easy to reconcile with the Christian virtues. Thus duelling was prohibited by Canon Law, but the knight who refused a challenge lost his honour. It is undeniable that the chivalric style of life set the tone for Spanish society, inspiring imitators even among the lower classes. It combined personal dignity with a contempt for purely material values and a self-sacrifice in the pursuit of higher ideals. Look at the proud emblems of certain noble houses: 'Death less feared gives more life' (Garrigo), 'Better to fly high' (Pimentel, Téllez Girón), 'Death to life and long life to glory' (Cerralbo), 'Die, do not run' (Pellicer), 'Dare, die, thus live' (Escalante).

Unfortunately between the ideal and the reality there was always a gap, and a gap which grew wider with time. Testimony abounds that the seventeenth-century nobility were no longer what their fathers or grandfathers had been. At the beginning of the century, Cervantes, through the mouth of Don Quixote, deplored the fact that 'the majority of knights nowadays go rustling along in their damasks and brocades and their other fine apparel, but would never think of donning a coat of mail. Where is the knight now who would sleep in the open in all weathers with his armour about him?'[1] The contrast was particularly marked in Castile because of its proximity to the court and the neglect into which the profession of arms had fallen. The autonomous provinces, in this as in everything else, proved more traditionally-minded and slower to evolve. The *hidalgos* of Vizcaya and Navarre continued to lead a simple life in their own homes where they kept a good supply of arms. The Catalans and Majorcans went on waging their private wars and vendettas with true medieval fierceness.

Was the Spanish nobility an idle class? Such is the reproach which is most frequently levelled against it, and even in those days its critics were not wanting. But one must beware of generalization. A large part of the poor *hidalgos* of the north worked by the sweat of their brow because they had no alternative. As for the well-to-do *hidalgos*, *caballeros* and titled nobility, they did not necessarily live in idleness because they lived *noblemente*. The professions of arms, letters or public office were open to them and many took advantage of the fact. A great lord had to place his person and property at the king's disposal, even for missions which were not to his liking. Don Fadrique de Toledo was severely punished by Philip IV because he refused to take command of a fleet which was manifestly unfit to put to sea. If disorders threatened, then the nobility were expected to restore order, for they were looked upon as the mailed fist of the community and as having the greatest stake in preserving the existing structures.

The *caballeros* took a leading role in municipal government, and not always out of mere self-interest. Most of them had estates to run; some even turned their hand to business in the few towns where there seemed to be a suitable opening – in Bilbao, Burgos, Barcelona, Seville and Cadiz one comes across many merchants with noble names. It is a moot point whether the decline of the spirit of enterprise is to be blamed just on the nobility or on society as a whole. Contempt for the 'mechanical' professions was a generalized phenomenon, and not only in Spain. What can be objected to the Castilian nobility is that by losing their military vocation and their capacity for government, from around 1620–30 they created the growing impression that they were a race of parasites. But the impression was never a wholly true one, since there were so many exceptions. In the economic sphere perhaps the greatest responsibility of the higher nobility was to have squandered their money so lavishly when the volume of their rents made them the class most apt to invest productively.

The clergy, like the nobility, enjoyed numerous privileges, including immunity from taxation. Consecrated ground was open to any criminal who wanted to take refuge there, and the law could not follow him, except in specific cases. Nor had it the power to arrest or punish a cleric, even one who had only minor orders, since he answered only to the ecclesiastical authorities. But in other respects the clergy was less exclusive. Anybody could become a member and, free as it was of the concept of privileged descent, it roused none of the racial prejudice which frequently envenomed relations between the nobility and the common people. Its numbers were not as big as those of the nobility. Around 1600 there were just over a hundred thousand clerics, friars and nuns in Spain,[2] and though their number went up in the seventeenth century while that of the laity went down, they continued as individuals to be well below the figure of 137,000 noble families.

Their distribution too was very uneven. They tended to be concentrated in the wealthier regions of the centre and south rather than in the north. This was particularly so in the case of the religious orders of more recent foundation, whereas in the north there were numerous Benedictine monasteries of remote origin. Nowadays one is amazed at the total lack of planning which left some districts with too many clergy and others with too few, some individuals or institutions in the lap of luxury and others without the means of keeping body and soul together. Such anomalies were taken for granted; an exaggerated respect for tradition and established rights prevented any reform.

At its highest level the ecclesiastical estate comprised some fifty archbishops and bishops. These were presented by the king to the pope and drawn nearly equally from the regular and secular clergy. The right of presentation, stemming from the royal supremacy or *Patronato*, covered many other high offices of the church. It was defended on the grounds that the monarchs had furthered the propagation of the Faith and the recovery of the national territory from the Moors. In fact it was the outcome of a violent struggle between the crown and the Holy See over a right which in the early church had belonged to the people and the chapters. The partial triumph of the crown was due to the firm stand taken by the Catholic Kings against the Renaissance popes who sought to reserve the rich Spanish sees for their relatives or dependants. But their victory was bought at the price of important concessions. The papacy, in effect, would no longer oppose the king's nominees, but levied considerable fees on the dispatch of the bulls and laid claim to *espolios* (property of deceased bishops) and *vacantes* (the net revenue of a see in the interval of the appointment of a new holder). The *Patronato* and other rights of the king over the church were known as the *Regalías* and were exercised through the Cámara of Castile, which was a committee made up of experienced members of the Royal Council of that kingdom. They not only drew up lists of candidates for the king but kept a check on clergy in office and had the power to punish them with admonishments, fines, or exile if they were found wanting.

In the provision of the wealthier sees favouritism existed

beyond all shadow of doubt. Toledo, seat of the Primate of Spain, was usually reserved for someone of high birth, like Don Bernardo de Rojas Sandoval, uncle of the duke of Lerma, who was succeeded by the Cardenal Infante Ferdinand, brother of Philip iv. In Seville, too, illustrious names abound. More than one natural son, whether of a king or a great lord, found a niche in these wealthy archbishoprics. In Santiago, Fonseca, a grandson of Ferdinand the Catholic, and Maximilian of Austria, grandson of the Emperor Maximilian ii, followed each other. These are facts, deplorable of course, and yet at the same time exceptions to the rule. In general the Habsburgs sought to raise to the episcopate men who were worthy of it, often men of humble origin, like Cardinal Siliceo, tutor to Philip ii and subsequently archbishop of Toledo. The Spanish bishops were not so exclusively aristocratic as the French, nor so secular in their outlook as the German. They were not permitted to reside outside their dioceses without good cause, they were generous in almsgiving, and most of them fulfilled the arduous duty of the pastoral visitation. Their revenues varied according to the yield of the tithe, their basic source of income. Around 1600 they were reckoned to total a million and a half ducats; but there were great contrasts between the wealthier and the poorer sees. The majority had from fifteen to thirty thousand ducats; but while Seville had as much as a hundred thousand, and Toledo two hundred thousand, the majority of the Galician and Catalan bishops got less than five thousand, a sum which barely allowed them to maintain the dignity of their station.[3] From these poorer bishops the king took no contribution, but the rest were made liable to pension charges which absorbed between a third and a quarter of the total revenues of the see. These pensions were used to reward the services of deserving ecclesiastics, and sometimes of courtiers as well.

The cathedral chapters comprised *dignidades* (the dean, one or more archdeacons, lector, master of schools, penitentiary), and varying numbers of canons, prebendaries, beneficed clergy, chaplains, musicians and lesser fry. The numbers involved can be calculated at some four hundred dignitaries, twelve hundred canons, eight hundred prebendaries, and over three thousand lesser benefices. There were in addition some one hundred and fifty collegiate churches which had a chapter but no bishop. Within the ranks of this intermediate clergy, too, there was much inequality, between rich churches and poorer, and within each between the well-endowed dignitaries and the lesser men who received a pittance. This lack of consistency resulted in frequent clashes and lawsuits. The chief dignities were coveted by the great lords for their own sons. The canonries usually went to the alumni of the *colegios mayores*, distinguished priests, or busybodies at Rome. Lower down the scale was a veritable proletariat of humble extraction. And yet they would all unite in defence of their rights against any bishop. Though Trent was a victory for the bishops the chapters were strong and had their protectors. If the bishop was an authoritarian any pretext was good enough for taking him to court: matters of precedence, seating, bowing at the start of the sermon, the administration of a few revenues. . . . The zeal for litigation so characteristic of the age was reinforced in this case because the canons felt their position threatened and because the small number of their obligations left them too much free time. Some, like Góngora or Alonso Cano, used their leisure for creations of great aesthetic value. But the majority, lacking any cure of souls or any pressing material cares, tended to attach exaggerated importance to the trivia of their tranquil existence. The expression 'to live like a canon' has become a proverb in Spain, and it gives a fairly accurate picture of the state of affairs as it once was.

The parish clergy were the real backbone of the Spanish church. There were nearly twenty thousand of them, scattered with the same appalling unevenness to be found throughout the ecclesiastical structure. The tiny province of Álava had over four hundred parishes, as many as the whole of Extremadura and more than the kingdom of Seville. Toro had as many parishes as Madrid. In Huete there were ten parishes, and only one in some towns which were bigger and wealthier, like Denia, Manzanares and Villarobledo. The result was that there were very wealthy parishes to which an important person might aspire and others where the priest had to rely on the charity of his flock to keep him from dying of hunger.

There was a similar variety in the way provisions were made. The majority of parishes were in the gift of the bishop to be provided either at his discretion or depending on the results of a competition. But, particularly in the traditionally-minded provinces of the north, there were many parishes which belonged to Benedictine monasteries. The monasteries served them either with their own monks or by appointing vicars at low rates of pay. Many others belonged to lay lords. In the Basque country especially there were several which were exploited along genuine commercial lines. The patron would nominate his son or some poor relative or bring in an ill-paid vicar and keep the rents of the church over and above a certain amount for himself. The rents of the parishes usually consisted of the *primicia* (a measure of grain which had to be delivered by each farmer); the tithe itself went almost entirely to the bishop or chapter. The priest could supplement his earnings with the dues he collected at certain liturgical acts or the administration of certain sacraments, chiefly baptism and matrimony. Despite the aversion of canonists these dues came eventually to have official recognition and their rates were fixed. Prayers for the dead was another source of income, as were the offerings which the faithful deposited every Sunday at the principal mass, consisting usually of crops they had harvested, a portion of grain, a hen, a jar of honey.

At the lowest level the secular clergy included a host of chaplains and beneficed priests without cure of souls. These men relied for their maintenance on pious endowments, which were generally meagre, on what they could get for masses (a *real* or two in stipend), and on a variety of other expedients not always compatible with the dignity of the priesthood. Many of these benefices required of the holder no more than minor orders or the simple tonsure. Many took minor orders just to use a family right to the presentation, or in order to take advantage of clerical exemption from taxation, military service, and so forth. The greater the pressure of the state became, the more attractive seemed these exemptions.

The majority of complaints about the excessive numbers of the clergy and their lack of training were directed against this lowly class. The recommendation of the Council of Trent about the setting up of seminaries was followed in only a few dioceses, and then but slowly. The majority of priests continued to receive their training in the grammar schools and universities, whence many of them emerged crassly ignorant and morally warped. More than one bishop refused to ordain them, but they would keep coming back, looking for a more lenient prelate or waiting for a vacancy when discipline would be relaxed. There was even the case of a foreign bishop denounced to the Council who had apparently come from Greece and who made his living by ordaining anyone who applied to him. The enormous contrast between the wise and virtuous cleric and the man who could hardly care less, the ignoramus who only wore the cloth to hide his evil ways, was intimately linked with the whole spiritual climate of the Ancien Régime.

The regular clergy was composed of monks, mendicant friars, and regulars properly so called. The majority of monks belonged to the Benedictine Order which in its two branches of Cluniac and Cistercian (or more popularly *benitos* and *bernardos*) accounted for some 120 monasteries. The Carthusians, with twenty-one houses, and the *Jerónimos*, a purely Spanish order, were later foundations. In the modern period only one new order emerged, that of the *Basilios*, who never attained much importance. There were some two hundred monasteries in all, as well as a hundred houses for women.

Then there were the mendicants: Franciscans, Dominicans, Augustinians, Carmelites, Trinitarians, Mercedarians. These were by far the most numerous and their number kept growing thanks to an intense spirit of religious revival which found only a faint echo in the monasteries. The revival came long before the so-called Counter-Reformation. A sign (not a cause) of this new vitality was the energetic reforming movement of Cisneros, coinciding with spontaneous efforts at reform within the orders themselves. The reforms centred round groups which desired to observe the rule of their order more strictly and cut themselves off from their brothers in the attempt, founding separate, even rival organizations. This was the origin of the Observant Augustinians, the Discalced Carmelites, Trinitarians and Mercedarians, and within the Franciscan order the Alcantarines and Capuchins. All of these except the last two originated in Spain.

At the same time as the old orders were being reformed new ones came into being: Jesuits, Escolapians and Hospitallers of Saint John of God. They sought to meet changing conditions, wearing no special habits but instead the soutane of the ordinary priest, whence their name, *regular* clergy. They did not give themselves over to a life of reclusion and penance, nor did they spend long hours in communal prayer. Instead they devoted themselves to works of a social character – preaching, teaching, missions, and helping the sick. They carried a stage further the process of adapting to the world and serving society initiated in the thirteenth century by Saint Francis and Saint Dominic, who established their followers in the towns rather than the countryside, enjoining them to look after their neighbour's salvation as well as their own.

It was these new or reformed orders which were behind the great expansion of the regular clergy in the sixteenth and seventeenth centuries. It is not easy to illustrate this expansion statistically, since we lack figures for 1500. But we may reckon their numbers tripled over the two centuries, so that by 1700 there were 1,608 mendicant houses (as well as 811 for women) and 278 for regulars. At that date the total number of monks and friars can be calculated at 50,000, while the figure for nuns is about half that. Nowadays the situation is reversed, for it is the 'pious sex' which furnishes the higher contribution to the regular life. Probably what restricted the admission of women in those days were economic difficulties, since they could not fend for themselves as well as men.

The great age of the religious foundation was the second half of the sixteenth century when unusual religious fervour and economic prosperity were fortuitously combined. Numerous lords were ready to sacrifice a piece of their property in order to pay for the foundation of a convent.[4] The new orders for their part had plans to cover the length and breadth of the country and fix themselves in towns whose wealth guaranteed support for a new foundation. If no patron came forward the arm of the public could be twisted by the provisional installation of the community in some small comfortless building, on the usually correct assumption that the sight of piety in such straits would move men's hearts.

Towards the end of the sixteenth century opposition began, and the strongest critics were the clergy themselves. The parish priests were none too pleased that the faithful neglected their churches for the convents. In the convents they were given a better reception, were offered new and attractive devotions and a service which no parish priest, even if he had two or three helpers, could provide on the same scale as a community. The parish was now used only for the obligatory rites of baptism, matrimony, burial, and annual communion which had to be certified by the parish priest. For everything else people went to the convent. A situation so prejudicial to the moral and material interests of the secular clergy caused serious misgiving. More than one bishop viewed with displeasure the proliferation of communities over which he had no authority. Even the friars were worried at the great number of convents which competed with one another for clients. Among the laity criticism was mounting of the growing strength and riches of the clerical body, and the burden this implied for the rest of society.[5] A law was introduced prohibiting any new monastic foundation which had not the permission of the Cortes as well as the ordinary licence issued by the king through the Council of Castile. However the pressure was so great that many establishments were founded right into the reign of Philip III and the first half of that of Philip IV. It was after 1640 that the number of new foundations were restricted under pressure of the economic crisis and the fact that saturation point was being reached. However the situation was already so extreme that many existing houses had great difficulty in supporting their inmates.

It was the nunneries that came off worst. They depended upon entrance dowries, *juros* and *censos* whose value fell relentlessly, and the yield from a few badly run estates. The monasteries on the other hand were quite well off since they had extensive lands and manors. Some of them were very rich indeed, like the Benedictines of Osero and Sobrado in Galicia, those of Ripoll and Poblet in Catalonia, the *Jerónimos* of the Escorial, Guadalupe and Santa Catalina de Talavera, or the Carthusians of Jérez, Seville and Granada – though one must remember that most of their possessions consisted of buildings, works of art and lands leased out in perpetuity for small sums of money. As for the mendicants, one must qualify the meaning of the term. Almost the only ones who still held firmly by the holy poverty laid down by their founder were the Franciscans. The other orders amassed property by purchase or donation, so that the public collection of alms was nothing more than an exercise in humility or a secondary source of income. There were even those, like the Dominicans, who had abandoned it altogether.

There were similar differences in recruitment. The monasteries would only admit persons of a certain social standing. They put difficulties in the way of those who had engaged in 'base and mechanical' occupations, or, depending on the circumstances, they might exclude them altogether. They were the resort of many a poor *hidalgo* from the north, while occasionally they managed to recruit some high-born noble, like the eighth count of Lemos who after being viceroy of Naples and ambassador in Venice was professed in San Benito de Sahagún. The mendicants were not concerned about ancestry. Now and then they admitted to their ranks some great lord whose motives were genuine enough; but the majority were men of humble origins. Indeed it was frequently asserted that many of those who made their vows did so in order to escape the rigours of the lay life and not have to worry about earning a living.

The case of the Jesuits is different from the others. Right from the start they were dogged by opposition. Great ecclesiastical princes like Cardinal Siliceo persecuted them relentlessly, while among the other orders they met with scant sympathy. They had the universities as well to reckon with. And yet they triumphed over every obstacle, with such speed that by 1600 there were already over two thousand Jesuits in Spain, not counting the Indies. Thereafter the figure did not change very much. They were set apart from the other orders by the novelty of their Institutes, their refusal to consider themselves friars, and their undeniable ability which gave them great popularity among those who were weary of the well-trodden paths. The pious were attracted by their *Spiritual Exercises*, those zealous for learning by their colleges which in their conception incorporated better teaching methods and curricula than their predecessors; while men of the world were happy to find learned and experienced counsellors who would make understanding confessors. For these reasons they won powerful protectors like Queen Margaret, spouse of Philip III, or the Conde Duque of Olivares. They did not attain the position of royal confessor until the eighteenth century, but long before that they had charge of the consciences of very influential people.

The clashes between Jesuits and Dominicans deserve a paragraph to themselves. In the intellectual sphere they had repercussions which went beyond the boundaries of Spain. The Dominicans were not so much worried about economic competition, though this was an additional grievance,[6] as by the presumption of these newcomers, who aspired to chairs in disciplines hitherto monopolized by them. The Jesuits, while remaining within the bounds of Scholasticism, were keen to emphasize their differences, to the point of forming a school of their own, both in pure metaphysics, as over the distinction between essence and being, and in moral theology, with the theories of Molina on grace and the interminable dispute over probabilism. In the reign of Philip III arguments about the Immaculate Conception were the reason or pretext for a confrontation between Dominicans and Jesuits in which headstrong spirits indulged in some incredible pulpit oratory.[7]

The ecclesiastical estate was much more integrated with society than that of the nobility, not only because it recruited its members in every social class but because it adapted better to its surroundings. The average Spaniard did not regard the ecclesiastic as someone socially remote: he himself could become one, or his son, and no doubt there actually was one somewhere in the family. Despite his frequent moans and irreverent wisecracks he felt himself closely tied to the church and its ministers. The gap between the secular and clerical worlds was not yet so disastrously wide as it was later to become. The distinction between the cleric and the layman was not all that clear, not only because the mere tonsure was the only basic qualification needed but because there were numerous inter-mediate and ill-defined positions – sacristans, hermits, *beatas*, knights of the Military Orders (religious in theory), lay brothers and helpers, and so on. Are we dealing with laymen or clerics in the persons of the duke of Lerma, who at the end of his political career procured himself a cardinal's hat, and the Conde Duque of Olivares, who was a canon of Seville, and Don Juan of Austria, natural son of Philip IV, who was loaded with ecclesi-astical prebends just for the rent he could get from them?

This intermingling of the two worlds is also revealed in the constant intervention in religious matters of the secular authority with the consent, indeed sometimes at the demand, of the clergy. First, there was the intervention of the king himself, whose *Regalías* caused protest in Rome but hardly ever in Spain. On the contrary there were constant appeals from superiors or church courts to the royal justice (*recursos de fuerza*). True, the custom of sanctuary and taxation of the clergy led to innumer-able incidents; but these were protests within the system and often the president of the Council who ordered a bishop to lift the excommunication he had decreed against some *corregidor* was himself a bishop. It is also significant that many dioceses continued to admit representatives of the lay estates to their synods,[8] the reason being that many of the questions arising there concerned the body politic as a whole – fixing holydays of obligation, the qualifications of schoolmasters, tariffs of ministrations, punishment of public sins and so forth. And after the synod's resolutions had been approved, it was the Council of Castile which had to sanction them.

This very lay-oriented church was matched by a very church-oriented state, over which presided a monarch who had a heavy sense of his responsibilities in these matters. The intervention of the state in church affairs had as its counterpart the active participation of the church in the state, almost always on terms of friendly collaboration. It was frequently a prelate who held the office of President of the Council of Castile, the most important one in the kingdom. Many others became viceroys, like Saint Juan de Ribera, viceroy of Valencia, or ambassadors, like the marquis de la Cueva, implicated in the Conspiracy of Venice and later a cardinal and bishop of Málaga, or councillors, like the Dominican, Fray Iñigo de Brizuela, who was an expert in the affairs of Flanders, and so on. The post of royal confessor, which was usually given to a Dominican, was of vital importance since the holder had a voice in every matter touching the Church and even in political questions which presented some moral problem, as most of them did. Some combined this position with that of Grand Inquisitor, which was very influential as well. The court preachers (and others) could not refrain from talking politics from the pulpit, going so far on occasion that they brought punishment on themselves. The majority of political writers were ecclesiastics, and their interest in these questions was more than just academic: they took part in every movement of a social character, indeed as in Catalonia even in revolts, demonstrating a feeling for local conditions which was the best guarantee of their popularity and influence.

9
TOWNS AND THE
URBAN POPULATION

The distinction between people living in the countryside and people living in towns is not one that can be drawn precisely, for all the criteria that have been proposed so far have some drawback. In France two thousand inhabitants or more are held to constitute an urban nucleus. In Spain this limit is unacceptable, particularly in the south where the population tends to fall into large village groups which despite their size are definitely rural in character. A list of occupations rather than overall figures would provide us with a safer means of classification. Where the primary sector predominates, especially agriculture, then the population is by and large a rural one.

The difference can be seen more clearly in the economically backward regions. In the age of the Habsburgs it was the relatively little urbanized north and northwest where the town as such stood out, small in size but perfectly self-contained, against a background which was wholly rural. Santiago, an administrative centre and spiritual capital of Galicia thanks to its university and archbishopric; Corunna, a seaport and site of an *Audiencia*; Oviedo, historic capital of Asturias; Santander and Bilbao, busy ports – all these were towns pure and simple. By contrast, Zaragoza, Córdoba, Murcia, even Seville, had a considerable proportion of rural workers. And there are cases, like Osuna, Motril, Valdepeñas, Arévalo, Calahorra, and many others, where the presence of landowners and rentiers, administrative functionaries, small artisans, merchants and suchlike, conferred an indisputably urban character on the town, despite the fact that the majority of the population were engaged in agriculture. Facts like this make us realize the difficulty of classifying mixed centres of population.

From the juridical point of view the distinction seemed clear: 'a city must have a bishop and walls'. This definition was of medieval origin but it was still quoted in the age of the Renaissance. It laid the emphasis on the military and ecclesiastical functions of a town. In law the title *ciudad* (city) was a distinction conferred usually on the capital of a kingdom and – though not always – on towns with a vote in the Cortes. The title of *villa* (town) in itself sufficed to ensure municipal autonomy and independence from any other territorial authority. The privilege of *villa* was reputed highly because it meant something; on the other hand few communities paid the crown to grant them the title of *ciudad*, which was rather an honorific one. Madrid always insisted on her status as *villa y corte* (town and court). These legal definitions, then, do not get us very far.

Our modern criterion of an urban centre as a place where industry and the service trades predominate is inapplicable to an age in which there was hardly any industry in the strict sense of the term. Instead, every neighbourhood had its artisan manufacture which combined with a lower level of consumption to make even very small communities self-sufficient or nearly so. When we further take into account that the artisan often engaged in agricultural pursuits when the need arose, or was the owner of a parcel of land, we get some idea of the complexity of the problem and the impossibility of settling it precisely.

Trade was more widely spread than industry. Small local capitals – El Barco de Ávila, Coria, Nájera, etc. – were above all market towns. But only the existence of a permanent commerce in uncommon goods marks off the real urban centre. The maximum degree of urbanization is reached where trade passes to the interregional or international plane and is accompanied by the indispensable financial apparatus of banks and insurance. But just as there were no purely industrial towns so there was no such thing as a mere commercial centre. Those which came nearest the mark were a few places in the north like Bilbao, though perhaps the best example would be Cadiz. In the towns of the Mediterranean, even those with very active ports like Barcelona, Alicante or Málaga, trade went hand in hand with other activities of equal or greater importance, deriving from their administrative functions or the presence within them of a healthy artisan class or of nobles and bourgeois who spent their rents there.

The rentier was an essential feature of most Spanish towns. Braudel was prompted to say that 'no town could really feel comfortable without a healthy agricultural balance'. Towns lived off their countryside, whether on an exchange basis by selling their goods and services or as parasites draining off rents, tithes and taxes. With a few exceptions, like Madrid, Segovia or Cadiz, which drew their wealth from other sources, the size of towns was determined by the richness of the surrounding agricultural district and of course by the degree of pressure brought to bear on the peasantry. After all the *balance* was often what the peasant needed for himself, but was wrested from him by the seigneur and taken to the towns. If the towns of Cantabria were few and small in size this was partly because the peasant was not in such an unfavourable position in those parts as he was in Aragon, Castile, Andalusia or Extremadura. There was also the fact that urban agglomerations had less of a tradition in the north, with proprietors and *hidalgos* tending to live on their lands. This may be contrasted with the situation in Cáceres, for example, where out of a population of two thousand families four hundred had entails.[1] The parasitic character of towns was a general phenomenon. One notices it in antiquity; and it is only now beginning to disappear thanks to a fall in the rural population combined with a rise in agricultural production. It made the towns closely dependent on the fortunes of agriculture, both tillage and pastoral, and it is the prime explanation of the collapse of the towns of Castile after 1640.

The supremacy of the town over the countryside was strengthened on the legal plane thanks to state pressure, especially in fiscal matters; for it was the urban oligarchies who were the agents of the state and who administered its revenues. There did seem to be a remedy: the crown was ready to sell villages the right to become *villas*, separating them from their townships and granting them judicial autonomy within a district of their own. But the remedy was not complete, since the new *villas* not infrequently tyrannized in turn over their own satellite villages. The prime movers behind these reorganizations were the rural proprietors, many of whom had grown prosperous during the boom of the sixteenth century. The change which had come over the economy since then could be seen in the fact that more and more townspeople were buying up land in the vicinity of their home towns, including even whole manors. This led during the seventeenth century to the growing dependence of the rural communities on the larger towns.

What did the towns give in return for the rents they squeezed from the countryside? Not much, is the answer, for the big town was very exclusive. Jobs in its manufactures were reserved to guild members. Charitable or educational foundations gave preference to native-born citizens. Prices of farm products were strictly controlled, for if the municipal oligarchy were not above forcing people to buy their goods first, they also had a consumer's interest in keeping prices as low as possible. The villager usually only came to a big town as a servant or a beggar. At times of disaster the towns were overrun by the starving, and the civil and religious authorities had then to resort to emergency measures which were not always sufficient to keep people from dying in the middle of the street.

The towns were enclosed by walls within which a desperate struggle went on for living space. The only luxury they could afford in this respect was a *Plaza Mayor*, square-shaped and often colonnaded, around which municipal life revolved. Fine examples remain today of some of these. There, or in the adjacent streets, would lie the commercial centre; there the most varied festivities took place, from bull-fights to *autos de fé*. Frequently the plaza was the only open space amid the maze of little streets which dated back to the Middle Ages. Within the community traces are extant to this day of distinct and separate towns: the *morería* of the Moors, or the *judería* of the Jews, which continued to have separate walls of their own even after they had been abandoned by their former inhabitants; or the trading quarter, also walled on occasion, as in the *alcaicerías* of Seville and Granada; or finally, the nucleus of defence constituted by the *alcázar*. If it was an episcopal city it would also have its well-defined ecclesiastical quarter. Problems of expansion rarely arose; but what could happen was that the amount of space available began to diminish through the erection of religious edifices, as in Toledo. The surrounding wall, though it had no military importance in the majority of towns at any distance from the frontier, was indispensable for policing purposes. Thanks to it a watch could be kept on those going in and out. The gates, closed at the sound of curfew, served not only as forts and guard-posts, but also as a police headquarters and a prison for the nobility. It was there that taxes on consumer articles were collected. In times of plague, flooding or other accident, each citizen was assigned responsibility for a gate.

Beyond there were usually some small suburbs, hermitages or holiday homes; but in general the suburban zone was then tiny or non-existent.

The distinction between a full citizen and a mere resident was still a very real one in the towns of the north. In the rest of Spain it was much more vague or did not exist at all. Society was less hierarchical in these parts, but another factor was that municipal administration had fallen into the hands of an oligarchy and civic rights had gone into abeyance, making it less necessary to control the composition of the electorate. Residence in the big city had therefore a certain attraction for the persecuted and the disfranchised, for those who sought to hide their origins or change their name. It brought the added advantage of more favourable treatment by the government in the matter of levies, *quintas* and taxes. In not a few big towns like Toledo, Granada, León or Seville, no list of classes was kept, nor was there any payment of the direct tax known as the *servicio ordinario*, or it was paid out of municipal funds. If in spite of everything the towns remained small, this was due to the factor indicated above: the meagreness of the agricultural surplus did not admit of large towns. Only two had more than one hundred thousand inhabitants. Madrid reached this figure in the seventeenth century as a result of becoming the capital of the country. She did not suffer from a shortage of living space, being surrounded only by a mud wall put up for fiscal purposes, a wall which enclosed ample waste right up to the middle of the nineteenth century. Despite her opulence Madrid gave the impression of being rather hastily built and not quite finished. She had no university and no bishop. Nor did she ever become the largest town in the empire, for Naples was bigger with over two hundred thousand inhabitants. A purely residential and administrative town, she lacked an economic base of her own.

Seville was in a stronger position, a town whose importance was enormously boosted by the Discoveries, though it antedated them. For a century it was the centre of the world economy, the place where, in Braudel's phrase, 'beat the heart of the world'.[2] And yet its population did not expand overmuch, rising from 60,000 in 1530 to 122,000 in 1588, or perhaps 150,000 if we count the floating population.[3] It never got beyond this figure. In the reign of Philip IV a slight decline set in, becoming catastrophic owing to the plague of 1649, and the level settled at around 85,000. Seville was a many-sided urban phenomenon, being the centre of a rich agricultural region, the home of a large nobility, a great administrative metropolis, an industrial nucleus, and the only inland port in the peninsula, one magnificently situated for transatlantic trade. Only Lisbon could compete with it for importance and range of activity.

The other cities of the peninsula hardly came near the hundred thousand mark. Barcelona, Granada and Valencia had about fifty thousand each; Zaragoza, Córdoba and Málaga somewhat less, perhaps forty thousand. Valladolid climbed above this figure in the few years it was a capital city at the beginning of the seventeenth century, but later sank below it. The rise of Madrid was achieved at the expense of Valladolid and Toledo, two cities which before 1560 nearly ranked as capitals. The crisis of Toledo, aggravated by the difficulties of its traditional industries, was so acute that the fifty or sixty thousand inhabitants of the time of Charles v had fallen to a third of that number in the reign of Carlos ii.

There were numerous medium-sized towns in Andalusia: Jérez, Antequera, Écija and Jaén had between fifteen and thirty thousand inhabitants. Cadiz was not as big as this; its expansion came later, when it supplanted Seville as the chief port of the navigation of the Indies. In the rest of Spain these medium-sized towns were very scattered: Salamanca, Badajoz, Murcia, Segovia. By contrast there were a lot of small towns with around a thousand households, perhaps five thousand inhabitants: in this category belong the Cantabrian ports, some others in the Mediterranean like Tarragona, Alicante and Almería, and several inland centres.

The general crisis of the seventeenth century manifested itself in a decline of the town, particularly in the central regions. The case of Toledo was linked, as we mentioned, with the competition of Madrid. More dramatic was the fate of Burgos, whose commerce was dealt a mortal blow by the rupture with the countries of northern Europe and by the withdrawal from affairs of its middle class. It was never a populous town. At its zenith in 1560 it had only 4,280 households, which cannot give a total of more than twenty thousand inhabitants. In 1595 it had already fallen to a half of that number, and by 1638 its households were calculated at eight hundred – that is less than five thousand inhabitants. Another drastic decline was that of Medina del

Campo, consequent on the ruin of its famous fairs. Segovia did rather better, though as the only industrial town at that time it suffered greatly by the decline of its famous cloth manufactures. Murcia suffered considerably by the expulsion of the *Moriscos*, and Extremadura by the war with Portugal. By 1660 only Madrid could show a large increase in population as compared with the preceding century. Some other towns remained static. But the majority lost a large number of inhabitants and were littered with the ruins of houses. Homes which were still standing had dropped so much in value through lack of demand that they were hardly worth while repairing. The situation favoured the poorer classes who could find dwellings virtually free; but it was a blow to the established families and institutions which owned property in towns and which had already suffered by the depreciation of the *juros* and the fall in rural rents. In the second half of the seventeenth century Spanish towns had not only fallen in size but, because they were so impoverished, were no longer capable of attracting immigrants.

The fact that the towns were so small did not prevent them enjoying a dominance which they owed to their cultured and wealthier citizens who were so well represented among the ruling classes of the country. Thus the upper crust of the privileged classes of nobility and clergy was largely urban. So too were the most economically enterprising sectors of the Third Estate, officials, merchants, members of the professions, and at a lower level the master craftsmen in the guilds. Trade was almost exclusively urban, for the countryside had only its fairs or occasional markets, its pedlars, or its sordid grain speculators, who belonged more to the world of usury than genuine commerce. In the towns, on the other hand, there was trade all year round, there were merchants with their own specialized branches, there were streets, even whole quarters, specially set aside for it. In some towns of the north there still survived the archaic touch of marking off the *hidalgo* from the peasant, the distinguished citizen from the *ruano* or merchant.

These merchants, with a few exceptions, were not interested in handling foodstuffs. A Jesuit missionary wrote that the tunny fisheries of Cadiz attracted 'wealthy merchants, each of them worth over twenty thousand ducats'.[4] But this was the exception. The policy of the towns was to fix prices, sell direct to the public and supply themselves by a monopoly contract, thus leaving little room for anyone but the small retailer. There was no place either for a specialized commerce in articles like furniture, shoes, hats, etc., which were manufactured by artisans and sold by them on the premises. The merchant's prime interest was in textiles, which accounted for a large part of the family budget in those days. He would also handle imported or luxury articles, paper, haberdashery, wax, cosmetics, hardware, books, jewels.

On a more lofty plane, the wholesale merchant (*mercader de grueso*) engaged in long-distance trade and might if he chose freight whole shiploads of wool or wine, or import wheat at a time of scarcity. The bigger the capital involved the more socially respectable was the business. Everybody looked askance at the retail trader. The merchants constituted an intermediate class. Their ambitions lay in the sphere of municipal government and they frequently rose by the purchase of office. They were in a position to marry into the families of the nobility by supplying their daughters with a big enough dowry. And on reaching the pinnacle of their social ascent they could always retire from business. Even some of the titled nobility of Castile were not above dabbling in wholesale commerce. But many of the greater merchants were foreigners, which continued to give the class a certain social cohesion.

While the old commercial bourgeoisie of Catalonia and Valencia demonstrated a certain apathy, that of Castile began to expand in the middle decades of the sixteenth century. The expansion, if hardly dazzling, was at least promising. There already existed a class with a mercantile tradition behind it, shaken perhaps but not destroyed by the expulsion of the Jews. Many of the latter of course stayed on as *conversos*; but it is an old fallacy to see a Jew behind every piece of business, for several of the merchants came from Christian backgrounds anyway.[5] In this period two things happened to stimulate commercial activity enormously, at least for a while, namely the trade with America and the expenditure abroad brought about by imperial policy.

It was approximately between 1535 and 1575 that Castile seemed closest to developing, if not as a nation of shopkeepers, yet as a country where trade mattered. The great merchants could not resist now and then acting as financiers or bankers to the king. The expression 'men of affairs' (*hombres de negocios*) covered both activities, which were closely interrelated at the period. The commercial renaissance of course was far from affecting the whole of Castile. It lay along an axis running from north to south through fertile country, for at bottom agriculture was still the determining factor. The axis can be divided in two. One part covered the wool route of the north – Burgos, its commercial centre, a few ports like Santander, Laredo or Bilbao, and farther to the south Valladolid, Medina del Campo and Medina de Ríoseco. The other was oriented towards the Atlantic and linked Córdoba, Seville and Cadiz, forming another very rich agricultural area. Seville stood head and shoulders above the rest. It was there that the local trades in wine and oil from the surrounding countryside reached their destination, there that silk found its way from Toledo and Granada, there that other articles came from even farther afield. Both axes were connected, with Madrid standing at the point of intersection. Madrid did not owe its position to mere chance. It would have been out of the question for the capital to have been sited, for example, in Murcia or Salamanca, towns which originally had had much greater importance than the future capital of Spain.

It was in these years that Zapata wrote of Medina de Ríoseco, property of the Admirals of Castile, that it was the richest town belonging to any lord, 'for they say there are over a thousand men worth a million'.[6] It was at this time that there flourished the important nucleus of Old Castile businessmen, Rodrigo de Dueñas, or Simón Ruiz, the man who accumulated over three hundred thousand ducats in capital,[7] or the Burgos fraternity, Lerma, Curial, Salamanca, Quintadueñas. Many of these men were in contact with France and the northern countries either in person or through agents. Among the Castilians established in Flanders, whose names have been noted by Vázquez de Prada, were Cuéllar of Bruges, a Segovian by origin, the Maluenda and Bernuys who came from Burgos and had very extensive contacts, the Andalusians Pérez, Palma, Carrillo, the Basques and Navarrese, Gauna, Peralta, Anastro.[8]

The period of their greatest prosperity was short and hollow: they were not in the same class as the great figures of international capitalism. The state bankruptcy decreed by Philip II in 1575 was greeted with enthusiasm in Castile because it represented the most determined effort yet made to break free of the tutelage of the Genoese bankers. But it was when the king tried to replace them with Castilians that he had to admit that the latter lacked the experience, the network of contacts and the huge fortunes of the former.[9] The Castilian men of affairs retired into the background and the majority of them were not long in leaving the stage altogether.

The expenditure of the monarchy abroad, which had served as a stimulant in the first instance, soon began to have more undesirable effects on the economy. Then came the great plague of the beginning of the seventeenth century, which fell with particular severity on Castile, aggravating the existing difficulties of her agriculture. There followed the expulsion of the *Moriscos* in 1609, and after 1621 a falling-off in the volume of trade with the Indies. How far the decline of the middle class was determined by its desire to ape its betters or by scruples of conscience over profits is a matter open to debate. But it is surely significant that these scruples seem to become more acute just as the profits from business begin to fall. Burgos witnessed the disappearance of its commercial middle class, whether through emigration to other parts or cessation of activity. The commerce of Medina del Campo ground almost to a standstill. This town in its heyday had numbered over twenty thousand inhabitants in addition to a big floating population which came in for the fairs. Apart from the exchange of goods of every description, especially luxury articles, the town gained its reputation as a great financial centre because of the bankers who used it for clearing purposes. According to Lapeyre,[10] it was not the crisis of 1575 but the one of 1594 that ruined Medina. It rallied only briefly in 1601 as a result of the transfer of the court to Valladolid, but afterwards sank into irrevocable decline. Madrid inherited part of its functions as a business centre. In the Crown of Aragon the revival in Mediterranean trade was not sufficient to halt a downward trend. The real state of affairs was made plain in 1614 with the bankruptcy of the *Taulas* or municipal banks of deposit of Valencia and Barcelona. The numbers of the mercantile community in Barcelona remained stable – 154 in 1625 as against 146 in 1552 – but their turnover was smaller.[11]

At the turn of the century, when the reversal of the economic trend was already apparent, a modest but observant author denounced as fatal the ruin of the 'middling sort' (*los medianos*): 'Our commonwealth has reached a point where there are only

F

rich or poor and no harmonious mean, where the rich live at their ease and the poor cry out, and there are none of the middling sort.' He attributed the disappearance of this intermediate class to the psychological factor above all. One part of the middle class had been assimilated by the upper class, had set up entails, arranged profitable marriages and invested its money in fixed rents. The rest, in the attempt to do the same, 'flew too high . . . so that their wings of gold melted away', and they fell into the depths of poverty.[12] Superficial as the outline may seem it was essentially accurate – it did put its finger on one of the most important causes of the decline of Castile's towns.

The case of Seville deserves special mention because it was so unique. It could boast no great middle-class tradition, which explains why most of the merchants we come across there were from the north of Spain or overseas. The corporation of shippers to the Indies, part of the *Consulado* of Seville from 1543, was the most powerful organization of its kind. For all that we cannot help remarking a certain lack of self-confidence, which may stem from the absence of any tradition or an insufficiency of capital, or the great risks of a traffic which was as much subject to the caprice of the authorities as of nature. Vilar outlines the drama thus:

It is in Seville that the great fortunes are made, in banking, in commerce, or in the American odyssey. In commerce, the foreigner bulks large, and his importance will grow during the course of the century. The same could be said of banking. Spanish names are not wanting indeed – Espinosa, Iñiguez, Lizarrazas, Loardos, Negrón, Morga. But one has hardly begun to tell their story before it becomes the tale of their bankruptcies, and this as early as the first half of the century. . . . If the period of gestation for Seville banking is 1536–40 when the precious metals begin to flow in, the first phase of multiple bankruptcies occurs in 1552–55, the years that Gresham found Seville so short of capital. No Spaniard makes a fortune from the silver of the Indies on the scale of those of the great houses of Augsburg, Genoa, or Florence. Is the reason incompetence? Or lack of tradition? More than anything, it is lack of time, for the risks are very great due to the greediness of the foreigner and the sovereign, and to the irregularity of the *flotas*. And yet . . . What about the treasures of the Conquistadores, the profits of the small or smallish trader, of the initial purveyor of wine and oil, of the manufacturers of woollen and silk goods? Capital did accumulate. Is it possible to chart its course? Not very easily as regards its point of departure, but fairly well by the closing stages. What did not go into public or private display, into land or houses, went into *censos* and *juros*, that is fixed rents, particularly into government bonds which often disguised a foreign loan. Bankruptcies diminished the interest on these bonds, while the capital began to shrink as prices rose.[13]

And yet very large fortunes *were* made in Seville, like those of Claudio Irunza or Juan Antonio Corzo Vicentelo de Leca, a native of Italy of whom it was said he was 'richer than the *Corso* (main street) of Seville'. In 1567 he purchased three manors which cost him a total of 56,776,993 *maravedís* and acquired the title of count of Cantillana. On his death in 1597 he left 1,600,000 ducats in his will.[14] More than one great merchant obtained a habit of the Military Orders, which was the supreme mark of nobility. Among these was Miguel Mañara who left a large part of his fortune for the erection of the palatial Hospital de la Santa Caridad. At the beginning of the reign of Philip IV, when the golden age of the bourgeoisie of Old Castile was no more than a fading memory, the Consulado of Seville still numbered hundreds of shippers among its members. But by 1639 the Casa de Contratación was already warning Madrid that, whereas in past years three to four hundred members would have assembled for the election of the prior and consuls, now only seventy-five could be scraped together after much effort.[15] And the worst was yet to come with the disasters which occurred after 1640. None the less it was the Seville-Cadiz region, with secondary centres like Sanlúcar, Puerto de Santa María and, at a distance, Málaga, which preserved their commercial middle class better than any other part of Spain, until the coming of happier times in the eighteenth century.

The guild craftsmen were another typically urban phenomenon. There was no lack of artisans in the smaller towns; indeed there are later signs of a growth of rural manufactures stemming from a desire to be free of guild regulations. But the guild as a corporation only existed in the bigger towns because only these possessed the numbers required for its formation and the authority essential to its development and control.

There is a widespread opinion that the guild movement was related to the medieval spirit of association. But this spirit of professional association has always existed, and though it began to wax strong in the Lower Middle Ages it has only reached its fullness in our own day. Barcelona, the city with perhaps the strongest guild traditions in Spain, had thirty-two guilds as early as the beginning of the fourteenth century. At the end of the sixteenth there were sixty-four, and by the beginning of the eighteenth seventy-two. In other towns the increase during the sixteenth centuries is even more marked. The reasons for the expansion lay in the advantages enjoyed by guildsmen, in particular protection against intruders or unfair competition. The guild also undertook responsibilities which would now fall to the care of social welfare – protecting the sick, the widowed and the orphaned, etc. Frequently the guild had a fraternity for the veneration of its patron saint and for dispensing charity. Many had hospitals for their members.

The guild hierarchy was not as clearly defined as it was in France, where the journeymen constituted a numerous and frequently disaffected class prominent in social disturbances. In Spain the category of journeyman is not a very clearly defined one. In the majority of cases the master worked on his own or with the help, at most, of a pair of apprentices or journeymen. The small numbers of journeymen, combined with the fact that they were not absolutely excluded from the mastership, prevented their developing any marked sense of class. No strikes or mutinies of journeymen are recorded. The only clue to the existence of a certain tension is a decree of 1552, included in subsequent legislation on the subject, prohibiting the formation of journeymen fraternities. Thus the only body whose rights were recognized at law were the masters.

The path to the mastership was a long and difficult one. It started at the apprenticeship stage. For four or six years the apprentice was entirely under the master's thumb and shared his table and his home on a strict living-in basis. Then he became a salaried journeyman, and at this level he might remain for the rest of his life if he had not the skill to execute the masterwork (*obra maestra*) which was the main part of his master's examination. Once he had reached this stage he could reckon on a decent secure income which would never make him rich but would never leave him poor either. The zeal for equality reached such extremes that in some guild ordinances it was laid down that the master who was a bachelor should get half as much raw material as a married man, each to receive according to his needs. The master usually had a little house in the street where the rest of the guild lived. It served him as an abode, a workshop and a sales premises all rolled into one. If the workshop was not big enough or badly lit, custom allowed him to take his work out into the open street which all day echoed to the clang of tools and the singing of busy voices.

As the towns began to fall under the control of aristocracies the guilds lost most of their influence on government, to which their relationship became one of duty rather than privilege. The town approved their ordinances, fixed the price of their goods, intervened in examinations, and told their inspectors what to do. On public holidays each guild had to make its contribution, whether by marching in procession behind its banner, building a gala coach, putting up illuminations or erecting triumphal arches. Though these obligations were sometimes burdensome they gave the artisan a sense of participation and responsibility and an idea of his own worth. When the guild officials marched in procession with their uniforms and ceremonial swords they too could have the feeling of belonging, in however small a degree, to the urban ruling class. The exclusivism of the guilds and their desire to achieve social prominence is revealed by other details, like the prohibition on admitting slaves or coloured people as apprentices. From the beginning of the seventeenth century clear signs began to appear of a decline in the guild system, and there was a steady deterioration thereafter.

The guilds of merchants, by sheer economic importance, overshadowed those of the artisans and forced them into their service, especially for working up expensive raw materials like silk for fine wool. Some guilds like the shoemakers or carpenters tried to avoid this danger by forming cooperatives for the purchase and distribution of material. But there were numerous weavers who became little better than hired hands: they were supplied with their raw material by merchants who bought up their finished product. Not all guilds suffered this fate. But few managed to avoid the favouritism which gave a preference in examinations to sons or sons-in-law of existing masters, or the routine which crushed any spirit of innovation and left them increasingly helpless in the face of foreign competition.[16] Despite its positive features the guild system proved unable to move with the times or bridge the gap between the world of the artisan and that of industry.

Administrative functionaries and members of the professions were also an integral part of any urban community. The latter were few in number and of little social consequence except when they had reached the top of their profession. Apart from Madrid, a city of bureaucrats, Granada and Valladolid were 'courts' on a smaller scale[17] thanks to their *Chancillerías* or supreme tribunals of justice, composed of a president and *oidores*. The latter were very conscious of their dignity and believed they had a universal right of precedence, and they were great opponents of the ecclesiastical authorities with whom they frequently clashed. The host of lesser officials beneath them and the multitude of litigants they attracted were notable factors in the prosperity of these towns. The same was true of Seville and Corunna, where the *Audiencias* were hardly less jealous of their privileges than the *Chancillerías*. This upper crust of lawyers who sat in the Councils, *Chancillerías* and *Audiencias* defended their authority with a rigour which shocked even contemporaries. One fine fellow who threw his hat in a fit of anger at an *oidor* of Granada was sentenced to eight hundred (*sic*) lashes. Two *regidores* were put in prison for not saluting an *oidor* of Corunna.[18] And for having boxed the ears of a mere *alguacil* Don Carlos Mendoza, a nobleman, was whipped in public and sentenced to the galleys.[19]

If the chronicles of the time are full of events of this character it was because the civil service of lawyers, who were often lesser *hidalgos* and even commoners, felt itself threatened by the increasing hunger for office of the untrained nobility. In the Councils the number of places reserved for noble *capa y espada* officials was growing at the expense of the lawyer class, and the same was true with respect to the appointment of *corregidores*. One has also to remember the new bureaucracy which was in process of formation as a result of the sale of offices in the sixteenth and especially the seventeenth centuries, when the government stood in great need of funds.

This was a development which, without going to the French extreme, went further in Spain than in other European countries. Yet even at the periods of greatest stress the Spanish government tried to avoid the alienation in perpetuity of the higher offices of government. In Spain therefore there emerged nothing comparable to the *noblesse de robe* whose overweening ambition kept the French throne itself in check. Thousands of intermediate and lesser offices were however sold, especially in Castile. Few of these had any real importance. The majority pertained to municipal government, a favourite being that of *regidor* which from being annually renewable and representative in character became a hereditary freehold. There were many lesser posts put up for sale, some specially created for the purpose – watchmen, inspectors of weights and measures, etc. The judiciary was another sphere affected by the sale of office. Judges were immune, but trafficking took place in such appointments as secretary, clerk, attorney, and so forth, and collectors of public revenue. Some of the posts sold in this connection had a salary attached, but the majority had to be satisfied with what they could take licitly or illicitly from the general public.

No good came out of this multiplication of offices, the greater part of which had no useful function to serve. They augmented public expenditure, created a class of idle drones, made government more complicated and led to dissensions within the urban communities. More than one town preferred to suppress the new offices by indemnifying the holders. The venality of office had no political consequences; it did not for example endanger royal authority. But it did have important economic repercussions through an increase in fiscal pressure and a drain of money towards unproductive investments. For the purchase of an office which yielded an income and could be sold or hired came to be one of the favourite investments of the seventeenth century. No less evident were the social consequences in at least two respects. It offered the rich bourgeois the prospect of ennoblement if he bought a post in some big municipal government or other major office. Secondly it created an intermediate class of small functionaries whose self-importance was out of all proportion to their usefulness. In other words, the service sector experienced an enormous inflation in the manner characteristic of economically underdeveloped societies.

The professions did not enjoy too high an esteem, because by the prevailing aristocratic standards of the time it was undignified to live by a calling or be remunerated by the general public. Science and the arts conferred prestige when they were pursued for their own sake, but no regard was paid to an author who lived by his pen or an artist who lived by his brush. There were no professional scientists or technicians. Jurisprudence brought distinction and gain to its higher practitioners; but advocates, attorneys and clerks, while forming a fairly solid middle class and owning, some of them, their own appointments, had not much of a standing in society.[20] There was no counterpart in those days to the great names of the modern bar. Only the judge mattered, and the other servants of the law had to be satisfied with the crumbs.

Physicians too were far from enjoying the importance they later acquired. Their numbers were small, they came from modest social backgrounds, and though there were some eminent medical practitioners the majority had to be satisfied with a small income.[21] It did not help matters that their discipline proved fairly unreliable in its application, and that the profession as a whole still bore the taint of Judaism. So the doctor, like the merchant, would usually like to see his son climb the social ladder by becoming a lawyer or living off an entail.[22] Surgeons and chemists were worse off, since they had to struggle for the recognition of their profession as a liberal rather than a manual occupation. The difference was that they would not be classed with artisans in the tax lists or involved in the prohibitions against certain symbols of social prestige like coaches or silk clothes.

The considerable numbers of foreigners coming into Spain made their greatest impact on the towns. The reasons for the influx were basically twofold: a shortage of labour and high wages, the very same factors which now lead the Spanish worker to emigrate. There had always been colonies of foreigners in Spain but up to 1500 they had been limited to small groups of merchants in the principal ports. The economic prosperity of the sixteenth century intensified the movement and now besides the bigger and smaller traders there came artists, clergymen, artisans and workers of no particular calling. The immigrants came from the highest to the lowest levels of society. The economic recession of the seventeenth century, instead of checking the movement, accelerated it as an attempt was made to fill the vacuum left by the expulsion of the *Moriscos*, plague and war. The wage gap remained as high or higher than ever. The immigrant, even if he did not go into business, might do well as a lackey or indeed a beggar, if he could get his hands on the silver coin which was much in demand outside Spain.

Public opinion was against the entry of foreigners, partly because it led to an exodus of silver. But there is a distinction to be made between temporary immigrants (soldiers, servants, itinerant salesmen) and others who settled down in Spain and were a source of wealth. The Consulado intervened on several occasions on behalf of those foreigners who resided there, and Bilbao, Burgos and Santander did likewise.

The favourite resorts of the foreigner included the capital, Madrid, with its large floating population and the plentiful opportunities it afforded the businessman or the adventurer. They included the ports as well, particularly those of lower Andalusia where the powerful attraction of the Indies trade made itself felt. In Seville the proportion of foreigners was nearly ten per cent, and it was as high or higher in Cadiz. It was also considerable in Aragon and Catalonia owing to the low density of population and the proximity of France whence most of the immigrants came. As Nadal and Giralt have demonstrated,[23] it was in the poorer regions of France, especially the Massif Central, where the pull of Spain was most strongly felt. The frequent wars between the two countries, accompanied as they were by confiscations of property, were a great blow to the French mercantile community. To safeguard themselves many sought naturalization, which they obtained after ten years' residence if they owned landed property and were married to Spaniards. Flemings, Englishmen and Hanseatics were other immigrant groups who made up in quality what they lacked in number. Special mention should be made of the Genoese, whose commercial genius earned them a privileged place. Several of their families – the Cataneos, Centurión, Strata, Serra and Spínola – married into the Spanish aristocracy and rose to high positions in government.

There are no reliable figures for the overall number of foreign immigrants. It is possible that they were never more than 150,000, of whom at least half would have been French. But since they arrived in successive waves and often stayed on in Spain, they left their mark on certain districts. Clashes of interest occurred from time to time, but there was no racial antagonism. Those who wanted to integrate found no difficulty in doing so. At most there does appear to have been a widespread anti-French feeling in the lands of the Crown of Aragon, stemming from the nearness of the two countries, their frequent conflicts, and the really high numbers of those crossing the Pyrenees.

THE RURAL WORLD AND THE SEIGNEURIAL REGIME

We have grouped these two headings because the seigneurial regime, while hardly affecting the towns, had a profound influence on a large part of the rural population. This rural world comprised by far the greater part of Spain. Over eighty per cent of her inhabitants lived in villages or small towns or in isolated farmsteads. Yet we know so little about these vast, mute masses for they did nothing worthy of note and for a long time were ignored by the historian. It was Viñas Mey who initiated a study of the question from the Spanish point of view some thirty years ago. Subsequent interest has been aroused among both Spanish and French historians who include Giralt, Anes, Ponsot, Bennassar, Vilar, Amalric, Salomon and others. Some have already published the results of their researches; others have not yet been able to do so as fully as they would like. It is probable that thanks to their efforts it may not be too long before we know what life was like in the Spanish countryside. But for the time being the data at our disposal is fragmentary, and any conclusions we draw of a general nature must necessarily be tentative.

Before we make any generalization we must remember too that circumstances were not everywhere and always the same. Geographical location has to be taken into account. The prevailing conditions in Galicia, Catalonia, Andalusia or the Meseta vary widely, and indeed even within a particular region the way of life of one community might be very different from that of its neighbours. There was also variety of a sociological kind, for within the same town there would generally be some great lord, a class of small or medium landowners and a greater or lesser number of wage-earners. And finally there is the time-span involved: the state of Castilian agriculture changed drastically, especially in the Meseta, in both attitudes and resources, between the sixteenth and seventeenth centuries.

The bigger rural proprietor might often be the lord of the manor. Perhaps he was an absentee, away at court. Or perhaps he was a townsman who had bought land in the vicinity because it was a secure investment, conferred respectability, or enabled him 'to go off for relaxation' (*salir a recrearse*, in the phrase of the time); for holidays and weekends are not a modern invention. The church, universities and hospitals were also big landowners. All these types of proprietor, administering their lands usually by means of a steward, do not properly speaking belong to the rural class.

Let us turn instead to the *labrador*. The word *labrador* is hard to define exactly. It was frequently used in opposition to *hidalgo* as a way of distinguishing the noble from the lowly commoner or serf. But for all practical purposes it meant a comfortable peasant proprietor who might be as well off as most *hidalgos*. Some of them appear to have been very wealthy indeed, like those we hear about in Utrera, near Seville, who kept three hundred oxen for ploughing and 'there are many who sow 1,500 to 2,000 *fanegas* of wheat and more'.[1]

Though less common than in Andalusia the well-to-do farmer was no rarity in Castile, though there it was the medium-sized property which predominated. As a historian of la Rioja put it: 'There are no big fortunes of the kind to be met with in other parts. But there is a generally equitable distribution of property, such that everybody has what he needs from his own harvest. However bad the year, they can almost always manage, and no one ever leaves his land.'[2] These medium-sized holdings were rare in Andalusia where the typical division was between the big proprietor on the one hand and the wage-earner on the other. They were probably more common in Catalonia and the Cantabrian provinces where the comments noted about la Rioja would also hold good. The Basque *caseros* are another case in point: though some were poor, none were desperately so.

The smallholder, whose endless debts forced him to sell his recently harvested corn at bottom prices and buy it dear when his own stock had run out, was the chief victim of the rural drama which was acted out in Spain from the end of the sixteenth century. A major factor was the worsening of the climate signalled by the disastrous harvests of 1576 and 1584.

To this was added increasing taxation, coupled with an odious exploitation practised against the small farmer by his wealthier neighbours, who used their control of municipal office to shift the weight of taxes on to his shoulders. They ruined him further by loans at usurious rates of interest until finally they got his property into their hands and made a beggar or a hired labourer of him. But oppression and injustice were not the only factors involved. It is a simple fact that a man's faculties are liable to decline, and that smallholders once they had reached fifty years of age grew less capable of coping with the heavy agricultural round. If they had no sons to help them, or if they could not afford hired hands, they were forced to beg or take themselves off to a home.

Extensive tracts of waste land, rugged in parts but elsewhere capable of improvement, had no big proprietor, yet the inhabitants lived in misery. Of the Santander region, now a very rich pasture zone, its bishop said in 1617: 'The poverty of the land is immense. The wealthy have at most four cows, and people count themselves lucky with a piece of bread.'[3] In the mountains of León many small proprietors of noble birth had to send their sons to serve in Andalusia to keep them from dying of hunger.

The fact of owning one's land, then, did not in itself determine social or economic standing. Many leaseholders enjoyed unlimited tenure on a low rental guaranteed by contract or custom and were better off than the small proprietors. There were quite a few examples of this in Castile. But the classic case of a people which did not own its land yet enjoyed a high standard of living is to be found in Catalonia. Here Ferdinand the Catholic by the *Sentencia de Guadalupe* (1486) had converted the *pagesos de remensa*, former feudal vassals, into free men holding their land in virtual freehold on payment of an emphyteutical due (i.e. a fixed rent). This sturdy middle class, in Vilar's view, gave the Catalan region its inherent stability. One may contrast this with the fate of the settlers who replaced the *Moriscos* after their expulsion from Valencia and Aragon: they had very heavy seigneurial dues to pay. In New Castile, according to Noël Salomon,[4] these constituted between twenty-seven and forty-one per cent of gross output – and of course they were proportionately heavier on poorer land. Combined with taxes and tithe, they left the leaseholder barely enough to subsist on. In Galicia the *foreros* enjoyed a position analogous to the Catalan *pagesos* in theory but not nearly as good in practice. They were bound more closely to their lords, had reached a lower level of technical advancement, and were plagued by an overpopulation problem. Originally a sort of emphyteusis in perpetuity, the *foros* came to be restricted to a term of years in the seventeenth century at the same time as the curse of subletting began to make its appearance. The Galician peasantry were looked on as the most depressed in Spain. Many went harvesting in Castile during the summer season in order to earn some money to take back home.

The landless labourer was the most unfortunate of all, though even he does not fit into any simple category. In the Crown of Aragon he was a useful part of the system of big and medium-sized properties. There was no surplus of labour in those parts and he was probably not too badly treated. During the sixteenth and seventeenth centuries many agricultural workers immigrated from France. In New Castile, according to Salomon, they must have comprised half the rural population. They were an unstable group, perpetually on the move from one town to another in search of work. Lacking any means of saving they had no chance of social betterment. Even larger must have been the proportion of hired hands in western Andalusia, traditionally a country of big holdings. They led an uneasy existence though no doubt they were not as badly off as they later became with the growth of population. They could take advantage of seasonal labour shortages to demand increases in wages, as some deputies complained in the Cortes.[5] The owners revived a law, originally introduced at the request of the Cortes of 1373, empowering local authorities to fix wages 'in relation to the current price of foodstuffs'; the owners of course *were* the local authorities. Thus the town council of Oñate, by decree of 1567, prohibited wages above twenty *maravedís* a day in addition to a meal.[6] At Cifuentes in Guadalajara they fixed the wage of a labourer at one *real* in February and two in May and June (1588).[7] But there were other more expeditious methods of dealing with potential rural trouble-makers: those workers who refused to do as they were told or demanded too high wages were arrested and put in the pillory.[8]

We should be on our guard though against overemphasising the dark side of the picture. Life, to be sure, had little in the way of refinements, but those who had grown up without them were not aware of what they were missing. Their predominantly vegetarian diet, once deemed inadequate, we can now see as more healthy and balanced. Their work-load was not excessive. Some people, as for instance Alonso de Herrera, author of a famous agricultural treatise, even accused the peasant of idleness. Here again one must take account of marked regional differences: whereas in some parts of Aragon it was customary to work only in the morning, in many other places they had to work ceaselessly to eke out a wretched existence. But even the latter had to observe the great variety of church holidays, whose number was for ever increasing for one pious motive or another – devotion to a particular saint, thanksgiving for deliverance from an epidemic, and other less justifiable ones which varied from community to community. In Almonacid the neighbours were coming out of mass on Saint Blas' Day when the church door caved in; since no one was injured it was decided to observe Saint Blas' Day thenceforward. Four years later (1570) the town council, seeing that the neighbouring towns kept Saint Anne as a holiday, determined to follow suit.[9] Matters reached such an extreme that many towns later petitioned for a dispensation from their commitments, for these voluntarily-imposed holidays had to be added on to the holydays of obligation which were plentiful enough in themselves. In the diocese of Ciudad Rodrigo there were forty-eight holidays to be added to the fifty-two Sundays of the year. In Salamanca, even after the suppression of twenty-nine, there still remained thirty-eight in 1654. Many of these holidays were accompanied by pilgrimages, processions, bullfights with *novillos* and other festivities. In almost every town there were fraternities which combined rustic banquets with devotion to a particular saint.[10]

Then too there was a great number of charitable foundations. Nearly every little town had its hospital where the traveller and the destitute could find a bed. Great importance was attached to charity and almsgiving was very popular. The enormous quantity of communal land helped to alleviate the plight of the poorer classes, for even the labourer had the right to draw for them, to cut wood, or bring his few sheep to pasture on the public heath. Though the *poderosos* (*lit.* powerful) usually took the plums for themselves they could not exclude their fellow citizens entirely. Gleaning the olives or the stubble, the right to the crude oil from the olives, and other little rights sanctioned by custom were a great help to the poor and the widowed.

Only in the rare event of a major catastrophe, like that which struck Galicia in 1626, did people die of hunger in the fields. The smaller farmer benefited greatly by the system of *pósitos*, which were a kind of seed bank organized by the authorities. They advanced seed in the sowing season which had to be paid back with a small interest at harvest time. In years of famine or scarcity they would also bake bread on their own account. It was thanks to safety measures like these that more than one Castilian village pulled through the period of depression, when so many lost their population and towns all over the country experienced a disastrous economic and demographic decline. Take the case of the village of Guinicio, to the northeast of Burgos, where the sixteen households of 1491 had become seventeen by 1560, were still seventeen in 1654, and finally sixteen again in 1784.[11]

It was not the labourer, critical though his position was, but the small proprietor or leaseholder who was in men's minds when they complained of the miserable condition of the peasantry. It was he who was favoured by one or two decrees, while the labourer was just ignored. The words of Fray Benito de Peñalosa in a work published in 1629 have been quoted more than once:

> The condition of the peasantry of Spain is the most wretched and downtrodden to be met with. You would almost think there was a conspiracy on the part of everyone else to ruin and destroy him. The word 'peasant' has such a bad connotation that it is used of taxpayers, rustics, uncouth or sly persons, and worse. It is associated with coarse food, garlic and onions, crumbs, tough salt meat, old meat, bread of barley or rye, sandals, belted tunics and hoods, rough collars and shirts of yarn, satchels and jackets of hide dressed with oil, huts and cottages, and dilapidated mud-built houses. . . . When a farmer comes to the city, who can count the misfortunes he endures and the tricks everyone plays on him, making fun of his clothes and his way of speaking? And who can recount his sufferings at the hands of judges and soldiers who visit his poor village. . . ? So why are we surprised at the marked fall in population in the country towns, villages and hamlets? What I marvel at is that there is anyone left at all.[12]

Allowing for the exaggeration apparent in this analysis we do nevertheless get some idea of the size of the gap separating town and country. As the towns became more wealthy, elegant and powerful in the course of the sixteenth century there developed an unflattering, burlesque image of the backward peasant masses. The most ignorant, poverty-stricken and primitive elements were singled out and taken as typical, without consideration of the evidence. Even the impoverishment of the towns in the seventeenth century did not change the assumptions about their superior living standards.

Cattle farmers, like tillers of the soil, could be divided into rich and poor. On the one hand there were the wealthy proprietors of Salamanca or Seville who owned hundreds of head of cattle, or flocks of sheep in the *Mesta*. On the other, shepherds and suchlike were living on the borderline of subsistence. Then there were the other lowly groups belonging to the rural world, the woodcutters and charcoal-burners, who rarely came into contact with civilization, those who lived by hunting the abundant game then available, the carters and muleteers who ceaselessly plied the highways of Spain, the taverners, and of course the millers. Some millers were quite well off. But in the Sierra de Guadarrama a friar who was quite well acquainted with rural life said of them: 'All their days they will be in need. Their bed is no more than a few skins, where they sleep as close as they can to a little fire. They pass their lives in such hardship that they would not be able to keep going but for the fact that they have been reared in privation since childhood.'[13]

On the material plane the great disparity of conditions was visible in dwellings. The Catalan *masia* and the Basque *caserío* were large and solid, as befitted the homes of prosperous peasants. The country houses of Galicia were very poor. The contrast between them and the seigneurial *pazos* is a measure of the gap between the narrow upper class and the mass of the peasantry. In the towns of Castile, Extremadura and Andalusia there was also a big contrast between a small number of large and comfortable houses, occasionally emblazoned with a coat of arms, and the lowly dwellings of the labourers. In the *Relaciones* of the towns of New Castile ordered by Philip II, a distinction is made between well-built houses with tiled roofs and those made of clay (*tapial*) with roofs of wood. It is in the mid-sixteenth century too that the cave dwellings of the Granada-Guadix region took shape, becoming a typical feature of the area.

Parallel to the authority of the king or town council (which in the exercise of its powers was also deemed royal) was that of the territorial or jurisdictional lords. It is not easy to convey a clear idea of the seigneurial regime in Spain since it involved such an overlapping of authority and differed in some respects from one region to another, indeed even within the same province. But we cannot afford to ignore it, for it represented one of the basic features of the Ancien Régime in Spain as in the rest of Europe.

Confining ourselves for the moment to the historic limits of Castile, we must be clear at the outset that feudalism had never really taken root there. True, the weakness of some kings had led in the Lower Middle Ages to extensive alienations of land and rebellious attitudes on the part of the nobility. But the crown never surrendered its supreme control of the national territory as a whole, nor did the nobility enjoy sovereign rights like the minting of money. On the other hand they received, or usurped, certain royal revenues like the *alcabala* and some even kept private armies. The Catholic Kings put a check on the alienation of land. They created no new lordships save in the recently conquered lands of the kingdom of Granada. They did away with the more odious abuses, razing the castles of the rebellious lords, recovering certain of the alienated revenues and affirming their right to legislate for the national territory as a whole as well as to hear appeals from the seigneurial courts. In a word, they abolished the political aspects of feudalism while leaving intact the enormous economic and social influence of the nobility, based alike on its wealth and its power over its vassals.

In strict law this power arose from a delegation of royal authority. It was compared by jurists to the case of a *corregidor* whose office had been conferred, as it were, for life or in perpetuity. This argument may have had some importance in the realm of theory, in upholding royal authority and subordinating the nobility to the crown. But it did not make much difference in practice. Millions of vassals saw in the *señor* their direct superior, whose capacity for good or evil was greater than that of the distant monarch.

As the age of the Habsburgs opened more than half of all towns belonged to some lord. The proportion was rather less as regards population, for these towns and villages usually had few inhabitants, the majority of big towns being in *Realengo*, that is, directly under royal authority. Within the category of *señoríos* one has to distinguish a subdivision, the ecclesiastical lordship, further divided into *abadengos* (lands belonging to monasteries, most of them Benedictine) and episcopal domains, which were few in number and often met with challenges to their authority. The lands of the Military Orders were also theoretically ecclesiastical; but after the incorporation of their headships in the crown it was the crown which distributed their *encomiendas* and disposed of their revenues.

Charles v and Philip ii sought to increase their income by alienating ecclesiastical lordships with papal approval, and new secular lordships were created out of the domains formerly belonging to bishops, monasteries and the Military Orders. The purchasers were generally members of the higher bureaucracy, like the royal secretaries Don Francisco de los Cobos, Eraso and Garnica, or foreign merchants and bankers who by this means moved up the social ladder or agreed to this method of payment offered by the king in settlement of debt. Although he gave the church *juros* in return, Philip ii had scruples on his death-bed about these alienations, and succeeding monarchs, without following his advice to restore them, did not pursue the policy.

Philip iii only alienated a few towns to the duke of Lerma and other courtiers. By contrast, in the reign of Philip iv numerous sales took place in order to raise funds. With the prior approval of the Cortes a decree was issued in 1626 for the sale of twenty thousand vassals, augmented in 1630 by a further twelve thousand, and in 1638 by another eight thousand. A total, then, of forty thousand families were assigned to 169 new lordships.[14]

In order to appreciate the limitations to which these new lordships were subject, one must bear in mind that whereas the old-style *señor* owned some or all of the land in the neighbourhood the new were only being sold rights of jurisdiction – the power of appointing or confirming the municipal authorities, of issuing decrees and ordinances, of holding a court of first instance. The property structures continued as before. So the operation was not very profitable financially for the purchasers, who paid at the rate of fifteen or sixteen thousand *maravedís* per family yet had no power to demand a rent in return. Those who sought the right to collect the *alcabalas* – an operation whose profitability was not in doubt – had to make a separate financial transaction. If despite the disadvantages buyers were not wanting, it was because many of the middle class aspired to the prestige conferred by ownership of a *señorío*. Though the title 'lord of vassals' did not carry ennoblement, it was a first step on the road from being a commoner to becoming a noble, perhaps even a titled noble. Of course, unscrupulous *señores* were also enabled to play the tyrant by selling office, usurping common land, and so forth. In effect more than one lord gradually extended his control over the lands of the town, making them an empty *coto redondo* and fusing ownership with jurisdiction.

The majority of villages sold off lay in the vicinity of the court or of towns with a wealthy urban bourgeoisie like Seville, Córdoba or Granada. Among the purchasers we find, very occasionally, members of the old nobility, more often Italian *asentistas* like Carlo Strata and Lelio Imbrea, royal councillors like Miguel de Salamanca and José González, generals and admirals of the Indies fleets like Carlos Ibarra and Díaz Pimienta, together with numerous members of the urban patriciate. The process cannot properly be classified as a feudal reaction: for the crown they were simply financial operations, for the purchaser a striving for nobility characteristic of the age.

The situation of the older type of vassal did not change appreciably in these centuries. Personal services had always been few and far between in Castile. They included such things as the obligation to find lodgings for the lord and his retinue; but by now they were commuted for a small cash sum. Some rents were indisputably feudal in character, like the *humaje* or *fogaje* which was a sort of poll tax, or the *martiniega*, a tax which was due to the lord on Saint Martin's Day. But none of these was very important compared to the rents which the lord received in his simple capacity as owner of the land. In many cases the confusion of feudal dues with agrarian rents prevented any clear differentiation and caused interminable litigation when the *señorío* was abolished in the nineteenth century. Unquestionably feudal in nature were the tolls on passage, by boat, road or bridge, as well as the monopolies of ovens, mills, wine and oil presses, and inns. In some parts of Andalusia the requirement that olives be brought to the lord's mill for pressing led to frequent protests and litigation. Seigneurial game reserves were practically non-existent, while as regards the use of the common waste the lord was considered to have a share equivalent to that of two vassals.

The jurisdiction of the lord and that of the community existed side by side in very varying proportions. There were towns where the lord appointed all the magistrates. More often he would nominate the *alcalde mayor* and choose the other magistrates from a list of candidates submitted by the community, including two or three names for every vacancy, or he might just ratify the results of a popular election. Justice was dispensed in the lord's name and to him went the proceeds of fines; but it was his duty to pay the salaries involved. This feudal justice was still very common in Aragon where they were empowered by old statutes to impose the death penalty, even though they rarely made use of it. In Castile their power was greatly limited by the system of *Chancillerías* and *Audiencias* to which vassals could have recourse if they believed themselves oppressed by the sentence of a feudal court.

On the whole the feudal system in Spain was not as harsh as it was in some other countries. It gave rise to abuse and injustice, but it often proved a safeguard for the community, especially if the lords were powerful or influential. Many set up fairs and free markets, others attracted craftsmen, whence for example the flourishing cloth manufacture at Béjar or silk industry at Pastrana. The duke of Lerma, marquis of Denia and favourite of Philip III, distributed his favours equally between Lerma and Denia and traces still remain of the handsome edifices he erected in these two places. The university of Osuna was founded by its dukes, as was its collegiate church. Sanlúcar de Barrameda was taken away in 1645 from the duke of Medina Sidonia after his conspiracy against Philip IV. It had no reason to welcome the change to royal authority, for the dukes animated the town by their presence and turned a blind eye to the profitable activities of the smuggler. In their own interests the *señores* endeavoured to preserve their communities from the worst effects of billeting or tax collecting.

The other side of the coin is reflected in the perpetual strife between some towns and their lords, leading to litigation and demands for reversion to the crown. The suits usually dragged on interminably in the Councils of Castile and Finance. The lords generally claimed that it was the most troublesome citizens who brought these suits forward, with an eye to their own interests rather than those of the community at large. It is true that the *hidalgos* and the middle class disliked living in subjection to a lord, whereas the poor and the workers were not bothered. In Andalusia the lord was likely to be a great figure who could protect his vassals, in Old Castile a lesser man, a rapacious exploiter. The ordinary people generally preferred powerful lords to men of lesser stature and lords who resided locally to those who governed by means of stewards. But circumstances varied so much that it is impossible to be dogmatic. What we can say is that despite the advantages the feudal regime conferred the great majority of towns preferred to belong to the *Realengo*.

The former lordship of bishops over their towns, especially in the north of the peninsula, had almost ceased to exist thanks to the growing independence of the communities in question. Tarragona refused obedience to its archbishop. Santiago had sixty thousand vassals; but if his authority was still respected in the villages it was certainly not respected in the city itself. The disputes of the bishop of Orense with his town were interminable. The majority of bishops made do with the retention of a few honorific rights and the receipt of some token offerings. The monasteries, by contrast, usually held extensive *señoríos* which if not all that numerous in Andalusia were a feature of Castile and more so of Galicia, Aragon and Catalonia, since the majority of endowments were due to the early monarchs of the *Reconquista*. These *abadengos* were also plagued by confusion between ownership and jurisdiction. The *Jerónimos* monastery of Lupiana (Guadalajara) owned half the cultivable land in the town, but in its capacity of feudal overlord only had a right to three pairs of hens at certain holidays in the year. At Guadalupe (Cáceres) the monastery appointed most of the municipal officeholders, collected the tithes and rents from the municipal butchery, ovens and taverns, was paid five thousand *maravedís* at Martinmas, and had other different dues.

It was in Galicia that the *abadengo* developed most fully. A large part of the region belonged to Osera, Sobrada, San Martín and other powerful monasteries, which in addition to their temporal jurisdiction exercised a spiritual one as well over their vassals. But their authority was far from being uncontested, and the litigious Galicians kept the royal *Audiencia* of Corunna very busy. The greater part of the land had been given out by the monks *a foro*, that is, on payment of a kind of emphyteutical due over a very long period, usually three lives. As this due was paid in cash its value fell so greatly that the middlemen got more than the monastery. The settlers were ejected, leading to further protests, as the monks tried increasingly to place the land under direct cultivation, with a monk and several helpers in charge of each property. The irregular lives led by these farmer monks (*monjes graneros*) gave rise to much criticism.

The Basque country was hardly touched by the *señorío*, while the kingdom of Navarre had a very limited acquaintance with it. The Crown of Aragon, by contrast, was throughout a classic home of feudalism. Of the 2,385 towns and villages in Catalonia only 660 belonged to the king, though it is true that this number included Barcelona and other major towns. The nobility held 1,200 and the rest belonged to the church. Of the fourteen Benedictine abbeys some, like Poblet, Ripoll and Santes Creus, had very extensive domains. Santa María de Ripoll (Gerona) by itself owned six thousand vassals and was engaged in an interminable legal battle with the towns of Ripoll and Olot which wanted to become townships.

Nevertheless the feudal system in Catalonia was mild compared with its harsh counterpart in Aragon, where the vassals were often *Moriscos*. Even the Christians found the yoke intolerable, an indication of this being the rising of the inhabitants of the lordship of Ribagorza against their lord, the duke of Villahermosa. Philip II, worried by a revolt of this kind in a district bordering on France, annexed the lordship to the crown and compensated the duke (1590). The harshness of the feudal regime in Valencia can likewise be explained by the fact that it was exercised over downtrodden *Moriscos*. These were liable to various dues, including a share of their harvest which was sometimes as much as a third of the gross yield. This they were obliged to carry to the lord's dwelling. After the expulsion of the *Moriscos* the lords replaced them with Christian settlers on similar terms. But the new vassals proved to be less long-suffering. The Valencian *huertas* were the scene of incidents, even open conflicts, for example towards the end of the seventeenth century and during the War of the Spanish Succession, which in these parts came to resemble a class struggle.

No judgement on the feudal regime – in so far as it is possible to formulate one – would be complete without taking one fact into consideration: regardless of whether the lord was deemed owner of the land (*solariego*) or mere *señor jurisdiccional*, custom rather than law prevented the arbitrary eviction of the tiller of the soil. It was this security that he could remain on the land worked by his fathers which basically interested the peasant most.

SOCIAL
OUTCASTS

On or beyond the fringes of established society, lived groups disfranchised because of their legal, religious or economic circumstances. The *pícaro*, the criminal or the vagabond are not included, since their problem was a personal one: once they mended their ways society would take them back into the fold. This was not the case with the slave, the *Morisco* or the gypsy, who regardless of their conduct as individuals were collectively isolated. The reasons for this state of affairs were several. In the case of the *Moriscos* the basic motive was the religious one. No one believed in the sincerity of their conversion, and this was sufficient to exclude them from office and promotion. As regards slaves, though the racial factor had some importance, the decisive consideration was that they were legally and economically inferior. The gypsies came up against all these objections. They were considered bad Christians, they came from foreign parts, they behaved like delinquents, and their material circumstances were precarious.

Moriscos and slaves lived on the fringes of society but served it and accepted integration in spite of themselves, whereas the gypsies refused any integration. Legally the gypsies were the most deprived of the three groups, and the most feared and hated by society; yet they outlasted the others and kept their identity right into modern times. The *Moriscos* were the most numerous: in 1609 when the decree was issued for their expulsion they numbered over three hundred thousand. There were never more than one hundred thousand slaves, and only a few thousand gypsies. In all then there were half a million malcontents, which was hardly excessive in a total population of eight millions. But their uneven distribution made them a problem, even a threat in certain regions, as with the *Moriscos* of the kingdom of Valencia, or the slaves and gypsies of the big towns of Andalusia. One must not forget that for lack of an organized police or standing army internal order depended on a mere handful of forces.

Slavery, which had never wholly disappeared from the West, received a considerable impetus towards the end of the Middle Ages and the beginning of the modern period. This was due to an increased demand for cheap labour, in part to pander to the taste for luxury and refinement of the nobility and indeed the middle class, who required large retinues of servants. Slavery, then, was associated both with economic exploitation and an extravagant style of living. While in America the former aspect was the more important because of the great mass of slave labour employed in agriculture, slavery was essentially an urban and domestic phenomenon within the Iberian peninsula.

Aside from a few Levantines and the *Moriscos* taken captive during the war in Granada, Africa was the principal, almost sole supplier of slaves, both black and white. The differences between the two colours ran deep. The whites were Turks or Berbers, captured in the merciless struggle which Christian and Moslem waged with each other throughout the Mediterranean. The Negroes were purchased from the Portuguese, being but a fraction of those embarked for transatlantic ports. The first group was rarely converted: savage and dangerous, they were more harshly treated than the Negroes, who allowed themselves to be baptized without any difficulty. Not a few of them made sincere, even fervent Christians: in some towns of Andalusia they banded together in special fraternities and paid reverence to a particular image.

Slavery probably reached its zenith in the closing decades of the sixteenth century. In the following century it began to decline, shrinking by the end to a shadow of its former self. There were various reasons for this. The sources of recruitment were drying up, for the seventeenth century knew no windfall equivalent to the capture of eighteen thousand prisoners by Charles v at Tunis or an even higher number at the Battle of Lepanto. The loss of Portugal made the acquisition of black slaves very difficult and raised the price of the merchandise. Furthermore, it is an established fact that the reproductive capacity of slaves is less than that of free men. Severe measures such as the prohibition on Moslem slaves from living near the coast or the dispatch of slaves to the galleys, ordered in 1637 owing to a shortage of oarsmen, further lessened their numbers. And there were frequent manumissions for good behaviour.

The geographical distribution of the slaves presented great contrasts. There were large areas which had hardly seen one, notably the whole of the north and the poor and mountainous regions. They were not very numerous in the centre, except in the vicinity of the court where there was a big concentration. Bennassar has documented their presence in the rich mansions of Valladolid during the sixteenth century, while in the seventeenth they abounded in Madrid. But it was Andalusia which had the greatest number, though they were never more than a modest percentage even there. In 1565, of 429,362 inhabitants of the archbishopric of Seville only 14,670 were slaves – that is 3.4 per cent. The proportion increases if the towns are considered separately. In Seville itself there were seven thousand of them, or seven per cent of the total. Another focal point was Cadiz, with the harbours along its bay. There is evidence for the presence of slave-dealers in other Andalusian cities, like Granada and Málaga, testifying to the volume of transactions.

It became the fashion in the houses of the wealthy to keep slaves. Inventories list them together with pictures, furniture and other chattels. Many survived to become trusted counsellors of their masters, while in the comedies of Lope de Vega we find mulatto slave women acting as confidantes to their mistresses and aiding and abetting their amorous escapades. Nunneries occasionally had slave girls in their employ. The treatment meted out to domestic slaves was mild: they were looked on as members of the family and sometimes found a place in the family tomb. Much harsher was the lot of the king's slaves, who were put to work on public projects and sent into the mines or aboard the galleys.

An intermediate situation was that of slaves belonging to private masters who used them for gain. This was frequent in Andalusia. They were allowed to live at liberty and follow any calling provided they handed over a fixed part of their earnings. The remainder was at their disposal and enabled them to save with a view to purchasing freedom for themselves and their children. As the majority of trades were organized by guilds which forbade the entry of slaves, they were reduced to the most menial and burdensome of occupations, such as carrier or worker in a soap factory. Only in very rare instances do we find slaves working in the fields.

Gypsies made their appearance in Spain at the time of the Catholic Kings. From the beginning their nomadic existence, their reluctance to mix in Spanish society, and their contempt for religious observances aroused popular hostility. The pragmatic of 1499 was the first of a series of laws on the subject; their frequent repetition is the best proof that they had no effect. The gypsies were ordered under grave penalty to choose a fixed abode, take up tillage, stay away from cattle trading, abandon their language and style of dress, and lead a common life with the other vassals of the monarchy. The Cortes of Castile made repeated demands that they be punished for the outrages they committed in deserted regions and small villages. The town of Madrid expelled them over and over again. The kingdom of Navarre prohibited their entry on pain of a hundred lashes. But it was all in vain. They stayed on, and not only that, they grew in number. This was partly because the genuine thoroughbred gypsy was being joined by others from the oppressed classes of society – fugitive slaves, *Moriscos*, even Christians wanted by the law, criminals, adventurers and vagabonds.

They became fairly numerous in Castile and most of all in Andalusia. In certain populous towns like Seville and Granada they put down roots and took steady jobs. But the majority continued to lead a wandering life, partly because the only heed the government paid to them was when it gave out punishments, which were not always justified. In 1575 Don John of Austria threw them into the galleys 'because of the need for men at the oars'. Similar steps were taken in 1639. Neither the state nor the clergy made any serious effort on their behalf, and the problem instead of resolving itself got worse. A memorandum of an Andalusian priest summed up the situation in 1674: The gypsies have not been known to give any sign of being Christians. They do not baptize their children unless they are forced to. They never serve His Majesty in peace or war. They are guilty of innumerable murders and robberies and are much in demand as paid assassins. They are vagrants and have no calling, while if some become blacksmiths it is in order to make files and false keys. They roam in bands of fifty and more, terrorizing the small towns, and it is their fault that there is no security in the countryside.[1] The Habsburgs bequeathed the problem to the Bourbons, who did nothing to solve it either, apart from repressive measures which were as cruel as they were ineffective.

The importance of the *Morisco* group was much greater than either of the others. Thanks to the study of Lapeyre their numbers and distribution are now well known. Although some individuals or groups escaped to North Africa, they increased steadily in number owing to a high birth rate. Christian writers of the age were aware of the phenomenon, attributing it to the fact that they did not have a celibate clergy, did not emigrate to the Indies and did not join the army. Nearly three hundred thousand *Moriscos* were expelled in 1609–14; their overall number would therefore be somewhat larger, if we allow for those who managed to escape the expulsion order. In the Crown of Castile there were no more than a few small communities. In the kingdom of Granada they were numerous until the rising of 1568. The great mass of them were located in the kingdom of Valencia – some 135,000 or a third of the total population. And there were a further 64,000 in the fertile plains of Aragon.

The *Moriscos* of Aragon and Valencia were mostly peasants living under a harsh semi-feudal regime. The nobility of these regions drew the greater part of their income from the tribute of *Morisco* vassals. In return they gave them a self-interested protection against the administration, the Inquisition and the populace, whose attitude towards the *Morisco* recalls that of the 'Poor Whites' of the southern United States towards the Negro. When the upheaval of the *Germanías* occurred in Valencia with its overtones of class conflict the *Moriscos* remained loyal to their lords. The rebels, reacting with a mixture of class and religious hatred, forced the *Moriscos* to accept baptism on pain of death. Once peace was restored a junta of theologians suggested that the baptisms must be considered valid.

In Castile *Moriscos* (also known as *Mudéjares*) had lived peacefully for centuries alongside the Christians. They were almost non-existent in the north, scarce in Old Castile, more numerous in New Castile, Extremadura, Murcia and Andalusia. When the kingdom of Granada was conquered the Catholic Kings promised to respect the religious liberty of the inhabitants, a promise which was not kept. The rising of 1499 furnished the sovereigns with the pretext for declaring the agreement null and void and offering the *Moriscos* a choice between baptism or emigration. The majority opted for the first solution. In their desire to achieve religious unity the sovereigns issued the same instructions to the Castilian *Moriscos*, although they had not been guilty of any disturbance. People could not help but be aware of the nominal value of these conversions, but it was hoped that they would become sincere in time. The case proved to be otherwise.

Each of the three *Morisco* groups (Valencian-Aragonese, Castilian, Granadan) might have its own distinctive features, but they all resembled one another in rejecting the religion imposed on them from above. The ecclesiastical authorities showed a rather lukewarm zeal in trying to get them to become sincere converts. There were prelates who made praiseworthy efforts: parishes and colleges were founded, prizes were instituted, special catechisms were printed for the *Moriscos*. But the most usual attitude was simply to require them to attend mass and fulfil the letter of their Christian duties on pain of a fine or other punishment. These methods resulted in some individual conversions, and even one or two whole communities like the Valle de Ricote (Murcia) seemed on the way to becoming genuine Christians. But the great majority remained loyal to their old faith. The fact was so notorious that the church did not force them to receive communion for fear of sacrilege.

Religious assimilation was so difficult because it was only a part of a much wider problem – the integration of the *Moriscos* with a society which rejected them. Like other groups which are discriminated against, the *Moriscos* might live side by side with the Christians but they kept themselves very much apart. Numerous towns in Valencia, Aragon, or the Alpujarra of Granada were inhabited only by *Moriscos*. There would be one or two Christians at most living in them – the mayor, parish priest or landed proprietor, symbols in their eyes of the forces of oppression. Many other communities were mixed, with a Christian quarter separate from the *Morisco*. Even where the *Moriscos* numbered only a handful they tried to live together in the same district, the same street or the same house. In this voluntary segregation the racial factor hardly entered. Though the Hamitic strain was more pronounced in the *Moriscos* than other Spaniards there is abundant testimony that it was not easy to tell the two groups apart by physical appearance. It was a wide range of social and cultural factors which gave them their closed, inassimilable character as a group.

Of these, inbreeding was one of the most fundamental. Mixed marriages seem to have been very rare. On the other hand there was no great barrier of language since Arabic was disappearing. Only in certain communities of Valencia and Aragon was Arabic spoken, and probably a very corrupt form of it at that. Elsewhere Castilian was the spoken tongue, though of a very picturesque kind owing to faults of grammar. The written language proved more resistant, resulting in a curious *Aljamía* literature consisting of Castilian texts composed in Arabic characters.

A geography of Spanish food would have to take account of the contrast between the dietary habits of the Christian, who liked meat, wheaten bread and wine, and those of the *Moriscos*, who were not very fond of meat and consumed great quantities of rice, fruit, vegetables and greens, which earned them the derision of their neighbours. But there was no disguising the fact that the *Moriscos* usually enjoyed a healthier and longer life than the Christians, for reasons which were a mystery to the unenlightened physicians of those days.

The occupations of the *Morisco*, besides agriculture, were handcrafts, small-scale commerce and cartage, by means of mules or *burros*. The rise in the cost of transport after 1609 was blamed on the disappearance of five thousand *Morisco* muleteers because of the expulsion.[2] There was a modest *Morisco* middle class in certain towns of Castile. In Granada there were even noble families which boasted descent from the old Arab kings and nobility, and some of these enjoyed honorific positions. When the *Moriscos* of Granada were banished to Castile the Cortes demanded that they should not engage in trade or the professions. There were some teachers and writers of *Morisco* origin – Casiodoro de Reina from Granada, a Protestant and a translator of the Bible, was of that stock, and Fray Alonso Gudiel, tried together with Fray Luis de León for preferring the Hebrew version of the Bible to the Vulgate, was *Morisco* on his father's side and Jewish on his mother's.[3] Occasionally one comes across mention of wealthy *Moriscos*, who were generally traders.[4] However on the whole they were a poor and illiterate group.

It would be wrong to assume that because of their lowly condition the *Moriscos* were a gloomy people. The clothes they wore were many-coloured and swirling; they had a great love of festivity and merrymaking, dancing and bull-fighting, and played a wide range of musical instruments. Many of the features attributed to the *Morisco* by contemporaries recall those of the Spanish gypsies of today, with whom some refugees from the expulsion probably merged.

The obstinacy of the *Moriscos*, their inbreeding, adherence to tradition and determination to stay together in a hostile world were more potent than the efforts aimed at their assimilation. They accepted a Christian name at baptism but among themselves they used another of Moslem origin. They attended the compulsory mass and listened to the sermon, but were not impressed. Their last wish was to die without the Christian sacraments, and to this end the family would delay calling in the priest, pretending that death had been sudden. They were allowed to have their own cemeteries until quite late.

This sociological structure of which religion was only one element, the *Moriscos* of Granada sought to safeguard by getting Charles v to agree in 1527 not to make any change in their customs for forty years. The emperor was persuaded by a subsidy, and perhaps also by the enquiries which had been made at his order revealing the injustices to which the *Moriscos* had been subject. When the limit expired in 1567 they tried to get Philip II to renew it, but the monarch followed the advice of his councillors and refused. This disappointment, combined with the harsh measures of the authorities in Granada and the grave crisis facing silk, one of their chief means of livelihood, decided them on revolt. The revolt affected mainly the mountain district of la Alpujarra. It was marked by horrible displays of cruelty on both sides. The few Christians who lived in the *Morisco* villages were assassinated and the churches and sacred images smashed in fury. Ninety priests and some fifteen hundred faithful lost their lives.[5]

The government lacked trained troops with which to combat the rising and there were great fears of a Turkish landing in Andalusia. In the event a few contingents landed from Algiers in support of the *Moriscos*. A summons was issued to the great lords to assemble their vassals and to the towns to call out the militia. These irregular forces were not worth much, and the war – a series of skirmishes, sieges and terrorist activities over a difficult terrain – dragged on for three years. The two leaders chosen by the *Moriscos* were assassinated by their own followers.

The command of the Christian troops also passed through several hands until it was given to Don John of Austria who eventually managed to pacify the devastated region. By order of the king the fifty thousand or so survivors were banished to other regions of Andalusia or Castile. An equal or greater number died in the fighting or were taken as slaves. The repopulation of the devastated zone was a very slow process. Some twelve thousand families were brought in from various parts; but many abandoned the villages assigned to them and the kingdom of Granada was a long time recovering its former population.

Philip II's intention in ordering the dispersal of the *Moriscos* of Granada was to achieve their assimilation. With this aim in mind he gave orders that they were not to live in groups but were to mingle with the Christian population. This attempt came to nothing. The exiles soon regrouped, abandoning the villages and concentrating in the chief towns in certain streets and quarters. Perhaps the merger would have succeeded if there had been a more friendly attitude on the part of the Christian population or a longer trial period. As it was, there was little time for it to take effect because within forty years occurred the general expulsion, decreed in 1609 not by the stern Philip II but by his son, the bland and spineless Philip III.

The *Moriscos* of the other regions of Spain had not given any trouble during the ferocious conflict in Granada. But the authorities were uneasy all the same. What would happen if a powerful Turkish fleet disembarked in Valencia and put arms in the hands of the *Moriscos*? There was no question but that certain elements were plotting against the monarchy. The religious consideration as well carried great weight with the pious king. The archbishop of Valencia, Juan de Ribera, after great efforts made to convert the *Moriscos*, grew indignant at their obstinacy and came to support the idea of expulsion. His views had the backing of some circles at court. But they were countered by weighty arguments of an economic order; so that discussions dragged on for years and any decision on the subject was postponed. Eventually the policy of rigour carried the day. This was not a triumph of the church, hopelessly split as it was on the subject, much less of the nobility. It was the army, preoccupied by the military danger, that won the king over to the idea of the expulsion. If the underlying causes were religious in nature, the immediate motive was political.

The expulsion was carried out in stages, starting with the main nucleus in Valencia. There was only a tentative resistance in the sierras, which was soon overcome. The unfortunate *Moriscos* were embarked at various ports for North Africa. They were allowed to take on board their money and jewels. Various stories got abroad of the fate awaiting them. News circulated in Spain that the majority died of their privations and hardships, and there is no doubt that in many cases this was so. The nomadic tribes of North Africa stripped those who fell into their hands of whatever possessions they had with them. But it appears too that they were well received in other parts, especially in Tunis, where they came to form compact communities.

The consequences for Spain varied from region to region. They were serious in Valencia, which lost a third of its population and was faced with a major problem of reconstruction. They were also serious in the *huerta* of Murcia and the *vegas* of Aragon. They were insignificant in Catalonia and Cantabria. In Castile properly speaking, considerable damage was done to towns like Toledo, Córdoba and Seville where there had been a fair proportion of *Moriscos*; but there were whole areas where the measure passed unnoticed. All in all, the departure of three hundred thousand industrious inhabitants meant a notable loss of wealth.

What Spain lost in human potential was a gain for the Berber states. Since 1492 they had been the resort of refugees from Spain, fleeing individually or in groups. The massive entries of 1609–14 animated whole areas and changed the face of the land for years to come. The middle class expanded in the towns of Morocco. Thousands more were to be found in Algiers. And round Tunis they transformed the countryside, cultivating it much more intensively than other parts of the Berber states. Right into the eighteenth century Spanish was still current in the region.[6] Braudel compares the role of these exiles to that of the Huguenots who fled from the persecution of Louis XIV.[9] Their contribution of an energetic and industrious population gave a new stimulus to African Islam, leading to expansionism in the south towards Black Africa as a way of compensating for losses in the Mediterranean. Some *Moriscos* missed their former homeland, and took enormous risks in order to return. But

others, full of hate, intensified the piratical activities which were
the curse of the Mediterranean. The *Moriscos* of Cherchell had
become specialists at this kind of warfare and the exiles from
Hornachos, a *Morisco* town in Extremadura, formed a pirate
base at Salé on the Atlantic coast of Morocco. But even these
offered to hand the fortress over to the king of Spain if he would
pardon them and allow them to return. For at heart, despite the
difference of religion, the *Moriscos* were, and felt themselves to be
Spaniards.

THE ECONOMY OF HABSBURG SPAIN: I. THE STRUCTURES

The Spanish empire was not an economic unit. To make it one more was needed than the few facilities which existed for the interchange of goods among its component parts – facilities that were not much better than those some foreign countries obtained by treaty. Even Spain itself was not an economic unit. Castile, Navarre and the countries of the Crown of Aragon had their own regulations, currency and customs barriers separating them from one another. There was likewise a great disparity in the stage of economic development each had reached, with Catalonia and Valencia having made more rapid progress in earlier centuries, as shown in certain superior forms of economic life – the municipal banks or *Taulas* of Barcelona and Valencia, for example, or the widespread use of maritime insurance, even of the letter of exchange. But by the sixteenth century these provinces had passed their peak and entered a period of stagnation. This explains a feature of society in those parts which was not yet apparent in Castile – the conversion of the old bourgeoisie into a sort of aristocracy living off its rents. Castile, by contrast, gave proof of greater dynamism and youth, invigorated as it was by the initially stimulating effects of the military expenditure required by imperial policy, but most of all by the annexation of an immense overseas dominion. For this reason, because they are that much bigger and have a more interesting story to tell, the Castilian territories will be the focal point of this brief summary. Our study makes no claim to being exhaustive and is liable to the corrections inevitable in a subject which is only now receiving critical scrutiny.

The cornerstone of any structural analysis is population size, for man is the prime source of a country's wealth and alone capable of activating everything else. We have not the information which would enable us to determine the active population of Castile, but we do know with a fair degree of accuracy the overall total for the sixteenth century thanks to a series of statistics of remarkable exactness for the period. These statistics have been known in outline for some considerable time,[1] and have recently been supplemented by Felipe Ruiz.[2] On the basis of this information we can deduce that Castile, in the widest sense, had 891,467 *vecinos* or households around 1530. This is equivalent to 4,457,335 inhabitants, if we adopt the coefficient of five persons per household, which is rather high but acceptable if we allow for the inevitable omissions. As for their distribution at the time, the high density of the central Meseta stands out, particularly in the northern half or Duero basin, whereas Andalusia and the Cantabrian coast, with more potential, were less well populated.

The above-mentioned date of 1530 saw the beginning of a phase of demographic expansion, particularly noticeable in New Castile, which for half a century was to have the highest rate of growth. This detail is confirmed by the *Relaciones* of towns in New Castile, drawn up in the first half of the reign of Philip ii, the majority of which point to an increase in population. It is difficult to determine the point at which this expansionist phase comes to an end. The date probably falls somewhere around 1580, at which time there began a series of bad harvests coinciding with epidemics, the most serious of which killed half a million people, chiefly in the central provinces, between the end of the sixteenth and the beginning of the seventeenth century. Before this catastrophe, in 1591, Philip ii had ordered a census to be made for fiscal purposes. It is the most detailed of its kind for the period, unmatched anywhere else in Western Europe. This census gave a total of 1,148,674 taxpaying *vecinos* as well as 133,476 *hidalgo* families and 33,087 of the secular clergy. Friars and monks of course could not count as families, only as individuals. On this basis we can reckon the population of Castile in that year to have been 6,600,000 inhabitants. That of the non-Castilian kingdoms was much less. Navarre, Vizcaya and Guipúzcoa may have had some 350,000 inhabitants, and the Crown of Aragon 1,400,000. Valencia, its population expanding rapidly before the expulsion of the *Moriscos*, was in the forefront with over 450,000 people, a figure slightly higher than that of Catalonia. Aragon, whose 47,000 square kilometres contained a bare 400,000 inhabitants, gave travellers the impression of being a semi-desert region.[3] The Balearic Isles, better populated despite the continual threat from pirates, had 135,000.

The total of 8,350,000 inhabitants seems very small to modern eyes: barely seventeen inhabitants per square kilometre. But it put Spain in a leading position at the time: markedly below France whose sixteen million inhabitants made it the most populous country in Europe, but above England and on a par with Italy or Germany. The demographic preponderance of the central regions explains why the court was sited in Madrid, while the smaller numbers of the Crown of Aragon underlines its satellite position *vis-à-vis* a powerful Castile.

The demographic evolution of the seventeenth century is less clear, for lack of statistical material of comparable exactness to the above. There is no doubt though that the population underwent a major decline. Since in the rest of Europe it remained stationary or increased slightly, this made the relative position of Spain that much worse. The chief blame for the fall lay with poor sanitary conditions. In normal circumstances there was an excess of births since the birth rate was high, higher than the death rate which also took heavy toll, especially of the new-born. This surplus determined the rise in the Spanish population in the sixteenth century. The trend altered in the seventeenth because of killer epidemics which seem to have been of foreign origin. Besides those which affected only a particular locality or were not very severe, three epidemics spread very widely indeed, though their importance has only been recognized in recent times.[4] The first has been mentioned already; it extended over almost the entire peninsula but was particularly severe in Old Castile, whose former prosperity disappeared for good. The second ravaged the east and Andalusia between 1647 and 1651. The third affected more or less the same area between 1676 and 1685. Spain was not the only country to suffer these outbreaks. They struck throughout the Mediterranean and could be frightful on occasion: one has only to think of the plague of Milan evoked by Manzoni, or that of Naples. In Spain however they kept recurring and took hold in the most populous zones. Their virulence was probably related to a general state of diminished resistance on the part of the population, caused by dietary deficiency, which would explain why the poorer classes were hardest hit.

Other causes of depopulation were the expulsion of three hundred thousand *Moriscos*, emigration to the Indies, losses on the battlefield, together with a lowering of the marriage rate owing to the high number of clergy and to economic difficulties. These losses were only partially offset by the entry of numerous foreigners, of whom a part put down roots in the peninsula. On balance, the net loss was of the order of a million and a half souls: from almost eight and a half million at the death of Philip II the Spanish population fell to barely seven million by 1700. It is probable that the level was even lower around 1660. Nearly all the gains made in the sixteenth century were wiped out in the course of the seventeenth century. In terms of *active population* the loss was even greater. The sources agree that an increase took place in the numbers of the idle, vagabonds, and beggars, owing basically to a shortage of jobs. The Spain left by Philip IV at his death not only lacked people but employment even for those few who remained. A vicious circle had formed: falling population led to a drop in demand, while low productivity prevented the economic development which was vital to any increase of population.

Not every region of Spain suffered equally from this decline in population. Most seriously affected was the heartland of Castile, the Meseta, which had been hardest hit by the concentration of property and by fiscal pressure. Andalusia showed an upward trend, offset by an exceptional mortality, which produced a position of equilibrium. Galicia and the Cantabrian coast, under-developed regions, sent what surplus population they had inland. Galicia, a poverty-stricken rural province, provided Castile with reapers, the youth of Asturias took service at court, and the large class of poor *hidalgos* from Cantabria and the Basque country supplied page-boys, esquires and secretaries. In the eastern provinces the expulsion of the *Moriscos* had rudely interrupted the progress of Valencia; in 1700 the province had still not made up the numbers of a century before. Aragon and Catalonia, after a low in the middle of the seventeenth century, registered small increases. To sum up then, the chief incidence of the decline was felt in the inland provinces, whereas in the coastal regions the population remained stable or began to expand with increasing momentum as time went on. It was an enormously decisive watershed in the history of Spain. The unification brought about by the Catholic Kings corresponded to the hegemony of a wealthy and populous Castile; now the preponderant position of the coastal provinces would open the door to centrifugal tendencies which were to become significant in our own day.

In this period economic structures were remarkably dependent on the geographical infrastructure over which technology had no control. Indeed it was not merely a question of technical backwardness but of lack of interest and resources on the part of the government. The Imperial Canal of Aragon begun by Charles v was the sole hydraulic work of any importance, and even that was interrupted for lack of funds. The construction of roads and bridges was left to private enterprise, with the state generally limiting itself to granting the municipality involved some tax or duty towards the cost. Lords or public bodies who levied tolls on public highways were supposed to look after their repair, but they were not usually over-zealous in this matter. The result was that the roads were in a lamentable state, making communications even more difficult over a terrain which was rugged enough already, and increasing the cost of transport.

The dismemberment of the bigger townships following the royal policy of allowing villages to become autonomous *villas* was an added disadvantage, for the towns had no longer the means of subsidizing works of general interest. In addition the portioning out of common land or waste caused many woods to be brought under the plough or otherwise abused. As early as the reign of Philip II the impoverishment of the forest was so apparent that orders were given for it to be restored. Some results were achieved: thus, for example, the extensive pine-woods of the left bank of the Duero seem to date from this period, according to Bennassar. But it was in the northern provinces, which were accustomed to rule themselves, that the woods were best preserved. The very inadequacy of communications was often a safeguard against the excessive felling of trees, because it was not easy to sell the wood unless it was near the coast or near some big river where it could be floated downstream. The Tagus served this purpose for the pine trees of the Sierra de Cuenca and the Guadalquivir for those of the Sierras de Cazorba and Segura, of which so few remain today. While discounting the notion that Spain was then one vast woodland, there is no doubt that the forest covered a larger area than it does today and was of a better quality. Many zones which have been replanted in our own day with conifers were then the home of the beech, oak, chestnut, walnut and other types of solid timber which takes a long time to grow. The woods were open-handed, almost democratic with their riches. They did not in general belong to private individuals but to the community, which had common rights of use. When one thinks that even today, after the immense losses which have occurred, some townships pay their way from the profits of the woodland and have a surplus which they divide out among the inhabitants, one can form some idea of the enormous heritage of pasture and timber enjoyed by even the most destitute regions.

The Spanish terrain being what it is, only two-fifths of the soil can be cultivated in our day. At the beginning of the modern period the proportion was even smaller. More land was given over to the type of farming which seemed to suit it best: mountainous terrain or poor soil to pasture and woodland, heavy soils to tillage. A glance at a geological map of Spain will show how the country falls roughly into the 'three Spains' suggested by Hernández Pacheco. The west is granitic, with a preponderance of peneplains and ancient mountain ranges. Then a hilly calcareous zone stretches in a double bend from the Basque country to the straits of Gibraltar. Finally there are the clay soils of the plains of Old and New Castile, lower Aragon and the valley of the Guadalquivir. This 'clay' Spain, with its complement of *vegas* and coastal plains, is the part which is really suited to agriculture. It underlay the prosperity of Old Castile, Toledo, Andalusia and the levantine *huertas*, whereas before the tardy introduction of maize Galicia and the Cantabrian coast had an impoverished and deficient agriculture.

Unlike nowadays, land might then go uncultivated for lack of labour or marketing facilities or because of some legal impediment which prevented the ploughing of the common. The privileges of the Mesta, the powerful association of transhumant sheep-owners, also interfered with the ploughing of pasture. A fair part of the Mediterranean coast, some of it good soil, was left untilled for fear of pirate attacks, against which the regular line of towers whose remains are still to be seen amid the hotels and blocks of luxury flats were a very poor defence indeed. The bounds of agriculture were further restricted because apart from the regularly irrigated land (*regadío*) there were few areas cultivated every single year. The normal practice was *año y vez* – that is, a harvest was reaped one year and the year after the land was left fallow and used only for pasture. There were some lands that lay fallow only one year in every two; but there were many others that gave only one crop every three. The really productive agricultural area was probably hardly as much as twenty-five million acres, a fifth of the surface area of the country. We have only fragmentary data about yields but there is no doubt they were as low as in the rest of Europe. In the tables of Slicher van Bath, used by Braudel and Mauro,[5] Spain figures jointly with Italy and France with a yield of 6.3 on seed over the period 1500–1820. This is an average which appears acceptable, since though there were poor soils that yielded less there were richer areas where the harvest was ten times the seed.[6] In these cases we are dealing with quinquennial or decennial averages, for the Mediterranean climate is capricious and the ups and downs characteristic of its agriculture were even more pronounced in the days before the technological revolution.

Though statistics are lacking everything goes to show that cereals occupied three-quarters of the cultivated surface area. The tyranny of wheat, the 'king cereal', was absolute. Only in the poorer or less hospitable soils was it substituted by rye or millet. Barley was grown as animal feed, while rice, very little eaten in Castile, was confined to the levantine *huertas*.

The transformations which took place in Spanish agriculture during the sixteenth and early seventeenth centuries were extremely important and may be summed up as follows:

The increase of population led to a growth in consumer demand which could not always be satisfied. Years of poor harvest and of scarcity occurred, which the government tried to counter by the imposition of a fixed price, the *tasa*, on grain. The *tasa* was introduced as an emergency measure in the time of the Catholic Kings and became permanent after 1558 in every part of Castile except the non-grain-producing regions of the north and northwest, 'because they are supplied by imports from elsewhere'. The *tasa* edict was renewed from time to time during the second half of the sixteenth century, raising the tariffs (wheat from nine to eighteen *reales* per *fanega*, a figure which thereafter remained constant), and making the penalties for infraction more severe. Though the *tasa* was never strictly observed it did hinder the expansion of cereal cultivation and was a nuisance for the farmer.

Growing demand caused a land-hunger which despite the laws making for the stability of rural property led to a series of holdings being put under the plough for the first time. Sometimes the ploughings were legal, sometimes illegal, occasionally of good land, occasionally of poor soil which was soon suffering from erosion.[7] The extension of the arable proved insufficient, perhaps because of adverse climatic conditions, so that major imports of wheat had to be arranged from the Baltic and from Sicily after 1580.

Another probable cause of inadequate harvests was that vast corn-growing areas were replanted with more remunerative crops of a marketable kind which were not liable to the *tasa*, like the olive for example, and above all the vine. The heavy demand for wine in America explains the extension of vine-growing in the old kingdom of Seville and particularly round the bay of Cadiz. But the phenomenon was a generalized one, so that this simple explanation will not suffice. There must have been a growth of domestic consumption which allied to the increase in population caused the vine to spread over the whole south of Spain. On the other hand it was receding in northern districts where it had been grown for ages past. A similar fate overtook oranges and lemons, though these were still being dispatched to England from Asturias and Galicia in the first half of the seventeenth century. It is an open question whether the decline was due to a worsening of the climate at the beginning of that century or to a growth of specialization. What appears beyond doubt is that there was a trend towards concentration and specialization in farming, accompanied by a decline of self-sufficiency both at the family and district level and an increase in marketing and trade. No doubt this development was connected with the investment of the urban capitalist in the purchase of land and the rise of the great domain.

In this evolution there were certain positive features: an expansion of the area under cultivation, a more favourable balance between soil and crop types, a generous infusion of capital part of which, as Viñas suggests, may have come from the Indies. These investments took one of two forms: direct purchase or improvement, or else a sort of loan against mortgage, the *censo*. The *censo* carried high interest-rates, but was not ruinous for the farmer as long as demand stayed high and prices continued to rise.

A radical change took place in the seventeenth century, slowly at first and then very rapidly from 1640. The basic factor was a fall in demand, which occurred for a number of reasons: a drop in the export of wine and oil to the Indies, where local production was beginning to get under way, a decline of population, a slump in the purchasing power of the consumer, and a steep rise in taxation which channelled income into non-productive sectors. Prices became increasingly erratic. In bad years no one observed the *tasa*, not even the clergy. But this development favoured only the bigger proprietor, the speculator and those who collected rents in kind, not the small farmer who had to buy grain for sowing or to keep himself fed. Conversely, when prices fell below the *tasa* the bigger proprietor stored his grain whereas the smallholder had to sell for less than cost price. As farming became less profitable so the burden of *censos* grew heavier. In addition, as Felipe Ruiz points out, there had been a fall in agricultural investments for some considerable time before the seventeenth century owing to the pull exerted by the *juros* market, which absorbed much capital in the reign of Philip ii.

The increasing concentration of property favoured the ecclesiastical communities and owners or lords who held rights of jurisdiction. The old feudal dues yielded very little, and these groups turned more and more to the income to be derived from ownership of land. The concentration of property was accompanied by a concentration of rural dwellings. A large number of small villages were abandoned and their inhabitants became labourers or went to swell the ranks of the urban proletariat, while their lands served to swell the lord's domain. But the time when great fortunes were to be made had passed and money was in short supply, so that hardly any investment took place and the lands so acquired were turned into game reserves or farmed in extensive fashion. Whereas in the sixteenth century the possession of a great domain was a profitable affair, in the seventeenth it was often no more than a showpiece for those who aspired to a title, for the *parvenus* who had become lords of vassals.

There are two other developments which should be mentioned: the substitution of the mule for the ox in ploughing in the dry lands of Spain, and the decline of pastoral farming. The former occurrence was widely deplored, on the grounds that the mule was an inferior and sterile animal compared with the ox which could be put to a variety of uses. The great advantage of the mule was its agility, which meant it could plough a larger surface area, if not in such depth. A contributory factor may have been the consolidation of property and population, which obliged the peasantry to make longer and longer trips to get to their workplace. The decline in the number of cattle was ascribed to the shrinkage of pasture. It is very probable that cattle-farming witnessed the same concentration in favour of a few bigger proprietors as had taken place in agriculture. One thing is clear: complaints of the scarcity and dearness of meat became frequent after 1600. Thus by the middle of the seventeenth century a very unfortunate state of affairs had come about. Arable had expanded at the expense of pasture, but it was so badly cultivated that its yield was no greater than before. So the overall balance at the end of a century and a half of rural development was an unfavourable one.

Industry had a plentiful variety of raw materials to draw on: iron mines, though only those of Vizcaya were exploited systematically (fifteen to twenty-five thousand tons output as against a total of slightly over a hundred thousand for Europe as a whole); copper and lead; alum from the coasts of Murcia, used in the preparation of textiles; mercury, exported to the Indies except for what went into medical compounds and cosmetics; marine salt, of which Spain was one of the chief producers; saltwort and soda, used in the making of glass; forest products; an abundance of high-quality wool; a large-scale production of silk, inherited from the Arabs, centred mainly on Valencia, Murcia and the kingdom of Granada; leather and hides; building materials, and so forth. Despite these advantages and despite the availability of skilled labour and of an extensive home market, Spanish industry proved unable to compete with other countries of Western Europe. After a period of prosperity which coincided roughly with the expansion of the population and of agriculture (1530–80) it sank to a position of inferiority. The Cortes as well as economic writers demanded that the export of raw materials be prohibited and foreign competition restricted, but they failed to grasp the root of the problem. Even now it is not easy to explain what happened, for the failure of Spain to industrialize was a product of several different factors which are difficult to evaluate exactly.

One of these factors seems to have been the strength of the guild system, with its spirit of localism, its strict regulations and its hostility to any concentration of the means of production or any technical innovation. The guilds played a very important social role, but by the very fact of their being were an obstacle to the birth of a modern type of industry. Industry could only make its appearance in a few towns in exceptional circumstances, as for example the manufacture of arms, which enjoyed state protection. The frequent presence of foreigners here is indicative of a certain backwardness in metallurgical techniques. There is no other explanation for the intervention of Flemish engineers in the armaments factories of Liérganes and La Cavada (Santander) which were set up in the reign of Philip IV.[8] The royal armaments factory of Seville developed apace thanks to the need for fitting out the vessels for the navigation of the Indies. Though it was functioning as early as the sixteenth century, it too expanded during the seventeenth.[9] On the other hand the production of sharp-edged weapons, lacking state protection, fell into decline. When Seville wanted to replenish her stock she had to send to Milan to buy them. Even in Toledo, by the middle of the seventeenth century the famous sword manufacture was but a memory.

Mints, though operated on behalf of the general public, were state enterprises of the type which Colbert would later create. That of Seville employed nearly two hundred workers in its heyday. That of Segovia was reorganized by German technicians called in by Philip II who produced new machines which improved the speed and quality of the minting. Working conditions were harsh by our standards, but not more so than was normal at the time. The working day lasted from five in the morning to seven at night, with two hours for meals – in other words twelve hours' actual working-time.

Ship-building, though not a state enterprise, was also kept going in part by state orders. Despite heavy demand and the undeniably high quality of much of their output, the Spanish yards were losing ground to their competitors in northern Europe who proved more progressive. Around 1600 Spain had something like an eighth of the 600,000 to 700,000 tons of shipping in Europe at that time. This put her in a respectable position, though outdistanced of course by little Holland. The Cantabrian coast, Portugal and the Seville–Cadiz region were the main centres of construction. The north had a better quality timber in its favour. The Seville yards were mediocre, specializing rather in repairs and auxiliary trades like the manufacture of sails, casks or biscuits. The situation was similar at Cadiz. The yards were all regulated along completely different lines from the guild system in that they employed a fairly numerous proletariat on a piece-work basis. Though wages were high,[10] the workers were badly off because the periods of unemployment were more frequent than those in which they had work.

The manufacture of soap, paper and glass and printing were other industries which had no place in the guild system owing to their dependence on large-scale operations and investment. All of the export industries had need of a commercial organization, which brought them within the capitalist orbit. Such was the case with Andalusian wines and their preparation, and perhaps also with the embossed leather industry (*cordobanes*), though on this point information is lacking. Toledo bonnets, very popular in the north of Africa, and Toledo and Ocaña silks and gloves remained subject to the guild system at the manufacturing stage but were under the control of merchants who organized manufacture and distribution and furnished the raw material to the master-craftsmen. Perhaps it was the high cost of the raw material which was the principal factor in this development, which is noticeable in the silk industry of Seville and Granada as well as of Toledo. A chronicler of Granada relates how in 1642, when a revaluation of the coinage was expected, the merchants cancelled their orders to the master silkworkers, the latter dismissed their helpers and a riot ensued which was only quelled when the *corregidor* advanced money to the merchants from the royal coffers.[11]

Like agriculture, Castilian industry benefited during the sixteenth century by an infusion of capital and experienced a similar process of consolidation which tended to turn artisan manufactures into veritable industrial enterprises. Since it was difficult to obtain a licence for the export of gold or silver the bankers who undertook the *asientos* of Philip II had to look outside Spain for credits held against foreign merchants which might enable them to fulfil their contracts. This placed a premium on export. Bills of exchange against purchasers of

Castilian products were brought up by the royal bankers, so that for a short period Castile financed its foreign policy by exports, principally of raw materials but also of certain manufactures like gloves, swords and textiles.

All this changed after 1568 (rising in Flanders) and particularly after 1575 (state bankruptcy and sack of Antwerp). The system of *asientos* was thrown momentarily out of gear, there was a slump in exports, gold and silver replaced commodities as the medium of exchange, and industry, deprived of capital, went into decline. There was the odd exception, like Segovia, whose traditional woollen industry reached its peak in the last third of the sixteenth century, perhaps as a direct outcome of the crisis in the export of wool. The studies of Carande, Bennassar and Felipe Ruiz[12] demonstrate the existence in Segovia of a curious hybrid system: the guild organization and the family workshop persisted, but were controlled by the merchants, who as in the case of the silk industry supplied the raw material and bought up the finished product. It even appears that there were some workshops of a modern kind, employing a large body of workers. It was the only purely industrial town in Spain, with seventy-seven per cent of its population workers, almost all of them employed in the clothing industry, whether textiles, finishing trades or leather. It was also the only town with anything approaching an industrial proletariat as we know it today, with its restless character and heterogeneous background. A local chronicler, Colmenares, excused the excesses committed during the revolt of the *Comuneros* by laying the blame on this proletarian class, most of which was not from the town originally. Seville too had a genuine proletariat of unskilled labourers, *Moriscos* and slaves who worked in the soap factories or in the preparation of esparto-grass or tobacco (the first tobacco factory to be set up in Spain was in Seville in 1620). But these masses were diluted in a much greater population, whereas the textile workers left their mark on a small town like Segovia. The cloths of Segovia sold well because of their high quality until changing taste and the introduction of French fashions led to their decline.

Other towns (Barcelona, Cuenca, Valencia, Córdoba) had also a wide range of manufactures, principally textiles, understandable enough in an age when despite the sumptuary laws expenditure on clothing was very great. In all of them one notices the downward trend of the seventeenth century, even in

Catalonia which was less affected than Castile by the upheavals of the period but nevertheless lost two-thirds of its weaving looms between 1600 and 1630.[13]

To sum up then, Spain experienced a modest industrial development during the sixteenth century comparable to that which J. U. Nef calls, with some exaggeration, the 'first English industrial revolution'. But whereas in Great Britain it was maintained and intensified during the seventeenth century, drawing on new techniques and capital investment and the growing use of coal, Spanish industry was in a sickly state and only at the end of the century developed a new impetus, centred on the modern industry of Catalonia. The classic explanation of this industrial decline concerns the price differential – that is, prices rose more rapidly in Spain than abroad, thus depriving her industries of the means of competing. No doubt there is some truth in this explanation, but it is not the whole story, since many of the foreign goods sold in Spain and the Indies were luxury articles where the buyer was more interested in quality than price. Foreign cloths had more variety and brighter colours and were therefore more in demand in those circles which could afford them; the humdrum article, meanwhile, continued to be manufactured throughout Spain, even in very small villages, for the undemanding local customer. The same thing happened with paper: the basic article was produced in Spain, the better quality came from Genoa. Printing had the reputation of being more carefully executed in Lyons, Venice, Cologne or Antwerp than in Spain. Other articles like watches, needles, scissors, and in general also haberdashery, hardware and ironmongery were almost a foreign monopoly.

The direst blow suffered by the textile industry was the turning away of the rich merchants, who instead of pursuing their programme of controlling national production found it easier and more remunerative to import foreign goods, which were in greater demand among the better-class customers of Spain and the Indies. In every controversy about the import of foreign goods the mercantile community of Seville supported them in preference to the home product. It is difficult to believe that the reason was domestic shortage when the artisans of many Spanish towns were working for starvation wages rather than give up jobs which no longer kept them fed. Nor can the contempt for manual occupations have been a decisive factor; contempt which those involved, naturally, did not feel. A foreign traveller might be surprised to see a master shoemaker at the end of his day's work strapping on his sword to take a stroll like any *hidalgo*.[14] But this only goes to show that the Spanish artisan did not consider himself debased by his calling. More to blame was the lack of business drive among the upper classes. In a word, the causes of the collapse of Spanish industry appear to have been lack of manpower and capital as well as the snobbishness of the upper classes who preferred the foreign article, which no doubt was more attractive and in many cases the only one of its kind on the market.

The most obvious consequence of the bankruptcy of the industrial sector was that apart from the short period of prosperity mentioned above the overseas trade of Spain came to depend on the export of raw materials – iron, fruit, wine, wool, salt. Imports were not restricted to manufactured goods: after 1578 large purchases of wheat were also made. Fish too was often imported, an incredible state of affairs in a country with such an extensive coastline. Galicia was a major producer and consumer of sardines and shell-fish; but the Basque fishermen stopped frequenting the Newfoundland banks as a result of the outbreak of hostilities with the powers of northern Europe, while the import of cod by the French and English became one of the most expensive import items. Around the straits of Gibraltar there was rich tunny fishing, which was a monopoly of the dukes of Medina Sidonia and fetched them up to eighty thousand ducats in profit in some years. In the Mediterranean, by contrast, fishing underwent a sharp decline owing to the deadly threat of the Berber pirates.

The deficit in the trading balance has to be added to expenditure on foreign policy and to the considerable sums which went to the Roman Curia in respect of bulls, pensions, dispensations and so forth. Much money also left Spain in the pockets of labourers, pedlars and beggars from other countries, who were attracted to Spain by high prices and a sound currency. By contrast, *invisible earnings* were limited more or less to the rents which a few great lords drew from Naples and Sicily, and the sums which viceroys and other high functionaries accumulated. Though important perhaps in a few individual instances, such earnings were insignificant compared to the national deficit.

Some money flowed in through the purchase of *juros* by foreigners in the reign of Philip II; but after the forced conversions decreed by Philip III and the seizure of the *medias anatas* by Philip IV, buyers were frightened off.

This huge deficit in the balance of payments was made good by the silver of the Indies. Or put another way, the favourable balance which Spain enjoyed with the Indies served to right her unfavourable balance with the rest of Europe. This mechanism functioned badly in the seventeenth century for two reasons: the quantity of silver arriving for the king fell markedly, while much of it arriving for private individuals escaped abroad, since the goods sent out were often of foreign origin. It may seem strange that a country could go on indefinitely with such a large deficit in its balance of payments. In order to understand the situation one must remember the considerable differences between the monetary system then and now. Nowadays a country faced with similar problems would devalue, thus making imports difficult and assisting exports. This safety measure did not exist in former times because there was no paper money. When silver was in short supply, it meant not a gradual deterioration but a sudden interruption of commercial life. Payments were stopped, bankruptcies followed and imports ground to a halt, unless the foreign merchant would take the country's products in exchange – an indirect bounty on exports.

Another thing hard to understand at first is why the Spanish government did not introduce higher tariff barriers, with the double aim of protecting national industries and raising revenue. Political considerations were uppermost here. The Spanish–American market had the greatest international importance at the time, and the Spanish crown took advantage of the fact for its own political ends. It did not wish to alienate friendly powers nor the other parts of the empire by raising the modest entry dues which were usually not more than ten per cent. Where its enemies were concerned, it tried on several occasions to enforce a total ban on commerce: this happened with the Dutch and English after 1585 and with the French under Philip IV. Some of these prohibitions were accompanied by confiscations which ruined many merchants of these nations established in Spain. But the prohibitions themselves had little effect thanks to an active smuggling trade and to the connivance of third parties. The Dutch in particular showed great skill in passing their goods off as French, German or Flemish. Powerless as it was to stop it altogether the Spanish government tried to make some profit out of this clandestine trade, and in 1603 laid an extra thirty per cent duty on any import or export where the party in question could not prove a point of origin or destination other than Holland. This decree provoked a fierce outcry and had little effect. France secured exemption. England obtained very favourable commercial terms by the treaty signed shortly afterwards. As for the Hanse, it was very much in the interest of the Madrid government to keep them friendly, and in 1607 they were granted the same rights as the English. Any attempt at a protectionist policy foundered with the wreck of Spain's political and military strength. The Dutch, by the treaties of Westphalia, received the same advantages and privileges enjoyed by the English and Hanseatics, and the French, who had never wholly interrupted their commerce even at the height of the war, were given full satisfaction as well in this respect by the Treaty of the Pyrenees. Thenceforward Spain became a sort of open house where the foreigner could sell what he liked, thus making it impossible for Spanish industry to make the slightest recovery. The situation was more or less the same in America, even though Spain held on to her legal monopoly in those parts.

THE ECONOMY OF HABSBURG SPAIN: II. THE TRENDS

Studies of the movement of the Spanish economy in the sixteenth century have aroused much interest among specialists since, for the first time in history, one can follow the trend of prices in detail, thanks to a wealth of documentation, at a time of crucial importance for the economy of the West, indeed of the whole world. Following the great Discoveries a world economy existed already in outline, as is shown by a series of related movements which cannot be the result of mere chance, not least the appearance of Spanish coin as far away as the Far East. From the Iberian peninsula the new developments spread out at variable speed to all quarters of the globe, at least to those parts of it which had any contact with the major currents of interchange.

There are however two qualifications to be made. The pre-capitalist type of economic development, where linked to the American output of precious metals, was centred on Castile. The lands of the Crown of Aragon, with a more traditional economy and reduced exposure to the harsh fiscal pressure of the Habsburgs, followed developments but played no leading part in them. The Spanish economic environment, then, was a Castilian environment. But Castile itself was a large and very diversified area; within it there were really two economies: that of arable and pasture farming, much influenced by climatic fluctuation and affecting the country as a whole, and that of trade or finance, very sensitive to political conditions and directly affecting only the commercial or financial centres. Of course these two worlds were not entirely independent of each other.

Agrarian trends depended in the long term on the combination of factors indicated in the previous chapter, but the annual cycle was conditioned first and foremost by climate.

Most important was rainfall, whose scarcity and uneven distribution are the curse of the zone known as 'dry Spain'. In those parts prayers for rain go back to a time out of mind. But in some years the patron saints had to be entreated to stop the rain, since an inopportune rainfall can also have destructive effects on crops adapted to a fixed seasonal cycle. No scientific meteorological data is available for the period; but even if we knew the total annual rainfall we would also have to know the monthly distribution. Abnormally low temperatures can also bring disaster. Trees of a typically Mediterranean variety, like the olive, have a poor resistance to prolonged frost: thus it is that the olive has retreated in historic times from the central provinces of Spain. At other times lack of heat, without killing the plant altogether, will check the formation of the buds. We have no statistics on temperatures and must rely on the odd observations of documents or chroniclers, for example about the freezing over of rivers normally free of ice. Dates when crops ripened or harvesting began have also been noted by researchers; but such information must be handled with caution because the date of the wine harvest, one of the indicators used, may be influenced by commercial considerations.

Such studies have barely begun in Spain, but we can draw on the studies made in other European countries, principally in France, since the range of these phenomena is always much greater than political frontiers. In fact the major fluctuations affect the northern hemisphere as a whole. Despite the meagreness of information on the subject at the moment, two facts seem beyond doubt: first, the climate of the sixteenth and seventeenth centuries was not *substantially* different from what it is today; second, the great variety in the annual cycle falls into cycles of ten years or more, and these in turn into much longer trends. What is known of climatic fluctuation in Spain is in general agreement with the illuminating survey of Le Roy Ladurie:[1] the climate of the first half of the sixteenth century was dry and sunny; it worsened in the second half, reaching a marked low round 1600.[2] A temporary improvement followed; then came a new downward trend in the second half of the seventeenth century culminating in the very harsh winters of its closing years.[3] But this pattern may be deceptive. Since cold years are usually also wet ones, a winter which was disastrous for the Meseta through a lengthy frost might prove of benefit to the south by reason of a generous rainfall. At most then, one can say that the greater part of Spain, including the urban population, depended on the fluctuations of a capricious climate, and although these may have contributed to the misfortunes of the seventeenth century we should beware of drawing conclusions which in the present state of knowledge would be premature.

Financial developments by contrast, can be illustrated by precise statistics, but none the less present us with formidable problems of methodology. Prices are expressed in terms of coin and this too is a commodity. Independent of its volume, its changes of tale or fineness, the wear and tear to which it is subject and so forth, coin has a value which varies from region to region and period to period. It is not a criterion by which we can measure other goods. In reality such a fixed criterion does not exist, although the Spanish monetary system was perhaps the most stable anywhere between the reform of the Catholic Kings and the end of the Ancien Régime. In good times as in bad the Spanish government staked its prestige on maintaining unaltered the prestige of the Castilian gold and silver currency. Very difficult moments arrived in the seventeenth century when within Castile itself there was little more than a bad copper coin in circulation with an intrinsic worth well below its face value. But this discredited coin never passed the frontiers; abroad, the Spanish silver *reales* were held in esteem for their fineness and the fact that their intrinsic worth was higher than their face value – a phenomenon which prompted the French to remark: 'In Spain everything is dear except silver.'[4]

The coexistence of a strong stable currency alongside one that was weak and fluctuating further complicates an already involved situation. In the seventeenth century, with the appearance of the *premium* or added value (legal or illegal) on silver as against copper, every commodity had two prices, a theoretical one in silver and a real one in *vellón* or copper coin, which was the actual medium of circulation. Of the two, silver prices are obviously handier, but *vellón* prices are more real. This initial problem, if it does not arise in the sixteenth, is fundamental in the seventeenth century, for prices in silver hardly moved at all over this period whereas in copper they underwent severe fluctuations and displayed an unmistakable upward trend. It may be objected that it was not the commodities which rose, but the coinage which was devalued. But for most people, who received their wages in copper coin, this reply would have had no meaning, especially if their wages were not going up in proportion.

For the moment the problem may be ignored since it did not arise in the sixteenth century. In that century the fundamental development was the general inflation of prices which, coming after the long recession of the Later Middle Ages, revolutionized economic life. What was the cause of the rise? For Hamilton, whose classic study continues to be indispensable,[5] it related entirely to the volume of precious metals coming into Spain from America and from Spain spreading to other countries. This was not a new idea. Bodin, and before him the economists of the school of Salamanca, had glimpsed the connection. But Hamilton was the first to set it on a scientific basis by comparing two sets of statistics: Spanish prices and the entry of precious metals. The correlation between the two is beyond question. During the first half of the sixteenth century Castilian prices more than doubled, reaching a marked peak around 1530 and another around 1545–50. In the second half they doubled again in a very steady upward movement. Over the century as a whole prices increased more than fourfold. To men of our generation, accustomed to galloping inflation, it would not seem anything out of the ordinary; but to contemporaries it was an unheard-of phenomenon. From 1600 the price rise became less regular, often illusory, since it was expressed in terms of a depreciated *vellón* currency.

The conclusions of Hamilton have aroused objections from various specialists. Some take exception to the method employed: his price series are not homogeneous, nor do they reflect retail price movements, nor refer to rural areas where prices were lower than in towns. Other objections relate to his interpretation of the rise itself. Is it certain that it was due solely or mainly to the increase in the volume of bullion? There were other means of payment: credit existed, though on a rudimentary scale. Other factors would have to be taken into consideration, factors which it is difficult or impossible to evaluate exactly: how much bullion was smuggled in, how much was hoarded, how quickly specie circulated, how long American bullion remained in Spain. Often the bullion was dispatched abroad, legally or illegally, before it had a chance to influence Spanish prices. Further, the volume of coin is only one factor in the equation: the other is the volume of goods and services which can be procured with it. An increase in production can lower prices just as market shortages can raise them, even though the volume of coin remains constant. Nadal, Vilar and Cipolla, among others, have criticized the exclusively monetary theory of the price rise. In general, then, the work and interpretation of Hamilton remain fundamental, but need clarifying and amending.

Chaunu in his magisterial work[6] and in others of a lesser kind has touched on the question by way of the movement of the port of Seville. The connection of Seville with the entry of American bullion is a very close one, for while part of the bullion arrived under the heading of rents, taxes or aids, the greater part came in exchange for commodities sent to the Indies. Where Hamilton saw the rise as a steady one, Chaunu is more cautious and differentiates between short-lived intercyclical fluctuations. A steady rise up to 1550 is followed by a slump in the next decade; the upward movement reasserts itself until 1592 and is followed by a period of equilibrium as far as 1620. He sees a close correlation between American developments and the foreign policy of the Habsburgs, going so far as to write: 'The decision to enter The Thirty Years War was, to some extent, a consequence of the prosperity of Seville in 1616–19.'[7]

It is an open question whether the transition from the expansionist sixteenth century to the stagnant seventeenth should be located round 1600 or 1620. There was a slight fall in prices in the first decade of the century, coinciding with some uncertainty in the Seville trade, but both sets of figures began to rise again as far as 1620. It is after this date that the curve starts to descend, slowly at first, then in catastrophic fashion from 1640. Ruggiero Romano[8] sees the crisis of 1619–22 as one affecting not just Spain but Europe as a whole. This is indicated by the fact that figures for the port of Seville agree with those of shipping through the Sound, silk production in Venice, Dutch trade with the Levant, and other data. According to his interpretation, the phenomena which mark the reversal of the trend are: the cessation of the demographic and agricultural expansion of the sixteenth century, exhaustion of credit, upsetting of the ratio of gold to silver, which had hitherto favoured silver, decline in the output of coin and in rates of interest, and the apparent inflation in terms of cash which disguises an actual deflation in terms of silver. It is the beginning, then, in the real as well as the symbolic sense, of an 'age of copper'. All these developments are effectively present in Castile, and perhaps more in evidence there than anywhere else, both because of the nature of her economy and because of political decisions. The crisis of 1627–8, a crisis of dearth and rising prices accompanied eventually by a devaluation and a *tasa* on prices and wages, derived in part perhaps from natural causes but also from excessive fiscal pressure (bond conversions and the over-minting of *vellón*). As for the political roots of the great crisis which began in 1640, they are so patent as to be hardly worth stressing. The interrelationship between politics and the economy and the dominant role of the former emerge nowhere so clearly as in a study of imperial Castile.

Another debated question is how far wages followed the evolution of prices. In Spain the two were in fairly close harmony, wages keeping pace to a fair degree with prices. If they fell in real terms in the first half of the sixteenth century, by the end they had recovered most of the lost ground, and in any event the discrepancy was less than in other European countries. Hamilton, under the influence of Keynesian ideas, sees in this high level of wages one of the causes of Castile's failure to industrialize, because it prevented an accumulation of capital. This point too has aroused objections. As Vilar has pointed out,[9] there were other ways of accumulating capital, particularly for the urban *bourgeoisie* who administered royal taxes. It was the recipient of fixed rents and the official whose salary lagged behind the rise in prices who were the chief victims of inflation, rather than the wage-earner, who took advantage of the shortage of labour to insist on a bigger pay-packet.

Though this inflationary movement would appear mild by contemporary standards (a cumulative rate of 2.5 per cent per year is near stability), it not only claimed attention at the time but provoked outbursts of dismay when it passed through occasional acute phases. One of these phases was the year 1553, mentioned by the chronicler Florián de Ocampo. In 1567 the municipality of Barcelona raised the wages of all its officials, 'since every article of human need is incomparably more expensive than it has ever been'.[10] The plague marking the end of the sixteenth century caused a shortage of labour and an increase in real wages; the same thing happened after the expulsion of the *Moriscos*. In 1613 the Inca Garcilaso de la Vega compared prices then with those he had found on his arrival for the first time in 1560 and found everything much dearer, except *censos* – that is the interest on loans, which had fallen by a half. The crisis of 1627 provoked a further rise. Thenceforward the prevailing climate was one of inflation, for although prices in silver remained stable, they rose as regards *vellón*, the usual coin in circulation. In 1637 the English envoy Hopton protested against the attempt to reduce his daily ration from six to four pounds as in the time of his predecessor under Queen Elizabeth:

All the diet of table and stable is three times as dear as in Sir Charles Cornwallis's time when the two pound a day was first added. A loaf of bread was then worth twelve *maravedís* and is now worth thirty-four. An *azumbre* of wine was then worth twelve *maravedís* and now sells for thirty; a pound of mutton which was then worth seventeen *maravedís* is now worth forty; a *fanega* of barley then cost six *reals* and sixteen now.[11]

Though Hamilton's wage series are not as full as those of prices they give some idea of the upward trend. A carpenter who was earning 48 *maravedís* in 1520 got 72 in 1590, 238 in 1620, and in 1650, at the height of the inflation, as much as 340. Over the same period the wages of a farmhand in Old Castile rose from 35 *maravedís* to 249, and those of a Valencian master mason from 60 to 272.[12] Caja de Leruela at the beginning of the seventeenth century affirmed that the cost of living had doubled in twelve years: a student of Salamanca who needed sixty ducats to keep himself and a servant now needed one hundred and twenty. Masons' wages had risen from four to eight *reales*, and those of an unskilled labourer from two to four.[13] Reducing these figures to terms of real wages, we find they did little more than follow the price rise of the sixteenth century, at a distance. In the seventeenth century the shortage of labour led to a real improvement, but this gain had to be offset against growing unemployment in some sectors.

It is no easy task to compare these wage levels with those of today, in the hope of obtaining some idea of the standard of living, because no established criteria of comparison exist. In normal years the wages of an unskilled labourer were more or less equivalent to eight kilos of bread, and those of a skilled worker to sixteen. If capacity to purchase meat is taken as the norm, then the standard improves, because meat was cheaper in those days than now. The tremendous fluctuations in prices placed workers, in bad years, in situations of genuine hunger. Agricultural wages were undoubtedly lower than those in the towns, but carried the advantage of being paid often in kind, so that they were less sensitive to the economic barometer. Once again one must take into account the regional diversity which is so marked in Spain. If in Galicia, for example, an agricultural labourer could be hired for half a *real*, this must be related to the point made by Mercado, a sixteenth-century economist, that a thousand ducats went further in Castile than in Andalusia.[14] How much greater the difference would be with regard to Galicia, which was almost bare of specie! This situation would favour public officials (the magistrates of the *Audiencia* of Corunna lived in great splendour); on the other hand many a native of these poorer regions went to work or beg in the wealthier parts to be able to return home with a sackful of coin.

Is it possible to calculate the national income of Castile in the period under review? Figures for production are scarce and very uneven, and prices too were liable to sudden radical alterations. Marketing outlay was small, since many homes were to a large extent self-sufficient. Other services are difficult to evaluate. Despite these difficulties calculations have been attempted then and now, some of which are reproduced below with the aim of establishing an order of magnitudes. In the Cortes of 1596 a representative of Burgos declared that there were ten thousand households in the kingdom worth 20,000 ducats, twenty thousand worth 10,000, fifty thousand worth 5,000 and a hundred thousand worth 2,000.[15] Small value attaches to these optimistic calculations; but the point to remember is that the representative of a commercial metropolis (and therefore a man likely to know what he was talking about) believed that at that date there existed in Castile a very numerous and well-to-do middle class.

In 1630 the total income of Castile was calculated at 110 million ducats, of which the church took 10,410,000.[16] This calculation and others like it were based on an estimate of ten millions as the value of tithe; but it reckoned without other goods and services which were not subject to tithe. So the total would have to be raised by at least a third, making the gross national product of Castile 150 million ducats and that of Spain as a whole nearly 200 million. Of recent calculations only that of Gentil da Silva will be considered here. Working on the basis of data from New Castile he estimates the average consumption of a peasant family at 15,500 *maravedís* (forty-one ducats). For Castile as a whole, 'in any year of the third quarter of the sixteenth century', he arrived at the following totals:

Primary sector:	42,586,666 ducats
Secondary sector:	10,666,000
Tertiary sector:	16,000,000
Gross National Product:	69,252,666[17]

Castile had six million inhabitants at the time; so the *per capita* output was a bare 4,340 *maravedís* (equivalent to eleven ducats per year). To move from these figures for 1570 to those of 1630 an increase of fifty per cent would have to be added to allow for the rise in prices, supposing output to remain constant. This would raise the gross national product of Castile to 105,000,000 ducats and *per capita* income to fifteen ducats per year, after deducting state taxes – equivalent perhaps at the present day, in terms of purchasing power, to eighty dollars.

These figures are possibly on the low side, not least since contemporaries reckoned that thirty *maravedís* per day was the minimum needed to keep body and soul together in the first half of the sixteenth century. Though there were many who never reached this level, others rose far above it. There is also the fact that the annual yield of tithe (including tithe in seigneurial hands) was put at ten million ducats by trustworthy witnesses. In view of all this, the present author would prefer to place the *per capita* income of Castile before the disasters of 1640 on a par with 120 dollars at the present day. Such a figure nowadays would relegate Castile to the bottom of the list of under-developed countries; but any comparison between monetary standards then and now may lead to inadmissible conclusions.

RELIGIOUS LIFE:
I. ORTHODOXY

When studying the religious life of Spain or of any other country in Europe during the modern period, it is first of all essential to empty one's mind of ideas which seem evident enough now but were not so evident then. One of these is the distinction, so clear nowadays, between the ecclesiastical and the layman, between the sacred and the profane. The separation of the two concepts, though it had started centuries before, was still far from being complete. The church was the body of all the faithful and not just the institutions of the clergy as it later became in the Latin countries, where the name 'church schools' is still given to those belonging to the clergy. The dividing line between laity and clergy was not yet clearly defined. The temporal order was church-orientated, and the spiritual order lay-orientated. When the Catholic King of Spain fought with the pontiff in Rome the clash was not one between opposing worlds. The two of them were mixed sovereignties, and Philip II was not mistaken in thinking that he defended the interests of the church better than certain popes, and that in doing so he was not only in his right but fulfilling a strict obligation. Only from this point of view can Spanish regalism be seen in its true perspective. To be sure, the Council of Trent implied a drawing-in of the Catholic church, accompanied by a growth of clericalism and a conscious move away from the temporal world apparent in the setting up of special training centres (seminaries) and in the efforts to adopt a separate style of dress and mode of existence. But this was an extremely slow process and it would still be a long time before it reached its fulfilment.

Trent took the path it did because there were already forces at work in this direction. One was a growth of centralization, especially in the matter of clerical provisions, which Rome tried to reserve for itself. The bishops tried to compensate for this increasing dependence at the expense of the lower clergy and the ordinary faithful, whom they deprived of their former privileges in the election of the ecclesiastical authorities. In the end the people were reduced to being the 'flock of the faithful', a mere passive instrument. There were many vested interests checking this development. Many lords were patrons, many towns enjoyed the privilege of reserving ecclesiastical benefices to their own sons, thus ensuring a close alliance between clergy and people. But the seed had been sown and would not fail to grow.

The rapid development of the religious orders worked in the same direction. By their very being they were less tied to the temporal world than the secular clergy; they dedicated themselves to the world, but at the same time they accentuated the differences separating them from it. They were highly specialized sectors of the church, whether as teachers or ascetics, and were well to the forefront of the struggle against any heterodox tendencies. They had a zest for combat which the secular clergy had lost, living as they did like laymen and in close dependence on the state.

Though dogma and basic attitudes remained unchanged Spanish religious life underwent an evolution which may be roughly divided into three phases. The first extends from the end of the Later Middle Ages to the beginning of modern times as far as the Tridentine reaction. It was characterized by a widespread interest in religious questions and an acute sensitivity to them on the part not only of exceptional individuals but of the masses as a whole. The reform of the church was the centre of men's preoccupations. An important though not essential part of this was the reform of the clergy, a programme on which Cisneros, with royal support, worked with great energy. But more important than any improvement in clerical standards was the aspiration towards an inner religion which would be less tied to rites and ceremonies. This religious awakening, which derived in part from Italy, manifested itself in various forms: reform of the religious orders, interest in the writings of Erasmus, diffusion of mystic and ascetic literature, whether of an original kind (Juan de Ávila, Fray Luis de Granada, Fray Francisco de Osuna) or in translation (*The Imitation of Christ*, the works of the Carthusian Dionysius). This widespread interest was not confined to mere speculation. Groups and conventicles of the faithful were formed to seek salvation along paths which sometimes led off the beaten track and away from traditional guides. The reaction of the Spanish hierarchy preceded the decisions of Trent. *Alumbrados* and Erasmians were persecuted, the Jesuits came under suspicion, the Bible was forbidden to be read in the vernacular, and a list of prohibited books was drawn up displaying great severity in matters of doctrine but considerable laxity in the sphere of morals. Protestantism was not the cause of this reaction, which would probably have come about anyway; but it made it harsher than it would otherwise have been.

The second phase began around 1560 and lasted until the beginning of the seventeenth century. It was characterized by a yearning for an intense religious life, purified and disciplined by the hierarchy. From it sprang a militant Catholicism which found its most typical expression in Spain and manifested itself in a variety of fields: teaching, missions for the people, charitable institutions, a flowering of religious art, and so forth. If lacking in the spontaneity and initial impetus of the earlier phase, this later period is one of maturity and fullness, both as regards doctrine and organization.

Some time between the second and third decades of the seventeenth century Spanish Catholicism began to display symptoms of decay of an increasingly serious kind. Accompanying the intellectual decline there was a virtual halt to the publication of new works, while the older ones fell into neglect thanks to a narrow-minded and stifling moral code which stood in sharp contrast to the prevailing climate of earlier days. The question at issue was no longer truth but human conduct, interpreted in its narrowest sense as little more than the relationship between the sexes, which was now hemmed in by an incredible series of taboos. The coexistence of the chivalric and the religious ideal, which had seemed possible a century before and had even taken shape to some extent in individuals like Saint Ignatius, gave way to a diametrical opposition between the two, with certain religious orders formulating a new concept of religion. This new religion was gloomy and lachrymose, obsessed with death and damnation and hostile to the world and its pleasures; it was given to the practice of a series of complicated rites which among the less exalted were allied with not a few forms of superstition. It is possible that a large part of the blame for the degeneration must be laid on the general atmosphere of decline. Part too may be due to the attitude of King Philip IV, that gallant and pleasure-seeking youth who in middle age ordered the theatres to be closed, sins to be punished and public prayers to be offered time and again in the hope of staying the wrath of heaven. But even without his intervention everything suggests that events would have taken the same course, for the situation remained unchanged long after Philip IV's day.

The dividing line between phases two and three is rather harder to draw because unlike the earlier division it does not coincide with a watershed in institutional life comparable to the Council of Trent, whose impact on the Catholic church was so great that it determined its evolution over the next four centuries. Charles V thought of the Council as a means of healing the religious schism; but it ended in the definitive separation of Catholics and Protestants, thanks to the intransigence of the leaders on both sides. It is not to our purpose to give here an account of the actual course of events. Suffice it to say that it was summoned at Trent in 1545 as a compromise between the wishes of the emperor to have it in Germany and those of the papacy to keep it under its own control, and in 1563 it ended its deliberations after numerous interruptions which reduced its effective working time to four years.[1]

In composition the Council had a marked Mediterranean character, with the Italians enjoying a large numerical superiority. The Spaniards came second, though in respect of the eminence of their representatives perhaps they should be given first place; for they had outstanding names, like the Jesuits Laínez and Salmeron, pontifical theologians, the Dominicans Domingo de Soto and Melchor Cano, and the Franciscans Alfonso de Castro and Andrés de Vega. The bishops played a less distinguished role, though they had some notable spokesmen. The pontiffs accepted wholeheartedly the Spanish theologians' contribution to the defence of orthodoxy and gave their opinions definitive form in the decrees on doctrine. But they were less happy about their insistence on dealing first of all with the reform of abuses which had crept into the organization of the church. In the end Rome resigned itself to discussing reform at the same time as doctrinal questions. If the legislation on residence, pluralism and other matters had been strictly enforced, the state of the clergy would certainly have improved. As regards the bishops in particular there was another point separating them from Rome, that concerning the divine origin of the episcopate, a question which vexed the assembly greatly in its closing sessions. If the Spaniards, in agreement with the French bishops, had succeeded in obtaining ratification of a decree to this effect, their authority would have been strengthened *vis-à-vis* the papacy. But the papacy had the Jesuits, and even Philip II, on its side, and the final wording of the decree read simply that as successors of the apostles bishops are superior to mere priests.

Trent was not the defensive reaction of a cornered Church. On the contrary, even before the Council the Catholic Church gave signs of renewed vitality, at least in Spain. It would be to distort the picture to attach too much importance to stories of the corruption of the clergy, some real, others invented, and to infer from them that it was in irremediable decline. For the clergy was not the whole church, nor did the failings of individuals affect its membership as a whole. Already before the Council was convoked, in 1540, Pope Paul III gave his approval to a religious order of a new kind which was to become the symbol of the militant attitude of the regenerated Church: the Society of Jesus. Its founder, Ignatius of Loyola, belonged by birth to the Basque country, a region which was late in receiving Christianity but was to make up the lost ground by a boundless enthusiasm and loyalty. As a young man he followed the normal *hidalgo* career of the age, the profession of arms. In later life he sought a higher ideal which could satisfy the inner passion consuming him. Wounded in the defence of Pamplona against the French, his imagination was fired by what he read of the lives of the saints, whom he saw as knights errant of the divinity. He hesitated for a few years as to the path he would follow, practising asceticism in the cave at Manresa, making a dangerous trip to Jerusalem, then devoting himself to study in the University of Alcalá, where he aroused the suspicion of the Inquisition that he might be an *alumbrado* or false mystic. It was while studying at the Sorbonne that his vocation took shape. He gathered six fellow students about him and together they pronounced monastic vows of poverty, chastity and obedience.

However as yet (1534) Ignatius had still no clear idea of what his mission and that of his companions would be; his overwhelming zest for action lacked any precise objective. An attempted pilgrimage to the Holy Places ended in failure, and it was then that he decided to set himself and his companions at the disposal of the pope for any task which might prove useful to the church. His organization was not to be just another order: its originality would lie in the militant character with which it was conceived. Its resemblance to an army is evident not only in the name, Society or 'Company' of Jesus, but in its iron organization and tight centralization. Only the General is elected, on a life tenure and he is the fount of all authority. Without neglecting the inner perfection of its own members the rule subordinates everything to the propagation and defence of the Faith. Hence the importance attached to religious instruction, whereas the practices of personal asceticism, fasts, mortifications and long prayers, occupy a secondary place and must not get in the way of the main objective. The abolition of the long hours of collective prayer in the choir was one of the innovations which caused most questioning and opposition, but the founder stood his ground. He also demonstrated his independence of spirit in the recruitment of his companions by taking no account of class or caste. He expressly forbade the exclusion of the descendants of Jews, and one of these, Laínez, even rose to be General. This ruling caused the Society great trouble in Spain and in the end had to be repealed.

Despite this breadth of vision, efficiency required that in practice Jesuit recruitment should be highly selective, with a preponderance of the middle and upper classes. The tasks undertaken by the Society were of the most varied kind. Some, like Francis Xavier, dedicated themselves to missions among the heathen. Others undertook missions within the Catholic countries themselves. Others devoted themselves to study and teaching. The *Ratio Studiorum*, published at the end of the sixteenth century and drawing on half a century's experience, represented a major step forward with respect to the teaching methods then in use. Pure and applied mathematics were among the disciplines introduced which had barely figured in the older school curricula; the quality of Latin was improved; and the arid study of grammar was rounded off with exercises in poetry and rhetoric. Dramatics, sports, public debates, the prize system, personal contact with the pupil and the comparative absence of corporal punishment were other innovations which established a reputation for the Jesuit colleges and brought their staff friends in high places.

The little guide to *Spiritual Exercises* is the personal work of Saint Ignatius. Based on a profound insight into the human soul, it is not aimed at the privileged few who are capable of rising to the heights of contemplation, for in fact the *Exercises* stop at the first stage of mental prayer, the stage which any normal person can reach without difficulty. In them every aid of the imagination is brought into play. It is not enough to know that Christ suffered for us, or that the torments of hell are horrible; as long as these truths remain on the intellectual plane they have little effect on the will. The individual must conjure up the picture of Christ scourged and crucified, must see the damned, hear their screams, smell the sulphur, feel the scorching flames. It all seems a bit too primitive, but it can serve as a first step towards a heightened awareness and a strengthening of the will. Tirelessly repeated, the *Exercises* have proved an effective instrument for the spiritual development of large groups of people.

The other religious orders, whether new or reformed, had no such intense influence on Spanish society, because they were not expressly oriented towards external activity. The Franciscans of Saint Peter of Alcántara, like the Carmelites of Saint John of the Cross (San Juan de la Cruz) and Saint Teresa, were concerned above all with their own salvation and only afterwards with that of their neighbour. Nor did the Escolapians of Saint Joseph of Calasanz or the Hospitallers of Saint John of God attain a comparable influence. They lacked selective recruitment and the successful techniques of winning men's minds; above all they lacked that ambitious, universal zeal implated in the Jesuits by Saint Ignatius which found them at one and the same time among the persecuted Catholic groups in England, in the universities of central Europe, in the forests of Paraguay and at the palace of the Emperor of China. Their unshakeable will-power, their efficiency, based on flawless organization, their inflexibility on fundamentals combined with an accommodating approach on non-essentials, all this is diametrically opposed to what is usually represented as the Spanish character. People take this type to be a mixture of savage individualism, inefficiency and blind intransigence. Yet, we are told, Saint Ignatius and his Society are the perfect expression of the Spanish character – a contradiction which shows how little attention should be paid to so-called 'national characteristics'.

It is hard to know how far the masses in Spain were affected by the great movement of religious renewal in the sixteenth century. The prevailing opinion, backed by the weighty authority of Menéndez Pelayo, is that practically the entire Spanish people shared in it. This 'population of theologians' not only crowded the squares where the *autos de fe* were held (where they might be supposed to have come for a free show) but were capable of understanding the *autos sacramentales*, plays based on theological symbols which take for granted an unusual degree of religious instruction on the part of the audience. On the other hand we have numerous and impartial witnesses who speak of widespread religious ignorance, of villagers who do not even know the Paternoster, and even of clergy who do not know the rudiments of the Faith. Probably there was exaggeration in both claims. The upper and middle classes were imbued with a very considerable religious culture, as continual quotations and allusions make plain. The urban masses were probably satisfied with knowing the catechism. In certain poor and remote parts of the countryside even this minimal instruction was probably absent, a logical outcome of the uneven distribution of the clergy.

More apparent and more shocking were moral discrepancies, for the majority of people in those days believed and sinned at the same time. Crimes of bloodshed were common, owing to the concept of honour which extended to the lowest classes, to the general practice of bearing arms, and to the inefficiency of the forces of public order. Sexual licence was common, increased by the very prohibitions against it. Moralists complained about young people who arranged rendezvous in churches – no doubt because the strict seclusion of the unmarried woman made it difficult to meet anywhere else. The repeated admonitions that engaged couples should not behave as man and wife before receiving the sacrament suggest that the practice was common in some rural districts. Abandoned infants were plentiful, though it is not possible in this instance to distinguish reasons of poverty from those of sexual misconduct. Civil and canon law, intransigent in matters of faith, were tolerant towards the weaknesses of the flesh. Unnatural practices were the only ones to be rigorously punished: bigamists were subject to Inquisitorial procedures and homosexuals were to be sent to the stake by the laws of the kingdom. Though a lenient view was often taken of the latter, in many cases the terrible penalty took its course, even where individuals of high birth were concerned. Public concubinage was supposed to be punished and frequently was, though in an unfair manner: the guilty woman was banished, the man was fined or escaped scot free.

In this frequent contradiction between belief and practice there was no hypocrisy, but instead a humble or unthinking acceptance of the gap between the ideal and real worlds. It was only later from the middle of the seventeenth century, when moralizing pressures grew, that the difference also grew between what one did and what one pretended to do. At any rate, if Spain in the Golden Century was not a terrestrial paradise it was certainly not the den of iniquity which some have depicted, using literary evidence which must be treated with caution or the orations of preachers who saw in their surroundings nothing but good reasons for God's anger. The lives of ordinary folk, as glimpsed through the pages of notarial acts, particularly wills, were on the whole given over to family and professional duties, and there is no reason to doubt the sincerity of the piety reflected in their last provisions.

These provisions usually recapitulated a life in which religion had marked every event from the most solemn to the most trivial. Birth had to be followed by baptism at an interval of a very few days in case the baby should die without this indispensable requisite for salvation, as was all too likely in those days of high infant mortality. There was much argument as to the fate of infants who died without baptism, and quite a few theologians still adhered to the harsh opinion of Saint Augustine who consigned them to the penalties of hell, though of the most moderate degree. Baptism was the real birth certificate of the new citizen: since there was no Civil Register until 1868 it was the parish books which fulfilled the function instead. Many Spanish parishes were already keeping these before Trent, and some have still complete registers of births, marriages and deaths from the beginning of the sixteenth century. Names were given according to family traditions or to the custom, still alive in certain regions, of giving the name of the saint on whose day the birth occurred. As regards family names (*apellidos*), there was considerable freedom: the usual thing was for the father's name to come first, as at present, but many preferred the mother's name, especially if it denoted greater nobility.[2]

The first communion was not in those days the social occasion which it has since become. It was made late, around fourteen years of age; but some time before, from the 'age of discretion' (generally eight years of age), the child would be going to confession. The obligation of annual confession and communion at Easter was attended to very strictly. For this purpose every parish priest had a list of his parishioners, and as they fulfilled their obligation he would hand them a certificate to the effect and make a corresponding entry in the list. Later he would send the bishop a note of those who had not fulfilled their duty: they might be admonished, fined, or in cases of contumacy excommunicated. Since the obligation of confessing to one's own priest was often painful the custom was introduced of accepting certificates of confession issued by other priests. It was not always easy for the inhabitants of small towns to find someone else; for this reason the missions offered by unknown religious, to whom it was easier to confide one's more intimate secrets, were greatly appreciated, especially by women. One of the consequences of this system of strict vigilance was the frequency of sacrilegious confessions and communions. There is general agreement in the reports of missionaries that they had confessed hundreds and thousands of persons who had been hiding sins in the confessional for years past.[3] The majority of these people were sincere believers, and the inner dramas they experienced as a consequence were so intense that they occasionally led to psychoses and even suicides.

Matrimony, another of the decisive stages in a man's life, was also governed by ecclesiastical rulings. The Council of Trent prohibited clandestine marriages – that is, those celebrated simply by the consent of the parties before witnesses, and without the canonical formalities. Such marriages were valid but unlawful. Occasionally the influence of some magnate managed to twist the immutable doctrine of the church, as when the marriage of the illegitimate son of the Conde Duque of Olivares was annulled on fairly insubstantial grounds. Where the Roman Curia came under attack it was not over cases like these, which were rare, but for the variety of impediments most of which had no other purpose than to force people to buy a dispensation for cash. In addition to the canonical impediments the tyrannical if unwritten laws of social convention imposed others which could not be broken except at the price of social ostracism. The case of the son of Olivares, mentioned above, is a good example of such prejudices, which were not peculiar to that age. Since he had no legitimate succession Olivares legitimized a bastard by the name of Enrique de Guzmán shortly before his fall, and wishing him to succeed to his line managed to dissolve the marriage he had contracted with a young nobody so that he might marry Doña Juana de Velasco, daughter of the Constable of Castile. In the documents instituting entails a clause was frequently inserted barring anyone who had stained the nobility of the line by a *mésalliance*. Occasionally the bar applied also to those who were not of pure blood – that is, not Old Christians. Father Arbiol went further: he designated such marriages as mortal sins, since they prevented the offspring enjoying the honours due to those of pure, noble blood.[4] This mingling of the sacred and the profane, this attempt to turn religion into the prop of a determined social order is another characteristic feature of the age. And not only of that age, of course.

At the approach of the supreme moment of death, which according to Christian dogma is not a final conclusion but the reckoning of one life and the start of another, the majority of people faced the ordeal with serene strength, making whatever provisions seemed suitable for themselves and their families. Testaments give an extremely valuable insight into the mentality of the age. They usually begin with a profession of the Catholic Faith and an expression of resignation and of confidence in the divine mercy. An inventory of goods follows, of a very detailed kind; instructions are given as to what is to be done with them; credits are to be recovered and debts paid; there are almost always legacies for the servants and for charitable works, and occasionally there is an order for the manumission of slaves. Finally instructions are given for the burial and prayers. Burials always took place in consecrated ground. The graves of the poor would usually be in the church porch or in an adjoining garden, those of the rich in reserved sites within the church, marked by memorial tablets and statues. The receipt of the last sacraments with the due disposition guaranteed salvation. Hence the anxiety with which confession was demanded by those who sensed they had been mortally wounded in the all-too-frequent clashes and brawls of the time. It was considered inhuman savagery to finish off a wounded man without heeding this anguished cry, for it meant repentance did not ensure immediate entry into paradise; the soul might undergo long suffering in purgatory. To guard against this eventuality devout persons accumulated indulgences throughout their life. Indulgences were easy to obtain, even after the Council of Trent placed some limit on their profusion. The best safeguard was to order as many masses as possible to be said for one's intentions after death. It was not rare to come across middle-class people who had paid for hundreds, in addition to responses and anniversaries. In the case of the wealthy, the masses for the dead might run into thousands. Frequently too such persons would found a chantry endowed with certain revenues, where a priest would say masses in perpetuity for their soul. A not inappreciable part of the rural and urban wealth of Spain was set aside for this purpose.

Between these two milestones of baptism and the last sacraments life passed in sustained and intimate contact with religion. Mass, the rosary, and other devotions were daily practices among the well-to-do, and even many poor as well snatched time from their work to attend to them. The calendar regulating work and play was the result of many centuries of Christianity. Contracts, payments and leases were made with reference to a feast-day. The academic year, for example, was not said to begin on 18 October, but on Saint Luke's Day. When people amused themselves, too, the excuse or the justification was some religious festival. Frequently these were tinged with superstition or gave rise to excesses, as in the case of the town fraternities with their gargantuan repasts, or of pilgrimages which offered couples the chance of losing themselves in the woods, or of the Holy Week processions where sincere piety and profane elements mingled. All this was inevitable from the moment that the populace as a whole, including the most undesirable elements among it, took part in these celebrations. The church tried to remove the pagan residue from festivals of remote origin, like the *mayas* or May festivals, and the Saint John's bonfires, which marked the summer solstice. She prohibited the use of churches for the staging of plays or for meetings of the town council, and the adjacent field for bowling or ball games. The reiteration of these prohibitions is indicative of their small success. The sacred and the profane existed side by side, and only an effort of the mind can separate them or detect points of friction which never really existed. Thus, rules which appear vexatious to us today, like fines for non-attendance at Sunday mass, were accepted as natural, like fines nowadays for infringing urban bye-laws.

Though this universal acquiescence had its advantages it also carried a danger for the church, that she herself might sink to the popular level – which was what happened in the seventeenth century. Various factors contributed to this: the change from an intellectual to an emotional outlook, the decline of the spirit of criticism, and the reaction against Protestantism. These and other influences led to excessive importance being attached to rites, images, devotions, relics, indulgences and other attributes of an external, formal religion. The new devotions in themselves were not an aspect of degeneration but rather of renewed religious fervour. This was the case with the devotion to the Immaculate Conception, which inspired so many demonstrations of popular piety and took shape in immortal works of art. The drawback here was that the discussion descended to street level and the populace tried to settle it by means of offensive ballads directed against theologians on the other side, almost all of whom were Dominicans. In order perhaps to combat their unpopularity and show that no one surpassed them in love for Mary the Dominicans gave a new impetus to the devotion to the rosary, which was traditional in their order. Public rosaries became so common that in the big towns processions were to be met with at any hour of the day or night.

The feast of Corpus Christi, though of medieval origin, assumed much greater splendour at this time. In every episcopal city the richly worked monstrances of gold and silver were preceded by long processions of civic and military dignitaries and of the guilds with their insignia, together with symbolic figures, and children, giants, even gypsies in some places, dancing, despite the protests of puritans. In Seville Archbishop Palafox attempted to suppress the dances; but after a lengthy lawsuit the town managed to retain them. From this period too dates the extraordinary rise of devotion to the souls in purgatory, testified to by countless pictures, altars and pious foundations, the aim of which was to free the souls from the flames by means of prayers.

That the church should add new saints to those already venerated at her altars was no novelty either; what was new was the ardour with which the orders involved pressed at Rome for the canonization of their outstanding members (Saint Ignatius, Saint Francis Xavier, Saint Teresa, Saint Peter of Alcántara), and not just they but the people and even the Spanish crown as well through its ambassadors, as if some grave affairs of state were at stake. The hunt for supposed saints became something of a national pastime. Whenever a holy person (almost invariably a friar or a nun) made a name for himself he was credited with the most extraordinary graces: he could read thoughts, be in two places at the one time, work miracles. This last above all: it is inconceivable the number of miracles worked every day in Spain, most of them trivial or easily explained away. But to attempt to explain them away was to lay oneself open to reproaches. Sensible people preferred to hold their peace, though perhaps they realized that it did not redound to the honour of the Creator to suppose him the author of natural laws which he was forever breaking on the most trifling pretexts.

The veneration felt for individuals who had the reputation of sanctity found an impressive outlet at their death. Their funeral was attended by the authorities and the populace, and bits of their clothing, hair or objects of personal use were snatched with such eagerness that genuine problems of public order arose. More than once it happened that the friars had to suspend the funeral of a brother who died in the odour of sanctity and bury him hurriedly, because the populace, after stripping the corpse, threatened to mutilate it in the scramble for relics.

The zeal for obtaining precious relics was a very old one, going back to the first centuries of Christianity. The more famous of those belonging to Spanish churches, like the chalice used at the Last Supper (the Holy Grail) of Valencia, probably date from the High Middle Ages. The number and variety of those appearing in cathedral inventories are impressive. A small remote cathedral like Coria in Extremadura could boast a jawbone of Saint John the Baptist, an eye-tooth of Saint Christopher, soil from the crib at Bethlehem and the Mount of Olives, and the tablecloth of the Last Supper. In Burgos there were eleven heads venerated of the eleven thousand virgins. Three famous crucifixes were believed to be the work of Nicodemus: those of Burgos, Osma and Orense. The men of the Golden Century not only preserved these inherited treasures but added to them continually and embellished them with every finery of art. The profusion of reliquaries of the most varied forms and materials became one of the characteristics of the religious art of the Baroque. Even laymen could own relics like these since every great lord had his oratory and chaplain in his own home, though the Holy See only granted the necessary permission with great difficulty and with inward misgivings in view of the irreverences and abuse to which it led.

It seems to be a fact that, but for the vigilance of the Inquisition which always showed itself sceptical of mystical raptures and manifestations of extraordinary graces, the scourge of miracle-workers and pseudo-mystics would have been even greater than it was. The venerable María de Agreda, the nun who became the trusted adviser of Philip IV, was not interfered with, though the realism and good sense of her advice to the king was allied to supernatural visions of an incredibly puerile kind.[5] Other obviously fake visionaries were punished. This was the fate of Sor María de la Visitación, a nun of Lisbon, who took in even Fray Luis de Granada. With others it could never be established for sure whether they were chosen and highly gifted spirits, fakes or hysterics. A case in point is Madre Antonia Navarro, a nun of Las Huelgas (Burgos), who suffered wounds in her hands, feet and side; every Thursday she lost consciousness and remained in this state until Friday; she conversed with Christ, the devil and her guardian angel. Her confessor believed that it was all an illusion, upbraided her and subjected her to severe penances. Apparently she was a victim of hysteria and in good faith.

In this summary account of religious life in Spain it is impossible not to mention the missionary movement, which as well as reflecting the prevailing emotional climate from the middle of the sixteenth century helped to mould the newer kind of religious devotion. Its precursors were the popular preachers of Renaissance times, who even then were expressing themselves with a vehemence which surprised foreigners. However it was in the seventeenth century that the missionaries perfected their techniques, which have remained unchanged almost to our own day. Whereas those preachers who were eager for renown went in for *culto* oratory, abounding in conceits and classical allusions, others, consumed by zeal for the salvation of souls, ignored rhetorical adornment and sought merely to move the hearts of their audience with the great themes of God's love, as shown in the sufferings of Christ, the intercession of Mary, the hideousness of sin, the sweets of heaven and the torments of hell. To reinforce the point they resorted to psychological aids and dramatic effects: they held up skulls, conversed with the crucifix, displayed canvases depicting the souls of the damned, wept, buffeted themselves, asked the audience to pardon their failings and urged their hearers to do likewise. If the orator was skilful and achieved the desired emotional effect the church or square where the whole populace had crowded together would re-echo with the cries of sinners demanding mercy, of enemies falling on each other's shoulder, of women fainting, of misers pardoning their debtors and of men who kept mistresses forsaking their evil ways. The mission, which usually lasted five or six days, finished with a general confession and a penitential procession. The missionaries were the first to admit that the results were not lasting, for it was difficult to sustain the atmosphere of excitement for any length of time. But by dint of constant repetition they left a profound imprint on Spanish Catholicism, which became highly emotional, moralizing, obsessed by sin (particularly sexual sins), hostile to the pleasures of this world whether lawful or not, ritualistic and anti-intellectual. No doubt the fact that religious orders, especially the Franciscans and Jesuits, inspired these missions played a large part in this development. If the piety they preached was not very secure, the moralizing effects were indisputable. The missionaries did not preach social justice in our sense of the word, but they promoted charity, checked the hatreds which tended to degenerate into bloody feuds, brought the different classes closer together and fostered a peaceful environment in the small towns, in contrast to the harsh primitive customs of the early modern period.

RELIGIOUS LIFE:
II. THE INQUISITION
AND HETERODOXY

In the eyes of many foreigners the inquisition is a typically Spanish institution. It is true that it also existed in France and Italy, but in Spain its activities continued into the early nineteenth century, at a time when ideas of religious tolerance had already begun to make their impact. In earlier centuries it carried through in an organized and spectacular fashion a task that was being less systematically tackled in other parts: the persecution of dissidents in the name of official orthodoxy. It is quite true that the witch craze or the Wars of Religion claimed many more victims than the Inquisition. But where the Inquisition can and must be blamed is for having maintained for centuries such a basically unevangelical system of repression in the name of a set of principles. It lacked the excuse of domestic strife or other collective outbursts of passion which can be invoked to explain occurrences like Saint Bartholomew's Day, the atrocity of which has no parallel in the legal and ordered procedure of the Spanish Inquisition. What was terrible about the Inquisition was not the number of its victims, which was comparatively small, but the fact that it presented its activities as an internal requirement of Catholic doctrine, and that it maintained this antiquated viewpoint after it had been abandoned in other countries and even in Rome itself.

During three centuries the Inquisition preserved, with minimal changes, the organization, norms and procedures accompanying its foundation by the Catholic Kings. No heed was paid to the representations, particularly of the lands of the Crown of Aragon where it was never popular, against its penal procedures, the abusive practice of confiscations and the arrogance it displayed in its relations with other tribunals. The bishops would have liked to recover their former jurisdiction over matters of faith; but they did not dare breathe a murmur of protest after seeing how the Inquisition was powerful enough to bring to trial an archbishop of Toledo and primate of Spain, who stood next in dignity to the king himself.

Yet, unchangeable though its procedures were, the nature of its enemies caused a variation in the style of its activities. The *judaizantes* or crypto-Jews, who had been almost its only prey in the earlier period and the real reason for its foundation, declined greatly in number. This led the Holy Office of the Inquisition during the reign of Charles v to take an interest in secondary matters, some of which concerned not faith but morals: cases of bigamy, witchcraft, *alumbrados* or false mystics, 'soliciting' priests, who used the confessional to seduce their penitents, and so forth. At the beginning of the reign of Philip ii some nests of Protestantism were uncovered and this gave new life to the tribunal. But these were quickly destroyed and trivial questions came to the fore once again. It would be a mistake to imagine that in the Spain of Philip ii the bonfires were permanently lit. On the contrary, the growing shortage of delinquents meant that the Inquisition was no longer able to live off the proceeds of its confiscations, and had to ask the king for the rent from one canonry in every cathedral church.

Where the Inquisition did display great activity from the middle of the sixteenth century was in preventing the introduction of heterodox books. In this, as in everything else, it acted in complete accord with the royal authorities, which in 1558 had decreed very severe penalties against those who introduced foreign books without licence. For works printed in Spain there was a double censorship, ecclesiastical and civil, which proved tolerant with regards to works of a literary character and intensely suspicious where dogma was concerned. The Council of Trent had already resolved that an Index of prohibited books be drawn up. The Roman Index never applied to Spain, where the Inquisition formulated one of its own. The latter was certainly more liberal than the Roman, which condemned authors out of hand, whereas the Spanish attempted to save the greatest possible number of works by drawing up a list of corrections and excisions. Once these had been made books which were deemed useful could circulate, regardless of whether the authors were dubious characters or heretics. The difference emerges clearly in the case of Erasmus, whose works were placed en bloc on the Roman Index, 'until they shall be corrected', which they never were. The Spanish censors, by contrast, undertook the long and thankless task of revising his entire works: the fruit of their labour fills twenty folios in one of the Spanish Indexes.[1] Other works suffered only the excision of a paragraph or two. One still comes across many such copies in libraries, with passages scratched out. Other books were condemned to be destroyed or reserved to a special section of the libraries or to persons who held a licence to read banned books. Among those prohibited totally was the Bible in the vernacular, until the end of the eighteenth century, for fear of the effects of 'free enquiry'. The prohibition was enforced with such rigour that one of the most serious charges laid against Fray Luis de León was translating into Castilian the 'Song of Songs'. To prevent the introduction of banned books a guard was mounted at the frontiers and functionaries of the Inquisition checked every foreign boat arriving in a Spanish port. Despite all the precautions a certain number of prohibited works circulated secretly and were kept in private collections. Kamen cites the case of Don José A. de Salas, a knight of the Order of Calatrava, who at his death was found to possess two hundred and fifty banned books, a tenth of his total collection.[2]

The extraordinary authority of the Inquisition derived to a large extent from the unconditional support given it by the crown. So intimate was its relationship with the secular power that some have seen it as an essentially political force, decked in religious trappings. This is by no means certain. The Inquisition was a religious tribunal and the authority which the crown had over it came by delegation of the pontiff. What happened was that its dependence on Rome became more and more theoretical; in practice it looked to the king, who appointed the Inquisitor General, as he appointed the bishops too, the pope's role being confined to one of formal ratification. The king protected the Inquisition because it was part of his royal functions to protect the Church. This boosted royal authority enormously; but the Inquisition was very rarely used for purely political ends. The most obvious and best-known instance is the arrest of Antonio Pérez by the Inquisition of Aragon. It was also used at a later date for the purpose of neutralizing the political influence of the Protonotario Villanueva, henchman of the Conde Duque of Olivares.

As has been said, Judaists were the favourite target of the

Inquisition. The expulsion of 1492 and the bloody persecution conducted against those who retained their Jewish faith under a veneer of Christianity reduced them to small groups and isolated individuals after the death of the Catholic Kings. Not a few were torn between the forces of family tradition and a social environment that pushed them towards Christianity. In this conflict of ideas and emotions there were many who felt the attraction of a vague theism or total unbelief, while there were even those who attempted an unrealistic reconciliation of the different dogmas. Many who had been forcibly baptized ended by accepting in all sincerity the faith imposed on them.[3] These types, who were rare in the first generation of Judaists, were to become common in the second and third, until Spanish Judaism all but vanished. It only recovered its vitality when as a result of the unification of the peninsula Spain became the resort of many Portuguese Jews, the greater part of whom had remained faithful to the law of Moses.

These Portuguese Judaists, many of them descendants of Spanish refugees from 1492, were harshly treated in their own country but had managed to corner its commerce and wealth. For this reason attempts were made to stop them leaving the kingdom: they were a prize which neither the crown nor the Inquisition wished to lose. From 1580 they began to negotiate an indult which would safeguard them from the persecution of the Inquisition and allow them freedom of movement. Both requests were granted, thanks to the more liberal policy of the Habsburgs, thanks too to the subsidies with which they won the mind of the kings and their ministers. Rome was not deaf either to such arguments. The result was that during the reign of Philip III a large number of these *marranos* began to come into Spain.[4] Under Philip IV the movement gathered momentum, since the king and his first minister Olivares proved well-disposed. Many turned their hand to farms of the royal revenues, or even became royal bankers. In 1643, on the fall of Olivares, things changed. The Inquisition, which had treated them so far with some respect, became increasingly severe; and since too the state of the Spanish economy was no longer so propitious to business many emigrated to France, Germany, England and above all Holland, where Amsterdam became eventually the 'Second Jerusalem'.

But for the entry of the Portuguese Jews it is probable that

Spanish Judaism would have become extinct in a short time. However, the decrease in the risk of religious contamination was accompanied by an increase in the precautions taken to isolate the *conversos* and their descendants on the social level – a fact which has aroused comment and provoked a variety of explanations. No exclusion of an official character was ever decreed: of the thousands of laws included in the *Nueva Recopilación* none is directed against the *conversos*. But a vast number of private bodies and organizations added to their rules and ordinances a 'statue of purity of blood', excluding anyone who had a Jewish ancestor, however remote. The question of whether he was a genuine Christian was not at stake. The problem developed strong racist overtones, the supposition being that, just as nobility was inherited, so the tendency to relapse into Judaism was hereditary. If the concern to preserve the purity of the Faith against crypto-Jews may have influenced the early statutes, these eventually became an expression of the cult of 'honour' characteristic of that society, and not just at its highest levels. Many individuals who could not pretend to nobility found cause for pride in an ancestry purer than that of many aristocrats, whose genealogy was not without a few dark patches.

In the early statutes promulgated between the end of the fifteenth and the beginning of the sixteenth century there was a genuine religious motivation. The order of the *Jerónimos* issued a prohibition in 1486 against admitting *conversos* because some monks had been found indulging in Jewish practices. The cathedral chapter of Seville invoked similar arguments when it made its statute in 1516. The change of tone was signalled by the ratification of the statute of the cathedral of Toledo in 1547, after fierce disputes in which religious arguments were a mere pretext. The real reason behind the legislation was the hatred of Archbishop Siliceo, an Old Christian of humble origins, of those who mocked his lack of nobility.[5] After the triumph of the archbishop, backed as he was by Charles v and his son Philip, no opposition to the statutes was any longer possible on grounds of principle. Opponents confined themselves to publishing anonymous lampoons and memorials, or seeking a limitation of the statutes, for example, to the fourth generation. But since the general opinion was that one drop of Jewish blood carried a perpetual contagion (against *Morisco* blood there was no such great prejudice), almost all of the statutes were formulated without limitation.

What was at stake was social prestige, not religion, as is indicated by the fact that the Church proved more accommodating in this matter than other institutions. The majority of the cathedral chapters did not make statutes. Officially, purity of blood was never a requirement for becoming a priest or even a bishop, though in time this consideration came to tell, if the absence of purity were notorious. Among the religious orders some enforced an exclusive policy, others kept open house. The Jesuits were forbidden by their founder to take account of norms which invoked Christianity but were essentially anti-Christian; but social pressures were so strong that they had to give way in the end. The universities never examined the genealogies of their students, but the *colegios mayores* did, and of course so too did the Military Orders. People employed by the Inquisition were also required to prove purity of blood. This was one of the motives for the popularity of posts of 'familiar' of the Holy Office. These were a sort of religious police, and apart from certain advantages of an economic order and their exemption from the ordinary courts they could proclaim to the world that they had no contaminated blood. This could prove useful on many occasions, for example in arranging a profitable marriage.

In this way, after having made the greatest sacrifices to ensure religious unity, the Spanish people lived for centuries haunted by the phantom which they themselves had conjured up. Commissaries, responsible for 'proofs', trod relentlessly across the land, interrogating witnesses and collating documents in the home towns of those who aspired to a position governed by statute. All who were candidates for posts of this kind wondered anxiously whether the investigations would uncover, or enemies would invent, some unknown Jewish great-grandfather. There is no doubt that this specifically Spanish environment (for no parallel existed anywhere else in Europe, and even in Rome the mania came under attack) contributed to the pathos enveloping the Spaniard of the Golden Century, though to what extent is a matter of considerable debate. The *conversos*, in the strict sense of the world, were few in number, since the blemish was passed on indistinguishably among the educated middle class to which the *New Christians* usually belonged. But research carried out in the last few decades has shown that a great proportion of Spanish writers had Jewish blood. The list includes famous philosophers, like Luis Vives, friend and companion of Erasmus, whose parents fell victim to the Inquisition of Valencia; jurists of international repute, like Father Vitoria; some of the most famous poets, of whom Fray Luis de León is the most outstanding; historians like Hernando del Pulgar and González Dávila; Fernando de Rojas, author of the *Celestina*, one of the masterpieces of Castilian literature; novelists of the fame of Mateo Alemán; theologians, philologists, Bible scholars. Suspicion also attaches to other names in Spanish literature and thought, provoking debate as to whether they were of Hebrew ancestry: such is the case with Arias Montano, Melchor Cano, Góngora and Gracián, among others. Even the name of Cervantes has been put forward recently on the basis of evidence which does not carry conviction.

It may seem more surprising to find the names of some of the greatest religious reformers in the list: Blessed Juan de Ávila, Saint Teresa de Jesús, whose *converso* ancestry is beyond dispute. On the one hand this shows what a mistake it was to question *a priori* the sincerity of every *converso*'s Catholic Faith without distinction; and on the other it prompts the thought that their strong personality was due precisely to the fact that being sincere converts brought to Christianity by conviction and not by routine or family tradition, they sought to live 'in spirit and truth' and were not happy with external rites. Their aspirations placed them on the borderline of orthodoxy as it was then understood; if some remained within the fold and acted as a vitalizing force, others placed themselves (or were placed) outside, as the trials of the so-called *alumbrados* and Protestants indicate.

It was not only those, like Vives, whose four quarters were Jewish, but those too – the majority – who had merely some remote ancestor, who brought their reforming, nonconformist thought to bear on civil society. For the strain common to both did not depend on physical inheritance but on the insecurity they felt in a society which distrusted them and barred the way to their promotion. It is hard to deny that these circumstances contributed to the bitterness and pessimism some showed, to the highly developed critical sense to be found in all of them, and to their denunciation of the external and the conventional both in religious and in social life. It is this bond of fate alone which gives unity to writers of such differing temperaments. Their only common ground was the painful circumstance which lead some to conceal their origins, others to criticize an unjust order of things. Fray Luis de León, in *Los Nombres de Cristo*, wrote that kings

not only do attack their own honour when they seek devices with which they may stain that of the people they govern, but do greatly attack their own interests and place in manifest peril the peace and security of their realms . . . (for) the realm where many orders and sorts of men and many private households feel, as it were, a sense of injury and resentment, and where the divisions created thus by fortune and the law prevent them from coming together and living in harmony, such a one will surely sicken and fall to fighting at the first opportunity which offers.

Judaists and genuine converts in Spain constituted groups whose boundaries are vague and whose number it is impossible to calculate exactly. The only important minority which was clearly recognizable and well defined and challenged the unity of the Faith in Spain until it was driven out in 1609, are the *Moriscos*. However, the Inquisition hardly bothered with the *Moriscos*. They rarely appeared in the *autos de fe*, and when they did it was often as witches, not as sectaries of Mohammed. The reasons for this paradoxical situation are several. The unbelief of the *Moriscos* was so notorious that it would have been necessary to put them all on trial, which was out of the question for reasons of humanity and self-interest. When any tribunal showed itself too harsh, there was an outcry from those who lived by exploiting the labour of the *Moriscos*. Thus the kingdom of Valencia, where the great mass of them resided, procured the signing of a contract between the *Moriscos* and the Inquisition in virtue of which, in exchange for an annual tribute of 2,500 ducats, the Inquisitors would not pry into *Morisco* affairs except in the case of some scandalous offence.

Abroad, it was not the treatment of Judaists and *Moriscos* which earned the Inquisition its fearsome reputation, but the trials of Protestants, though the numbers of the latter were comparatively small. Around many of the best-known Spanish Protestants hovers a doubt as to whether they really were such: in the view of Bataillon they were reformers influenced by

Erasmus. It is appropriate first of all, therefore, not least in the interests of chronology, to give some account of that curious chapter in the spiritual history of Spain associated with the influence of the Dutch philosopher. The story is now well known. It was Menéndez Pelayo who summarized it first. More recently, drawing on a greater wealth of information and a more dispassionate judgement, Bataillon wrote his *Erasme en Espagne*, which is a compendium of the whole religious life of Spain in the sixteenth century. The works of Erasmus aroused an unusual interest in Spain because they dealt with all those topics which in the days before Trent most vexed men's minds – the value of faith and works, the Bible and tradition, the role of the monk and the layman in the church.

As Eugenio Asensio aptly remarked, we have rediscovered Erasmus the pietist, buried as he was beneath Erasmus the mocking, destructive force.[6] The jokes against friars, pilgrimages and relics were but the superficial side to his teaching, which in essence was aimed at a reform of the church by a return to the founthead, rejection of later accretions, and respect for the church as an organization without letting it come between the soul and God. Erasmus the humanist, the defender of human freedom, would not ally with an early Protestantism which placed too much emphasis on an uncompromising Augustinianism and sacrificed free will to the omnipotence of grace and the awful mystery of predestination.

The university of Alcalá, founded by Cardinal Cisneros in accord with modern humanist ideals, became a centre of religious renewal along very Erasmian lines. From it came the Polyglot Bible, a collaborative undertaking by the *conversos* Alfonso de Zamora and Pablo Coronel, the Hellenist Hernán Núñez and the Latinist Antonio de Nebrija, prince of Spanish humanists, who fell foul of the Inquisition for his attempt to revise the Vulgate. In 1516 Erasmus, having just published his New Testament, was invited by Cisneros to Spain. It is not clear why Erasmus refused this invitation and why he never wanted to visit a country where he had so many admirers. It appears that he considered it a land full of Jews, a strange idea which may have been prompted by his frequent contact with the *converso* Vives. The list of Spanish Erasmians is a very long one and includes many of the most notable names of the age: Vives, the Valdés brothers, the Hellenist Juan de Vergara, and

Archbishop Manrique, the Inquisitor General, who eased his gout pains by laughing uproariously at the friars' tales in the *Praise of Folly*. Finally, Charles v himself was among his admirers and invited him to Spain, offering to protect him against his detractors. The informed public as well, the middle classes, enthused over the works of a man who not only denounced abuses in outspoken fashion but in the *Enchiridion* depicted the ideal of a Christian gentleman.[7] This work and the *Colloquies* were translated into Castilian, going through an unusually large number of editions for the period. The fame of Erasmus was such that Spanish travellers to the Netherlands included a visit to the great humanist on their programme. Hernando Columbus, son of the discoverer, was no exception and he received a present of a copy of the *Antibarbus*.

The whole ethos changed as the Protestant menace began to rear its head, for many saw in it a consequence of the attacks of Erasmus on traditional religion. His fiercest opponents were among the friars, not only because they had been satirized but because their concept of the church was not that preached by the critic of Rotterdam. A colloquy arranged at Valladolid in 1527 witnessed heated disputes between his supporters and opponents, and was suspended by the Inquisitor General before it had reached any conclusion. Two years later Charles v left for Italy. The anti-Erasmians took new heart while the Inquisitor Manrique, frightened at the turn events were taking, made no move. The Holy Office began to bring suits against Erasmians, not as such but as *iluminados* or *Lutherans*. The confusion was easily arrived at, since both had points in common with Erasmism, namely their demand for an inward freedom which seemed incompatible with the guide-lines laid down by the ecclesiastical hierarchy. Some, like Juan de Vergara, were brought to trial; others fled abroad. Pedro de Lerma, the venerable chancellor of the University of Alcalá, despite his advanced years had to follow the path to exile, ending his days in France. When Erasmus died in 1536 his numerous circle of Spanish disciples had been dispersed; and though traces of its influence could be discerned until much later, for example in the work of Cervantes, these were embers, not a living, active flame.

The Inquisitorial reaction was already very apparent in the closing years of the reign of Charles v. It could count on the support of the great mass of the Spanish people, who were Old

Christian and instinctively hostile to the middle class of Hebraic descent, its love of innovation and its protectors in high places, like the Admiral of Castile. Two factors had helped discredit the reforming movement associated with Erasmism. One section of the mystics, the so-called *alumbrados* (*lit*. 'illuminated', since they believed themselves illuminated from within by the divinity) had degenerated to the point where they were involved in common moral offences. It was established that in Extremadura and elsewhere sexual excesses had occurred in their conventicles; some clerics had persuaded their female followers that when a person reached an exalted stage of union with God, nothing he did was sinful. These perverted or deceived individuals were punished and the whole movement fell under a cloud – though finally Juan de Ávila, Ignatius of Loyola and Teresa de Jesús succeeded in placing their bona fide mysticism above suspicion. Offshoots of another mystical heresy, linked to some extent with the preceding, soon sprouted forth: these were the *dejados*, (*lit*. 'abandoned') who strove to suppress the will and the personality and took refuge in a passivity in which the ego was totally enslaved to the divinity. The last and most famous representative of this trend (so greatly at odds with the dynamic character of true Spanish mysticism) was the Aragonese Miguel de Molinos, author of a *Spiritual Guide* which exerted widespread influence. Brought to trial by the Inquisition in Rome, he died in prison after a lengthy detention (1696). In the view of some biographers his memory has been unjustly blackened and his ideas are susceptible of an orthodox interpretation.[8]

The other factor which helped to compromise the position of the Erasmians was the growth of Protestantism. In practice the frontier between the two movements was not easily defined, as appears from the fact that certain persons cannot be categorized under either heading. Juan de Valdés is a case in point. While his brother Alfonso, Secretary of Latin Letters to the Emperor, remained within the Catholic fold despite the violence of his verbal attacks on the pope and the monks, Juan was the leading light of a circle of exalted spirits in Naples which included Julia Gonzaga and which discussed the most delicate spiritual questions. Valdés died without being molested. The fact that some of his disciples were subsequently condemned as Lutherans prompts the suspicion that their master had similar tendencies.

There is no question, though, of the Protestantism of Francisco de Encinas, a native of Burgos and like Valdés gifted with a profound insight into the secrets of the Castilian language, into which he rendered the New Testament on the advice of Melancthon. Imprisoned in Brussels, he managed to escape from gaol and from there roamed across Germany, Switzerland and England until his death in 1552.

Though Spanish Protestantism is not a purely imitative phenomenon and can be partly explained in terms of internal developments, it was logical that it should appear in civilized and wealthy regions which were in close contact with foreign countries. These conditions were present in Old Castile, and particularly in Burgos, Valladolid and Salamanca, and lower Andalusia. Thus Seville and Valladolid witnessed the great *autos de fe* which heralded the growing repression of the early years of Philip II. The Seville nucleus was the most important through the number and distinction of those involved. It included Antonio del Corro and Cipriano de Valera, *Jerónimos* monks; the former eventually held a chair of theology at Oxford, while the latter translated Calvin's *Catechism* and corrected the Bible translation of another Seville refugee, Casiodoro de Reina. Many others who could not or would not flee were caught in the *auto de fe* of 1558, when twenty-one people suffered the death penalty and eighty were given lighter punishments. On the same occasion the bones of two prebendaries of the cathedral, Doctors Egidio and Constantino, who had died some time before, were cast into the flames. Constantino had been a chaplain of Charles V and accompanied him to Flanders and Germany before he obtained the post of preacher in the cathedral of Seville.

Likewise the two *autos de fe* held at Valladolid in 1559 consisted mainly of clergy and nobility, and of a few women, who displayed great courage. The most important victim was Agustín Cazalla, who like Doctor Constantino had accompanied Charles V on his travels around Europe. Bataillon does not believe that these journeys made them Lutherans; they merely fostered the illuminist ideas which were already latent in some circles in Castile and which could be considered orthodox before orthodoxy became so rigid. Cazalla recanted in public before his death, thus earning the right to be strangled before his body was set alight.

The *autos* of Valladolid and Seville destroyed the seeds of what might perhaps have been a Spanish variety of Protestantism. Henceforward the Inquisition only came across the odd case, occasionally involving a foreigner since any baptized person could be tried on a question of faith. This was the fate of several pirates, prisoners, and indeed incautious traders or travellers of French or English origin during the second half of the sixteenth century. In 1604 the peace treaty with England included among its provisions a guarantee that English residents would not be molested for their religious beliefs as long as they did not vent them publicly. One by one the other countries of northern Europe obtained the same concession on behalf of their nationals.

Perhaps the most spectacular of the Inquisition trials was that involving the archbishop of Toledo, the Dominican Fray Bartolomé Carranza. He had accompanied Philip II to Flanders and England, distinguishing himself wherever he went by his hatred for heretics, their books and even their mortal remains. Philip II made him Primate of Spain. It is a mystery why he later turned so much against him; probably he began to believe he was a dangerous Lutheran. Carranza had many enemies, including his fellow Dominican Melchor Cano. Between them they took to pieces the *Catechism* which Carranza had issued years before and discovered certain ambiguities in it. The archbishop hastened to modify them, but all in vain. The prisoner was claimed by Pope Pius V, remaining in decorous confinement for many years to come. In the end he was forced to abjure a variety of propositions and was sentenced to several penances. If it would be an exaggeration to claim that the trial was wholly the outcome of personal grudges, it is not easy to believe that the actors in this shady drama were motivated solely by zeal for the purity of the Faith.

One other Spanish heretic remains to be mentioned, a victim this time not of the Spanish Inquisition but of the Calvinists. Miguel Servet (1509–1553), an Aragonese physician, went to France as a very young man. He had a wide range of talents, practised medicine in Paris with great success, edited an edition of Ptolemy's *Geography* in Lyons, and at the same time indulged in theological speculation and controversy. He belonged to no particular sect. The central point of his doctrine was a denial of the Trinity, in which he influenced the Socinians and other anti-Trinitarians. The appearance of the *Institutio Christianismi* of Calvin furnished the occasion for a violent rejoinder, the *Restitutio Christianismi*, in the course of which he mentioned, in sudden incongruous fashion, his discovery of the pulmonary circulation of the blood. Calvin denounced Servet to the French authorities. Put in gaol, he escaped, but inexplicably attempted to pass through Geneva, where Calvin, a species of dictator in those parts, had him condemned to the stake. If as a physician he left behind him a notable discovery, as a theologian his thought is confused and pantheistic in tone: Jesus, son of God and a manifestation of God, may also be regarded as God inasmuch as he partook of the creation at his incarnation.

There is one point at least on which the activities of the Inquisition merit praise. When all over Europe the witch craze was claiming thousands of victims, Spain was immune. It was not disbelief in the existence of witches; the populace believed firmly in them, especially in the north. The Pyrenean regions of Navarre and Catalonia were the only ones to share – to a limited degree – in the collective madness of the sixteenth and seventeenth centuries. It was in fact events in Navarre in 1527–8 which obliged the central organ of the Inquisition (the Supreme Council or the Supreme Inquisition) to issue a circular recommending prudence. At the beginning of the following century a series of bad harvests and unexplained deaths terrified the people of Navarre, who laid the whole blame on the evil practices of witches. A veritable hunt was mounted and the local tribunal of the Inquisition weakly heeded the accusations, so that six victims perished in the *auto de fe* of Logroño in 1610.

The Supreme Council then ordered an investigation which showed that the events were attributable to a collective psychosis, accompanied by self-accusations, involving mainly women and even children who claimed to have committed imaginary offences. On the basis of this report the Inquisition issued a set of instructions on the premise that such occurrences were imaginary, without excluding the possibility of their being real. In fact there were several trials for witchcraft during the remainder of the seventeenth and eighteenth centuries, most of them resulting in light sentences.[9]

LEARNING AND SCIENCE

Often but not always the political hegemony of a country is accompanied by a great flowering of its culture. The reasons for the coincidence are not very clear. It would seem evident that spiritual and material factors are both present – collective excitement aroused by the heroic feats which have been performed and the successes obtained, and, on another plane and not to be ignored, vast opportunities for patronage, upheavals in population and manifold contacts opened up by political ascendancy. Such an ascendancy usually leads to a propagation of the language of the dominant race, and to greater attention and appreciation being awarded its writers and artists. All these circumstances were present in Spain between 1500 and 1650, an era of political greatness which coincides with the Golden Age of arts and letters. The time-lag between the two phenomena has been pointed out often enough – the early period of imperial consolidation was less fertile in cultural achievements than the period of maturity and initial decline. Cervantes and Lope de Vega, Velázquez and Murillo produced their best work when the decline in the political and military power of Spain was already evident. There is nothing unusual in this: if we accept that intellectual and aesthetic production is partly the outcome of a particular infrastructure, then it must follow the latter in time. Anyway the discrepancy has been greatly exaggerated: the early imperial era was not lacking in works of great value, nor can 1600 be taken as the starting-point of an economic and political decline which only appeared irremediable after 1640.

To treat culture as a monolith would be as unacceptable as to break it down into partial facets and isolated topics. Within certain shared limits, a separate treatment must be reserved to intellectual activity (learning and scientific output), literature and artistic expression, while recognizing that the links between the last two are very close. All three are influenced by a series of factors which have to be examined in any attempt to explore the subject in real depth. One of these is the aristocratic character of Spanish society with its universal aspiration after nobility, its cult of valour, honour and personal dignity and its contempt for 'low and base' callings. Another is the profound religious ethos which is all-pervasive, including the nonconformist strain, struggling for expression within or beyond the limits of orthodoxy. It should not be forgotten that religion contradicted the chivalric ideal; despite attempts at reconciling them, the two outlooks were very different and their conflict finds expression in literature. The difference was partly a sociological one, since the church was not a closed caste and provided even the most humble citizen with a career open to talents. The economic situation influenced the higher reaches of culture: the irreparable decline after 1640 had a malign effect throughout. Nor can one overlook the enormous discrepancies between the progressive areas, where groups or schools of writers and artists sprang up (Seville, Granada, Valencia, Valladolid, and later Madrid) and the impoverished rural areas with little cultural activity.

Last but not least one must remember that this remote peninsula of Spain was never more united with the rest of Europe than it was in those days, by every kind of contact. There was a constant interchange of men and ideas, which acquired a particular intensity where Italy was concerned, for Italy was always a very active focus of cultural life. Religious schism and wars limited contact with the north of Europe without interrupting it altogether. The cosmopolitanism of the Enlightenment was unthinkable before the doctrinal disputes had been resolved; but the Renaissance and the Baroque proved to be universal phenomena, while still allowing for national diversity. Spain is an excellent example of this: she was very receptive but very clever at adapting the imported forms to her own particular genius. Within Spain itself one notes that the frontiers between Castile and the Crown of Aragon were sometimes a reality in the cultural sphere as well.

At the beginning of the modern period the role of the printed word and of centres of instruction was not as decisive as it was later to become. More than any teaching centre, it was the family, the church and society as a whole which formed character and provided most of the current stock of knowledge. Only a reduced minority received instruction in special centres. The masses, by contrast, imbibed a large amount of information by word of mouth (traditions, proverbs, sermons) and thanks to this the numerous illiterates of the time were not wholly lacking in education. Illiteracy was not considered a basic deficiency, because it did not prevent the individual being a skilled craftsman, a diligent housewife, a trusty servant or possessing considerable practical wisdom about life and mankind in general. This situation changed during the sixteenth century. There continued to be a very high proportion of illiterates among the lower classes, especially in rural districts and among the female population; but the proliferation of schools indicates a desire for instruction which stemmed in part from practical considerations – growing rationalization, the need for documentation, the custom of committing even unimportant agreements to paper. The notarial acts of the time are full of contracts of purchase, apprenticeship, business agreements, often for sums which would not warrant a visit to a solicitor nowadays.

Education in those days was not considered to be the responsibility of the state, which merely arrogated to itself a right of inspection and control. It was the church and private individuals who attended to the task, whether from a desire for gain or a sense of service to the community. Numerous charitable endowments existed for the maintenance of a primary or a secondary school run by the municipality or the patron. In the small towns it was usually the parish priest or the sacristan who provided a very rudimentary schooling based on reading, writing and catechism. In the bigger towns it was the duty of the municipality to hire primary school teachers, but this duty was irregularly fulfilled: whereas in a small town like Mondoñedo schooling was declared compulsory, other bigger towns seem not to have bothered with the problem.

Secondary schooling was better attended to, being provided by the 'grammar schools', an essential preliminary for those who wanted to become priests or go to university. There were some very good academies of this type, like the *Estudio* of Madrid run by López de Hoyos, which numbered Cervantes among its pupils; it provided a humanist education, gave instruction in poetry and organized competitions. But more common were the much criticized schools of the *dómines*, run generally by some failed student or some rural cleric who in order to earn his daily bread doled out a meagre education amounting to little more than an apprenticeship in Latin. Here the birch was the main instrument of instruction. These schools proliferated to such an extent that restrictive measures were introduced, because it was not considered desirable to allow an excessive increase in the number of students which would deprive the manual trades of recruits. Perhaps the Society of Jesus was another factor in the restriction, since from 1560 it had been setting up colleges of its own in every town of any importance with the aim of establishing a monopoly. This it succeeded in obtaining, on many occasions, by means of an exclusive contract with the municipality involved. A typical example was Madrid, which at first protested against the opening of the Jesuit college, but seeing that it not only kept functioning but won all the best entrants closed down its own school in 1619.[1] It has to be admitted that the Jesuit colleges were usually superior to the rest, as much in the content of their teaching in which the humanist heritage was combined with the occasional rudiments of the new sciences, as in their teaching methods which were based on competition rather than punishment.

The universities experienced a more spectacular increase still: from the beginning of the sixteenth century to the beginning of the seventeenth their number rose from eleven to thirty-two, a number which thereafter remained invariable throughout the period of the Ancien Régime. Apart from the odd one like Granada which was a royal foundation, most of them were instituted by municipalities, private individuals or religious orders. None of the new foundations attracted the prestige of Salamanca or Alcalá. Some of the so-called *minor universities*, sited in tiny localities (Irache, Osuna, Almagro), with few chairs and fewer students, hardly merited the name of universities and the degrees they conferred had no validity elsewhere. Even the universities of some bigger towns had a poor reputation: the citizens of Zaragoza preferred to study in Huesca university, which had a better name, and people of any standing in Seville went to Salamanca.

This variety is to be explained by the complete lack of any uniformity or centralization. Each university had its own revenues, curricula and governing body. The chancellor or master of schools represented the higher authorities (royal or pontifical), while the rector, who was then a sort of director of studies, was elected by the students among themselves. Don Gaspar de Guzmán, later favourite of Philip IV, was rector of Salamanca while studying there. The lecturers too were elected, whether by the patrons of the university or by the students themselves, with the concomitant incidents and abuses. These abuses only changed form when in 1623 the Council of Castile arrogated to itself the right of appointing professors; indeed, favouritism took on a new impetus, through the influence enjoyed at court by the *colegiales mayores*. These were students who boarded in one of the four *colegios mayores* of Salamanca, that of Santa Cruz of Valladolid and San Ildefonso of Alcalá. Instituted by distinguished patrons for the purpose of helping poor students in the higher branches of learning, these colleges became a monopoly of the nobility, who destroyed their ancient character. On completion of their studies these nobles obtained bishoprics, *corregimientos* and judicial posts thanks to the support of old boys of the colleges, who held key positions. It may be reckoned that half the higher civil and ecclesiastical appointments were in their hands. Meanwhile greater obstacles confronted the poorer student, called *manteista* from the cape he wore.

The numbers of the student body in the Golden Age have been the subject of exaggeration. Salamanca was the most popular owing to the high quality of the instruction given there and to the fact that it was a cheaper town to live in than Valladolid or Alcalá. Those enrolled totalled nearly seven thousand towards the end of the sixteenth century, but not all were students. Their servants and even their landlords registered as well, so as to be eligible for academic privileges. In the seventeenth century there was a big drop in the number of students, partly through the creation of new universities, and seminaries too, which catered for the formation of the clergy. By contrast, the student population of Alcalá increased in size owing to its proximity to Madrid.

A chair carried little remuneration and was usually not a career but an intermediate calling in which the individual could show his worth and aspire to a higher position. Physicians could find it useful for building up a reputation in their profession.

Some religious orders too had chairs in freehold for the purpose of defending their theological opinions. In this respect those who attached most importance to the university chair were the Dominicans, followed by the Franciscans. The Jesuits caused an upheaval at the beginning of the seventeenth century by instituting chairs of *Suarist* theology in the universities and creating in the *Estudios Reales* of Madrid a new kind of higher education. But subsequently, without abandoning the university world completely, they grew less and less interested in it and devoted greater attention to their colleges.

The university student had no trouble securing a pass. There were no examinations by subject; all that was needed was to attend the courses for a given number of years in subjects of greatest interest and to take part in a few public debates and ceremonies. The Faculty of Arts was a sort of preparatory school where the student perfected his Latin and studied Aristotelian scholastic philosophy. These studies earned him the degree of *bachiller*, which was more highly esteemed then than it is now. Those who continued with a more specialized programme could choose from among the Faculties of Theology, Canons (ecclesiastical law), Laws (civil law) and Medicine. The last was offered in only a few universities and its professors were less well paid. The conferring of the degree of *licenciado* took place at a special ceremony when the candidate presented a thesis and answered his objectors. It was a purely formal occasion, an excuse for feasting and merrymaking at the graduate's expense. This circumstance, added to high examination fees, made it very difficult for poor students to graduate.

The quality of teaching varied a lot. In the Spanish universities there were eminent men lecturing, but there were others too whose standard was abysmal. The most usual procedure was the reading and expounding of a text determined beforehand by the regulations. In the theological faculties the standard work was, naturally enough, Saint Thomas; in Laws, the *Corpus* of Justinian and glossators; in Medicine, Hippocrates, Galen and Avicenna. Sciences, in the modern sense of the term, living languages, history and national law had no place in these archaic curricula. The very good lecturer would bring his texts up to date and set a personal stamp on all he expounded, but the mediocre one whose type was a lot more common, would confine himself to delivering a series of notes worked up in advance. The use of Latin was compulsory; in Salamanca students were even fined for using the vernacular. But it was a lost cause: Spanish eventually carried the day even in the lecture room.[2] Latin survived as the educated language of scientific treatises, but the generally low standard indicates the effort it cost authors to manipulate this artificial tool, which still however had the great advantage of facilitating international communication. Doctrinal considerations also played a part in the retention of Latin, since it was forbidden to read the scriptures in the vernacular. It is in this light that one has to see the refusal of the Cortes of Castile to entertain the petition of Pedro Simón Abril, philosopher and pedagogue, to be allowed to teach philosophy through the vernacular. The grounds of the refusal were that philosophy 'is the basis of our Faith, and errors could spring from allowing it to be bandied about among the unlearned'.[3]

Great importance is commonly attached to the prohibition decreed by Philip II in 1559 against Spanish students studying in foreign universities, except those of Bologna, Rome, Naples and Coimbra, on grounds of the need to protect Spanish universities, prevent the export of specie from the kingdom and check the contagion of new ideas. It is usually held that this last reason was the fundamental consideration, and that the intellectual isolation created by this measure was one of the main causes of Spain's scientific backwardness. Without denying the great importance of the decree one should note that universities everywhere were traditionalist and backward institutions. The scientific movement owes little or nothing to them, being fostered by individuals and academies beyond their walls. More important was the law, promulgated at almost the same time, which forbade on pain of grave punishment the printing or importing of books except under licence. The fact that these restrictive measures coincided with the *autos de fe* of Valladolid and Seville was no coincidence. They were all part of a reaction against the intellectual freedom which had been the order of the day in Charles V's time and which, from making its initial impact on theology, had extended to other allied disciplines. Biblical studies came under suspicion, as is indicated by the trial of Fray Luis de León and his companions. Semitic studies declined from the high level which had made possible the Polyglot Bible; and when Arias Montano brought out a new improved edition (the *Royal Bible*) it appeared not in Spain but in Antwerp, and only the fact that he enjoyed the patronage of Philip II prevented his persecution and condemnation. It is true that the Spanish Inquisition did not burn men of learning; it does not have to answer for cases like those of Galileo or Giordano Bruno. But its Index of prohibited books, its trials however bloodless, of several members of the Spanish intelligentsia and the support it gave to pseudo-historical legend, all helped to cloud the atmosphere, blunt the critical spirit and frighten off those who had no wish to bring trouble on themselves.

One may admit as much and yet still be faced with the problem of the real value of Spanish science, a topic which before and since Menéndez Pelayo has caused a lot of ink to flow and which is not completely solved by a discussion of tolerance and reaction. Decades after the restrictive measures mentioned above the University of Salamanca had a scientific curriculum which was better than that of the other European universities and which included the Copernican system. In the Casa de Contratación of Seville, cosmography and cartography reached a high level. At the end of the sixteenth century Spaniards did not feel that they were living through a period of intellectual depression. On the contrary, a friar is found exclaiming in 1598: 'There have never been in Spain so many and such great lawyers, theologians and jurists in every discipline; never have the arts been so flourishing; never have so many books made their appearance; and never have learned men been so favoured or rewarded.'[4] Half a century later such statements would have been inconceivable; the men of the Baroque believed in the excellence of their talent in the sphere of arts and letters, but not in their scientific superiority.

To arrive at a just appreciation of the value of Spanish science one must define the limits of one's approach. No great name is to be found in physics or pure mathematics. The spiritual environment cannot be blamed in this instance, for mathematics has nothing to do with dogma. Whether it is because of a racial aversion to pure speculation, or a lack of tradition or of the right conditions, the fact is that Spanish mathematicians were very second-rate. When Philip II, aware of the practical value of such studies, invited those towns with a vote in the Cortes to set up chairs of mathematics, only Burgos showed itself willing.[5]

By contrast, there was a brilliant galaxy of observers of nature, geographers, cosmographers and naturalists, evidently linked to the maritime and exploring vocation of Spain. These intrepid navigators did not trust to luck in their voyages; they drew on the heritage of antiquity and the Middle Ages, modifying and amplifying it continually from their own discoveries and observations. In this way they aroused the critical spirit and shook the yoke of the classical authorities who had manifestly erred in such basic questions as the size of the earth, the distribution of the continents and the habitability of the equatorial regions. Unfortunately very little remains of the enormous treasury of maps and observations collected in the Casa de Contratación at Seville. But there still exist books on navigation and cosmography which were classics in their day, like the *Arte de Navegar* of Pedro de Medina (1545), in which the Atlantic is already delineated with notable accuracy. When in 1871 the hut where Barents wintered was discovered in Novaya Zemlya two books were found inside, both Spanish: Mendoza's *Historia de la China* and Medina's *Arte de Navegar*.

Spanish cartography of the sixteenth century was already surprisingly up to date: it used coordinates, dispensed with picturesque symbols and figures, and even sought to correct the distortions in flat maps by using trapezoidal or spherical charts. But still unresolved was the problem of longitude. As early as the beginning of the century Alonso de Santa Cruz listed the methods proposed: dead reckonings, declination of the magnetic needle, lunar distances, elipses. But despite the large prizes offered by the Spanish government the solution could not be found until the eighteenth century, with the manufacture of watches of great accuracy. The Discoveries also contributed to a large extent to the renewed interest in the natural sciences. Typical of the *ad hoc* naturalist, the simple enthusiast describing unknown species, was Gonzalo Fernández de Oviedo. Much more scientific is the *Historia natural y moral de las Indias* of the Jesuit Ascota. In this work, and that of the Seville physician Monardes, and those of Francisco Hernández (among many others), the educated classes found a vast storehouse of knowledge on the exotic species which had just been discovered.

Strictly speaking this was not enough to make up for the lack of great mathematicians and philosophers; but it would not be fair either to dismiss it as the work of mere routine enquirers, for the new knowledge opened the way to the growth of the critical spirit. Among the leading physicians of the time there were those who did not shrink from speaking out against the stifling authority of Galen. Special mention should be made of the Aragonese Miguel Servet (see above, p. 227–8). For a long time he practised medicine in France, bringing out a notable edition of Ptolemy in the interval. But curiously enough it was in a book of religious polemics called *Restitutio Christianismi* that he published a major physiological discovery, not only for its own sake but because it destroyed the theories of Galen: the minor or pulmonary circulation of the blood, which was later to be rediscovered by the Englishman Harvey.

The humanities afford a more inspiring picture and can boast names which enjoy a world-wide reputation. In philosophy there were several independent thinkers who cannot be assigned to any definite school. The Valencian Luis Vives, friend and companion of Erasmus, left Spain when he was very young, never to return, probably because of the Jewish origins of his parents who were condemned by the Inquisition of Valencia. He was at one and the same time a humanist concerned with the reform of education, a preacher of humanity and tolerance in a world of discord, and a thinker with moments of happy insight but no systematic corpus of thought. The work of other independent thinkers (Gómez Pereira, Francisco Sánchez) suffered from a similar lack of completeness, perhaps because they had not the necessary genius, as, indeed, few single individuals have had, to create as Descartes later did a system and a school of their own. The Jesuit and Dominican theologians started with two advantages: a doctrine which served them as a base (Aristotelian–Thomist Scholasticism) and the backing of their respective orders. In the measure that they were able to free themselves from excessive dependence on their masters, they produced notable works and revitalized a doctrine which seemed already moribund.

The Jesuits were the best adapted to this task of partial liberation since they were not required to pay such regard to Saint Thomas. Thus, it is not pure chance that the best-known Spanish philosopher of the modern period is the Granadan Jesuit Francisco Suárez (1548–1617). He was the representative of a neo-scholasticism which was ready to seek and receive truth from whatever quarter: in Aristotle and Saint Thomas of course, but in Ockham as well and in the thinking process of the author himself. Suárez' *Disputationes Metaphysicae* not only led to the formation of a separate school within scholasticism in Spain but exerted great influence in Europe, even in Lutheran Germany whose theologians found in the work an arsenal of polemics for use against Calvinists and Socinians.[6] Without attaining the fame of Suárez, other Spanish Jesuits extended their influence, by their personal teaching or their books, to a large part of Europe. These included Gregorio de Valencia, professor at Innsbruck, and Rodrigo de Arriaga, who from his chair at Prague made a name for himself in central Europe generally. From this late scholasticism, deeply tinged as it was with humanism, flows one of the currents which by way of Leibnitz gave rise to modern philosophy.

In this sphere as well one notes the contrast between the poverty of pure speculation and the richness of applied studies. Suárez may have been the only major metaphysician; but there were numerous theologians and philosophers who devoted themselves to a study of politics, morals, law and the norms of human conduct in general. Leaving secular jurists with their interest in Roman law to expound statute, Jesuits and Dominicans dedicated themselves to a study of the major themes of Natural Law and the Law of Nations. Such topics were made highly relevant by changing political conditions, contact with primitive races and in general the problems raised by Spain's imperial expansion. The originality and independence of judgement of writers on the subject place them among the great thinkers of the age. They cannot be called Renaissance writers, if by that one means the cult of the ideals of antiquity. In the judicial sphere, in fact, one can see how stultifying such reverence was: without the least historical sense, the lay jurists applied to the Europe of the sixteenth century the Aristotelian concepts of slavery, the Roman tradition of the *Lex Regia* and the precepts of Justinian and the glossators, referring a society in continuous evolution to a set of anachronistic legal norms. The Renaissance spirit may and should mean, among other things, the critical sense which does not despise authority or tradition but subjects them to examination, and a humanism which combines the best of antiquity and of the Christian heritage with the new currents. If this is so then Spanish authors too, despite their scholastic affiliations, must be considered men of the Renaissance. The different approach to human relationships was made plain in the famous dispute over the freedom of the American Indian between Sepúlveda and Fray Bartolomé de las Casas. The former, invoking the Aristotelian theory of *natural slaves*, maintained that it was lawful to enslave them; the latter, less erudite but also less chained to a supposedly infallible authority, advanced the argument that they were free.

The lectures delivered by the Dominican Francisco de Vitoria in the University of Salamanca and later published by his fellow Dominican Melchor Cano unquestionably constitute the beginnings of modern international law as subsequently developed by Hugo Grotius. The Dutchman in various parts of his work admits his debt to Vitoria and other Spanish theologians. Vitoria took as his starting-point the questions raised by the discovery and conquest of America. His penetrating examination of the 'just titles' of the conquest led inevitably to a study of the principles governing the community of nations, the right of war, its limitations, the freedom of the high seas, and other allied topics. He was helped in this task by Vázquez de Menchaca, Baltasar de Ayala and other theologians, philosophers and jurists, most of them connected with the University of Salamanca.

His enquiries also embraced a discussion of the origin, nature and limits of political power, and hence political liberty and the rights of citizens. The Roman lawyers upheld royal absolutism on the grounds of a supposed cession by the citizens of Rome of their original sovereignty to the emperor in virtue of a *Lex Regia*. The date and content of the pact could never be established, but with a total lack of critical sense it was supposed to be still in force. Scholastic theologians also referred back to a pact between vassals and monarch, but with a different emphasis. Some of them were close to the Roman lawyers in holding that the cession of sovereignty by the vassals was total and irrevocable. But the common school of thought was that the kingdom had reserved certain rights to itself which could prevent the king becoming a tyrant. It is probable that this relatively liberal viewpoint was emphasized in the reaction against the absolutism of certain Protestant monarchs who restricted the rights of their Catholic subjects.

On the vexed question of tyrannicide these writers took a stand which varied in detail from one to another despite their agreement on fundamentals. Buchanan in England and Bodin in France had allowed it in certain cases; in Spain Soto accepted it, but with so many restrictions that it was tantamount to a practical rejection; Molina and Suárez recognized the power of the private individual to kill a usurper, but only the nation as a body had the power to remove a legitimate ruler who behaved tyrannically. Mariana in his treatise *De Rege* (1598) put forward the theory of the partial delegation of power and the lawful killing of a usurping tyrant by a private individual. In this there was nothing particularly new; but his use of a laudatory epithet in connection with the murderer of Henry III and the subsequent assassination of Henry IV, in which men thought they saw a consequence of these theories, led to the condemnation of the book in France. It would be a mistake to think that these writers held democratic views; all of them attributed a divine origin to the power of the ruler, which was the same whether the monarch was absolute or bound by the privileges of his vassals. But compared with the doctrines which were then current in the rest of Europe and later became general within Spain as well, they did represent a definite stand against the unconditional absolutism later described by Bossuet.

The decline of these studies dated from their growing popularity outside the cloister and the lecture theatre, as happened after about 1600. The fashion of politico-moral treatises for the enlightenment or education of princes reached Spain, like much else, from Italy, where Machiavellians, anti-Machiavellians, followers of Tacitus and suchlike had been proliferating from the end of the sixteenth century. The crux of the controversy had some importance: how to reconcile the principles of Christian morality with the demands of *raison d'état*. On the strength of doctrinal orthodoxy Machiavellism had to be repudiated; but while there were those like Francisco Ribadeneira who rejected it out of hand, other authors sought some sort of compromise, often looking to Tacitus as a less compromising guide. At every level of society there was a tendency to examine the foundations of the government of states. Cervantes was not being whimsical when in the first chapter of the second part of Don Quixote he shows us the knight in animated conversation with the priest and the barber over 'this thing they call reason of state'. But once the great academic theses were replaced by trivial collections of quotes advanced as recipes for good government, the discussion fell to a lower plane. It became an excuse for retired officials and friars in search of a reputation to write books which have now fallen into merited neglect.

The same descent from the heights of speculation to paltry routine studies can be seen in the sphere of theology with the growing dominance of practical morality, which turned into casuistry. The Jesuit–Dominican controversy over the distinction between essence and being and other Thomist metaphysical points which Suárez had brought into doubt were not accompanied by anything like the bitterness of the confrontation over grace and predestination. The Dominicans attached greater importance to divine grace than to the human will, whereas the Jesuits elaborated a more balanced system, in part as a reaction against the theories of predestination which the Protestants had adopted and exaggerated. The publication of the Jesuit Luis Molina's *Sobre la concordia del libre albedrio y los dones de la gracia* initiated a theological battle which is still undecided, since the Holy See has never pronounced on the rival theses and the respective orders have no thought (at least until the change of climate in recent years) of abandoning their position. Though the question is no longer of interest to more than a few specialists, it was an important episode in the intellectual history of the time and one associated essentially with Spaniards.

This theological warfare became embroiled with another famous controversy between those who believed in following the safest opinion in any moral question ('probabiliorists') and those who thought it permissible to follow any opinion supported by two or more doctors of repute ('probabilists'). The Dominicans defended the former thesis and the Jesuits the latter, thus earning themselves the reputation of professing a lax and flexible moral code. It is not possible here to go into this controversy, which in its day inflamed western Europe; but one should note the close parallel in content and time between the degeneration of juridico-political literature and of theology, which was turning to mere casuistry. In reality the bad name of casuistry is due only to its abuses – for in principle it was sound and laudable – because it adjusted to individual cases a set of abstract moral rules which could not meet the endless variations to be met with in practical life and which if literally enforced would often prove unjust and inhuman. The Jesuits were in an excellent position to meet this need through their diligence in the confessional, their familiarity with every class in society, and their more flexible theological principles. They did actually produce works of considerable importance, until the scientific spirit and the sense of pastoral duty gave place to an obsession with the difficult, the novel or the paradoxical solution to cases which rarely or never arose in real life. For example, was it a greater sin to fornicate with an ugly than with a beautiful woman? Was a person obliged to fast if by doing so he grew incapable of fulfilling his conjugal obligation? Was it a sin for a person who killed his father in a state of drunkenness to rejoice at the fact not because his father was dead but because of the legacy he would inherit? Of course, the majority of questions dealt with were not so absurd; but these give the measure of the decline of a branch of learning which had held out considerable promise. Thus the diatribes of Pascal against Escobar and others of his kind (not all of them Jesuits, of course) were not unjustified, though exaggerated.[7]

The same process of degeneration is evident in historiography. The traditional, erudite kind of history had its disciples, like Zurita and Ambrosio de Morales, industrious and conscientious writers but lacking in general ideas. The discovery of America marked a new departure in this field as well. As Fueter pointed out, the chronicler soldier introduced into his narratives an element of spontaneity which had been lacking as much in the traditional medieval annalists as in the voluminous and rhetorical histories of the humanists, who were more concerned with form than substance. The letters of Hernán Cortés relating the conquest of Mexico, the extensive history of the same conquest by Bernal Díaz del Castillo, one of Cortés' soldiers, the general history of the Indies by López de Gómara, to mention but a few of the leading names, are true historical gems by virtue of the amount of first-hand information they contain and their absence of bias in favour of a doctrine or school.

Where Spanish topics were concerned the situation was not so satisfactory. The kings had their official chroniclers and expected from them a heroic narrative of their deeds. Those who ventured of their own accord into the domain of contemporary history exposed themselves to disagreeable incidents. Jerónimo de Zurita was able to relate the medieval history of Aragon without incurring grave reproach; but when his fellow

Aragonese Argensola tried to recount contemporary events in his country he came up against unsuperable political obstacles. Mariana wrote a history of Spain in classical Latin, then translated it himself into Castilian (1602), and it became the most widely read of its kind until the beginning of the nineteenth century. Yet he did not venture to go beyond the reign of the Catholic Kings, no doubt because he felt that he could not write with the necessary freedom about recent events. In the seventeenth century the distrust of the authorities for historians grew steadily stronger; prohibitions and measures of censorship proliferated, and the result is that for the later Habsburgs we have little more than a semi-clandestine literature comprising memoirs, news items and journals, few of which were intended for publication. To this category belong the writings of Almansa, Pellicer, Barrionuevo and others like them.

The seventeenth century, however, abounds in religious and local histories, some of them of interest, like the *Anales de Sevilla* by Ortiz de Zúñiga, but lacking, most of them, the critical apparatus whose principles had been established in the previous century by men like Vives, Vergara and Melchor Cano. False ideas of national honour prevailed, leading to the invention of a long series of mythical kings for the Spain of primitive times. Similarly, respect for the noble traditions of the great families resulted in the forging of remote genealogies. Love for the locality emerged in the claim of towns to have been founded by Noah, Japheth, Hercules or some other hero of antiquity. But what caused most harm was the number of myths fabricated about the origins of Spanish Christianity. To the men of those times the greatest glory of their town was to count saints and martyrs among its sons and to own precious relics. To such men the paucity of information about the early centuries was exasperating. A variety of forgers dedicated themselves to filling the gap; they dreamed up ancient chronicles in which Saint James and his disciples appeared journeying the length and breadth of Spain, preaching, founding churches and leaving their martyred bodies behind as relics.

In vain a small number of distinguished men like the bishop of Segorbe, Juan Bautista Pérez, or the great Seville bibliophile Nicolás Antonio sought to check the rising tide. Their objections were accounted irreverent temerity, circulation of their works was made difficult or brought to a halt, and the wave of myths rose to such a height that even today the ecclesiastical history of Spain is not free of them. The authors of these cheats (learned men like Tamayo, Father Román de la Higuera) sought to give them a gloss of realism. Incredible is the story of the forger, clearly a *Morisco*, who buried near Granada some calcined bones, supposedly of martyrs, and some lead tablets in which the Christian doctrine displayed Islamic overtones and the apostles were made to speak in Arabic. The clumsy deceit was greeted with enthusiasm by the archbishop of Granada and the learned men whose opinion was consulted either refused to comment or pronounced in its favour. Long afterwards the doctrine contained in the tablets was condemned by Rome, but the supposed relics are still venerated in those parts.[8]

The religious mania of the time cannot of itself account for this withering away of the critical faculty. Very few men now possessed the critical spirit, and they found themselves stifled by the atmosphere of the Counter-Reformation; the way was thus left open to credulity, the supremacy of emotion over reason and a deficient interpretation of the principle of authority, as it was formulated in *Don Quixote* when a canon ventured to deny the veracity of the romances of chivalry: 'That's a good one! Books which are printed under licence from the king and with the approval of those to whom they are referred, and which are read and talked about to the general pleasure, can such be lies?'[9] At bottom it was the same argument employed by the defenders of the slave trade: could a practice carried on with the tacit or express consent of the civil and ecclesiastical authorities be unlawful? In both instances there is a clear hint of a refusal to think independently.

LITERATURE

Spanish literature of the Golden Age is almost entirely Castilian literature. The political hegemony of Castile was accompanied and even preceded by a linguistic hegemony in which force had no role. Basque was without a literature. Galician had gone into eclipse after flourishing promisingly for a while. In these regions it is not surprising that Castilian carried the day. But it does causes surprise that Catalan, after bearing such ripe fruits in the Middle Ages, declined in the fifteenth century and that Catalan poets even before the coming of political unity were beginning to use Castilian. More eloquent testimony to the expansive vigour of Castilian is the fact that several of the most notable Portuguese writers were bilingual. The outstanding case is that of the dramatist Gil Vicente (1465?–1536?), who wrote with equal facility in his mother tongue and in Castilian, and even has plays where the two languages alternate in the mouths of his characters.[1] The rise of Castile as a political and economic force undeniably had a part to play in the widespread accept-ance of her language. Language had not then the political significance it had at a later date in the era of nationalism, but there was a certain connection between the two, as contempor-aries were aware. The words of Antonio de Nebrija, dedicating his first Castilian grammar to Queen Isabel the Catholic, are well known: 'Language was ever the fellow of empire and accompanied it everywhere, so that together they waxed strong and flourished and together they later fell.'[2]

The solemn installation of Castilian as an international tongue can be dated precisely: 17 April 1536, when Charles v in the Consistory Hall of the Vatican spoke in Castilian in the presence of Paul iii and the representatives of France for the purposes of justifying his policy and attacking that of Francis i, ally of the Turk.[3] It was the time when the Italian Renaissance was thrusting forcefully into Castile, so that it seemed that Castilian was receding on its own ground before Latin, the language of culture; there were even Spanish poets writing in Italian. No doubt it was the imperial power of Castile which exalted patriotic pride and prevented the language going out of use. By the end of the sixteenth century the struggle waged by Latin for monopoly of the universities and scientific studies could be considered lost; it came increasingly to be relegated to works of theology and legal tomes.

To the year 1597 belongs the Spanish grammar of César Oudin, who in his preface excused himself for teaching the French 'the language of their enemies'. This plea would have been superfluous some years later in the very Castilianized court of Louis XIII. The outbreak of hostilities did not bring Castilian into disfavour in France. The French fought the Spaniard while appreciating his language, not only as an instrument of culture but for its own sake, for its idiomatic richness and the facilities it offered for expression. If on a more modest scale because of the primitive state of communications, Spanish was up to 1650 what French and later English became: a language whose use conferred prestige as well as being a practical asset in itself. The enormous number of Spanish editions issuing from foreign presses indicates a widespread knowledge of Spanish over a large part of Europe, regardless of political or religious barriers. Very revealing is the fact that Mazarin, the great enemy of the Spanish monarchy, kept his notebooks in a mixture of Italian and Spanish; as they were intimate jottings they prompt the conclusion that Mazarin *thought* in Spanish. This perhaps was a legacy of his Italian upbringing, since in Italy the prestige of Castilian was even greater than it was in France. When it is remembered that in the first half of the sixteenth century Spain was in danger of becoming a cultural colony of Italy, one is forced to the conclusion that this change in the respective positions was not caused solely by the prestige of military power but to some extent by the quality of the literary production then emanating from Spain.

The political and economic axis of Valladolid–Toledo was a linguistic axis as well. The presence of the court in these cities and later in Madrid contributed to the triumph of the Castilian spoken on the Meseta, whereas the Andalusian variety remained in the background despite the large nucleus of writers coming

from the region. This was the time that Andalusian was
establishing itself as the dominant form of expression in Spanish
America, which it is to this day; but as a Spanish literary
medium it was of secondary importance, eclipsed by a form of
Castilian which was supposed to be more grammatically perfect.
The tendency of the great Andalusian writers to indulge in a
culto style of great artificiality was no help in popularizing their
native forms of expression. This contrasted sharply with Saint
Teresa, for example, who effortlessly raised the popular tongue
of Castile to heights of literary distinction. The differences
between Castilian (in the strict sense) and Andalusian were
anyway too slight to have furnished the basis of a new literary
form. Thus Castilian, without destroying individual variety in
point of style and vocabulary, attained a unity which very few
languages enjoyed at the time. This magnificent tool was forged
in the age of the Catholic Kings and of Charles v and reached
its perfection under Philip ii.

As in the plastic arts, the Italian Renaissance strongly
influenced Spanish literature, producing a certain initial
disorientation. The denial that there was ever a Renaissance in
Spain is sheer nonsense, to be explained only by the belief that
Spain is a cultural world cut off from the rest of Europe.[4]
What can be said is that the Renaissance in Spain, which
began with the importing of foreign forms, provoked a nationalist reaction which led to a synthesis combining national and
imported elements. This synthesis is usually given the name of
Baroque, which in Spain was rather more complete than
Renaissance culture.

A strong classical tradition had never died in Spain, as is
attested by the works of Alfonso the Wise. In the fifteenth
century began the invasion of Italianate forms, which did not
spread beyond a circle of intellectuals: refined, artificial,
bookish, their culture was divorced from the people. The reign
of the Catholic Kings seemed about to witness a synthesis of the
traditional and the novel, the down-to-earth and the refined, the
national and the exotic. In the plastic arts such a synthesis was
about to bear fruit in the so-called 'Isabelline' or 'Cisneros'
styles. Nebrija represented similar possibility for the humanist
current: the first Latinist was also the author of the first Castilian
grammar. But neither Nebrija nor the learned men gathered at
Alcalá by Cisneros were capable of creating new perspectives in

literature. The *Celestina*, considered by many the greatest work in Castilian literature after *Don Quixote*, was an isolated phenomenon and left no school to follow it. As regards literature this reign was one of unfulfilled promise.

In this uncertain situation, when the developing new forms had not yet found a means of expression, there occurred in the reign of Charles v the invasion of Italian poetry, an event comparable to the Roman influence on painting. In both instances the Spaniards took lessons from the foreigner, and, rather neglectful of their own tradition, produced works whose technical mastery cannot conceal the fact that they are the expression of something alien, something that struck no deep chord in the heart of the community as a whole. The date is usually fixed exactly as 1527, when Boscán, a Castilianized Catalan, conversed with the Venetian ambassador Navagiero and adopted the eleven-syllable metre. Boscán also translated the *Courtier* of Baltasar Castiglione, a manual for the perfect man of the world according to the model of the small and refined courts of Italy; this work enjoyed a great vogue in Spain. At almost the same time the *Enchiridion* of Erasmus was reaching a wide reading public, a work which also aimed at offering a model for living, though of a more profound kind. The popularity of both suggests the variety of currents that met on the parched soil of Castile. The Flemish influence and that of the north of Europe in general might have been very useful in checking the mannered and purely formal elements coming from Italy, but political and religious factors intervened to weaken this northern strain to an ever greater extent.

Italian lyric forms found a masterly exponent in Castile in Garcilaso de la Vega from Toledo – warrior, courtier, man of arms and letters, who met a premature death while fighting the French. His eclogues, sonnets and ballads are unsurpassed for perfection of form, and reflect a tender and passionate nature. He exalts love, idealizes nature, and in line with the classical conventions introduces us to lovelorn nymphs and shepherds, acclimatizing the myths of Greece and Rome to the banks of the Tagus. The same Italianate strain, influenced to a considerable degree by Petrarch, appears in the Andalusian Cetina, while Cristóbal de Castillejo represents the traditional popular currents which paid no heed to the new forms or the new themes.

Attractive as it was, the poetry of Garcilaso afforded few

perspectives in which the Spanish genius might find true expression. But in this same reign two genres were initiated that were destined to flourish. It was no trial effort which gave them birth, but works that are masterpieces of their kind: the picaresque novel with *Lazarillo de Tormes* and mystical literature with the treatises of Juan de Ávila, which are linked in time with the works of Saint Teresa de Jesús and Fray Luis de Granada. The picaresque novel has no exact equivalent in any other literature. It is the genre which best exhibits the union of the coarse with the refined, or better, the exaltation of the coarse, which is one of the characteristics of Spanish literature in the Golden Age. Its protagonists are the *pícaros* – that is, the lowest members of the lowest social strata. They are not however slaves, gypsies or *Moriscos*, but genuine Castilians, Old Christians whom vice or poverty drives to a wandering existence and a life of falsehood and cheating. Not for them the loftier passions; they do not kill, they are not interested in love, being all the time preoccupied with the problem of getting enough to eat without having to take a steady job. They are social misfits rather than products of an economic crisis: the picaresque flourished in the period of Castile's maximum prosperity, when there was a demand for labour and wages were high. It is wrong therefore to see in it the reflection of an economic and social order; rather it is the description of urban outcasts who exist in any affluent society. The writers of picaresque novels had no didactic aim; they confined themselves to observing and sketching, with a tolerant eye and an implacable trueness to life, different types whose bizarre way of life marked them out within a strongly conformist society. The earliest and perhaps the most perfect of these novels is the *Lazarillo de Tormes*, published in 1554; its author is unknown. It follows the adventures of an abandoned child, first as a blind man's guide then as servant to various individuals – a famished *hidalgo*, a miserly priest, until he obtains the post of town crier in Toledo.

Ascetic and mystic literature is another very Spanish genre, though one with strong Flemish and German influences (Eckhart, Tauler, Suso, the Carthusian Dionysius, Thomas à Kempis). The irrational strain in these authors was calculated to appeal to those souls who found the religion of their day too cerebral and too institutional. This trend towards a freer and more individual religion, towards a direct and intimate contact with the Deity, was what made one part of the official church suspicious of such mystic currents. This was particularly true after the Reformation, since though the roots of the two movements were distinct they had certain superficial resemblances. It explains why several of the Spanish spiritual authors were molested by the Inquisition, though none seriously. Only Miguel de Molinos, author of the *Guía espiritual*, was actually convicted, not by the Spanish Inquisition but by the Roman. There was anyway a notable difference between Molinos and the rest of the Spanish mystics, inasmuch as he followed the 'quietist' path of the *iluminados*, whereas Saint Teresa or Juan de Ávila were able to combine mystical rapture with the most intense temporal activity.

Blessed Juan de Ávila, a tireless missionary in the Andalusian region and a director of consciences, took part in the foundation of the University of Baeza. He wished to become a Jesuit but was prevented by the stain of his Hebrew ancestry. He spent a few months in prison in Seville on suspicion of Lutheranism. In his treatise *Audi, filia* and in his *Epistolario* he laid down rules for the guidance of souls: first, their preparation by means of asceticism (sacrifice, penance), and then their mystical experience or union with God. Mysticism reached its height in the second half of the sixteenth century; but the term mystic, bordering on heterodox, could also be applied to Juan de Valdés, of whom mention has been made above, for his *Comentarios a la epístola de San Pablo a los Romanos* (Venice 1556) and the *Consideraciones divinas* (Basle 1550). However as a stylist his best work is the *Diálogo de la Lengua*, which is written in an exquisite Castilian.

Garcilaso, Valdés and the anonymous author of *Lazarillo* are the outstanding trilogy of the imperial period. However the writer who at the time and for quite a while to come had the greatest popularity was the mediocre Fray Antonio de Guevara. Nowadays one is baffled to learn that his *Reloj de príncipes* went through editions in French, German, English, Dutch, Italian and Latin. Perhaps the secret of its popularity was not so much its literary value but the fact that it was one of the first examples of a didactic political treatise. This was a genre which would later proliferate, reflecting popular interest in the problems raised by the birth of the nation state and the growth of absolute monarchy.

It is doubtful if the transition from the universal monarchy of Charles v to the national type of Philip ii with its emphasis on monarchical power and Catholicism decisively influenced the evolution of Castilian literature, for it appears to have followed laws of its own. In fact the basic genres were already in existence: poetry, religious and didactic prose and the picaresque novel. Drama was less well developed, only coming into its own in the seventeenth century. The second half of the sixteenth century witnessed the gradual assimilation of the foreign forms of the Renaissance and an attempt to synthesize them with purely national elements, though the synthesis would only reach its fullness at a later stage.

Mysticism in the age of Philip ii was associated with writers who had been trained in the first half of the century, when the deep and passionate religious feeling of the Spanish people was seeking to express itself within the limits of orthodoxy with a freedom which was later to suffer considerable restriction. A Dominican, Fray Luis de Granada (1504–88) was the author of the *Guía de pecadores* and the *Introducción al símbolo de la fe*, written in impeccable Castilian prose. Saint Teresa of Ávila, reformer of the Carmelite order, related her mystical experiences in *Las Moradas* and the *Libro de su vida*, while in the *Libro de las Fundaciones* she told of the trouble and opposition the reform of her order cost her. Her style, despite its lack of literary pretension, is highly attractive by virtue of its spontaneity and expressive force. San Juan de la Cruz, companion of Saint Teresa and born like her in the mountainous heartland of Castile, is one of the most profound of poets. No one can match him in describing the painful ascent of the soul towards the heights of mystic union ('Subida del Monte Carmelo', 'Noche obscura del alma') and the superhuman joy which intoxicates it when all the obstacles have been overcome and it achieves union with the divine essence. There is a marvellous balance between the profundity of emotion and the perfection of form in his poems, which strive to express by means of exclamation, symbol and metaphor what is an intimate, personal experience and therefore incommunicable.

Fray Luis de León (1527–91) was not, properly speaking, a mystic. His very diverse output is the most successful attempt made at combining the Renaissance heritage with the Christian legacy in its fullest sense. His interest in the Bible was perhaps a throwback to his Hebrew ancestry, while his Augustinian platonism is a far cry from the arid reaches of scholastic philosophy. In addition to translations from the 'Book of Job' and the 'Song of Songs', two other works of his were deeply influenced by the Bible: *La perfecta casada* and *Los nombres de Cristo*. The poetry of Fray Luis combines the most perfect classical form, sculpted in the manner of Horace, with a robust inspiration.

From the point of view of his poetry Fray Luis belonged to the lyrical school of Salamanca, which included other lyrical writers of much less merit. The other great school of poetry in the peninsula was that of Seville, of which Fernando de Herrera was the leading exponent. Author of compositions in a sonorous, full verse, ornate and betraying Latin influences, he heralds the Baroque forms of the next century. Some of these poems which are epic in tone ('A la muerte del rey Don Sebastián', 'A la batalla de Lepanto') have become classics and objects of innumerable imitations.

The work of Cervantes, like that of Goethe, falls between two centuries and two styles. The sixteenth-century heritage is evident in the Italianate classicism, the traces of an almost forgotten Erasmism, the polished and unaffected prose. In fact almost the whole of his output belongs to this century; but *Don Quixote* is already Baroque. Miguel de Cervantes Saavedra was born in Alcalá de Henares near Madrid in 1547. He experienced life in its many facets, as a soldier (he was wounded at Lepanto), as a captive for five years in Algiers and in a variety of unspectacular occupations which never lifted him above the threshold of poverty. As a collector of the royal revenues he travelled for years round the south of Spain, gaining an intimate knowledge of urban as well as rural life. He was imprisoned for debts in Seville and died in Madrid in 1616 as poor as he had always lived. It is curious how Cervantes deceived himself as to the relative value of his various works. *Galatea* and *Persiles*, novels which he held in high esteem, are the work of a skilled craftsman but not much more. He had illusions about his talents as a writer of plays and noticed how Lope de Vega overshadowed him. His poetry is by no means brilliant. On the other hand, his twelve *novelas ejemplares*, though uneven, would on their own have earned him an important place in Spanish literature. But it is *Don Quixote* which puts him in the front rank of authors. A work of the mature, indeed ageing man (the second part was published a year before his death), it is for all that a serene and optimistic work. It is not likely that his intention was to uproot the fondness for romances of chivalry, for this fondness was already disappearing fast. He took from them the idea of a hero struggling against crude reality so as to ennoble (on the pretext of satirizing) the eternal human aspiration to establish the reign of good in a world where evil frequently triumphs. The contrast between fiction and reality, the shifts from one side to the other of the vague boundary between them, do not just occur in the person of the leading character but pervade the whole plot of the novel, so that the reader is dealing with a 'true story' at one moment and a figment of the imagination at the next. This technique of illusion is wholly Baroque and has its parallel in the optical devices used in painting and other plastic arts of the time. It would be a mistake however to regard *Don Quixote* as a purely Baroque work; there are many uncharacteristic features, not least the fact that it is set entirely in the countryside.

The final years of the sixteenth century mark the emergence of a new world of ideas and expression. It is a gradual process, not a brusque transition. The themes change: mysticism, after a magnificent flowering, declines almost to the vanishing-point, for the *Mística Ciudad de Dios* of Madre Agreda is a mere jumble of puerile dreams and visions, and the *Guía espiritual* of Molinos does not appear until 1675. Poetry undergoes a major transformation: the earlier balance is upset and two currents emerge, one popular and the other refined. The novel, didactic literature and above all drama, the most characteristic genre of the seventeenth century, all take a great stride forward.

This is the century of the Baroque, a term that being made to mean so much means almost nothing. The attempt to stretch it to cover the many-sided activities of a whole century has caused it to lose all precise meaning. To some critics it is the expression of courtly life; to others it is first and foremost a popular phenomenon. There are those who see it in terms of post-Tridentine religious feeling, others who maintain that it marks a secularization of life and society. At one moment we are told that it is connected with the economic depression of the period, at another that it is a culture based on ostentation and wealth. Rather than lose ourselves in abstractions, we would do well to look at some particular instances of conflict which appear in the literature of the time.

One of these is regional contrast: as with painting, literature was concentrated in specific urban centres. The sterility of the north is very marked: Galicia and the Cantabrian provinces produced very few writers indeed; Catalonia likewise very few; Aragon, the odd outstanding figure (Baltasar Gracián). The Valencian region was average; but it was the two Castiles with Andalusia that were the creative centres. Of forty-seven major writers of the sixteenth century sixteen – a third – were Andalusians, and the proportion was maintained and even increased during the seventeenth century. The proportion of Castilians is even greater, but with certain differences from one century to the next: whereas in the sixteenth there is a certain equilibrium between Old and New Castile, in the seventeenth the Old Castilians all but vanish and the production of New Castile increases. A closer analysis however indicates that within New Castile it is Madrid, home of Quevedo, Lope, Tirso and Calderón, which is responsible for the lion's share. The court and Andalusia account for nearly all the intellectual output, a fact which may perhaps be more clearly grasped by relating it to what Don Luis de Haro said when he asked the *ayuntamiento* of Seville for a subsidy: 'Madrid and Seville are the greater part, or, better, the whole of this Monarchy.'

Literature does reflect class and caste feelings, though not to any marked degree. There is the odd detail which indicates Christians of *converso* ancestry, but the considerable debate as to the significance of details of this kind suggests that they were not too clearly marked. Then there are wholly Jewish authors, like Isaac Cardoso, Enríquez Gómez or Miguel de Barrios, whose thought and style resemble those of the Old Christians. Among the latter too there is no clear differentiation of ideology, for all sectors shared a common attachment to Catholicism, the monarchy and chivalry.

Ecclesiastics were preponderant in speculative writing, but less important in pure literature – only thirteen out of forty-seven major writers of the sixteenth century were clerics. In the following century the proportion rises somewhat – twelve out of thirty-seven. It should be noted, though, that several of the examples chosen mean very little because of the vagueness of the boundary between the lay and ecclesiastical spheres. One thinks of Fernando de Herrera, who never got beyond minor orders, Lope and Calderón de la Barca, who were ordained priests later in life when a large part of their work was already done, and others like them. The distinction appears with greater clarity if the regular clergy alone is taken into account. In general, there is a more pronounced difference in the later Baroque than in the classical period, though in the seventeenth century itself a friar, Tirso de Molina, was busy writing plays most of which were very secular in character. A divorce also emerges between arms and letters at the later stage; the knight who can handle the pen and the sword with equal dexterity, like Garcilaso or the historians of the *Conquista*, becomes increasingly rare.

The contrast between popular and refined literature assumes special relevance in Spain because popular literature was so good. Not only did it influence the novel and drama to a considerable degree, but it created two exclusive genres of its own: *refranes* and *romances*. Spain has a rich collection of *refranes*, short proverbs or sayings which condense centuries of observation and experience. The *romances* were poems, flexible as to metre and historical, fictional or lyrical in theme. The term 'popular literature' does not mean it was confined to the lower classes. No doubt it was thanks to it and to sermons that the common people built up a considerable stock of information; even the illiterate benefited, because this literature was passed on to a large extent by word of mouth. But this did not stop the upper classes taking an interest in it as well, as is shown by the collection of *refranes* assembled and edited by philologists from the sixteenth century onwards, and by the contribution of poets of repute to the popular ballads, which were also collected in *cancioneros*. The romances of chivalry, an escapist literature anticipating the adventure novel and the serial broadcast, appealed to every class in society. In writing them, obscure literary hacks worked alongside writers of great talent, as the unknown author of the first *Amadís* must have been.

Erudite and Italianate culture, evident from the fifteenth century but most influential in the first half of the sixteenth, widened the gap between refined and popular literature, though never to any marked extent. A reaction soon set in. The best prose writers, including even Cervantes, gloried in the use of the plain language of the people; distinguished poets wrote *romances*, and a New *Romancero* took shape, which was no less inspired than the Old or medieval. If some genres declined, like religious drama or the novels of chivalry, they were replaced by others of an equivalent standard and similar universal appeal. But the opposition of the traditional and the imported refined forms was just tending to fade when it was given a new lease of life. The reason may have been the universal tendency to seek new forms when the old become inherently less creative, or it may have had something to do with social and educational factors. The odd individual like Guevara was writing in a precious and mannered prose as early as the age of Charles v: some critics have seen in him the origins of English euphuism. But it was towards the end of the sixteenth century that the poets of the Seville school began to adopt a hermetic, aristocratic poetry which sacrificed clarity of concept and directness of expression to an affected and highly *recherché* style. This trend came into its own in the seventeenth century, though it never wholly extinguished the popular forms; indeed, some of the greatest *culto* poets, like Góngora and Quevedo, expressed themselves with equal mastery in both styles.

But the consequence was a growing divorce from reality and from the perennial roots of culture, though not to the same extent in every branch of literature. Drama, eminently a community form, might be influenced by the new trend but had to remain on a level which all could understand; but poetry fell into the hands of minority literary groups or erudite salons dominated by clerics and jurists whose training permitted them to savour allusions to classical mythology and appreciate neologisms and involved metaphors. No doubt they were pleased to feel themselves set apart from the *profanum vulgus*. Pulpit oratory (the only sort there was) split in two: preachers who saw as their prime aim the spiritual welfare of their audience continued to express themselves in the traditional forms; those who sought to build a reputation before distinguished audiences followed the example of the court preacher Fray Horacio Paravicino, an opulent and immoderate orator.

This growing divorce meant the decline of literature. The popular forms atrophied as they lost contact with the educated classes in society; the educated were given to exercises of mere skill and their creations became artificial and academic as the life blood of reality ebbed away. The work of Góngora (1561–1627), despite the enormous talent of the man, was purely personal and was followed by no more than mediocre imitators. The 'Polifemo' was still comprehensible to the majority of the public, but pursuing the same line, Góngora wrote the 'Soledades', which, despite its formal beauty, afforded no promising perspectives, not even for the cultivated minority, who needed a learned commentary in order to understand its hidden delights. Though there was much versifying, the poetical panorama of the second half of the seventeenth century is pretty arid.

The picaresque novel after *Lazarillo* yielded some important works during the sixteenth century. Several of the short novels of Cervantes are masterpieces of the genre, especially *Rinconete y Cortadillo*, an unsurpassed picture of the Seville underworld. The *Guzmán de Alfarache* of Mateo Alemán is a bitter, pessimistic work, very far removed from the ironic satire of *Rinconete* and *Lazarillo*. In the seventeenth century the genre went into decline, again because of a growing divorce from reality. Only one work of genius stands out: the *Vida del Buscón* of the many-sided Madrid author Francisco de Quevedo (1580–1645). Quevedo led an active and stormy life. A prolific prose and verse writer, he bowed to fashion in the occasional piece of affected prose but never fell into pure estheticism. He was always attentive to the reality of his age and criticized it mercilessly.

The Aragonese Jesuit Baltasar Gracián was, like Quevedo, a critic of his times, though more intellectual, less passionate and without the latter's satirical vein. In style he was a sort of Góngora, but without Góngora's felicity. His works set forth a human type, humanist, Christian and man of the world all rolled into one according to the Jesuit educational model (*El Héroe*, *El Discreto*, and *El Criticón*); as such they enjoyed a wide popularity within Spain and abroad, until in the eighteenth century they were replaced by another human ideal.[5]

Only one genre instead of declining actually rose to heights of popularity and brilliance in the seventeenth century: drama. Drama had always been a vital art form in Spain in one form or another. The religious play, though driven from the churches, retained a firm hold on popular affections. At certain festivals there was an open-air staging of scenes from the Passion, or *autos sacramentales* at Corpus Christi. Italian influences inspired middle-class or pastoral comedies or classical tragedies. None of these resulted in a major work. Not even Cervantes, despite his *Numancia* which had literary merit of a national kind, managed to found the great school of Spanish drama. Two conditions had first to be present: an urban public with a distinguished middle class with leisure and literary interests, and a group of writers of great talent who would have to preserve the union of aristocratic and popular culture, of experience and erudition. It was no accident that the best of these dramatists were from Madrid (Lope, Tirso, Calderón), for it was the court which could provide the fullest audiences. The attitude of the various kings was also important. Philip II had little interest in the stage and while he lived it did not develop much. Nor was Philip III a devotee of plays, but since he was not a commanding personality this was no great obstacle; many exalted persons began to frequent the theatre and acting circles without fear of damaging their careers. Philip IV was very keen on the stage. He had a theatre built for himself in the palace of the Buen Retiro, patronized distinguished authors and even, it is rumoured, wrote plays himself. The early period of his reign is the most brilliant in the history of Spanish drama. Circumstances changed when public and personal disasters darkened the king's mind and led him to take steps against a form of entertainment which the stricter moralists regarded as sinful. In 1644 play-acting was forbidden, and though it was allowed once more a few years later the climate had changed in the interval. The campaign of one part of the clergy against the theatre was so intense that a copious bibliography has actually been compiled of works for and against.[6] Only by assigning part of the takings to the upkeep of charitable institutions were the principal towns able to secure authorization for their theatres to remain open. Censorship became steadily more severe. When Calderón died in 1681 the great Spanish theatre died with him.

Lope de Vega (1562–1635) condenses and symbolizes the most brilliant period of the Spanish stage. Trained in the classics, he abandoned them (not without a plea for pardon to the scholarly) in favour of the freer style to which his own bent as much as the preferences of his audience prompted him. He was incredibly prolific: he seems to have written nearly two thousand plays, of which only four hundred are extant, and still found time to compose works outside the theatre and lead a very busy life. Such a vast output of course is necessarily uneven:

the flawless masterpieces are few in number, though in all his plays, even the most mediocre, he shows his technical mastery and his comprehensive grasp whether of the world of letters or the secrets of the human heart. In his plays he combined the earlier genres, like pastoral, mythical and the comedy of manners, and created or perfected various others, like the drama of intrigue or 'cloak and dagger' or the *comedias de santos*. The most numerous are those dealing with historical subjects. He ransacked old and contemporary chronicles and national and foreign histories in search of plots. In the interests of variety he set his scenes in the most exotic surroundings, though his characters continue to think and talk like Spaniards of the period; for if there was ever a faithful portrayer of the Spanish people with all its virtues and failings, its cult of honour, monarch, woman and love, it was this womanizing priest, this some-time soldier whose faith was mighty and his sins mightier yet. His fame survives still thanks to his social dramas – *Peribáñez, Fuenteovejuna, El mejor alcalde el rey* – though his philosophy is sometimes distorted by attributing to him revolutionary ideas which he certainly never held.[7] He was a *hidalgo* and never disowned his class; but he believed in the fundamental unity of all Spaniards, equal before the law as embodied by the king.

As Charles V. Aubrun points out, the Spanish stage was at its most brilliant in the year of the death of Lope. Calderón, Tirso and Juan Ruiz de Alarcón were in full flow and until the suspension of 1644 were to bring out some major works; there were other dramatists like Rojas Zorilla who were in the second rank but would not have been overshadowed in any other age. The Mercedarian friar Fray Gabriel Téllez, who adopted the pen name of Tirso de Molina, wrote with much greater licence than might have been expected of a man of his calling and earned himself reprimands in the process. In *El condenado por desconfiado* he confronted his public with the most intricate of theological problems and one hotly contested at the time: that concerning grace and predestination. The dénouement comes as a surprise, though it is in the best orthodox tradition: the repentant bandit is saved, while the virtuous hermit who had despaired of the divine mercy is damned. The other great masterpiece of Tirso has made an enormous impact on the world's literature, for it is from his *Burlador de Sevilla* that the immortal figure of Don Juan derives, whose demoniacal grandeur is at once repellent and fascinating.

Don Pedro Calderón de la Barca was another who combined the callings of priest and soldier in a way we find strange nowadays. Lope was Spanish in his outlook but at the same time universal, human and tolerant. These qualities are less apparent in the works of Calderón, where (sexual) honour reigns absolute, regardless of laws of compassion, justice or religion. Events like those he describes in *El médico de su honra* and *El pintor de su deshonra* did occur in the Spain of those days, but they were the exception. *El alcalde de Zalamea* portrays this conflict of honour from a more congenial angle: the rustic who avenges his daughter who had been seduced by an insolent officer relying on his privileges. In this play too the monarchy intervenes as the supreme fount of justice taking no account of class. The most profound and universal of Calderón's works, *La Vida es sueño*, sets out the really basic problems concerning life and the destiny of man, but has no solution to offer. Calderón also wrote a great number of *autos sacramentales*, allegorical compositions in which he managed to breathe life and interest into abstractions like Grace, Faith and suchlike.

This short summary is inadequate to convey a complete idea of the poetic and human treasures of the Spanish stage of the Golden Century. Contemporaries everywhere acknowledged its merit by translating and imitating its masterpieces, particularly in France, regardless of political hatred and rivalries. Often mentioned is the fact that the Paris of 1636, threatened by Spanish troops, was applauding Corneille's *Le Cid*, which was based on a play by the Valencian Guillén de Castro.

ARCHITECTURE, PAINTING AND SCULPTURE

For all her apparent remoteness Spain actually stands at a crossroads of itineraries and influences. This is particularly noticeable in the development of her art and, above all, her architecture. At the beginning of the modern period the still lively recollection of *Morisco* decorative forms joined to the opulence and technical maturity of late Gothic and the first fruits of the Renaissance had given rise to original art-forms of which the best known is the so-called *Isabelline* style. This contained the promise of a wholly national form, and one which could be developed in any number of ways. Unfortunately the Renaissance strain coming from Italy grew so strong that it ended by supplanting every other type. The *Morisco* tradition, relegated to auxiliary tasks, began to disappear; even the Flemish or north European influence, which had been so strong in the reign of Ferdinand and Isabel, declined; and the creative impulse which seemed on the point of ushering in a distinctively Spanish style yielded to an imitation of foreign models. It was only much later, with the rise of the Baroque, that Spain once more found her own means of expression.

The economic expansion of Castile in the sixteenth century was reflected in a series of monuments erected in the Meseta and Andalusia, whereas the Cantabrian coast and the eastern lands witnessed less activity. Noble materials were employed in profusion on constructions whose great solidity shows the concern of a society inspired by high ideals to build for eternity. The decorative details, by contrast, exhibit the traditional features of exquisite woodwork, wrought iron, traditional *Morisco* ceramics and glass then beginning to cover the open spaces in stately homes. It was the age of the last cathedrals, of the seigneurial palace which took the place of the cheerless and antiquated castle, and of charitable and educational foundations like hospitals, universities and *colegios mayores*. The accumulation of rents in the hands of the church and of a few great families, the tradition of patronage among them, their will to immortalize their names, indeed the difficulty they had finding profitable investments that were compatible with the noble way of life, were factors which combined to divert a large part of the national product towards buildings in the grand manner.

It was at this time that the last major Gothic monuments took shape: the cathedral of Segovia, which had been all but destroyed in the struggle of the *Comuneros*, and the new cathedral of Salamanca which by a happy inspiration was built alongside the old and not on its ruins. Deplorable, though, was the demolition of the central naves of the great Mosque of Córdoba to make way for a small Gothic cathedral. The conquest of the kingdom of Granada furnished the occasion for the erection of cathedrals in the new lands and of palaces for the magnates who had received lordships there. One of these, the marquis of Cenete, built the palace of La Calahorra at the foot of the Sierra Nevada; another, the marquis of Los Vélez, erected a handsome edifice within the forbidding fortress of Vélez Blanco (Almería) that recalls the ducal palace of Urbino. Through these monuments the architecture of the Italian Renaissance was brought to Spain. The cathedral of Granada, with its vast dimensions, was planned along Gothic lines; but when Diego de Siloe took charge of the work in 1528 he replaced the Gothic pillars with clusters of classical columns whose proportions he was obliged to distort in order to achieve the required height. The cathedral of Granada inspired those of Jaén and Málaga, though they were closer to the Renaissance style.

In these major constructions of the early period the actual architecture was still greatly influenced by Gothic traditions. The Renaissance, apart from the odd exception like the above-mentioned Calahorra palace, entered Spain in the form of *Plateresque* – that is, pure ornamentation – and only gradually began to affect building techniques. This is the explanation of the paradox that Spanish architecture in the sixteenth century moved from the ornate to the sober, from the complex to the simple, contrary to the general rule governing the evolution of styles. Plateresque was the name given to the fine carving, comparable to that of silversmiths, which was executed on the surface of buildings, with its inspiration classical motifs –

candelabra, garlands, weird heads, cornucopia, arms, medallions with busts and so forth. Fine examples of this style are the façade of the University of Salamanca, the convent of San Marcos of León and the *ayuntamiento* of Seville.

As the century advanced the Renaissance began to influence architecture and construction to an ever-increasing extent, while Plateresque decoration diminished or disappeared. To this more sober style belong, in addition to the cathedrals of the kingdom of Granada, a series of monuments erected under the auspices of Charles v – the *alcázar* of Toledo, destroyed in 1936, the old *alcázar* of Madrid, subsequently a residence of the Habsburgs, of which nothing remains either, and the fine, very Italianate palace next to the Alhambra at Granada, which was left unfinished for lack of funds.

The process of simplification culminated in the second half of the sixteenth century in the style known as *Herreran* or, more properly, *Escorial*, since it appears that the role of Juan de Herrera in the building of the Escorial was not as crucial as was once supposed. The plans were drawn up by Juan Bautista de Toledo, an artist trained in the Italian style; but on his premature death Herrera took charge of the project. Herrera modified the plans according to the wishes of the king so as to increase the size, but this obliged him also to raise the height. The result was that while the exterior is well proportioned the patios appear inadequate, drowned by the massive granite walls. In this immense quadrilateral, which is a mixture of royal monastery, museum, residence and pantheon, architecture becomes pure geometry. It is at the opposite pole from the Alhambra, which conceals its filigrees within; the grace and harmony of the pure lines of the Escorial are best appreciated from a distance. It is said that this monument reflects the ascetic spirit of Philip ii, who took a keen interest in the building process and chose a suitable site for the palace at the foot of a forbidding range of dark hills.

The Escorial is by its very nature a unique monument; it could not give rise to a school. The colossal element is an integral part of its being; interpreted on a smaller scale the effect is lost. The cathedral of Valladolid, also entrusted to Herrera, remained unfinished. The *Lonja de Mercaderes* at Seville, now the Archive of the Indies, is an excessively cold building on the outside but more handsome and lively from within. Some other buildings betray the influence of the Escorial; but barely was the threshold of the new century crossed than the pure, functional line began to alter, heralding the advent of the Baroque.

With the same force as in architecture, or even greater, the Italian influence manifests itself in painting and sculpture during the period of the first two Habsburgs. It is evident in the importation of works of art (paintings, tombs) and in the arrival of artists from Italy. After Fancelli, who was responsible for the tomb of the Catholic Kings in the Royal Chapel of Granada, another Florentine, Pietro Torrigiani, worked in Seville, where a magnificent Saint Jerome by him is still extant; there was Jacopo Florentino in Granada, and Leoni and his son, Pompeyo Leoni, who were court artists fetched by Charles v and Philip ii.

More in harmony with the Castilian spirit were two other foreign sculptors, Felipe Biguerny or Vigarni from Burgundy and Juan de Juni from France. In the first half of the sixteenth century Vigarni sculpted altarpieces and cathedral choirstalls in a style which still retains much of the Gothic tradition, while Juan de Juni, later in date, had a Mannerist style which recalls Michelangelo. Juni worked in Valladolid, then the greatest centre of sculpture in Spain. In the museum dedicated to him one can admire among other works the tormented figures of his *Santo Entierro*, wherein sorrow is no longer expressed in the restrained moulds of classicism. His sense of pathos, like his preference for using wood rather than cold stone, marks Juan de Juni as a Castilian artist in spirit, something which cannot be said of any of his Italian contemporaries working in Castile.

Greatly influenced by Italian and French sculpture, though not to the extent of abandoning their personality or their Castilian identity, were Becerra, Ordóñez, and, greatest of all, Alonso de Berruguete (1490–1561). The last, born in the heartland of the Castilian Meseta and trained in Italy, came to be known, not without some exaggeration, as the 'Spanish Michelangelo': Michelangelo in wood, more gesturing, less perfect, and more dependent on the surroundings in which his figures are set – for (a fundamental difference) whereas in Italy the sculptured figure had established its independence, in Spain it was still completely decorative and a part of a whole, generally a choir or an altarpiece. Even within these limitations Berruguete was a sculptor of genius and his figures are full of life and movement. His major work is considered to be the enormous altarpiece of the monastery of San Benito of Valladolid, preserved in sections in the museum of that city. More perfect perhaps, is his work on the choir of the cathedral of Toledo.

The eastern regions are less well-endowed, more backward in sculptural development. There is only one outstanding name: the Valencian Damián Forment who worked in the first half of the century on altarpieces of a Gothic inspiration (the Pilar of Zaragoza), and only in his later years came to be influenced by Renaissance currents. Forment died in 1540, and after him there is not much more to be said about sculpture in the lands of the Crown of Aragon, strange though it seems in view of its contacts with Italy.

While sculptors and architects were quick to assimilate the novelties arriving from Italy, Spanish painting in the sixteenth century showed a certain disorientation. This was perhaps because the Flemish influence, with its Gothic overtones, had been very marked in the earlier period, so that when the Italian style burst on the scene it came as too brusque a transition. In the paintings of the first third of the century 'primitive' traits are still apparent: perspective is imperfect, much gilt is used, and some figures still bear a halo or crown. In the following third Raphaelism triumphs, to be seen clearly in a number of painters: the Sevillan Alejo Fernández, Morales from Extremadura, Juan de Juanes from Valencia; artists who despite their merits must rank as secondary figures – good draughtsmen and colourers but lacking in originality. Nor did Sánchez Coello, painter to the court of Philip II, rise above this level.

The relative inadequacy of Spanish painting in this period explains the favour enjoyed by foreign painters like Kempeneer from Flanders, the man mainly responsible for Raphaelism in Seville; Antonio Moro, also from Flanders, who painted numerous portraits at the Spanish court; the Italian painters (none of them outstanding) summoned by Philip II to decorate the Escorial; and above all El Greco. Domenico Theotocopoulos, born in Crete, formed in Venice and transformed in Spain, stands on his own as an artistic personality: he belonged to no school and he left no following. He arrived in Spain in 1577 and painted a great canvas for the Escorial, the *Martyrdom of Saint Maurice and the Theban Legion*, which did not please Philip II because of its too-audacious execution. Far from losing heart at this setback or trying to adopt to the prevailing taste El Greco continued painting in an ever more personal style, employing clear, cold colours of a hitherto unknown range and a lighting not of this world. There is the same unearthly quality about his superhuman visions and his figures, so elongated that they appear symbols of disembodiment. The most varied theories have been advanced in the attempt to explain his style; but the one thing which seems clear is that he distorted reality because contrary to the tastes of his age he had no wish to copy it; he sought rather to interpret and transcend it. The most famous of his paintings, the *Burial of the Count of Orgaz*, is the one which best represents his style. It is like a drama in two acts: on the lower plane a group of monks and *hidalgos* dressed in black and with pointed faces surround the dead body of the count, which is shrouded by Saint Augustine and Saint Stephen; the upper plane introduces us to heaven, where the divine persons welcome the soul of the deceased. Toledo, where the artist lived, preserves this and many other canvases by him, a testimony to the identification of the painter with the city and the esteem in which he was held there. He never lacked commissions, nor was any pressure brought to bear on him to paint in a more conformist manner. Later on he fell into neglect and his art was dismissed as pure caprice. It was the men of the 'Generation of 1898' who rediscovered the genius of this artist, a foreigner by birth but a Spaniard by adoption and spiritual affinity.

The apogee of Spanish art lies between the end of the sixteenth century and the middle of the seventeenth – that is, at the time the political might of the empire began to decline. The reign of Philip III and even the greater part of that of Philip IV were of incomparable splendour in this respect. A large part of the credit is due to the patronage of the crown: the three Philips were devoteees of the arts, Philip III perhaps less so than his father or son. Both of these were informed critics, ready, despite the depleted state of the treasury, to pay for good artists and buy any work of merit which came on sale. A large number of nobles followed this lead, while the church for its part continued to be an inexhaustible source of commissions for every class of artist, from the dearest of painters to the humble rural stonecutter.

The phenomenon of artists grouping together in regional

centres whose activity was closely conditioned by economic development was already apparent in the sixteenth century, and became even more so in the following century. The wealthier areas not only had greater facilities for training and holding their artists but creamed off those who appeared in other less well-endowed parts. Northern Spain continued to have a low artistic output; so, even, did Galicia even though a large proportion of the wealth was in the hands of the church, for it was not merely a question of money but of tradition and aptitude as well. Within Castile, Valladolid and Toledo declined, while Madrid became a centre of attraction for artists from a variety of backgrounds. Andalusia was the most prolific region artistically. The studios of Seville, where artists of varied origins received their training, exported their products to every corner of Spain and even to the Indies. In lesser degree Granada too had a school which began to adopt Baroque with great gusto and originality. In the levantine region Valencia stands out as a centre; but Catalonia was still unable to recover the exalted position she had reached in the Later Middle Ages.

With the age of the great cathedrals past it was the extraordinary flourishing of the religious orders which furnished builders with most of their commissions. But the very abundance of the foundations placed limits on what they could afford to spend: only the Society of Jesus managed to accumulate in a brief period a great volume of possessions thanks to the donations of rich patrons. Lay monuments (palaces, colleges, town halls) were not often very elaborate. It should not be forgotten that the economic crisis was intensifying after 1600. No grand architecture developed in the seventeenth century; instead there was a great number of smaller buildings, newly erected or restored, in which the transition from the pure geometry of the Escorial to the craziest whims of the Baroque became steadily more pronounced as the years passed. The first step was to add trifling decorative details to enliven the bare façade; then the pediment was split down the middle and its two halves twisted; lines now became curved or broken, not straight; flat surfaces were ornamented, as were the shafts of columns. By virtue of the play of concave and convex, of mass and bays, of light and shade, an attempt was made to point contrast, depth and perspective. By the second half of the century the distortions were so marked that the three classical orders were on the way to disappearing, giving place to a completely new style, late Baroque, which in Spain is called *Churrigueresque*. The transformation was complete when columns, originally classical and then twisted, were replaced by the *estípite*, a pilaster of capricious shape, tightly throttled and stood upside down – that is, narrowing towards the base. But this final phase falls beyond the scope of the present study.

Restrained Baroque, which respects the basic lines of the classical orders while interpreting them with ever greater freedom, can be studied, for example, in the works of Gómez de Mora (Jesuit church of Saint Isidore, now the cathedral of Madrid) and the Italian Crescenzi, architect of the royal pantheon of the Escorial, which is elliptical in form and decorated with polychrome marble. Towards the middle of the century the Seville architect Herrera constructed his grandiose basilica of the Pilar of Zaragoza, and Alonso Cano the main portal of the cathedral of Granada which overall is still sober enough. By the middle of the seventeenth century one already encounters the theatrical touch, the *recherché* perspectives, the rich and varied ornamentation of church interiors, which were conceived as great festival halls of the divinity and came to be a sort of reproduction of the princely salons where the eye was charmed by paintings, light and crystal lamps, the ear by choice music and the nose by incense. But all this reaches its culmination at a later period, with the total breakdown of form and the triumph of the artist's whim or genius over every rule.

The altarpiece, a very Spanish creation, had grown as an adjunct to the altar until it almost took its place. The vast reredos of the cathedral of Seville, finished at the beginning of the sixteenth century, with its colossal proportions and its hundreds of figures, is the masterpiece of the genre. Built by carpenters and sculptors, the wooden altarpiece followed the changes and copied the styles of architecture; the volume of ecclesiastical rents permitted them to be replaced as tastes changed. Between the end of the sixteenth century and the beginning of the seventeenth a wholesale destruction took place of Gothic and Plateresque altarpieces, which were replaced by others of a Herreran style. This phenomenon is comparable to the removal two centuries later of many Baroque altarpieces in favour of cold neo-classical compositions. The order of Pius v that reredos be crowned by a crucifix may have influenced their removal or modification. Other instructions emanating from the Council of Trent on sacred art must also have had an effect, although their importance is still debated and has perhaps been over-estimated. The decisive factor was probably not liturgical rulings but the inherent laws of the evolution of styles and the inexorable tendency for the old to be shoved aside by the new. There is every reason to believe, for example, that the destruction of priceless medieval pieces was directly due to an order found in many synodal constitutions for the burning of images whose age or imperfection prompted derision rather than devotion.

Sculpture and painting reached a much higher level than architecture in the seventeenth century. Whereas the latter yielded no more than a small number of exceptional works, the former brought Spain to the forefront with a galaxy of artists of international fame. These artists had a high opinion of their own worth and sought recognition by a society which still considered them, at least legally, mere artisans. They were, after all, subject to guild ordinances and to municipal inspection; they did not work like modern artists according to the dictates of their fancy, but always by commission from clients who were very specific in the contract about the details of the execution. But in these contracts it is already apparent, from promises made to execute works of real merit for higher rates of pay, what a difference there was between the true artist and the mere hack. More than one dispute and lawsuit arose between a famous artist and a stingy client who would not pay the required price for a work.

This conviction that their profession was of a superior order and not manual underlay the painters' refusal to pay the *alcabala*, following the example of El Greco who was the first to fight a lawsuit for the purpose. In practice the distinction between the creative artist and the hack was impossible to draw, but they all enjoyed the prestige conferred by the great names. Cardinals and grandees of Spain were on intimate terms with the celebrities of the world of art. The Seville painter Francisco Pacheco kept in touch during his life with important political and literary figures and left us their portraits. Not a few rose to favour at court: Philip ii was on familiar terms with Sánchez Coello, while Philip iv treated Velázquez not as a servant but as a friend in whose company he would on occasion unburden himself of serious questions which had nothing to do with art. But it is typical of the ambiguous status of these men that in order to acquire a habit of the Military Orders Velázquez had to declare that he did not paint by trade but as a hobby to please the king. His office of painter was such a minor one that he held it jointly with that of *aposentador real* (officer of the household), which was more important in the hierarchy.

The architects of the seventeenth century, after the interruption represented by the Renaissance, had restored a climate of freedom and spontaneity in which the basic influences of Isabelline architecture were able to develop. So, too, painters and sculptors recovered a personality which if not altogether lost had been greatly compromised in the previous century, though they never abandoned the Italian heritage which remained always basic for them. In sculpture the differences are obvious: instead of the serene coldness of marble or stone constant use was made of painted wood, which gives a much greater sensation of reality and has a warmth and an expressive potential which stone cannot match. The difference in subject matter was no less radical. European Baroque was very religious but also very princely: the plethora of small Italian and German courts provided artists with numerous commissions to immortalize princes and princelings in studied poses, enhanced by pompous Latin inscriptions. In Spain there was no such longing to perpetuate one's image by statues and busts; even those featuring kings of Spain are surprisingly rare, and often the work of foreigners. Spanish sculpture was almost totally at the service of the church, to the extent that sculptors are frequently known as *imagineros* (image builders). In the sixteenth century images of saints usually formed part of an altarpiece; in the seventeenth, without abandoning the altarpiece completely, they win their autonomy. Many of the most famous images are processional, no longer meant to be looked at just from the front but to be admired from every angle; this had important effects on their execution. One should not forget the emotional climate fostered by the missions and the emphasis of preachers on the sufferings of Christ in his Passion and of his mother at his side. The processional images of Holy Week were conceived with the aim of impressing on the multitude the sufferings of the God-Man. The restrained, serene sorrow which the classically trained master was capable of expressing gave place to the contortions of Christs in agony. The canonization of new saints (Ignatius, Teresa, Hermengild) furnished extra material, as, on a grander scale, did new forms of popular devotion to Mary, particularly the Immaculate Conception, the innumerable portrayals of which are the lasting witness to the controversy and fervour it aroused.

The Castilian school of sculpture which had been so active in the preceding century produced yet another representative of merit in Gregorio Fernández, creator of the recumbent Christ of the Pardo. But it was Andalusia that carried the day, through its two schools of Seville and Granada. In Seville Martínez Montañés (1568–1649) produced works that distinguish him as the greatest Spanish sculptor. Trained in a classical environment, he worked at the height of the Baroque without abandoning his principles of proportion and restrained emotion, apparent for instance in the marvellous crucifix of the cathedral of Seville and the altarpiece of San Isidoro del Campo in the same neighbourhood. Of his disciples the outstanding name is Juan de Mesa from Córdoba. A much younger man, he was more open than his master to the spirit of the Baroque and captured it in processional images of great emotive force. The Seville school continued producing in the same vein until well into the eighteenth century.

The Granada school of sculpture has two names of great worth: Alonso Cano and Pedro de Mena. The first, a passionate individual who lived a turbulent life, received his artistic training in Seville, then went to the court of Philip IV and ended his stormy career in Granada. In the cathedral there, where he was beneficed, he left some of his best works. Like the great artists of the Renaissance he was a man of universal talents: painter, architect, designer of altarpieces; but he was first and foremost a sculptor. His images of the Virgin recall very clearly those of Montañés by virtue of their serenity and sweetness, while his male figures are full of determination and energy. Pedro de Mena (1628–88) was an artist of real spiritual depth. His Saint Francis of Assisi, with its pointed face and gaze lost in the infinite, is a likeness in wood of the creations of El Greco. One of his greatest works is the choir reliefs of the cathedral of Málaga. Like its Seville counterpart the school of Granada survived for quite a while, in fact until the changing climate brought about by the Enlightenment. It maintained a certain decorative standard but lacked figures of genius.

It is in painting that the contrast is most marked between a generally mediocre sixteenth century and the group of artists of genius who raised Spanish painting to a position of supremacy in the first half of the seventeenth. There are those who relate this change to the introduction (principally through the work of Ribera) of the style of Caravaggio. But this was merely one part of a reaction which set in throughout Europe and in Italy itself against a form of painting which, though very skilful in execution, had become mannered and unproductively academic. In Spain, as in Flanders, the native vein now came into its own after a long period of subjection, and without sacrificing the achievements of the Italian masters followed a separate course and managed to surpass the creations of its teachers. However although Spanish painting was like the Dutch and Flemish in hunting freely for new forms, a difference of subject matter, dictated by the dissimilar milieu in which the artists moved, led to major differences of style. The Spaniards did not cultivate landscape for its own sake, or middle-class interiors; non-religious painting was in fact confined to still-life (*bodegón*) and portraiture, both of which were in close harmony with the realist strain in Spanish art. Mythology, by contrast, vital to the culture of the age, was so unenthusiastically and unimaginatively tackled by Spanish painters that patrons preferred to place their commissions in Italy.

The religious subject was everywhere present. Not only in churches and convents but in the home as well, even the lowliest, there was a demand for representations of Christ, the Virgin, the better-known saints, Biblical stories and pious legends. The walls of shrines were covered with tablets on which those who had received favours caused spectacular events to be depicted (miraculous cures, dangers averted). The great Spanish painters found the means of reconciling religious inspiration, even mystical rapture, with the most stark and unyielding realism. The sublime and the ridiculous often figure side by side in the same picture, as in the theatre of the time. In the representation for example of the Last Supper artists would try to portray the atmosphere of grief and divine love, without however sacrificing elements of light relief, as in the drawing of table-cloths, crockery, food and even perhaps a burlesque detail or two, like two cats fighting over a fishbone. In general, physical details are depicted with a dignity which bridges the gap between matter and the spirit. The scarcity of female nudes, another feature of Spanish art, can hardly be seen solely as a deference to ecclesiastical rulings; it appears to be due rather to the instinctive modesty of a society in which a woman felt herself dishonoured if she showed the tip of her toe to the eyes of a stranger. Thus, when Valdés Leal painted the Temptations of Saint Jerome the courtesans appeared clad in rich, heavy clothing which exposed merely the face and hands.

With the change from formal beauty to a seeking after truth and life came a change from the universal, conventional lighting of the older masters to a lighting adapted to each particular setting. The reaction led to the appearance of another mannerism: the projection into the canvas of a narrow shaft of light which illuminated certain sections very markedly while leaving the rest in shadow. But the really great masters did not abuse the technique, which many lesser men adopted to hasten the execution of a work. *Chiaroscuro* was introduced into Spain by Ribalta and Ribera. Ribalta, a Catalan, lived around the end of the sixteenth century and the beginning of the seventeenth. Ribera belonged wholly to the seventeenth. A Valencian by birth, he was trained in Italy, where he mostly lived, without however ceasing to be very Spanish in expression and feeling. The Italians wondered at the temperament of this little Spaniard (*lo Spagnoletto*) whose paintings display a vigorous and cruel realism. But the depiction of physical deformities and bloody martyrdoms was only one aspect of his art. Ribera was able to transform rude beggars and peasants into holy penitents or philosophers of antiquity, portraying them with a nobility and dignity with no loss of the most vigorous realism. Because of the milieu in which he lived he cultivated the mythological theme more frequently than his colleagues in Spain; but it is his religious paintings (*Saint Bartholomew, La Inmaculada de Monterrey*) which give the measure of his genius. In Spain his pictures found a ready market; and because of this Ribera, despite living abroad, could be one of the most active agents of the revolution in Spanish painting.

Velázquez (Seville 1599-Madrid 1660) was the most complete

painter of the Golden Age. After an apprenticeship in the studio of his master and father-in-law, Francisco Pacheco, he took himself off to Madrid where he became the favourite painter of Philip IV. This new position allowed him to complete his training by studying the magnificent royal collections and making two lengthy visits to Italy. It also enabled him to escape the virtual monopoly which the religious theme held over other painters, for which he was not specially gifted. As a court painter his chief duty was to paint the king and his courtiers, a task which could have led him into a facile and mannered approach. Velázquez avoided this pitfall thanks to a constant striving for self-improvement. Though as a young man he could already look on himself as a master possessing every technique that mattered, yet he never ceased during his life to meditate on problems of depicting existence, space and the atmosphere surrounding figures. Ortega and Maravall have shown that the attitude of Velázquez towards reality goes far beyond esthetic or technical considerations and finds a place in the new mathematical, rationalist vision of the world which was the most important contribution of the seventeenth century to civilization. It is usual nowadays to draw a distinction between estheticism and science, the artist and the scientist. This was not the attitude of the artists of the Renaissance, and it should not surprise us that the catalogue of Velázquez' library lists a considerable percentage of scientific and technological works. The output of Velázquez was not very extensive, nor has it been scattered to the same degree as that of other famous Spanish painters. Some of his works are in England (the *Rokeby Venus*) and in Vienna (the portraits of the Princess Margarita); but the bulk of them are in Spain, or more specifically Madrid, for in his home town of Seville only two canvases of small merit have been preserved.

Only one of his religious paintings has become famous, the crucified Christ. More renowned are his mythological subjects, which Velázquez treated as genre paintings. In his *Bacchus*, the most notable feature is the precise characterization of a group of inveterate tipplers. In *Vulcan's Forge* he depicts with great accuracy an ironsmith's workshop in which the only false and postiche figure is the Apollo, who looks as if he has strayed from classical fable into our everyday world. The best works belong to the later years. During his second stay in Rome he painted the stupendous portrait of Pope Innocent x, and two little pictures in a style which without exaggeration can be called impressionistic. Velázquez interpreted reality not according to the dictates of temperament but of reason. Problems of perspective had been solved long ago; something infinitely difficult remained to be done – to paint the atmosphere in which figures moved, the air bathed with light which fills space. This was the great achievement of *Las Hilanderas* and above all of *Las Meninas*, pictures which convey an unsurpassable sensation of reality.

Despite the loss of Velázquez to Madrid, Seville continued as the greatest centre of painting in the peninsula. It was the workplace of Zurbarán from Extremadura, painter of saints in ecstasy and monks in white habits. His spiritual intensity was combined with a realism which delights in depicting rich clothing, leather seats, books and flowers. The *chiaroscuro* influence did not prevent his employing a full range of colours. Among his most celebrated works are the great collection of canvases of the monastery of Guadalupe, and the delightful Saint Margaret in the National Gallery in London.

Bartolomé Esteban Murillo (1618–82), the best known of the painters of the Seville school, for long enjoyed an esteem which impeded a more perfect appreciation of his work, since part of his output found its way into private English collections and could not easily be inspected. From the beginning of the present century, as the stock of Velázquez, Goya and Greco rose, that of Murillo declined and he was branded as mannered and sickly sweet. This reaction went too far: Murillo may not be the greatest of Spanish painters, but he is by no means a negligible figure. In sheer technique he is scarcely inferior to Velázquez, and like him succeeded on his own in finding a style which could be called impressionistic. His gentle, devout temperament made him the ideal artist for portraying the Immaculate Conception, through a series of sweet feminine figures surrounded by angels. Fond of the Franciscans, poor and humble like them, he painted a great deal for their convents, and it could even be said that he sacrificed his life for them, since he died as the result of a fall while working on an altarpiece in the Franciscan convent in Cadiz. There is no theatrical or pessimistic touch to his art, but instead a sincere faith allied to a healthy and sunny realism. This is typified by the street urchins eating fruit, who despite the rags which cover them brim over with life and happiness.

The tragic side to the Baroque, ignored by Murillo, was by contrast the favourite genre of Valdés Leal, a man of violent and gloomy disposition. His painting is uneven, but full of dramatic intensity. Some of it is decidedly macabre, like the two great canvases he painted for the hospital of the Santa Caridad at Seville by commission of its founder Miguel Mañara, a rich merchant who mended his ways after a stormy youth and left his money to charity. The instruction to portray the vanity and wretchedness of earthly existence and the inexorable triumph of death (a very frequent theme in the Baroque) is executed with unparalleled intensity. In one of the canvases a skeleton carrying the scythe and a coffin snuffs out the flame of life; the other takes us into a burial vault where amid the gloom we can glimpse the worm-eaten bodies of prelates and knights. Not even the most consummate art can make such horror beautiful.

THE POLITICAL EMPIRE OVERSEAS

The complexity of the history of Spain in the modern period is enormously increased by the fact that she was also the head of a great American empire. To give an adequate treatment to this subject is beyond the scope of the present study, but some reference to it, however brief, is indispensable since otherwise it is impossible to understand the political and economic life of Spain under the Habsburgs. The aim of these last three chapters is to consider the empire primarily in terms of its effects on the development of peninsular Spain. They attempt to cover the *Conquista* and the subsequent colonization, the more important economic development, and finally what we may call 'spiritual imperialism'.

By 1517 the initial exploratory phase was well advanced. In a quarter of a century the West Indies had been reconnoitred as well as almost the entire Atlantic coast of the continent from the peninsula of Florida, sighted by Ponce de León in 1512, to the Río de la Plata, where Solís met his death at the hands of the natives in 1516. A few years later Lucas Vázquez de Ayllón and Esteban Gómez explored the mean latitudes of the coast of the modern United States, linking the Spanish discoveries with those made by Cabot, Verrazzano and Cartier in the far north. The *Mundus Novus* was expanding in all its vastness before the astonished gaze of Europeans. The discovery of the 'South Sea' (the Pacific Ocean) by Vasco Núñez de Balboa in 1513 had put paid for good to the idea of Columbus' time that the discovered lands were dependencies of Asia. They appeared at first as a screen, a tiresome obstacle or at best a stepping-stone towards the regions where silk, ivory and spice abounded. The refusal to abandon the old idea of going west to reach the East meant voyages in search of the northwest passage, blocked by ice, and the southwest passage, eventually opened by Magellan. The true dimensions of the Pacific and the globe were revealed by this first voyage of circumnavigation. When on 8 September 1522 after three years at sea Juan Sebastián Elcano reached Seville at the head of eighteen exhausted survivors, geography was enriched by the most important contribution yet made to it by man. At the same time the dream of a short, easy route by sea to the Far East was dispelled. Instead of economic and cultural contacts with China and Japan a much more exciting prospect was set before Europe: to Europeanize an entire continent, thus establishing the bases for an enduring supremacy of the white races and of western civilization.

A task as great as this could have used the combined efforts of the European nations as a whole, but they were for a time unaware of the opportunities before them and anyway had no inclination to pool their resources. The affairs of the Atlantic interested only the powers of western Europe. The contribution of Italy was hampered by political weakness, that of France by the Wars of Religion, while Holland was too small to send settlers in any great number and confined herself to gathering the crumbs by exploiting the new lands economically. England, by contrast, founded authentic colonies, but at a later stage and with limited objectives, having no interest in what was going on across the Alleghenies. The result was that, ultimately, it was Spain and Portugal who were left with the task of exploring, conquering and peopling the greater part of the continent from California and Florida to Cape Horn.

It is hard to see how Spain could have claimed and maintained supremacy over the greater part of America. The decisive factor was that the undertaking was conceived from the outset as a state enterprise, and the Spanish state was strong, both in terms of military power and advanced administrative organization. If the disastrous reign of Henry IV had not been followed by the reforming period of the Catholic Kings the fate of the world would have been very different, for Spain would not have discovered America, or, having discovered it, would not have been able to hold on to it. With the same iron hand as he used to restore order at home Ferdinand the Catholic asserted the Spanish monopoly over the New World. This was the motive behind his attempt to obtain the famous bulls of Alexander VI, while the creation of the Casa de Contratación was to enable the state to control men and merchandise crossing the Atlantic. Subsequent kings yielded not an inch of their political and economic monopoly of the overseas possessions. This exclusiveness (which was not a Spanish invention but a feature of the age) explains the 'official secrets' law relating to voyages of exploration and to the maps recording discoveries, the censorship of historical and geographical works, and also the draconian orders against foreigners found without permission west of the Canaries (they were to be hanged on the spot).[1]

When America stopped being considered a route or a passage and became an end in itself, mere exploration gave way to conquest and colonization. In fact the *Conquista*, despite its overtones of myth, was but a brilliant, short episode (some twenty years long), a phase of the exploration involving some use of arms. At the beginning of the reign of Charles v only a tiny area of the continent had been occupied, just the Isthmus of Panama; humid, unhealthy, covered by dense jungle and unsuited to white colonization on any considerable scale. The situation in the islands was none too satisfactory either. The native population was declining at the same rate as the alluvial gold, and the settlers were not at all keen to become farmers: to come to this pass, they said, they need not have left Spain.

The organization of expeditions into the distant hinterland of the continent was due as much to a hankering after more promising horizons as to the thirst for action and adventure which kept these men continually on the move. The immigrant population of Cuba and Hispaniola was still very small: a few thousand men, almost all of military age, very few of whom had put down permanent roots in the West Indies. It was an amateur army in embryo, with an unsuspected capacity for war which was to be revealed very shortly in the shattering overthrow of the Aztec and Inca empires, the two great political formations of native America.

These two empires, despite their great size, covered less than a tenth part of the total surface area of America, most of which was uninhabited or populated only by tribes at a very low level of civilization. In comparison with these the Aztecs and the Incas had attained a high standard of development; but compared with the Europeans their inferiority was abysmal, for in certain vital respects they were even more retarded than the Celts and Germans of Tacitus' time. They were ignorant of the wheel; precious metals were the only kind they forged; they had no writings,[2] no scientific thought and no religion with any ethical content. These basic deficiencies outweighed their grandiose constructions in stone and the notable progress made by their spade agriculture. Their most serious fault, perhaps, was that these 'anthill civilizations' did not encourage the development of personality, so that when the supreme test came they showed themselves extraordinarily fragile. Once the nerve centre was destroyed the masses submitted, whereas other more primitive and more individualistic peoples held out stubbornly against the Spaniards.

The Aztec empire comprised only a part of the present state of Mexico. Its centre was the highlands of the meseta of Anahuac and its capital, Tenochtitlán, comparable in size to the biggest town in Europe at the time, rose where Mexico City stands today. The poor drainage of its waters meant that it was then a sort of American Venice. The Aztecs had conquered these territories at a comparatively recent date (the fourteenth century) and had formed a confederation of a strongly hierarchical and militarist character which exercised an often nominal control over outlying and disaffected tribes. At the moment the Spaniards set foot in the territory, Moctezuma II ruled the confederation.

News of the existence of this rich and powerful empire had reached the island of Cuba through the dispatch of short expeditions to reconnoitre the coast. Diego Velázquez, governor of the island, decided to try to conquer it. He gathered an expeditionary force together and placed at its head his former secretary, Hernán Cortés.

Just before Cortés set out his chief, sensing that he would not be content with a subordinate role, repented of his choice and attempted to replace him – too late. The first act of Cortés on putting foot on Mexican soil was to found a town, Veracruz; the step had a legal rather than a material significance, referring to medieval democratic traditions which conferred a wide-ranging autonomy on a municipality. In the presence of the town council formed by his comrades in arms Cortés resigned the command he held from Velázquez and was reappointed, with no obligation now to obey his former chief. This concern for legal forms is not just to be explained by the intellectual training of Cortés, at one time a student of law at Salamanca and an attorney: it emerges at every step in the great adventure of the *Conquista*, which at first sight seems to obey no other law than that of the strongest. It was present even in the laughable form of the *requerimiento*, a summons before seizing possession, read out to groups of ragged and astonished Indians who understood never a word.

Cortés' band was absurdly small: five hundred men with sixteen horses and a few firearms. They included the odd supporter of governor Velázquez and others who considered the enterprise hare-brained. To make sure no one thought of turning back Cortés had the boats scuttled in secret; this was a less spectacular affair than it was later portrayed in legend, but it served its purpose of leaving no alternative to death or victory. It is impossible to say what the outcome of the bold undertaking would have been if the millions of natives had been united; but many of them detested the Aztec dominion and joined the Spaniards. The warlike Tlascaltecas did so, after attempting resistance. The advance of the Spanish force on Tenochtitlán along a very difficult route was determined more by political considerations than by the imperatives of geography.

The Spaniards to all appearances were not coming under a flag of war; they manifested their desire to visit the Aztec emperor. But the emperor's embassies, laden with costly gifts, failed in their object of getting them to turn back. On 8 November 1519 they entered the capital, amid the curiosity, expectancy and fear of the natives, who saw in them the 'white gods' whose coming was foretold by an ancient tradition. Though the welcome was a friendly one Cortés realized that his position was unsafe, not to say desperate, isolated as he was in the middle of a vast empire. Only a stroke of daring could save him, and on the pretext of an attack on the garrison of Veracruz he seized Moctezuma and forced him to declare himself a vassal of the king of Spain.

There was not much hope of this unusual situation being resolved peacefully, as by the establishment of a protectorate. What hope there was was shattered by the impatience and brutality of some of Cortés' captains. Cortés had had to leave the capital in order to counter an expedition which the duped governor of Cuba had dispatched against his insubordinate lieutenant; he had little trouble overcoming the small force and incorporating it into his own. But on his return to Tenochtitlán he found the place in arms against the Spaniards, who had treated the natives roughly and destroyed their bloodthirsty idols, hungry for human sacrifices. This truly reckless act on the part of an isolated handful of individuals stemmed from missionary zeal, mixed with proud disdain for the native whose capacity for retaliation was unknown. Respect for the white man and his semi-divine aura had vanished, and bloody fighting ensued. Moctezuma, who tried to calm the revolt, was stoned to death and the Spaniards had to make a frantic escape by night in which they lost many men. However the Spaniards had so decisive a superiority that the feeble remnant of their retreating army vanquished the pursuing Indians at Otumba, though the Indians had a hundred times more men.

The support of the Tlascaltecas allowed Cortés to regroup his forces and with some reinforcements from Cuba to march on the capital once again. What had been planned as a sudden coup turned into a long and terribly bloody siege, for the Aztecs under their new sovereign Cuautemoc offered a desperate resistance. But once Tenochtitlán fell all the rest of the empire submitted almost without resistance (1521).

The conquest of Peru was largely a result of the exciting successes in Mexico and affords quite a few parallels with the Mexican campaign. Its leader, Francisco Pizarro, was not a young and cultivated man like Cortés but a rude *conquistador* who had reached maturity without attaining a position of any distinction. He and his comrade Almagro found a moneyed associate in the cleric Luque, and starting out from the Isthmus of Panama made voyages of discovery along the Pacific coast of South America, lured by reports of the existence of a fabulously rich native empire. On establishing the truth of the rumour Pizarro went to Spain for the purpose of legalizing his future conquest and obtained from Charles v the title of governor of the lands he would conquer. Almagro, meanwhile, was pushed into the background, and this sowed the seeds of a rivalry between the two partners which was to erupt at a later date.

Despite the brilliant promises in store the white population was so small, provisions in such short supply and the dangers to be overcome so great that the expedition which left Panama in 1531 was even weaker and smaller than that captained by Cortés: barely three hundred men, whose number was soon further reduced by hunger and the fatigue of the journey. After a lengthy voyage along what are now the coasts of Colombia and Peru the expeditionaries penetrated inland and found the Inca emperor Atahualpa in Cajamarca. The Inca empire was even more extensive than the Aztec, more paternalistic, less militarist, with a sort of state socialism which made possible the great monuments whose remains are a source of awe to this day, and the highways which cross the giddy heights of the Andes. But the Incas were to prove more passive than the Aztecs and incapable of challenging any authority, even one imposed by an act of force. Pizarro planned to take advantage of this trait in the native soul so as to carry through an enterprise which seemed at first sight sheer folly.

As in Mexico, the Spaniards made their entry to all appearances under a flag of peace, prepared to explain to the native monarch the reasons why he ought to accept the spiritual authority of the pope and the temporal authority of the king of Spain. But whereas Moctezuma awaited the Spaniards in his capital, full of apprehension and cowed, as it were, beforehand, Atahualpa went out to meet the Spaniards with such a numerous and well-armed following that his intention to arrest the daring visitors could scarcely be mistaken. The scene which took place on a November day in 1532 in the square at Cajamarca is one of those in which the facts are more incredible than the wildest fancy. When Pizarro learned that the Inca was coming at the head of 40,000 men he realized that only an act of daring could save him. He hid the 180 men and the few horses comprising his entire force in the buildings overlooking the square, while he took up his position in the centre beside a chaplain and an Indian interpreter. The great square filled with Indians, jammed so tightly together that they could hardly move. In the middle stood Atahualpa, flanked by his dignitaries. The chaplain advanced towards him with a Bible in his hand and told him they came from the other side of the ocean, where the most powerful sovereign on earth reigned, so as to inform him of the true religion and invite him to accept the sovereignty of the king of Spain. Atahualpa, who cannot have understood a word of this strange message, replied with words full of arrogance and contempt. He grabbed the Bible, flicked through it and threw it on the ground. It is more than likely – though the confusion of the moment makes it uncertain – that he then gave the order for his followers to seize the Spaniards. At a signal from Pizarro the Spaniards emerged from their hiding-places; the few who had fire-arms blazed away with their arquebuses, the rest attacked with their drawn swords, and the horses trampled the Indians who, in their surprise and terror, thought only of flight. The incident which decided the fate of a mighty empire had lasted only a few minutes. In the square there remained only the little group of Spaniards, the dead or wounded Indians, and the captive Inca.

What followed was but an epilogue – the attempt of Atahualpa to free himself by means of a large ransom, the vacillations over what to do with an embarrassing prisoner, his judicial assassination on feeble pretexts but in reality for reasons of state. The assassination is an indelible blot on the memory of Francisco Pizarro and even more on that of Almagro who insisted most on the execution. Finally there was the march on Cuzco and the easy suppression of feeble attempts at resistance. Cortés had built the Spanish capital on the site of the native one; but Cuzco, situated at 3,500 metres' altitude on a plateau of the Andes, was out of the way and inconvenient. Pizarro substituted it with a newly created capital, Lima, on the coastal plain (1535).

From these two centres of Mexico and Peru expeditions of exploration and conquest fanned out in every direction at such a pace that by the middle of the sixteenth century the general configuration of Spanish America was that which it was to keep for three centuries. The occupation was not uniform; instead there was a series of little islands linked together by a weak chain of strongholds, in the intervals of which stretched vast, empty spaces. The greatest of these empty spaces was the Amazonian region, whose limitless reaches separated the Spanish settlements of the Andes from the Portuguese on the coast of Brazil. The jungle, high mountains and arid lands were crossed often enough (even the Amazon was soon navigated by Orellana); but they rarely attracted much of a stable population.

The natural milieu, then, was a factor in the distribution of Spanish settlement on American soil. But as important, or more so, were sociological considerations, particularly the distribution and standard of living of the natives. Excellent arable land was ignored because it was uninhabited or occupied only by scattered bands of Indians. In their continual travels the discoverers were looking not so much for land, which was everywhere abundant, as for Indians, the wealthy Indian, civilized, submissive, ready to give his lord gold, or labour at least. The growth of this mentality was no doubt influenced by the sight of the large fortunes amassed by the *conquistadores* of Mexico and Peru. The continent was scoured from end to end in the search of other civilizations akin to these; but they did not exist, and the success of the other *conquistadores* was much less than that of Cortés or Pizarro. The Maya civilization of Yucatán was exhausted after centuries of splendour, Guatemala and the rest of central America were no more than an impoverished annex of Mexico. The islands, with their alluvial gold exhausted and the native population depleted, lost all their attraction, and their population fell so dramatically that foreign pirates were able to occupy several of them without any difficulty. The coast of Venezuela, though reconnoitred at an early date and boasting several towns, led a listless existence until the eighteenth century, and the interior remained almost wholly void. The present territory of Colombia was the seat of a native civilization which, if much less advanced than those of Mexico or Peru, was by no means negligible. This Chibcha culture depended on a rudimentary agriculture and the practice of a few trades (precious metals, ceramics). At this crossroads of several different routes a junction was effected by Belalcázar, a former captain of Pizarro, who had already conquered Quito and continued his advance north; Federman, one of the Germans to whom Charles v had made a grant in Venezuela; and the Granadan Gonzalo Jiménez de Quesada, who went up the Río Magdalena with his companions, amassed a rich booty and founded Santa Fe de Bogotá (1538).

The Spanish empire in America never had precise boundaries. In law the Spanish government believed itself the master of the whole New World apart from the coast of Brazil which had been assigned to the Portuguese by the Treaty of Tordesillas. In practice its shifting boundaries were determined by a no-man's-land beyond which there was nothing to attract the discoverers. The presence of rich mineral deposits brought the Spaniards to the north of Mexico, but in the immense plains which today form part of the southwest of the United States they found nothing of particular interest. After several deep thrusts into the interior which brought to light some of the basic features of the geography of that part of the world (Mississippi river, Colorado canyon, deserts of Arizona and New Mexico) these vast regions were left to themselves. It was only at a later period, when the human potential was greater, that several extremely feeble and scattered claims were staked, which were sufficient however to give the region an enduring Hispanic character.

In the extreme south, too, it was not the difficulties of the physical milieu which checked the advance of the *conquistadores*. The frozen heights of the Andes and the fearful solitudes of the desert of Atacama failed to deter Almagro's men, who sought in the present territory of Chile a prize comparable to that which Pizarro's band obtained in Peru. It was the presence of impoverished and warlike Indians rather than the rigours of nature which discouraged them, for no immediate profits were to be expected from these tribes. But the growing awareness that there were no more El Dorados to be found did not impede the Spanish advance: though at a slower rate, it continued in proportion as the permanent riches of the soil began to replace the lure of booty which was gained one day and gone the next. The territory of Chile, in fact, barren as it was of gold or serviceable Indians, was subjugated after a bloody struggle and an agricultural colonization was begun on the coastal plains, where the climate was like that of Castile. Agrarian settlements were also founded on the plains of the Río de la Plata; an early version of Buenos Aires came to grief, while the second and definitive foundation (1580) long remained a tiny oasis with very precarious communications linking it to upper Peru. Meanwhile Patagonia (like the southern tip of Chile) stayed as an unoccupied 'land's end' until the nineteenth century.

The few thousand men who in less than half a century managed to occupy territories which appear vast even to us with our modern means of communication must have been motivated by very compelling urges. The psychology of the *conquistadores* has been analysed often enough, with conflicting results: they have been seen as gangs of bandits and as crusaders for an ideal, and there is a whole range of intermediate interpretations. A certain number of objective facts exist, on which everyone must agree. Between 1500 and 1535, 5,500 persons left for America with official authorization. One must take into account those who had arrived earlier and those who went without licence, while discounting those who stayed on in the islands without adventuring on to the continent. In other words the New World was explored and conquered with the strength of one brigade; nothing gives a better measure of the distance between European civilization and even the most advanced Indian cultures. A large proportion came from Extremadura, a poor sheep-rearing region. Cortés, Pizarro, Valdivia and Orellana were Extremadurans. The Castilians came partly from lands bordering on Extremadura with a very similar physical and human milieu. Thus Almagro, though his birthplace is uncertain, appears to have been a native of the town of that name, and the Vázquez Coronado were from Salamanca. The Andalusians, though they furnished the majority of the settlers, can boast few outstanding figures. By contrast, there are several Basques of note, to be explained perhaps by their seafaring tradition. Catalonia remained on the sidelines of the discovery more from voluntary abstention than legal restrictions, which would not have been difficult to circumvent.

The social background of the discoverers, with rare exceptions, was not of the highest in society, but there was no preponderance of the low-born. The lead was taken by an intermediate class of *hidalgos* – second sons, soldiers and officials. Their cultural level was not as low as has been alleged. This is proved by the abundant historical writings of the *conquistadores* themselves; the fact that in such a small band of men one finds a respectable number of writers – some of them, like Gonzalo Fernández de Oviedo, Jímenez de Quesada and Ercilla, with a place of their own in Spanish literature – is an irrefutable argument against those who would represent the *Conquista* as the work of a horde of illiterates.

The very fact of engaging in adventures so full of peril itself involved a selection that weeded out the timid and even the prudent. The dangers and calamities suffered by these men passes all reckoning. The attempt to conquer vast empires with such unequal forces was a rash enterprise in itself. The possession of horses and of a few small-range firearms was a moral rather than a material advantage. As Parry says, referring to the army of Cortés: 'The arms and the equipment were as heterogeneous as the men; they included few weapons which in Europe would have been considered modern, and they certainly did not, in themselves, confer an overwhelming superiority upon the Spanish forces.'[3] It was rather moral factors that decided the struggle; and the Spaniards, who despised the Indians for their passivity and fatalism, had no hesitation about fighting against odds of a hundred to one. They respected the warlike qualities of the Araucanos and praised them in epic poems, of which Ercilla's 'La Araucana' is only the best known by virtue of its literary merit. Much more than by the arrows, clubs and darts of the Indians, they were scourged by the rigours of a hostile nature, by the icy and rarefied atmosphere of the high altitudes, the burning heat of the tropics, the swampy plains, the fevers, the swarms of insects, the hunger which occasionally forced them to eat the most loathsome creatures. The march of Almagro on Chile and that of Alvarado across the snow-capped Andes, from whose volcanoes ash rained down, were dazzling feats. What compelling motives could they have had for braving such dangers? The desire for gain, of course – not in the sense of greed, but as a way of asserting their identity, of obtaining positions of command and honours, of excelling and rising to become leaders. Only thus can we explain why many men who would have enjoyed a tranquil, easy existence engaged in new and terrible adventures. Ambition, the thirst for command, for acquiring nobility and renown, for leaving an honoured name behind – these were ideals of the Renaissance Spaniard, and he found in the Discoveries an opportunity to exploit them to the full. Religion was not a decisive factor with the *conquistadores*, but a feature of their lives which is apparent at every step. They did not conquer souls for Christ, like the ecclesiastics, but when they got the chance they replaced the pagan idols with Christian images and even preached sermons to the Indians. These men who scorned their own and others' sufferings were guilty of unjustifiable atrocities. But their Christian upbringing always came through in the end, even if only by way of a bad conscience, a tardy remorse, such as emerges plainly from the will of Pizarro, who bade masses to be said for the souls of Indians killed during the conquest.

Though the American continent afforded limitless horizons for the discoverers and conquerors the primitive obsession with the Asiatic East kept pushing them across the Pacific. Spaniards coming from America and Portuguese arriving by way of the Cape of Good Hope met each other in the antipodes of the Iberian peninsula, in those spice islands (*Maluco*, Moluccas) which Charles v recognized as belonging to Portugal in exchange for a cash indemnity. The Far East continued to be a preserve of Portugal, but with an important Castilian outpost:

the Philippine Islands, named after Philip II, in whose reign
Legazpi and Urdaneta founded Manila and began the colonization of that distant territory. All across the Pacific numerous
islands were sighted by Spanish sailors, but few were permanently occupied. The name of one of these sailors is preserved
in the Torres strait on the northern coast of Australia. It is also
a moot point whether the present name of the continent comes
from *Terra Australis Incognita* or from the House of Austria, in
whose name the navigator Fernández de Quirós took possession
of those lands in 1606 in nominal fashion and without any
sequel.[4]

These territories of the Pacific were not substantial enough to
be considered separate kingdoms and were amalgamated in the
Indies complex and governed by the Royal and Supreme
Council of the Indies. This body had been set up in 1524 when
it was clearly apparent that the discoveries were not a mere
territorial appendix but a New World. Their legal status within
the vast network of the Spanish monarchy was a very special
one. They were joined to Castile, not as another province, for
they had their own laws and organs of government, but
inasmuch as the hereditary royal title of Castile could not be
divorced from that of the Indies. This was the position regarding
the patrimonial rights of the crown. But in addition the kingdom
of Castile, with whose men and money the discovery had been
made, had the exclusive right of settling and trading in those
parts. Concessions and exemptions eventually granted to other
Hispanic kingdoms did not fundamentally alter the situation.

These territories were known as 'the Indies', and were
divided into two great viceroyalties, Mexico, or New Spain, and
Peru; but they formed an indissoluble whole for legislative
purposes. The same laws were in force from California to the Río
de la Plata, and all the territories were under the supreme
authority of the Council of the Indies, including the Philippines.
The crown looked on these territories as a second Castile, where
it would have liked to set up an ideal system of government,
taking advantage of the absence of historical precedents and
personal and local privileges. It sought for example to achieve
legislative unity, to which there were major obstacles within
Spain. It forbade the formation of a seigneurial regime which
leaned towards feudalism, principally by refusing to allow the
Indian *encomiendas* to become hereditary, despite strong pressure

and offers of money. It tried, though only half successfully, to keep Spanish colonization selective by prohibiting the emigration of elements then regarded as undesirable or suspect – *Moriscos*, Judaizers and foreigners. It also sought, this time with success, to end church-state quarrels over jurisdiction which caused so much trouble in Europe. The *Patronato Real* was instituted, giving it complete control over the church in America in every matter other than dogma.

But the Ideal Society stumbled on the limitations not only of inadequate supervision, administrative corruption and other failings inherent in human nature, but of something basic in the nature of the Indies themselves and their innately heterogeneous character. A fundamental separateness of interest had to be recognized, not from a desire for segregation or for the superiority of the white man over the coloured, but out of respect for the personality of the native and a realistic acknowledgement of the impossibility of subjecting him to identical laws and an identical way of life. Thus there arose the *República de los Indios*, with its characteristic institutions, communal lands, native authorities and peculiar language and customs, and the *República de los Españoles*, which in institutions, norms of government and ideals of conduct did not differ greatly from peninsular Spain. The main preoccupation of the government in Madrid was to see that these two communities, legally equal but distinct, coexisted harmoniously, that the balance did not swing to the detriment of the weaker half, and that a union of the two was fostered by every possible means – a Spanish education for the chiefs' sons, mixed marriages and missionary work that besides its spiritual goal had the auxiliary task of helping the integration of the Indians, which was inconceivable otherwise.

These lands were never termed *colonies*; this was a sophisticated expression which was rarely if at all used in the literature of the age. It would anyway have been very improper to use it in its later sense because the Spanish crown never considered the territories as subordinate. Legally they were no whit inferior to the other parts of the Spanish monarchy. In practice the theory has to be qualified to some extent. It seems evident that Ferdinand the Catholic failed to appreciate the true importance of the recently discovered lands and that he saw them first and foremost as a means of strengthening his finances. Something of this mentality persisted in the attitude of Charles v. But the three Philips who succeeded one another were fully conscious of the value of the Indies in themselves. True, they sought to extract as much money as they could from them (and from their other kingdoms), but they did not strangle their potential for expansion and defence. Ever greater importance was attached to the Atlantic, while Mediterranean problems, including the urgent question of piracy, were neglected. There was no repetition of Charles v's expedition against Algiers. By contrast, expenditure on the defence of the Indies rose to ever greater heights. During the seventeenth century this tendency for revenue to be spent locally combined with a diminishing yield from the mines to produce a drastic falling-off in the sums received by the crown from the Indies. The *volte-face* was complete when, with the loss of the European territories at Utrecht (1713), Madrid's policy concentrated on the defence of those in America.

THE ECONOMIC EMPIRE

For a minority the missionary ideal was uppermost; for the great body of the discoverers the economic consideration had top priority. For statesmen the economy was primarily a function of politics: in the eyes of the government at Madrid the Indies were important for their own sake but were also expected to help shoulder the tremendous burdens of the monarchy. Politically the Indies were very far away: the journey there took months and years. Only goods that weighed little and had a high value could make the crossing of such distances worth while: hence the role of American precious metals as a bond of union between the two parts of the empire separated by the Atlantic, and indeed in creating the outline of a world economy by their dispersal across the globe.

This exceptional importance of mineral wealth is not a feature of Spanish America alone: it is found even in more recent times, minerals being the most profitable and most easily exploited asset in a new country. In America this motive was strengthened by the desire not only of private citizens but of the government to amass as much treasure as quickly as they could and transport it to far-off places. The first means was the booty of the *Conquista* – that is, the expropriation of reserves accumulated over centuries. Then followed the working of mineral deposits. Agriculture and cattle-raising came later and very gradually, giving rise to a more solid economy, though the dream of El Dorado never faded.

The speed with which the economy of America influenced that of Spain and of the world came largely from the potential afforded by its numerous population. We now know, thanks to the model studies of the Berkeley school, that the pre-Colombian population of America was much greater than was once thought. It is true that immense tracts lay virtually empty and that these

comprised probably the greater part of the continent. But the
two great civilizations of Aztec and Inca corresponded to
centres of dense population; the fact has been documented for
Mexico and, less thoroughly, for Peru. By analogy we can sur-
mise that the numerous population of the islands and other
areas with a low cultural level was no figment of the chroniclers'
imagination. If, as appears probable, the Aztec empire had
twenty-five million inhabitants when the Spanish arrived,
America as a whole must have had at least two or three times
that figure.[1]

Comparing these probable estimates with later calculations
we see a dramatic decline which continues into the mid-
eighteenth century, only in the second half of which does the
native population begin to recover its numbers. The Mexican
Indians were a bare 6,300,000 in 1548 and a little over a million
in 1605. In the continent of South America the population
seems to have held out better; but even reducing the figures
proposed by Borah and his school (accepted by such magisterial
authorities as Chaunu and Braudel) one cannot dispute the
reality of the demographic collapse of the American population
after the arrival of the Europeans. The responsibility is only in
small degree attributable to the direct consequences of the
Conquista, which was accomplished in a series of speedy coups
involving a relatively slight number of human casualties. Nor
was there any systematic persecution of the Indians, not only
because of moral considerations but for selfish reasons, inasmuch
as the Spaniards aimed to live at the expense of the Indians.
Forced labour may have wrought havoc in certain places and at
certain periods. But the principal factors behind the mortality
were biological, especially lack of immunity to smallpox and
other diseases introduced by the European. The devastating
consequences of the epidemics of the second half of the sixteenth
century are perfectly documented in the case of New Spain. The
competition of cattle, man's rival for food, is another factor
which cannot be overlooked. *Mestizaje* also had a part to
play, since every mestizo (person of white and Indian parentage)
born was a potential Indian less. Lastly, the effect of psychological factors should not be neglected: the collective depression
which settles on a people subjugated by another whose cultural
level is too high for assimilation, so that it finds itself suddenly
deprived of the norms and ideals which had informed its life. It

is a well-known phenomenon which has been often repeated in history.

Compared with this massive decline in the native population the immigration of Spaniards represented only a feeble counterbalance. Castile could afford only small contingents. These provided the nucleus of an ascendancy, but were incapable of colonizing such vast territories on any intensive scale. Only in a few scantily inhabited areas where the climate was particularly favourable, like the temperate mesetas of Costa Rica or the plains of Río de la Plata, did white settlement geared to agriculture take place. These white islands are even today the exception in Hispanic America. In the majority of cases the Spaniards overlaid or mingled with the existing population, giving rise to mestizo masses which comprise the highest percentage of the population in Mexico and the countries of the Andes. At the same time, as a purely white minority their numbers grew with surprising speed, reaching perhaps 300,000 in 1600 and more than twice that figure by the end of the seventeenth century. This increase was attributable mainly to natural factors, because emigration was always sluggish and the Spanish government, except in special circumstances, tended rather to restrict than encourage it.[2]

The conquest introduced yet another racial element: the African Negroes, brought there to supplement the Indians, whom the crown protected as being its own vassals, unlike the Africans. There was another, more prosaic consideration as well: the inaptitude of the American Indian for labour, a fact attested by all the sources. The Negroes, though harshly treated, displayed greater vitality, greater capacity for survival, behaving, as Chaunu tells us, as masters towards the Indians, who had to be protected by legal enactments against those who were inferior before the law. Negroes, mestizos and mulattoes showed a healthy demographic expansion from the outset, filling the gaps left by the natives, who only slowly and some time later recovered from the loss of their manpower in the sixteenth century. It was Negroes and mulattoes who made possible tropical plantation agriculture (cane-sugar, above all) in a physical milieu which made sustained activity out of the question for white men.

In other areas it was not physical obstacles but social prejudice which prevented Spaniards from working. Where the climate permitted and the Indian population was scarce, as in the islands, Chile, Costa Rica and Río de la Plata, white settlements grew up with the primary aim of cultivating the soil. By contrast, where a coloured population predominated they were left with the most tedious tasks and work was deemed beneath the whites, just because it was being done by other races. The latter were judged inferior on social and legal rather than ethnic grounds: the Negroes because of their slave origin; the Indians, against whom in principle no racial prejudice existed, because of their apathy, personal neglect and the squalor of their lives; the mestizos and mulattoes because they bore the stigma of their origins. Thus in time a carefully differentiated hierarchy evolved which took pigmentation of the skin as its basis, though originally the classifications were made with regard to economic and social rather than racial criteria.

This unpromising development had its repercussion on the economy, augmenting the numbers and relative weight of the idle class while attracting a partly legal, partly clandestine immigration of foreigners who exercised the functions neglected by the Spaniards. The struggle for *encomiendas* and administrative appointments grew steadily more acute as well, with the opposition between creoles (Spaniards born in America) and peninsular Spanish becoming very plain from an early date. The bickerings and recriminations contained the unmistakeable germ of dissatisfaction and subsequent separation.[3]

If the peninsular Spaniard was above all a functionary, the high-ranking creole was an *encomendero* and rural proprietor. Europe saw America as a producer of precious metals, since this was almost all she exported; but cattle and tillage were much more important for the American economy. Cattle were practically unknown before the discovery, while tillage was improved by a great number of plants of European origin. F. Chevalier has given an unparalleled account of this development in the viceroyalty of New Spain: the formation of the great domains, the ruin of the little native holdings, the steady rise of the cattle *estancias* and their evident connection with the depopulation of the country, for as manpower grew scarce agriculture had to be confined to very extensive holdings or make room for the herds which needed even fewer hands. In turn this replacement of arable land by pasture, of man by beast, aggravated the crisis of the Amerindian population. In South

America the efforts of the rulers to preserve the agrarian patrimony of the natives met with better results, a development which should be related to the greater capacity for survival of the Inca race, as a consequence perhaps of the almost inaccessible refuges afforded by the Andes chain.

Only a small fraction of these riches and this population actually influenced the economy of Spain and the world. America was no longer the isolated world it had been before 1492, but it was still semi-closed and self-sufficient to a very marked degree. Even within it relations between the various parts were slight, and the metropolis had obvious reasons for hindering exchanges between northern and southern America. Access to the Pacific was also partly blocked, confined to the famous *Acapulco Ship* or *Manila Galleon*. Unrestricted communications with the Far East would have dried the stream of precious metals flowing towards Spain, since America had almost nothing to export apart from her silver.[4]

The Spanish government never tried to enforce a state monopoly in the American trade like that of the Portuguese with regard to spices. It confined itself to controlling the movement of men and merchandise, with the double aim of protecting the Castilian economy and the interests of the royal treasury. In order to get a true idea of the Spanish-American trade of the colonial epoch it is essential not to exaggerate its volume. In the most prosperous years the Spanish ships crossing the Atlantic came to hardly over 35,000 tons, the equivalent of a not very big boat of today. The number of Spanish immigrants to America during three centuries was not as great as that leaving Spain for the same destination in the first twenty years of this century. As for the output of gold and silver, the quantities registered on their arrival in Seville seem very modest by modern standards. According to Hamilton, 185,000 kilos of gold (less than the *annual* output of the mines of South Africa) and 16,886,000 kilos of silver (equal to two years' world production at the present day) reached Seville between 1503 and 1660. These figures will come as no surprise if we remember that the American commerce was in the hands of under half a million whites, and that the native masses hardly impinged on the world economy. Yet in spite of everything this trade did have a notable impact on the Old World, an indication of the difference in scale but also of the hypersensitive nature of the point of contact – the monetary medium, whose scarcity hampered the Renaissance economy.

In the climate of opinion of the Mercantilist epoch it shocked no one that Spain and Portugal kept the profits of the Indies trade for themselves. Far-sighted Spaniards, in turn, realized that it was impossible to exclude foreigners altogether. After Charles v no more concessions were made of the kind he had granted to the Welser in Venezuela; but numerous foreigners were able to engage in trade, whether directly by acquiring Castilian citizenship or indirectly by selling their products to Seville merchants for shipment to the Indies. While Seville (and later Cadiz) held the monopoly of commerce with the Indies, they favoured foreign importers and acted as their allies against Spanish producers and against the government which preferred to restrict imports to prevent the export of precious metals. Curiously enough, even an official body like the Casa de Contratación took the merchant's side in this affair. In this way the much-vaunted Spanish commercial monopoly became simply the right of collecting a trading commission and a few moderate fiscal dues on merchandise. Let us see, very briefly, how this situation arose.

As American demand grew after the conquest of Mexico and Peru, the production of the requisite foodstuffs, especially wine, expanded in the area round Seville. In the industrial sphere the repercussions were more widely reaching, extending to the major textile centres of Andalusia (Córdoba, Granada), of the Meseta (Toledo) and even the east (Valencian silks). For reasons examined in an earlier chapter this invigorating influence of the Discovery on Castilian industry was short-lived. Foreign industry, less affected by rising costs and guild impediments, produced more efficiently and more cheaply. For this reason the merchants of Seville were interested in buying articles of import, while the fact that many of these Seville and Cadiz traders were of foreign extraction (Genoese, French, Flemings, English) and kept in touch with their former homeland could not but assist this development. The inadequacy of domestic production became so manifest from the end of the sixteenth century that often enough the fleets delayed their departure because of the non-arrival of foreign shipping with the goods to supply them.

In the light of this situation it is not strange that many

Spaniards asked themselves if the Discovery had been really a benefit, if the treasures which had barely reached the peninsula before they disappeared beyond the frontiers compensated for the decline of population, the rising cost of living and other sinister effects for which, rightly or wrongly, it was blamed. Antonio Pérez claimed that the Discovery had been 'a punishment from heaven'.[5] González de Cellorigo thought that the Indies trade had ruined the commerce which Spain had hitherto engaged in with other kingdoms.[6] The *Junta del Almirantazgo* in a report submitted in 1628 suggested that the 'Indies have been the cause whereby these kingdoms find themselves with few inhabitants, no silver and a burden of commitments and expenses, serving as a bridgehead for the transfer of silver to other kingdoms, all of which would have stayed in these if what went to the Indies were of our harvesting or manufacture.'[7] In fact the silver arriving for the king promptly went to keep his endless wars going; while the greater part of the private silver flowed abroad in payment for the outward cargoes to the Indies and for imports into Spain herself, for Spain's favourable balance of trade with the Indies served to check her unfavourable one with the rest of Europe.

Since the participation of foreigners in the American trade was important and amply tolerated it may be asked why contraband grew to the extent it did. In part, it was aimed at avoiding payment of the commissions charged by Seville and royal taxes; in part too at exporting gold and silver freely from Spain, a practice which was discouraged by the government, who preferred foreigners to take payment in Spanish products. And to a large extent it was due to the semi-permanent state of war between Spain, Holland, France and England. Even despite the war they continued sending goods to Spain with the complicity of the authorities; but when the Spanish state grew feeble they preferred to put their commodities directly into the Indies, where they could be sure of a tolerant and friendly reception from those who shared in the profits of such unlawful commerce.

Contraband, then, took many forms. It could be conducted under entirely lawful semblances by means of Spanish intermediaries who lent their name and traded on behalf of the foreigner. Another form was to send merchandise in the legal manner and then, on the return of the fleets, transfer the silver before it reached Cadiz or Seville to boats waiting to take it abroad. A finer point was put on this practice by the Dutch after the Peace of Westphalia: their boats waited in the Bay of Cadiz for the fleet to collect and then loaded their goods aboard without registering them, and in the same fashion took off the silver on the return journey. All these manœuvres were facilitated by the complicity of the guards, who received a bonus on top of their miserably low wages in exchange. Another factor was the substitution of Seville by Cadiz as the point of departure and arrival for the fleets. It is true that the river of Seville was not adapted to a trade which was using ever bigger vessels. When ships of over five hundred tons became standard it was a difficult business putting to sea from the Guadalquivir; sometimes the vessels had to be towed by galleys. The return was worse still, with quite a few boats coming to grief on the sands at the mouth of the river. But aside from these natural obstacles the interest of foreign merchants in eluding efficient control also played a large part in the change-over.

When smuggling was not possible or not enough the nations at war with Spain resorted to armed attack. Against these attacks the Spanish Indies displayed an amazing capacity for resistance; they were protected by their very vastness, their remoteness, and the fact that their principal centres lay inland. Mexico and Peru were invulnerable. The ports of the West Indies suffered occasionally, but the Indies as a whole, with a minimum of resources, held out resolutely against a host of enemies. The attacks on the fleets had little success either: only on one occasion did the Dutch capture the *flota* of New Spain (Matanzas 1628) and only one other fleet fell into the hands of the English (Tenerife 1657). The losses inflicted by nature were higher than those caused by man. On the whole the system of merchant fleets escorted by men-of-war (the heavy galleons) functioned satisfactorily from its inception in 1563. As for private piratical assaults (freebooters, buccaneers) mounted from a few uninhabited islands, these were encouraged by the decline of the Spanish monarchy, which withdrew the *Barlovento* fleet in 1647 owing to political and economic difficulties. Only then did the golden age of piracy begin which, though a nuisance, never became a real threat to the Spanish dominion in the Indies.

Though the percentage of Spanish products in the exports to

the Indies fell right to the end of the seventeenth century, this was not the sole factor in the balance of payments between the two countries. Apart from sums arriving for the royal treasury there were important items classed as 'money for private individuals' which represented net income for Spain. These included *bienes de difuntos* (sums bequeathed by those who died in the Indies to their relatives in the peninsula or to pious endowments) and clerical alms. The most notable alms were those sent by the Mercedarians for the ransom of captives, though other orders also sent money to Spain (and Rome), in part without passing through the official channels.[8] Then there were the occasionally important sums of money brought back by Spaniards who had held ecclesiastical or civil posts in the Indies, as well as remissions in respect of pensions, *encomiendas* and so forth. As long as these items remain unreckoned no one can tell how economically profitable Spain's political control of America actually was.

While the American contribution to the Spanish private purse continued to be considerable, in spite of everything, the part destined for the royal treasury kept falling, for a variety of reasons highlighted by several authors. These reasons were the reduction of the native labour supply, the gradual exhaustion of the mines, the *quintos* from which constituted the soundest of the treasury revenues, and perhaps most important of all the increasing cost of maintaining, administering and defending the Indies themselves, including the Pacific dependencies which were wholly incapable of paying their way. Thus the overseas empire, affected by the seventeenth century economic depression in the same degree as Europe, yielded less and less, while expenditure on it rose to ever greater heights; so the balance in the king's favour, amounting usually in the prosperous years of Philip II and Philip III to two million ducats, fell subsequently to one million, and even less after 1640. The smallness of these figures would seem in conflict with prevailing ideas of the importance of the Indies wealth in the foreign policy of the Habsburgs. In fact it was much less than has been supposed; the greater part of the financial effort was made by peninsular Spain, not by America. However in one respect the American contribution has a major relevance: it furnished silver for foreign settlements, copper money, almost the only kind which circulated within Castile, being unacceptable in Europe.

Fiscal pressure did not produce such devastating effects in the Indies as in Castile. The factors in the Indies recession were, as already indicated, the reduction in the numbers of the Indians, the exhaustion of some of the best mines, and no doubt too, for New Spain, the increasing dryness of the climate towards the end of the sixteenth century, as attested by the study of tree growths. The tax potential of the Indies was low, the Indians being too poor and the whites few in number and less willing to shoulder heavy burdens than those in Castile. The possibility of a bid for independence was never far from the minds of the rulers and helped moderate their demands. This did not prevent sinister social and economic effects flowing from the sale of public office, an expedient which both reduced the competence of the officials and indirectly increased the tax load on the subject, as the illuminating study of Parry has shown.[9]

Taking into account the relatively tiny volume of Spanish-American trade and the important share foreigners had in it, can one talk of a Hispanic economic empire? It has to be borne in mind that just as the different parts of the Habsburg monarchy were autonomous as regards administration, so they constituted separate economic units divided from one another by customs barriers. The fact of belonging to one sovereign did not make for a free interchange of goods, nor did it prevent different monetary units existing side by side. Almost the only mutual commercial advantage was that they were free from the prohibitions, confiscations and surcharges which always threatened the goods of enemy countries. As the country was frequently at war this advantage was an appreciable one, but was not tantamount to constituting a sort of common market. Anything of the kind was far removed from reality and never entered the heads of the Castilian kings. They could not even reach the much more modest goal of fiscal equality among the different parts of their empire.

No economic empire existed, then, nor could it have done so, given the state of technology and transports. But there was a sort of Castilian monetary empire, based on the abundant gold and silver which that kingdom received from the Indies and on the excellent quality of its coinage, which made it prized throughout the world. This monetary empire was more wide-reaching and more enduring than its political counterpart. The golden doubloons and the silver pieces of eight (called also *pesos duros* and *piastras*) were accepted and held everywhere in repute, as the dollar is today and the pound sterling was before that. Throughout the eastern Mediterranean Spanish coin circulated alongside Austrian and Turkish. Delays in the arrival of the fleets at Seville were felt in those parts, and the 'squeeze' in Castile had its repercussions thousands of miles away. Asia as ever was the sponge which soaked up the precious metals of the West; only now it was not Roman *denarii* but Potosí silver which streamed into Turkey, Persia and Sumatra – 'the Spanish dollars are everywhere current', remarked a traveller there – and finished its long odyssey in China, where the king of Spain was known as the 'Silver King' and Spanish *duros* circulated until the last century. In this way American silver created a sort of economic unity in the world.[10]

A SPIRITUAL EMPIRE

As a political empire Spanish America collapsed in 1810–25, though a few bits stayed in place until 1898. The economic empire fell with it, apart from a few persisting links of an economic nature. As a spiritual entity, however, the empire gave proof of an extraordinary capacity for survival, for in the guise of a language, a religion, a personal and collective ethic and a style of life it exists almost unaltered to the present day, just as the Roman influence continued to exist and even expand long after the fall of Rome. André Siegfried wrote:

> Wherever [Spanish civilisation] has been introduced, it still survives. For the last five centuries its frontiers have hardly retreated; there has been virtually no betrayal on the part of those who have ever lived under its sign. At the very portals of the United States, a powerful centre of attraction, Cuba is Spanish, and Mexico too, to the extent that it is not Indian. Even within the forty-eight states, lasting traces of Latin civilization remain imprinted on Florida, Texas, Louisiana, Arizona, New Mexico, California and even Colorado. Spain as a political entity need not be loved; she may even be hated . . . but there is a Hispano-American way of looking at life which stays constant. All the prestige of the Anglo-Saxon world will have no easy task uprooting this preference.[1]

Even in the remote Philippine archipelago, where the Spanish presence was always feeble and Castilian has been brushed aside by English, the Hispanic imprint in terms of customs, norms of conduct, the Catholic religion and the sense of a bond with the western world, is very far from having disappeared.[2]

Nowadays one thinks of language as the strongest bond of this spiritual unity, but in those days religion was more important than language. The case of the Philippines indicates that it is in fact a more sturdy socio-cultural element. At one time it had very pronounced political overtones, since by a chance of history the enemies of the Spanish empire in America were non-Catholics almost without exception. For this reason, even apart from supernatural considerations, the Spanish government strove to impose religious unity while refraining from using pressure to bring about linguistic unity. No doubt it was the friars who paid most attention to the native languages in the effort to spread the gospel; but in the University of Lima, a royal not an ecclesiastical foundation, a chair of Quechua was set up. It was not until the eighteenth century with its incipient nationalism that the government in Madrid manipulated language as a political instrument.[3]

The motivation of human actions is very complex, which makes it futile to debate whether the motives behind the Discovery were of a material or spiritual order. Both had their part to play in differing degree; missionary zeal was no doubt uppermost in the mind of Isabel the Catholic, while in that of her husband Ferdinand, of Columbus himself and of the explorers in general, it took second place to political and economic interests, without being ever totally absent from their cares. The crown did not base its dominion in America on the bulls of Alexander VI, but this did not mean that they were used as a mere diplomatic counter against foreign claims. Their instruction to convert the natives was fulfilled, even to the detriment of the royal finances. In this regard there is nothing improbable about the anecdote attributed to Philip II, who on being told of the high cost of preserving the Philippines compared with what could be got out of them replied that to maintain the Catholic religion in the Philippines he would spend all the revenues of his kingdoms.[4]

The conversion of the natives went through two phases, one violent, the responsibility of the *conquistadores* themselves who cast down idols and banned pagan rites, the other based on preaching and example and associated with the secular and regular clergy. Of course these two phases are not always clearly distinguishable, for there were soldier-missionaries capable of improvising a sermon and ecclesiastics who employed methods of violence. In any event, it is a cause for surprise that so little resistance was put up by the Amerindian religions, in contrast to the stubborn resistance of Islam in Europe, Africa and the Far East, where that other Christian spearhead, the Philippine Islands, could not dislodge it entirely though it did check its advance. At the outset the belief in the divinity of the new arrivals facilitated the acceptance of their religious message; even after it was proved that the whites were mortal they were surrounded by an aura of prestige, and their beliefs were deemed more successful. The rise of the mestizo, as well as political pressure and the example of the traditional authorities, contributed to the rapid spread of the new faith, though its exotic concepts proved hard to assimilate and met with a certain resistance and hostility. The contemptuous words of Atahualpa in Cajamarca have an echo too in the rare literary fragments relating to Indian reactions on first coming into contact with the white man and his gods. They acknowledge that their gods have died, but they are not happy with the gods of the bearded man, 'this True God who comes down from heaven and talks of nothing but sin'.[5] Many things which had been hitherto considered permissible or praiseworthy would from now on be sins. All the vigilance of the authorities and the missionaries would not prevent many of the old rites lingering on as customs or superstitions, barely tinctured with a superficial Christianity, or old beliefs persisting in the less urbanized zones.

The Spaniards had no illusions about the degree of authenticity of the Indian's Catholicism; but they knew that their case was not comparable to that of the *Moriscos* or Judaizers, and hence they did not take a harsh line or subject them to the jurisdiction of the Inquisition. Offences of superstition, witchcraft or idolatry, which would have entailed very heavy penalties for a Spaniard, were punished much more lightly where Indians were involved. The counterpart of this mildness was that, not being recognized as fully responsible persons, they were not full members of the church either. The political distinction between the *República de los Españoles*, full citizens, and the *República de los Indios*, wards and treated as minors, was reproduced on the spiritual plane. The clearest manifestation of the difference was that the Indians were not obliged to compulsory communion once a year since they were deemed to lack the necessary preparation.[6] There were several odd attempts to form a native clergy, but they failed for reasons which are not easy to determine. One thing is certain: the present difficult position of the church in America stems to a large extent from the lack of native clergy.[7]

As a recompense for the toil of the Spanish monarchy in spreading the Gospel, a series of pontifical documents issued by Alexander VI and Julius II granted the kings of Spain the universal patronage of the church in the Indies. How far the pontiffs used this concession to repay favours received from Ferdinand the Catholic is a matter for debate. What can be said is that the Holy See was not aware at the time of the magnitude of the concessions involved, and when it subsequently sought to limit them it was too late. The kings of Spain admitted no restriction of their prerogatives in this respect. So far-reaching were the crown's powers that it had a right to the whole tithe, and virtually no ecclesiastical appointment could be made in the New World, from the archbishop of Mexico to the humblest parish priest, without its participation. In theory the pope could refuse to ratify an episcopal candidate; in practice he very rarely put up objections. The privilege was an exorbitant one, repugnant alike to the modern mind and to canonists, if for different reasons. However from the point of view of the interests of the Catholic Church it proved useful, and Rome therefore resigned itself to a situation which was without parallel in any other nation.

Royal intervention was more marked in the case of the secular than the regular clergy, since the religious orders enjoyed ample internal autonomy. It would be false to conclude from this that the lower moral standards of the former were due to their closer links with the secular power. The most probable explanation of the difference is that the Spanish religious orders were in the process of reforming themselves just at the time of the *Conquista*, and their zeal for holiness and their proselytizing spirit carried them across the ocean; the secular clergy meanwhile were more lukewarm in their faith and more worldly in spirit, and far from improving got even worse in surroundings which encouraged every kind of backsliding. The episcopate, though carefully selected, was not always of a standard in keeping with its mission. Though there were distinguished figures in plenty, like Fray Juan de Zumárraga, first holder of the see of Mexico, or Saint Toribio de Mogrovejo, apostle of Peru, there was no lack, especially in the seventeenth century, of men who displayed an excessive attachment to wealth and returned to Spain with a large fortune, using their exalted station to avoid paying duties on it. Typical of the mentality of some of these prelates is the letter which Don Fernando de Vera, archbishop of Cuzco, wrote to a nephew in Spain in 1636:

In the Indies everything has gone badly for me. . . . As regards money matters, too, I have done very badly, for the riches of the Indies is one big lie. Though this land bears gold and silver, the Indians will not say where it is even if put to death. Their lot is a very hard one, and since the Spaniards here do not work, very many of them are poor and have to be given alms. This bishopric is the third see in the Indies, and has a return of 20,000 *pesos*, which are 14,000 Spanish ducats. Consider, now, that the poor are numerous, the price of everything here is extremely dear, and the vanity of wealth is so rooted since (the *Conquista*) that a man who would be given eight *reales* in alms in Spain gets fifty *pesos* here; just tell me, then, how I am going to manage.[8]

Under the remote and not always conscientious control of the bishop the rural parish priests, especially those in charge of Indian parishes, were exposed to a series of temptations (greed, lewdness, abuse of power) which not all of them could resist. Chaunu points out, as proof of the mediocre character of these clerics, that cases of 'soliciting' penitents constituted half those brought before the American Inquisition, and that only those who repeated the offence were severely punished. But in the complaints of the communities it is the rapacity of the priests, their tendency to take advantage of the ignorant and defenceless Indian, which one comes across most frequently. One must beware however of over-generalization – correct behaviour does not usually leave a trace in the archives.

This secular clergy, as well as being rather inefficient, was too few in number. Hence the religious orders often assumed duties in connection with the cure of souls which were normally none of their business. The activity of the religious orders is perhaps the most positive aspect of the Spanish achievement in America. It was not the contemplative orders who went there, for they would have been out of place; the intensely energetic were the ones needed to carry out the missionary task the crown had in mind. Franciscans, Dominicans and Jesuits took the lead, though the contribution of others, like the Carmelites and Mercedarians, should not be ignored. The Franciscans included Fray Pedro de Gante, author of the first Aztec grammar in 1528, his companion Fray Toribio de Benavente, known as *Motolinia*, which in the Mexican tongue meant poverty, the intrepid explorer Fray Marcos de Niza, Archbishop Zumárraga, and many others. The missionary labour of the Franciscans was rivalled, even surpassed by the Jesuits alone. Already at the beginning of the seventeenth century they began their famous *Reducciones* in Paraguay, a sort of Christian version of the Inca socialist state, which have been the object of very diverse judgements, though their advantages for the cultural development of the Guarani tribes cannot in fairness be denied. The Jesuits included Father Kino, with his mission in Lower California, Saint Peter Claver, the 'apostle of the Negro' since he devoted his life to them in Cartagena de Indias, point of entry for the slave masses arriving from Africa, and Father José Anchieta, a native of the Canary Isles, though he is usually taken for a Brazilian since his labours were focused on Brazil where he founded São Paulo. And since the Far East was regarded by Spain as a prolongation of the Indies it is not out of place to mention here the greatest missionary figure of all time, the Navarrese Saint Francis Xavier, who preached in India, Indo-China and Japan, and died (1552) within sight of China where he also longed to make his way.

The missionaries often enough relied on the civil authorities in carrying out their task; but often too they ventured alone among hostile populations, risking their lives and losing them fairly frequently. They showed the Indian the other face of the white man; unlike che *conquistador*, the bureaucrat and the *encomendero* who exploited him, the missionary was the man of God who sought his welfare, respected his personality, learned his tongue and tried to reconcile his customs and mentality with the new faith in everything which was not clearly incompatible with Christian morals. Just as the first archbishop of Granada authorized the recently converted Moslems to use their traditional songs and musical instruments in the Christian service, so the love of the Amerindians for music was amply exploited in the effort to attract them to the new beliefs. The missionaries did not seek the cultural assimilation of the native; on the contrary, as in the particular example of language, they aimed to keep his personality alive. This did not prevent the process of Christianization bringing with it fundamental changes in native life, promoted in every case with the best of intentions – 'ut Indi politice vivere instituantur', as the Council of Lima ordered in 1583. As a first priority this involved 'reducing' them to a stable and sedentary population, because the small, scattered and nomadic groups of the Californians, Guaranis and inhabitants of the Orinocco and Amazon jungles made the task of evangelization well-nigh impossible. Sedentary life meant learning new techniques: agriculture, cattle-raising, and the more indispensable crafts. The demands of Christian morality forced them to abandon their innocent nakedness. The old taboos regarding food and sex were replaced by new norms and prohibitions. The distribution of time took on a new significance: they were taught the difference between festive and working days. All this implied a real revolution in Indian life, most of it of a healthy kind. But as the modern sociology of civilizations has shown, in specific instances it often had destructive effects on populations not accustomed to such drastic changes. Often enough, as in Lower California, the zeal of the missionaries proved to be the opposite of productive.

One of the dangers of the *Reducciones* was that the Indians on coming into contact with so-called civilization fell a prey to authorities who exploited them and were exposed to the contagion of the white man's vices and diseases. This explains why the missionaries made such efforts to keep the Indian *Reducciones* more or less isolated and as little as possible under the control of the white authorities, though of course motives of self-interest must also have played their part on occasion. At other times the friars had to make good the shortage of secular clergy, and taking charge of a rural parish fell victim to the temptations of their environment.

The general decline and backsliding of the seventeenth century made itself felt within the religious orders as well, and on both sides of the ocean. The missionary flame was never extinguished; there were always intrepid and generous spirits ready to make the necessary sacrifices. But the urban communities were governed by routine and getting steadily richer, and the climate there was no longer what it had been in the heroic age. The scandalous disputes between creoles and Spaniards were a sign of how the worldly spirit was infiltrating the cloister. The struggle for office between the two factions led to the *alternativa* – that is, they took it in turns to hold appointments. But this did not cure the basic friction between the two groups or prevent them abusing each other.[9] As for evangelical poverty, really only the Franciscans stayed faithful to it.

Dominicans, Augustinians and Mercedarians accumulated considerable quantities of property, as did the Jesuits too, to a greater extent than any other order.[10] Of the odious results which followed this not the least grave was the dispute with the bishops and chapters over the payment of tithe, from which the regulars claimed exemption. This was the principal cause of the scandalous quarrel between the Jesuits and the famous bishop of La Puebla, Don Juan de Palafox.[11]

It was from the seventeenth century too that the religious orders slackened in their campaign on behalf of the native. Perhaps they were weary, having obtained appreciable results already, or more probably they had lost much of their early zeal, that righteous intolerance which so often pitted them against brutal *conquistadores*, rapacious settlers and none too benevolent local authorities. The higher authorities, whether in Spain or the Indies, in general supported the efforts of the religious, while tempering their idealistic and frequently utopian demands with a touch of realism. The outcome of the struggle for justice was a code of colonial legislation the like of which no other nation can submit to the judgement of history. If the actual conduct of the Spaniards departed considerably from the theoretical ideal, it was yet far removed from the mere balance of force which in that age governed relations between the European powers and their subject peoples.

In this struggle it was the Dominicans who played the most important role. One may think that the clergy, thanks to their ecclesiastical status, could speak out with greater freedom and less fear of sanctions. But the passions unleashed were capable of provoking serious reprisals, and more than a little conviction and courage was required in the effort to prevent force triumphing over right. The conflict can be said to have broken out at the very start, when Columbus, seeing how unimpressive were the material proceeds of his enterprise, sought to turn it to good account by using the Indians as human merchandise, as was already being done with Turks, Berbers and African Negroes. For medieval Europe had only ruled out the enslavement of Christians, not infidels; nor could infidels gain their freedom by subsequently becoming converts. The firm stand of Queen Isabel in defence of her new subjects prevented the New World turning into a New Africa. But the eagerness of the settlers to exploit the forced labour of the natives would inevitably lead to something very similar to slavery. A struggle developed over the next century, based on philosophical argument, legal texts and occasionally force of arms, between the crown supported by the clergy on the one hand, and on the other the settlers, aided by distance and all sorts of complicity. The outcome was the *encomienda*, which was very different from slavery and even from the feudal system, but nevertheless represented some concession to the demands of the *conquistadores*. The *encomendero* was a Spaniard who had the right to certain services from the Indians; in return he was to act as a sort of guardian to them. Never, not even in moments of greatest stress, did the crown consent to make the *encomiendas* hereditary and so make possible the development of a new feudalism. At most, it conceded them for three lives, that of the recipient of the favour, his son and his grandson. This brought about the final demise of the institution, which in itself would not have been objectionable if it had conformed to its strict legal limits and not led to frequent abuses.

The original *encomienda*, as established in 1503, was a system whereby the labour of the native was exploited to the benefit of the *encomendero*. The courageous protests of the Dominicans obliged the crown to modify its abuses by the Laws of Burgos (1512). But neither Ferdinand v nor his councillors were really interested in the fate of the Indian. It was the Franciscan Jiménez de Cisneros, governor of Castile and later regent of the kingdom, who made the liberal message of Isabel his own and dispatched a commission of three *Jerónimos* monks. They outlined measures which came too late to save the population of the islands from extermination. There now burst on the scene the most controversial figure in the history of the Indies, the Seville Dominican Fray Bartolomé de las Casas, who had watched with indignation the conduct of the early explorers. The first fruits of his activities was the decree of 1520 recognizing the complete freedom of the Indians, who were to live directly subject to the crown and their own municipal authorities.

Charles v and his Erasmian circle were well disposed towards the ideas of Las Casas. This he showed by the above-mentioned decree and by the ruling of 17 November 1526, by which no new explorations or conquests were to be made thenceforth without royal approval. The explorers were to proceed in all cases in a peaceful manner; they would speak their message to the Indians and invite them to submit. War, in any event, was only to be waged in self-defence. These proposals were excellent but unrealistic. What was to be done if the Indians refused to submit to the Spaniards in spite of the summons? Meanwhile, despite the decree of 1520, the *encomienda* had been reinstated, without the harshness which accompanied it in the islands but in a form which assured the *conquistadores* of Mexico and Peru an easy existence, to which they believed themselves entitled as a reward for their toil.

In 1524 the Council of the Indies was established, with a Dominican at its head, Fray García de Loaysa, who was opposed to anything which involved restricting the liberty of the Indian. Under his influence Charles v ordered the setting up of a junta to examine the question of the *encomiendas*. It should be noted that the Council of the Indies included men of experience, who feared the probable reaction of the *conquistadores*, and was not therefore dominated by the partisans of total abolition. But Charles ignored it and heeded only the generous and rather utopian opinion of the members of the junta; after many hesitations and delays he issued in 1542 the famous *Leyes Nuevas* which declared the *encomiendas* extinct. In Mexico the skill of the viceroy Mendoza and of Archbishop Zumárraga managed to allay the storm, but in Peru it broke out with a vengeance. There the insurgents went to the unheard-of extreme of taking up arms against the royal troops and killing the viceroy, Blasco Núñez Vela. But so firmly anchored in Castilians was the notion of loyalty that the emperor did not need to send armies to subdue the rebels. One cleric proved sufficient: Don Pedro de la Gasca gathered the faithful together, won over the waverers and isolated the intransigents, and managed to get their army to disband without any need of fighting. The leader of the rebellion, the youngest of the Pizarros, was left on his own and suffered the supreme penalty with resignation.

Despite this triumph Charles v realized that concessions must be made, in line with the promises La Gasca had already made in Peru. The royal Edict of Malines (1545) was in part a revocation of the *Leyes Nuevas*, but only in part. If the *encomiendas* were now allowed, they were stripped of any feudal character; the labour services of the Indians were suppressed and commuted to the collection by the *encomendero* of the tribute owed by the natives to the monarch. Thus they were reduced to a sort of pecuniary indemnification, and a well-deserved one at that, conceded by the crown to those who had vastly expanded its dominions. Apart from this partial revocation everything else remained in force: the prohibition on enslaving the Indians, the supremacy of the state, represented by the Council of Indies and the *Audiencias*, and the subordination to these supreme authorities of every new enterprise of exploration and conquest. Far from vanishing, the spirit which informed the *Leyes Nuevas* inspired the Ovando Code (1573) and, in general, all subsequent legislation with respect to the Indies. Emphasis was laid throughout on protecting the Indian and condemning any military undertaking of an aggressive character which had booty or personal gain as its object – the kind that was all too frequent in the first stage of the Discovery.

These considerable achievements cannot be attributed solely to Fray Bartolomé de las Casas, nor even to the Dominican Order as a whole, which for all its efforts could have done little without the support of the crown and a large section of the higher bureaucracy. But it is evident that no one stirred men's consciences to the extent that las Casas did. He is not a figure who can be judged dispassionately, for he himself was terribly passionate; and with the best will in the world one cannot absolve him of the tremendous injustices and exaggerations he printed in the *Brevísima relación de la destrucción de las Indias*, which became the most potent weapon in the armoury of anti-Spanish propaganda, though this was not the intention of the author. As with other great figures of controversy no unanimous judgement of him will ever be possible, for even after we have sifted every aspect of his life and ideas there remains the problem of interpreting and evaluating, in which subjective factors are always involved. What one can do is to avoid extremes, either of making of las Casas an exception who points the accusing finger at Spain and her achievement, or of trying to discount his testimony on the grounds of supposed mental deficiency. The best defence of the Spanish administration is precisely that it heeded and cooperated with a man who was not afraid to proclaim some home truths at the top of his voice.

Extolling las Casas is no reason for decrying Sepúlveda, the man who usually plays the role of the villain in the piece. In the famous controversy which pitted the two against each other the position of las Casas was closer to the human and Christian ideal, but Sepúlveda's had some truth in it as well. The latter is usually represented as an uncompromising defender of the Aristotelian principle of *natural slaves*, applied in this instance to the Amerindians. This is inaccurate, the position of Sepúlveda was not so crude. He did not assert that the Indian was naturally and racially inferior, and therefore destined to be a perpetual slave of the Spanish; he asserted that he was socially and culturally inferior, owing to heredity and environment. He could overcome this by living in contact with the superior civilization of the Spaniards, under whose tutelage he would have to remain for a more or less lengthy period of time. But this did not mean that he would have to put up with the greed and the brutality of the *conquistadores*. However, even this relatively moderate viewpoint caused a scandal in the progressive Erasmian milieu of Castile, and the work of Sepúlveda (the *Democrates Alter*) was not allowed to be published. Between the two opposing attitudes the Dominican Vitoria represented the voice of deliberation in his famous university lectures, *Sobre los Indios y el derecho de la Guerra*. Unlike las Casas, Vitoria had no personal experience of the Indies and did not deal with specific instances but with general principles. The principles, however, were common to both men: they were those of Christian freedom, applicable to every human being. The considerable difference in tone derives from the fiery, passionate temperament of the one and the serene objectivity of the other.

This 'struggle for justice', as Lewis Hanke has called it, continued for quite some time. Despite the laws in the Indians' favour their sufferings did not end overnight; they were still required to furnish personal services, and the terrible *mita* or compulsory labour in the mines was regarded with such horror that to escape it the Indians fled from the neighbourhoods affected. Philip II watched the pile of *consultas* and reports on these questions grow taller on his desk, but no solution could be reached. A bishop of Guatemala, Fray Juan Ramírez, distinguished himself by the vehemence of his reproaches. Philip III resorted to the common expedient of appointing a junta, which recommended measures alleviating the grievances without remedying the root cause, for to suspend work in the mines would have meant the total collapse of the American economy. Recommendations were made that the Indians should be well treated and be replaced by Negroes and volunteer workers, but no marked change occurred in their situation. The reforming ardour of the religious had grown lukewarm, consciences had fallen into accommodating ways, and the dominant attitudes were somewhere between the merciless exploitation of the first settlers and the good intentions of the government. The most glaring abuses were eliminated, but there was no complete cure – and this was the situation in Spanish America from that day to this.

NOTES

CHAPTER I : CASTILE, SPAIN AND THE EMPIRE

1 The quotations assembled by Miguel Herrero García *Ideas de los Españoles en el siglo xvii* (Madrid 1928), show that Portugal thought of itself as part of Spain, and also that the Portuguese felt an inveterate dislike for Castilians.

2 Chaunu brings out this point, and contrasts the inability of the monarchy to mount similar operations in the seventeenth century. See Pierre Chaunu, *La Civilisation de l'Europe Classique* (Paris 1966), p. 40.

3 Catalonia was governed, basically, by a standing committee of the Cortes, the *Diputació de la Generalitat*, which was chosen by drawing two names by lot every three years from among sixty-six members of the higher clergy, another two from 250 nobles of the *brazo militar*, and another two from the urban oligarchy which ruled the principal towns. J. H. Elliott, 'A Provincial Aristocracy . . .', in *Homenaje a Jaime Vicens*, Vol. II (Barcelona 1967).

4 A Castilian had this to say in 1620: 'Now that to the Crown of Spain there have been added Aragon, Portugal, Navarre, and all that is beautiful and splendid in Italy, Flanders, Lombardy, the East and the West Indies, such that with its land and its sea it lies along the whole path of the sun and the sun is scarcely lost to view from this monarchy, now that it is superior in territories, in riches, unequalled by those of Antiquity, superior in valour, loyalty, and the troth it keeps with its princes, and in firm religion and unswerving devotion to the church . . . the Ambassador of Spain has a patent claim everywhere and always to lay claim to precedence.' Vera y Zúñiga, *El Embajador* (Seville 1620), discurso 3, p. 54.

5 José A. Maravall, 'The Origins of the Modern State', *Cahiers d'Histoire Mondiale*, Vol. VI, 4, (1961).

6 Laws of between 1325 and 1528 which were included in subsequent legislative compilations. They usually refer to royal letters illegally issued to the prejudice of third parties, *Novísima Recopilación*, Vols. III and IV, laws 4 to 7. An example of a royal order obeyed but

not put into effect was that of Charles v that Columbus be buried in the Cathedral of Santo Domingo, Cuartero, *Historia de la Cartuja de las Cuevas*, Vol. i, p. 366 ff.

7   Quoted in B. Croce, *Storia dell'Età barroca in Italia* (Bari 1929), part i, ch. 3. Compare the words of Girolamo Giustiniani, ambassador of Venice to the court of Philip iv: 'The king of Spain has more of the forms than the reality of power, like some idol of antiquity who is the object of adulation, though his ministers make the replies,' N. Barozzi, and G. Berchet, *Relazioni degli ambasciatori veneti*, Vol. ii (Venice 1860), p. 131.

CHAPTER 2: THE DYNASTY

1   Shortly after the death of Philip ii the priest Baltasar Porreño published a collection of 'Words and Deeds' of the dead king, a work steeped in heartfelt admiration and much used by biographers. The little book is in some need of critical revision, since there are grounds for thinking that what Porreño intended was not so much a work of history as a model of the good king, which would serve at the same time as a veiled criticism of his successors, *Dichos y hechos del señor rey don Philipe segundo etc.* (Cuenca 1628).

2   'Go to your home, for I did not send you to kill kings, but to serve kings.' With equal severity he reprimanded a poor bishop who thought to please him by offering a ring snatched from the mummified body of King Alfonso viii. The town of Ávila he held in great aversion since it was there that Henry iv had been deposed.

3   Carlos Riba, prologue to *El Consejo Real de Aragón* (Valencia 1914).

4   More akin to the Spanish temperament was that of Don John of Austria. Once, when he organized a bull-fight in the Escorial, 'the king, Don Felipe, our lord, did not attend and refused to watch'. Codoin vii, 170, quoted by Valbuena, *Historia de la Literatura Española*, Vol. i, p. 563.

5   He is credited with saying: 'God who has given me so many kingdoms has denied me an heir capable of ruling them.'

6   Barozzi, and Berchet, *Relazioni*, vol. ii.

CHAPTER 3: THE INSTRUMENTS OF EMPIRE

1   Alvaro Castillo, 'Dette flottante et dette consolidée en Espagne de 1557 à 1600', *Annales* (1963). On the crisis of 1575 see also Henri Lapeyre, *Simón Ruiz et les 'asientos' de Philippe II* (Paris 1953), and Ramón Carande, 'Cartas de mercaderes', *Moneda y Crédito* (1944) as well as the introduction by Felipe Ruiz to *Lettres marchandes échangées*

entre Florence et Medina del Campo (Paris 1965), and of course the fundamental work of Modesto Ulloa, *La hacienda real de Castilla en el reinado de Felipe II* (Rome 1963).

2   C. Espejo, *El Consejo de Hacienda bajo la presidencia del marqués de Poza* (Madrid 1924), p. 64.

3   Domínguez Ortiz, *Política y hacienda de Felipe IV*, (Madrid 1960), p. 182-3; see also below, p. 197-8.

4   Take for instance the army of the duke of Alba in 1573, which was made up of 7,900 Spaniards, 25,800 Germans and 20,800 Walloons. That of Alexander Farnese was even more heterogeneous: 5,000 Spaniards, 3,000 Italians, 10,000 Germans, 8,000 Walloons, 8,000 men from the Franche Comté, 800 from Lorraine and 700 Irish. See L. van der Essen, 'Croisade contre les hérétiques ou guerre contre des rebelles', *Revue d'Histoire Ecclésiastique*, Vol. LI (1956), pp. 42-78.

5   Marcos de Isaba, *Cuerpo enfermo de la milicia española*.

6   A one-time soldier described the usual pattern of a mutiny as follows: 'These mutinies usually take place on campaign, and the men get the name of the "squadron of the disaffected". Their first concern is to occupy some stronghold from which they can roam the surrounding countryside, the which, to avoid worse trouble, agrees to pay them tribute. And then they elect a leader, whom they call the *electo*, who has several counsellors. The infantry is commanded by a *sargento mayor* and the cavalry by a *gobernador*. Offices are bestowed and decisions taken by a show of hands. The quarters of the *electo* overlook the square, and from a window he makes his proposals to the squadron. When they are fed up with him they pass from words to bullets. For this reason the *electo* has always a sentinel to watch over him. He can not receive or transmit correspondence without notifying the squadron which in all respects maintains strict military discipline, for they impale on their pikes or shoot down anyone who commits an offence. Most of their rules are savage, therefore, though some are just and legitimate.' F. Moles, *Amistades de Príncipes* (Madrid 1637), p. 42.

7   *Discurso Militar* (Valencia 1653), c. XXV.

8   At the outset of the war with France in 1635 the army of Flanders consisted of 8,863 officers and 60,840 soldiers, a very high total for the period. But deducting losses and garrisons which account for 44,000 men, there were only 11,000 on active campaign. AGS Estado, Flanders, legajo 2051.

9   AI, Indiferente, 782; *consulta* of 13 February 1671.

CHAPTER 4: CHARLES V

1   *Las Comunidades de Castilla. Una primera revolución moderna* (Madrid 1963).

2   J. Pérez, 'Moines frondeurs et sermons subversifs en Castille', *Bulletin Hispanique*, Vol. LXVII (1965).

3   J. Gutiérrez Nieto, 'Los Conversos y el movimiento comunero', *Hispania* (1964).

4   R. Carande, *Carlos V y sus banqueros*, Vol. III, (Madrid 1967), pp. 285–6.

CHAPTER 5: THE ZENITH OF EMPIRE: PHILIP II

1   A. L. E. Verheyden, *Le Conseil des Troubles: Liste des condamnés* (Brussels 1961).

2   *Histoire de Belgique*, Vol. IV (Brussels 1927). This work is the best summary of the history of the Spanish Low Countries between the beginning of the wars and the Peace of Westphalia. It is not entirely objective in its treatment of the monarchs of the House of Habsburg.

3   'Séville et la Belgique', *Revue du Nord* (1960). Parallel developments in Spanish America and in the course of the wars in Flanders, with observations which are sometimes bold but always suggestive.

4   This detail, and that on the *flotas* of 1595, in Ariño, *Sucesos de Sevilla de 1592 a 1604* (Seville 1873), pp. 24 and 34.

CHAPTER 6: THE PRECARIOUS EQUILIBRIUM 1598–1634

1   'El dominio del Adriático y la política española en los comienzos del siglo XVII', *Revista de la Universidad de Madrid*, Vol. II (1953).

2   *The Dutch in Brazil, 1624–1654* (Oxford 1957), p. 7.

3   Braudel, *Civilisation matérielle et Capitalisme* (Paris 1967), p. 300.

4   *La política europea de España durante la guerra de Treinta Años 1624–1630* (Madrid 1967).

5   *La política europea*, p. 181.

6   Montero de Espinosa, *Diálogos militares y políticos* (Brussels 1654), p. 26.

7   'Le rôle du Cardinal-Infant dans la politique espagnole du XVII siècle', *Revista de la Universidad de Madrid* (1954).

8   C. Federn, *Mazarin* (French trans. Paris 1934), p. 47.

CHAPTER 7: YEARS OF DISASTER 1635–59

1   On this debate, see José Mª Jover, *1635: Historia de una polémica y semblanza de una generación* (Madrid 1959).

2   G. Coniglio, *Il viceregno di Napoli nel secolo XVII* (Naples 1957), p. 283.

3   AGS Estado 2,093, *consulta* of 11 April 1658. The ordinary consignments for Flanders hitherto had been between three and four millions.

4 AGS Estado, 2,368. The king of Spain had an old debt outstanding with the Danish crown over the impounding of ships. It was paid in part with licences for the free export of salt.

CHAPTER 8: THE PRIVILEGED ESTATES: NOBLES AND CLERGY

1 Part II, ch. 1.

2 According to Tanner ms, xcix quoted in John C. Salyer, 'La política económica de España en la época del Mercantilismo', *Anales de Economía*, Vol. xxxi, there were 29,745 secular clergy and 32,698 regular. The number of nuns, which is not given, would have been less. These figures should be increased by roughly a fifth to allow for the non-Castilian provinces. One has also to take into account the lay servants of the religious and clerical households.

3 The relative poverty of the Catalan church is to be explained by the fact that there the greater part of the tithe belonged to lay lords.

4 And not only lords: 'There is hardly a shopkeeper', so runs an anonymous leaflet of the seventeenth century, 'who is not taken with the fancy of styling himself patron of a monastery and becoming lord of its principal chapel,' BN ms. 17,502.

5 The protest of Medina del Campo against the foundation of a convent of Discalced Carmelites ran as follows: 'Who would imagine that this particular vineyard of the Lord is untended for lack of hands, when for barely six hundred households still remaining the town has two collegiate churches, ten parishes, and seventeen convents?' Fray Silverio de Santa Teresa, *Historia del Carmen Descalzo*, Vol. x, p. 131.

6 The French Benedictine Bartolomé Joly, who travelled through Spain at the beginning of the seventeenth century, noted on his arrival in Zaragoza: 'The Jesuits teach there and are the envy of the other religious, because they seem more enterprising, and, though they are the most modern, they own more property than all the others,' *Voyage en Espagne*, in *Revue Hispanique*, Vol. xx, p. 533.

7 Stanko Vranich, 'Carta de un ciudadano de Sevilla', *Archivo Hispalense*, n. 137–8.

8 Among other examples one can cite the case of Pamplona in 1590, where the summons went out to 'the councils, justices, *regidores, caballeros, escuderos, hidalgos, hombres buenos*, and any other ecclesiastical or other lay individual whatever'; or Cuenca in 1626, with '*corregidores*, governors, justices, and *regidores* of the cities, towns, and villages of the bishopric'; or Segovia in 1648, where they invited 'the dukes, marquises, counts, and lords of the towns and villages, and governors, justices and *regidores*', and so forth.

CHAPTER 9: TOWNS AND THE URBAN POPULATION

1   Most, if not all these entails were founded on rural possessions.

2   *Civilisation matérielle et Capitalisme,* p. 63.

3   For a discussion of these and other population figures for Spanish towns see the present author's *Sociedad española del siglo XVII* (Madrid 1963), Vol. i, ch. v.

4   Pedro de León, S. J., *Compendio de algunas experiencias* . . . (ms of the University Library of Granada), Vol. i, ch. 13.

5   It is now agreed that this was not the case even in Amsterdam, Boxer, *The Dutch in Brazil,* ch. 2.

6   *Memorial Histórico Español,* Vol. xi, p. 56.

7   363,000 ducats by 1600 is the estimation of his biographer Lapeyre, *Simón Ruiz,* p. 81.

8   *Lettres marchandes d'Anvers* (Paris 1961), Vol. i, *passim.*

9   Felipe Ruiz, prologue to *Lettres marchandes échangées entre Florence et Medina del Campo.*

10   *Une famille de marchands: les Ruiz* (Paris 1955), pp. 498–9.

11   J. H. Elliott, *The Revolt of the Catalans* (Cambridge 1963), pp. 163 and 274.

12   M. González de Cellorigo, *Memorial sobre la política necessaria y útil restauración de la República de España* (Valladolid 1600), f. 54–6.

13   *La Catalogne dans l'Espagne Moderne* (Paris 1962), Vol. i, pp. 569–70.

14   S. Montoto, *Sevilla en el Imperio* (Seville 1940), p. 218.

15   AI, Indiferente, 760.

16   An instance of selfishness combined with a lack of far-sightedness is to be found in the case of the hatmakers guild of Zaragoza, which in 1601 refused a worker permission to carry on his trade not because he was incompetent but on the contrary because he brought in technical innovations from Italy which gave his workshop an advantage over the rest, Sancho Seral, 'El gremio zaragozano del siglo XVI', *Universidad,* Vol. ii (1925).

17   In effect they were known as *Corte* (Court) in official jargon, and the *Chancillería* was called *Regius Senatus.* The fact that they combined administrative with judicial competence greatly enhanced their importance.

18   Vedia, *Historia de la Coruña* (Corunna 1845), appendix XXVI.

19   The case occurred in Madrid in 1645 and provoked such a violent reaction on the part of the nobility that the king banished several *Alcaldes de Casa y Corte* who had been responsible for the degrading sentence. But two others were spared since they had only voted for the death of the offender, a more rigorous sentence which however was not deemed degrading to the victim or the army,

AHN, Consejos, 51,438. Also 'Cartas de Jesuitas', *Memorial Histórico Español*, Vol. xviii, p. 198, and Lucas de Torre, 'Un noble condenado a azotes', *Revista de Historia y Genealogía*, Vol. i, p. 343–8.

20 There was for example the case of the dramatist Rojas Zorilla who had to seek a dispensation from the pope in order to accept a habit of Santiago, since he was the son of a court clerk, Pérez Pastor, *La Imprenta en Madrid* (Madrid 1906), Vol. iii, p. 464.

21 Special cases existed, like the royal physician Luis de Mercado who according to Bennassar became wealthy indeed, B. Bennassar, *Valladolid au siècle d'or* (Paris, The Hague 1967), p. 363. But, on the other hand, there was the doctor in the little town of Cigales who was hired by the municipality for the extremely modest sum of 90,000 *maravedís, ibid.*, p. 364.

22 Suárez de Figueroa, *El Pasagero* (Madrid 1914 – original edition 1617), p. 171.

23 *La population catalane de 1553 à 1717* (Paris 1960).

CHAPTER 10: THE RURAL WORLD AND THE SEIGNEURIAL REGIME

1 Rodrigo Caro, *Relación* . . . *de Utrera*, f. 6. On the wealthy *labradores* of New Castile, Salomon, *La Campagne de la Nouvelle Castille à la fin du XVIème siècle* (Paris 1964), ch. 8.

2 Fray Manuel de Anguiano, *Compendio historial de la Rioja* (Madrid 1704), p. 24. In fact la Rioja, though historically incorporated in Castile, was geographically part of the Ebro valley. Its human problems are not those of the Meseta.

3 D. Mansilla, 'El Obispado de Santander', *Hispania Sacra*, Vol. iv, p. 93. Another very backward zone was the centre of the present province of Huelva, which was then part of the kingdom of Seville. Its inhabitants fed on acorns and lived in huts and caves, and according to Jesuit missionaries who preached there towards the end of the sixteenth century, in language, dress and style of living 'they resembled Indians rather than Spaniards'.

4 *La Campagne de la Nouvelle Castille*, ch. 6.

5 In the Cortes of 1602 a deputy complained that the wages for reaping were as much as eight or nine *reales* per day, 'and a plough-boy who received eight or ten ducats before now gets thirty or forty', *Actas de las Cortes*, Vol. xx, p. 415. There were renewed complaints about high wages in the Cortes of 1610, *ibid.*, Vol. xxv, p. 772 and xxvii, p. 237. It is probable that these sudden rises in wages were connected with the plague of 1597–1692 and with the expulsion of the *Moriscos*.

6 Zumalde, *Historia de Oñate* (San Sebastián 1957), p. 291.

7 Layna Serrano, *Historia de Cifuentes* (Madrid 1955), p. 151.

8　J. de la Torre, 'Como se solucionaba una huelga de campesinos', *Boletín de la Real Academia de Córdoba* (1931).

9　Matías Escudero, ms. quoted in Catalina García, *Escritores de Guadalajra.*

10　F. Mauro suggests that these rural banquets were designed to compensate for the frequent deficiencies of the ordinary diet, *Le XVIème siècle européen. Aspects Economiques* (Paris 1966), p. 177.

11　P. A. Goy, *El Espino y su comarca*, ch. 16.

12　*Libro de las cinco excelencias del español que despueblan a España* (Pamplona 1629), Vol. II, ii.

13　Fray Juan Martínez, *Discursos theológicos y políticos* (Alcalá 1664), p. 391.

14　Listed in the *Historia Nobiliaria de España* of the marquis of Saltillo, (Madrid 1951), Vol. I. Not all the sales gave rise to new lordships, since there were towns which bought their own jurisdiction. But others, overwhelmed by debt, sold themselves to individual lords with royal approval. In addition the crown had already exceeded the number of vassals it was authorized to sell by 13,089 by the reign of Carlos II. So the figure of forty thousand must be taken as a minimum.

CHAPTER 11: THE LOWER CLASSES OF SOCIETY

1　AHN *Consejos*, leg. 51,442, n. 6.

2　Zarco Cuevas, *El licenciado Caja de Leruela* (Madrid 1935), quoting a memorial of Pedro López de Reyno, BN ms. 1092, f. 305.

3　M. de la Pinta Llorente, *Causa criminal contra el biblista Alonso de Gudiel, catedrático de la universidad de Osuna* (Madrid 1942), p. 125–6.

4　For the case of a *Morisco* businessman who made considerable profits from a trade in silk fabrics, see Bennassar, *Valladolid*, p. 338.

5　F. M. Hitos, *Mártires de la Alpujarra en la rebelión de los Moriscos en 1568* (Madrid 1935).

6　'The Andalusians here as elsewhere were the civilizing influence *par excellence*', Agustin Bernard, *Afrique du Nord* (Paris 1925), p. 280. see also his note on 'Le Tell septentrionel en Tunisie', *Annales de Géographie* (1935), p. 549.

7　*La Mediterranée et le monde méditerranéan à l'époque de Philippe* II (Paris 1949), part II, ch. 5.

CHAPTER 12: THE ECONOMY OF HABSBURG SPAIN: I. THE STRUCTURES

1　Don Tomás González, archivist of Simancas, published in 1829 the results of the census of 1591, adding some findings from others of an earlier or later date. This publication is not free from error but it is the source of most of the figures used by later historians, *Censo de la población de las provincias y partidos de la corona de Castilla en el siglo XVI* (Madrid 1829).

2   'La población española al comienzo de los tiempos modernos', *Cuadernos de Historia*, Vol. I, pp. 189–202. This is an anticipation of a much more detailed study.

3   Guicciardini, crossing it in 1512, called it 'paese desertisimo, nel quale non si trova allogiamento alcuno'. A century later, a French traveller relates that 'en Aragon on marche des journées entières sans trouver aucun habitant', quoted in Braudel, *El Mediterráneo*, Vol. I, p. 350 of the Spanish edition (Mexico 1953).

4   These questions have been fully dealt with by the present author in his *Sociedad española del siglo XVII*.

5   Braudel, *Civilisation matérielle et capitalisme*, Part I, ch. 2. Mauro, *Le XVIᵉᵐ siècle européen*, p. 110–11.

6   A memorial of 1624 affirmed that sterile lands yielded six to one, and the good sort a lot more, Murcia de la Llana, *Discurso político*. Another author of the period asserted that in the countryside round Córdoba a yield of ten to one was common, Fray Cristóbal de San Antonio, *Historia de Bujalance*, p. 46. In reality we know very little about these questions; their exploration depends on work now in progress, especially that of M. Pierre Ponsot.

7   Salomon, *La Campagne de la Nouvelle Castille*, p. 95, note. He cites a series of complaints from the Cortes about the increase of new ploughings.

8   M. Ribas de Pina, 'Un antiguo éxito de la siderurgia española', *Boletín de la Real Sociedad Geográfica* (1951), p. 151–97. The need of foreign technicians is confirmed by Philip IV's order to the governor of the Low Countries about sending miners, engineers and gunners, copied in Cuvelier, *Correspondance de la Cour d'Espagne*, Vol. III, documents 1550 and 1551.

9   Jorge Vigón, *Historia de la Artillería Española*, Vol. I (Madrid 1947), p. 308 ff.

10   A document of 1644, probably with some exaggeration, put at two thousand the number of workers in the shipyards of la Carraca at Cadiz, with a wage of ten *reales*, AI Indiferente 436. Wages of eight and ten *reales*, unheard of in other trades, were recognized in this one by law, Veitia y Linage, *Norte de la Contratación de Indias*, Vol. I, p. 175 ff.

11   Enríquez de Jorquera, *Anales de Granada*, Vol. II.

12   R. Carande, *Carlos V y sus banqueros*, Vol. II, ch. 8. B. Bennassar, 'Economie et Société à Ségovie au milieu du XVᵉᵐᵉ siècle', *Anuario de Historia Económica y Social*, Vol. I, pp. 185–205. Felipe Ruiz has not yet published the result of his researches on Segovian industry, but he refers to it in several of his more recent writings, for example in

'Rasgos estructurales de Castilla en tiempos de Carlos v', *Moneda y Crédito*, n. 96. In this article he calculates that in 1584–9 Segovia achieved an annual output of 12,500 to 13,000 pieces of cloth to a value of 262 to 269 million *maravedises*.

13   Vilar, *La Catalogne dans l'Espagne moderne*, Vol. 1, p. 593. In Barcelona the silk spinners fell between the same dates from seventy to twenty.

14   Brunel, 'Voyage d'Espagne', *Revue Hispanique*, Vol. xxx (1914). His account was first published in Paris in 1655.

CHAPTER 13: THE ECONOMY OF HABSBURG SPAIN: II. THE TRENDS

1   Particularly in his *Histoire du Climat* (Paris 1967). Prior to this, in 'Le climat des XI et XVIème siècles', *Annales* (Sept. 1965) he gave a summary of the conclusions of the Congress on Climatology at Aspen (1962).

2   This deterioration at the beginning of the seventeenth century was felt even in the far south of Spain: in 1604 the sugar-cane froze on the coast of Granada, an extremely rare occurrence, AGS *Consejo y Juntas de Hacienda*, leg. 441. They froze on at least two other occasions in the seventeenth century, in 1651 and 1699.

3   Much information on the climate in history is to be found in local histories and chronicles, though no systematic study has as yet been undertaken. The lack of measuring equipment and scientific observation means that the greater part of the data is of a subjective kind; but there are objective facts which can be used with complete confidence, for example falls of snow in warm districts like Alicante, where on 29 December 1572 a palm of snow fell, 'a thing which we rarely see', and on 1 February 1624, a palm and a half, Bendicho, *Crónica de Alicante*, p. 191–2. In Seville it snowed twice between 1624–6, a phenomenon which was accompanied by heavy flooding. Similarly, the freezing of the sugar-cane on the coast of Granada in 1651 must be related to the overflowing of the Segura in Murcia in the same year. Another event of objective value is the freezing over of rivers in the southern half of Spain, for example the Tagus in 1536. These few instances show the profit to be derived from looking again at the available information on the subject.

4   A saying related in Joly, 'Voyage en Espagne', p. 470.

5   *American Treasure and the Price Revolution in Spain* (Cambridge, Mass. 1934).

6   *Séville et l'Atlantique*, esp. Vol. VIII (Paris 1959).

7   'Séville et la Belgique'.

8   'Una crisi economica: 1619–22', *Rivista Storica Italiana*, Vol. LXXIV (1964), and 'Encore la crise de 1619–22', *Annales* (Jan. 1964).

9 'Problems of the Formation of Capitalism', *Past and Present* no. 10 (1956); see also his valuable essay, 'Le temps du Quichotte', translated into Spanish and included in *Crecimiento y desarrollo* (Barcelona 1964).

10 Carrera, *Historia económica de Cataluña* (Barcelona 1947), Vol. II, p. 253.

11 Hume, *The Court of Philip IV* (London 1907), p. 321.

12 Hamilton, *American Treasure*, appendix VII.

13 *Restauración de la abundancia de España*, Part I, ch. 16 (Madrid 1632).

14 *Suma de tratos y contratos*, Part IV, ch. 4. The first edition of this classic work dates from 1569.

15 *Actas de las Cortes*, Vol. XV.

16 *Rentas de Castilla y León que goza el rey Don Felipe IV*, an anonymous work.

17 *En Espagne. Développement économique, subsistance, déclin* (Paris 1965), pp. 91–3. By the same author, 'Cálculos retrospectivos del producto', *Desarrollo Económico* (1965).

CHAPTER 14: RELIGIOUS LIFE: I. ORTHODOXY

1 On the Council of Trent a vast literature exists which cannot be cited here. Perhaps the best guide to a detailed study of this question is *A History of the Council of Trent* by H. Jedin (London 1961). Of the Spanish contribution a good summary is provided by the work of the Jesuit C. Gutiérrez, *Españoles en Trento* (Valladolid 1951).

2 It should be noted that contrary to the practice in most other countries a Spanish woman keeps her family name after marriage and passes it on to her children.

3 A very experienced priest estimated that a third of penitents kept back sins, and that this was frequent practice even among pious individuals. He counselled complete frankness on sexual matters because people had most trouble confessing these. It should be noted that for this father (and others), even the fact that a man squeezed a woman's hand could be a mortal sin, Fray José Gavarri, *Interrogatorio* ... (Granada 1676). Of interest too in this respect is the *Predicador Apostólico* by Fray Gabriel de Santa María, and in general any work of a missionary character.

4 *La Familia regulada*, Vol. IV, ch. 23.

5 The visions of Madre Agreda are contained in her *Mística Ciudad de Dios*, a work written in 1655 which aroused great controversy. Censured by the Sorbonne, it found ardent defenders in Spain. In this work Madre Agreda mingles subconscious reminiscences of the apocryphal gospels with the fruits of a not very fertile

imagination, and expounds in great detail the rebellion and fall of the angels, the deliberations of the Divine Persons regarding the Incarnation, the childhood of Mary, and so forth.

CHAPTER 15: RELIGIOUS LIFE: II. THE INQUISITION AND HETERO-DOXY

1   Francisco Murcia de Llana, a censor of books in the period of Philip IV, quotes this fact in order to demonstrate the greater tolerance and probity of the Spanish Inquisition in drawing up its Indexes compared with that of Rome, which by totally condemning lengthy works did serious damage to Spanish authors and publishers. There is a copy of this memorial in the university library of Granada.

2   H. Kamen, *The Spanish Inquisition* (London 1965), p. 97.

3   Some of these are mentioned by the Dominican Fray Domingo Baltanás or Valtanás in his very odd treatise, *De la discordia de los linajes*, included in his *Apologia sobre ciertas materias morales en que hay opinión* (Seville 1556).

4   The word *marrano* applied to Portuguese Judaists is of uncertain etymology. The most probable explanation is that it refers to the Castilian word for a pig, in an ironical allusion to the ritual prohibition on eating the meat of that animal.

5   On this and the other problems touched on here, see the bibliography referring to this chapter.

6   'El erasmismo y las corrientes espirituales afines', *Revista de Filología Española* (1952) p. 31-99.

7   A matter of some debate is whether Ignatius of Loyola was influenced by Erasmus. He read the *Enchiridion*, at least, and his biographer Ribadeneira says that it cooled his devotion. On reaching maturity the founder of the Jesuits not only rejected the ideas he might have imbibed from Erasmus but prohibited his followers from reading his works, R. García Villoslada, *Loyola y Erasmo*.

8   An analysis of the work and influence of Molinos (Molinism or quietism) falls outside the chronological limits of this book. An impartial and relatively favourable summary of the man is given by Paquier in the *Dictionnaire de Théologie Catholique*, Vol. x, 2. He laments the fact that the letters and other papers of Molinos are inaccessible, being locked away in the archives of the Holy Office in Rome.

9   Kamen, *The Spanish Inquisition*, ch. 11.

CHAPTER 16: LEARNING AND SCIENCE

1   J. Simón Díaz, *Historia del Colegio Imperial* (Madrid 1952), Vol. 1.

2   In the curious picture Miguel Servet painted of the Spaniards

in his edition of Ptolemy he remarked: 'In the universities they use Spanish rather than Latin, and Morisco words if the occasion arises,' quoted by Padre Iriarte, *Pensares e historiadores*, p. 353. A later author wrote: 'Hispani, etiam in scholis suo idiomate loqui maxime gloriantur,' Alejandro Aguado, *Política española*.

3   *Actas de las Cortes*, Vol. IX, p. 206–29, for the year 1587.

4   Fray Alonso Cabrera, *Sermones*, p. 701–2. Some years before, Juan de Mal-Lara had written: 'Man ought to give infinite thanks to God for placing him in an age when all things have reached a point of perfection, such that it seems that there is nothing more to be discovered in the arts, instruments and equipment that man has developed for different uses', from *Descripción de la galera real* . . . , in Gallardo, *Biblioteca española*, Vol. III, column 592.

5   *Actas de las Cortes*, Vol. XI, for the year 1590.

6   E. Lewalter, *Spanisch-Jesuitische und Deutsch-Lutherische Metaphysik des XVII Jahrhunderts* (Hamburg 1935).

7   The sad notoriety of Escobar is due to his having been the scapegoat of an entire school of thought. Not only was he not the most lax of the casuists, but in his definitive work (*Universa Theologiae Moralis . . . disquisitiones*) many of the propositions of his *Manual de confesores* do not appear. It was the latter, translated at Lyons in 1644, which was the chief target of Pascal.

8   An agreeable summary of this scandalous business is to be found in T. D. Kendrik, *Saint James in Spain* (London 1960), ch. 5.

9   Ch. 50 of the second part.

CHAPTER 17: LITERATURE

1   On the spread of Castilian in Portugal see the article by Eugenio Asensio, 'España en la épica filipina', *Revista de Filología Española* (1949), where he shows, contrary to H. Cidade, that it was not achieved by coercion. There were Portuguese poets who sung the praises of the empire and of peninsular solidarity and even acknowledged Castilian to be the more perfect tongue.

2   These words may be referred to Campanella's dictum on the three instruments of empire: language, the sword and money, quoted by Oliver Asin, *Historia de la lengua española* (Zaragoza 1939), n. 144.

3   Brantôme, a great hispanophile, relates in his *Rodomontades* how the bishop of Macon interrupted the Emperor with the allegation that he did not understand Castilian, to which Charles V replied: 'My lord bishop, hear me if you will but do not expect from me words other than those of my Spanish tongue, which is so noble that it deserves to be known and understood by every Christian people.'

4   On this now forgotten polemic one may consult Dámaso

Alonso's essay, *Escila y Caribdis de la literatura española* and Díaz Plaja's summary in *La Poesía lírica española*, p. 79 ff., in addition to the fundamental works of Geers and Aubrey G. Bell.

5   P. Hazard, *La crise de la conscience européenne*, Part III, ch. 7.

6   *Bibliografía de las controversias sobre la licitud del Teatro en España*, by E. Cotarelo (Madrid 1904).

7   Charles V. Aubrun in his notable study writes: 'Lope takes his stand beside the jurists who desire the abolition of seigneurial jurisdiction and the extension of that of the king', *La comedia española* (Sp. tr. Madrid 1968), p. 72. The present author confesses to ignorance of these jurists who desired the abolition of seigneurial jurisdiction. What dramatists and jurists sought was the equality of all before the law, and the castigation of injustices and abuse, not the transformation of a hierarchical society into a democratic form.

CHAPTER 19: THE POLITICAL EMPIRE OVERSEAS

1   The justification of this measure, which stands in contrast to the Spanish government's usual humanity in matters of war, was that they did not 'fight fair' – that is, that all the French and English found in those seas without licence were, in principle, suspect of piracy. *Cédulas* of 1598, AI Indiferente 747, reiterated in 1608.

2   The rare Maya inscriptions, only partially deciphered, and the Aztec rudimentary pictography are inconsiderable exceptions.

3   *The Spanish Seaborne Empire* (London 1966), Part I, ch. 4.

4   Carlos Sanz, *Australia, su descubrimiento y denominación* (Madrid 1963).

CHAPTER 20: THE ECONOMIC EMPIRE

1   In a short but luminous study, *New Spain's Century of Depression* (University of California 1951), W. Borah pointed out the correlation between the Aztec demographic collapse and the decline of the viceroyalty of New Spain. He supposed at the time that the drop had been from eight to one and a half millions. In subsequent works L. Cook and L. B. Simpson proposed even higher figures for the original population, and as their researches broadened the Berkeley historians have gone further in the same direction until they arrived at the figures quoted in the text. The results seem so astounding, so radical that they are far from having won the unanimous assent of scholars. See on this question, P. Chaunu, 'La population de l'Amérique indienne', *Revue Historique* (July–Sept. 1964).

2   In principle all passengers to the Indies had to be registered in the Casa de Contratación at Seville; these registers are not complete, and those which are extant contain very low figures – in three

centuries only 150,000 Spaniards appear to have crossed to America; that is, 500 per year. There was an important clandestine emigration which is difficult to estimate exactly but which perhaps tripled these figures. An exception to the hostile attitude of the government towards emigration was its policy of encouraging the settlement of Spaniards in the threatened West Indies.

3 As early as 1625 Gaytán de Torres was writing that office ought to be apportioned equally among Spaniards and Creoles, since 'as they are such varied types and have such just grievances, if they ever drop the mask . . . the Indies will never return to the yoke of Castile', *Reglas para el gobierno de estos Reynos y de Castilla* (Jérez 1625), p. 101. One of the best works on this fundamental question is Fernando Benítez, *The Century after Cortés* (Eng. ed. Chicago 1952).

4 Seville, and Lisbon as well, realized from the outset the dangers which the direct contact of the Indies with China via the Philippines could present to their commerce. The restriction on this trade was the outcome of these fears. A prohibition was enacted against navigating to Manila from southern America, and the north was limited to an annual fleet of two small galleons with a combined tonnage of 500 tons. Even so, given the small weight and high price of silk goods which were the principal object of the trade, turnover might have been high; so from the end of the sixteenth century the total value of purchases was limited to 500,000 *pesos*. Of course, this limit was not observed, and the merchants of Seville were perpetually complaining that the actual outgoings of American silver were at least four times as great. There is one piece of information which supports these claims: the only two occasions on which the Manila galleon was captured (in 1587 by Cavendish and in 1740 by Anson) the prizes amounted to two million and two million four hundred thousand *pesos*, R. A. Rydell, *Cape Horn to Pacific* (University of California Press 1952).

5 According to Marañón, going by the *Norte de Príncipes*, in *Antonio Pérez*, Vol. ii, (Madrid 1958), p. 203.

6 *Memorial . . .* (Valladolid 1600), f. 15.

7 Quoted in González de Salcedo, *Tratado jurídico-político del contrabando* (Madrid 1654).

8 Several cases of the kind are referred to in a *consulta* of the Council of Indies on 17 February 1658, lamenting the tolerance shown to 'so many millions in silver which comes unregistered to Spain under the control of religious, to the total ruin of the *averías* and of Your Majesty's treasury', AI Indiferente 772.

9 *The Sale of Public Office in the Spanish Indies under the Habsburgs* (University of California Press 1953).

10 F. C. Spooner, *L'économie mondiale et les frappes monétaires en France 1493–1680* (Paris 1956), ch. 1.

M

CHAPTER 21: THE SPIRITUAL EMPIRE

1 *Amérique Latine* (Paris 1934), p. 149–50.

2 See on this point the observations of P. Chaunu in *Les Philippines et le Pacifique des Ibériques* (Paris 1960), p. 21. Catholicism was so identified with Spain, until quite late, that Independence was accompanied by the anti-Spanish gesture of setting up a schismatic National Church, which had always a limited appeal.

3 In 1770 the Spanish government ordered the suppression of the chair of Quechua. The policy of linguistic 'castilianisation', begun in the peninsula, was being extended to the American dominions.

4 This was not mere talk. According to Chaunu, *Les Philippines*, the maintenance of the archipelago must have cost Spain a deficit of some twenty million *pesos* during the seventeenth century.

5 Prophecy of Chumayel y Tizmín, in *El reverso de la conquista* (Mexico 1964), by Miguel León Portilla, p. 81.

6 The junta administering the *cruzada* bull for Peru reported in 1603 that it was not possible to increase the collection because the majority of Indians could not afford the two *reales* which the bull cost, and because 'the indulgences are granted with the obligation of communion, and there are very few Indians who can receive it', AI Indiferente 748. There is a clear parallel with the *Moriscos*, who were forced to confess but not to go to communion, since their Christianity was in doubt. For a summary of the varying attitudes of the ecclesiastical authorities on this point see Ibot León, *La Iglesia y los eclesiásticos españoles en la empresa de Indias*, Vol. I, ch. 17.

7 The Roman See always advised that the natives should be admitted to the priesthood. The Spanish authorities, whether in Madrid or America, had no objection in principle, but occasionally issued instructions to the contrary since they did not regard them as fit for this mission; it is in this light that one must see the prohibitions of the Council of Mexico in 1555 and the Second Council of Lima. The attempts of some religious orders to admit Indians to their ranks also failed, through mutual inadaptability. This should not surprise us, since we know how difficult it was for Spaniards from opposite sides of the Atlantic to agree, even though they had the same colour of skin. Some important documents on this topic are contained in G. Figuera Marcano, *Documentos para la historia de la Iglesia colonial en Venezuela* (Caracas 1965).

8 *Biblioteca de Autores Españoles*, Vol. LXII, p. 71. Accounts of prelates returning from America with large fortunes in Pedro de Leturia, 'Antonio Lelio de Fermo', *Hispania Sacra* (1948), Vol. I, Pellicer, *Avisos*, 14 May 1641 (death of Don Feliciano de Solis, bishop of La Paz, leaving a million), and Barrionuevo, *Avisos*, Vol.

11, pp. 273, 298, and 301. On the money which religious brought back undeclared from the Indies, AI Indiferente 772.

9   The present author is not aware of any complete study of this interesting topic. The *alternativa* was introduced into the Franciscan provinces of Lima and Charcas in 1664. The Dominicans also accepted it, but it was never in use among the Jesuits. In a dispatch from the king to the Spanish ambassador in Rome the laxness of the province of the traditional Augustinians of Mexico was blamed on 'the lack of Spanish candidates of letters and training who could be drafted into the *alternativa*, since the best and the greater part of the posts are given to creole religious, as they are strongest in number and win the votes', Archive of the Spanish Embassy to the Holy See, legajo 140. In the previous legajo as well there are numerous documents on this matter from the second half of the seventeenth century.

10   F. Armas Medina, 'Las propiedades de las órdenes religiosas . . .', *Estudios Americanos*, Vol. XXIII. This statement is not invalidated by the fact that many Jesuit houses had debts, caused by bad administration, bad business or superfluous expenditure.

11   By apostolic concession the king collected tithe and provided the bishops with up to 500,000 *maravedís* annually; but if the tithes from their dioceses were more than this the bishops collected them themselves. This prompted Gaytán de Torres to say that the bishops in the Indies played 'heads I win, tails you lose' with the king, *Reglas para el gobierno*. . . .

ABBREVIATIONS USED IN THE NOTES:

Codoin	Colección de documentos inéditos para la historia de España
AI	Archivo de Indias (Seville)
AGS	Archivo General de Simancas
BN	Biblioteca Nacional (Madrid)
AHN	Archivo Histórico Nacional (Madrid)

BIBLIOGRAPHY

GENERAL WORKS

B. Sánchez Alonso, *Fuentes de la historia española e hispanoamericana* (2nd ed. Madrid 1952), three volumes: this is a bibliography of works relating to political history. *Indice Histórico Español*, a review founded by Jaime Vicens Vives and published by the Faculty of Philosophy and Letters of the University of Barcelona, is a guide to works published on all aspects of the history of Spain, with a brief criticism of their content. See also *Actas de las Cortes de Castilla*, published by the Academia de la Historia, 59 vols. (Madrid 1861–1968).

In view of the world importance of Spain in the sixteenth and seventeenth centuries, all the general histories give considerable space to her. Among others, the following are of interest: H. Hauser, *La prépondérance espagnole* (3rd ed. Paris 1948), Vol. IX of *Peuples et Civilisations*; R. Mousnier, *Les XVIème et XVIIème siècles* (4th ed. Paris 1965), in the *Histoire Générale des Civilisations; The New Cambridge Modern History*, Vol. I ed. G. R. Potter (1957), Vol. II ed. G. R. Elton (1958), Vol. III ed. R. B. Wernham (1968); P. Chaunu, *La civilisation de l'Europe classique* (Paris 1966), in *Les Grandes Civilisations*; F. Braudel, *Civilisation matérielle et capitalisme* (Paris 1967), in *Destins du Monde*; H. Lapeyre, *Les monarchies européennes du XVIème siècle* (Paris 1967), in *Nouvelle Clio*. About a half of the great work of Braudel, *La Méditerranée et le monde méditerranéen à l'époque de Philippe II* 2nd ed., 2 vols. (Paris 1966) refers to Spain.

The general histories of Spain also devote much space, as is only to be expected, to the age of the Habsburgs. The more important are those of: R. Altamira, *Historia de España y de la civilización española* 4 vols. (Barcelona 1900–11), which was in advance of its time by giving much greater space to socio-cultural topics than those of a purely political character. Also, the same author's *History of Spain* (New York 1949), A. Ballesteros, *Historia de España* 2nd ed., 12 vols. (Barcelona 1943–8) contains a great wealth of information, though it needs to be brought up to date. F. Soldevila, *Historia de España* 8 vols. (Barcelona 1952–9) is distinguished by the wealth of its illustrations and by the greater attention it pays to the outlying provinces. The great *Historia de España* undertaken by the firm of Espasa Calpe under the editorship of Don Ramón Menéndez Pidal is still far from completion. The volumes relating to Charles V and Philip II have appeared and are mentioned below. See also *Historia social y económica de España y América*, ed. J. Vicens Vives, 5 vols. (Barcelona 1957–9).

Short summaries but packed full of stimulating ideas are J. Vicens Vives, *Approaches to the History of Spain* (University of California 1969) and Pierre Vilar, *Spain: A Brief History* (Oxford 1967). Also interpretative, but more extensive and setting out from a different standpoint, are the very important *España: un enigma histórico* by Claudio Sánchez Albornoz, 2 vols. (Buenos Aires 1956) and Américo Castro, *The Structure of Spanish History* (Gordian 1970). Very useful, though not always convincing, is the *Diccionario de Historia de España*, published by *Revista de Occidente* (2nd ed., 3 vols.).

Good textbooks on the history of Spain are in short supply. P. Aguado Bleye, *Manual de Historia de España* (1927–) is very informative but lacking in general ideas. A more modern approach is provided by the *Introducción a la historia de España* by Ubieto, Reglá, Jover and Seco (Barcelona 1963). Though specialized in scope, the monumental works of P. Vilar, *La Catalogne dans l'Espagne Moderne*, 3 vols. (Paris 1962) and H. and P. Chaunu, *Séville et l'Atlantique*, 12 vols. (Paris 1955–9) cover a much wider field than their titles would suggest and are indispensable for a study of the age.

The best survey of Habsburg Spain is that of J. H. Elliott, *Imperial Spain 1469–1716* (London 1963). Also worth mentioning are J. Lynch, *Spain under the Habsburgs*, 2 vols. (Oxford 1964–9) and R. Trevor Davies, *The Golden Century of Spain 1501–1621* (London 1937). The now ageing study of R. B. Merriman, *The Rise of the Spanish Empire in the Old World and the New*, 4 vols. (New York 1918–35) may also be of use. On administration, see J. Gounon-Loubens, *Essais sur l'administration de Castille au XVIe siècle* (Paris 1860), and J. A. Escudero, *Los Secretarios de estado y del despacho 1474–1724*, 4 vols. (Madrid 1969); on the councils, C. Riba, *El Consejo Supremo de Aragón* (Valencia 1914), and the work of Schaeffer, quoted below.

CHARLES V (CHAPTER 4)

H. Koenigsberger, 'The Empire of Charles V in Europe', *New Cambridge Modern History*, Vol. II (Cambridge 1958); Karl Brandi, *Charles V* (Eng. trans. London 1965); Peter Rassow, *Die Kaiser-Idee Karls V* (Berlin 1932); Hayward Keniston, *Francisco de los Cobos* (Pittsburgh 1960); F. Walser, *Die Spanischen Zentralbehörden und der Straatsrat Karls V* (Gottingen 1959); H. L. Seaver, *The Great Revolt in Castile* (London 1928); R. Tyler, *The Emperor Charles V* (London

1956); *Charles V et son temps* (outcome of a symposium held in Paris in 1958); M. Fernández Alvárez, *Carlos V* (Madrid 1966), in the *Historia de España* edited by Menéndez Pidal. The same author has published a critical edition of the *Memorias del Emperador* (Madrid 1960); J. Mª Jover, *Carlos V y los Españoles* (Madrid 1963); José A. Maravall, *Carlos V y el pensamiento político del Renacimiento* (Madrid 1960), and the same author's *Las Comunidades de Castilla. Una primera revolución moderna* (Madrid 1963).

Also of interest are many of the monographs included in the two volumes of studies devoted to the emperor, published by the University of Granada on the quartercentenary of his death, *Carlos V: Homenaje de la Universidad de Granada* (Granada 1958). See too Joseph Pérez, *La Revolution des Comunidades de Castille* (Bordeaux 1970).

PHILIP II (CHAPTER 5)

H. Lapeyre, 'Autour de Philippe II', *Bulletin Hispanique*, Vol. LIX (1957) pp. 152–75; C. Bratli, *Felipe II, rey de España* (Madrid 1940); L. Pfandl, *Philippe II: Gemälde eines Lebens und einer Zeit* (Munich 1938, French trans. Paris n.d.); R. Altamira, *Ensayo sobre Felipe II, hombre de estado* (Madrid 1959); L. Fernández Retana, *España en tiempo de Felipe II* (Madrid 1955), two fat volumes in the *Historia de España* edited by Menéndez Pidal. Despite its title, it is little more than an antiquated apologia of the person of the monarch. *L'Espagne au temps de Philippe II* (Paris 1965) is an excellent popular work for which a variety of specialists were responsible. C. Fernández Duro, *La Armada Invencible* (Madrid 1884–5); K. R. Andrews, *Elizabethan Privateering* (Cambridge 1964); Michael Lewis, *The Spanish Armada* (London 1960); G. Mattingly, *The Defeat of the Spanish Armada* (London 1959); G. Marañón, *Antonio Pérez*, 6th ed., 2 vols. (Madrid 1958), abridged Eng. tr. London 1954; A. González Palencia, *Gonzalo Pérez, secretario de Felipe II*, 2 vols. (Madrid 1946); A. J. Loomie, *Spanish Elizabethans. The English Exiles at the Court of Philip II* (New York 1963); J. Reglà Campistol, *Felip II i Catalunya* (Barcelona 1956); J. M. Rubio, *Felipe II de España, rey de Portugal* (Santander 1939); M. van Durme, *Antoon Perrenot . . . Kardinal van Granvelle* (Brussels 1953), Sp. tr. Barcelona 1957; W. Stirling Maxwell, *Don John of Austria* (London 1883); L. Serrano, *La Liga de Lepanto* (Madrid 1918–20); H. Koenigsberger, *The Government of Sicily under Philip II of Spain* (London 1951).

PHILIP III AND PHILIP IV (CHAPTERS 6 AND 7)

C. H. Carter, *The Secret Diplomacy of the Habsburgs 1598–1625* (New York 1964); Bohdan Chudoba, *Spain and the Empire* (Chicago 1952);

C. Pérez Bustamente, *Felipe III. Semblanza de un monarca y perfiles de una privanza* (Madrid 1950); P. Marrades, *El Camino del Imperio. Notas para el estudio de la cuestión de la Valtelina* (Madrid 1943); A. Cánovas del Castillo, *Estudios sobre el reinado de Felipe IV* (Madrid 1888–9); F. T. Valiente, *Los validos en la Monarquía española del siglo XVII* (Madrid 1963); M. Hume, *The Court of Philip IV* (London 1907); G. Marañón, *El Conde Duque de Olivares* (Madrid 1936); R. Ródenas Vilar, *La política europea de España durante la Guerra de Treinta Años 1624–1630* (Madrid 1967); A van der Essen, *Le Cardinal-Infant et la politique européenne de l'Espagne 1609–1641* (Brussels 1944); José Mª Jover, *Historia de una polémica y semblanza de una generación* (Madrid 1949); V. Palacio Atard, *Derrota, agotamiento, decadencia en la España del siglo XVII* (Madrid 1956); J. H. Elliott, *The Revolt of the Catalans* (Cambridge 1963); J. Sanabre, *La acción de Francia en Cataluña 1640–1659* (Barcelona 1956); R. Villari, *La rivolta antispagnola a Napoli. Le origini 1585–1647* (Bari 1967); F. J. Routledge, *England and the Treaty of the Pyrenees* (Liverpool 1953).

SOCIETY (CHAPTERS 8 TO 11)

Salvador de Moxó, *La Alcabala. Sobre sus orígenes, concepto y naturaleza* (Madrid 1963) and the same author's *La incorporación de señoríos en la España del antiguo régimen* (Valladolid 1959); Pierre Vilar, 'Le Temps du Quichotte', *Europe*, Vol. xxxiv (1956); A Valbuena Prat, *La vida española en la Edad de Oro segun las fuentes literarias* (1943); M. Defourneaux, *La vie quotidienne en Espagne au Siècle d'Or* (Paris 1965); J. Beneyto, *Historia social de España e Hispanoamérica* (Madrid 1961); P. W. Bomli, *La femme dans l'Espagne du Siècle d'Or* (The Hague 1950); Marqués de Saltillo, *Historia nobiliaria de España*, 2 vols. (Madrid 1951); A Dominguez Ortiz, *La Sociedad española del siglo XVII*, 2 vols. (Madrid 1963 and 1970), and the same author's *La clase social de los conversos en Castilla en la Edad Moderna* (Madrid 1955); A Sicroff, *Les statuts de pureté de sang en Espagne aux XVIème et XVIIème siècles* (Paris 1955); A. M. Guilarte, *El regimen señorial en el siglo XVI* (Madrid 1962); J. H. Elliott, 'The Decline of Spain', *Past and Present*, no. 20 (1961), reprinted in Trevor Aston (ed.) *Crisis in Europe 1560–1660* (London 1965); B. Bennassar, *Valladolid et ses campagnes au XVIème siècle* (Paris 1967); Julio Caro Baroja, *Los Judíos en la España Moderna y Contemporánea*, 3 vols. (Madrid 1963), and the same author's *Los Moriscos del Reino de Granada* (Madrid 1957); A. A. Neuman, *The Jews in Spain*, 2 vols. (Philadelphia 1948); H. Lapeyre, *Géographie de l'Espagne morisque* (Paris 1959); Tulio Halperin Donghi, 'Un conflicto nacional en el siglo de oro: Moriscos y Cristianos Viejos en Valencia', *Cuadernos de Historia de España*, Vols. xxiii–viii (1955–7); A. Domínguez Ortiz, *La esclavitud en Castilla en la Edad Moderna* (Madrid 1952); Cecil Roth, *A History of the Marranos* (1932, reprinted New

York 1959). M. Fernández Alvárez, *La Sociedad española en la época del Renacimiento* (Madrid 1970).

THE ECONOMY (CHAPTERS 12 AND 13)

R. Pike, *Enterprise and Adventure: The Genoese in Castile* (Cornell U.P. 1966); M. Moret, *Aspects de la société marchande à Seville* (Paris 1967); J. Vicens Vives, *Historia Económica de España* (Barcelona 1959), English translation, *An Economic History of Spain* (Princeton U.P. 1969); F. Mauro, *Le XVIᵉᵐᵉ siècle européen. Aspects économiques* (Paris 1966), in *Nouvelle Clio*, Vol. XXXII, with copious bibliography; E. E. Rich and C. Wilson, ed., *The Economy of Expanding Europe in the Sixteenth and Seventeenth Centuries* (Cambridge 1967), Vol. IV of the *Cambridge Economic History of Europe*. Its information is incomplete with regard to Spain. J. Nadal and E. Giralt, *La population catalane de 1553 a 1717* (Paris 1960); Jorge Nadal, *La población española de los siglos XVI a XX* (Barcelona 1966); E. J. Hamilton, *American Treasure and the Price Revolution in Spain* (Cambridge, Mass. 1934): a classic work; J. Klein, *The Mesta. A Study in Spanish Economic History* (Cambridge, Mass. 1920); José Larraz, *La época del mercantilismo en Castilla* (Madrid 1943); H. Kellenbenz, *Unternehmerkräfte in Hamburger Portugal – und Spanienhandel 1590-1625* (Hamburg 1954); G. Lohmann Villena, *Les Espinosa: une famille d'hommes d'affaires en Espagne et aux Indes a l'époque de la colonisation* (Paris 1968). A. P. Usher, 'Spanish Ships and Shipping in the Sixteenth and Seventeenth Centuries', *Facts and Factors in Economic History. Articles by Former Students of E. F. Gay* (Cambridge, Mass. 1932); C. Viñas Mey, *El problema de la tierra en España en los siglos XVI – XVIII* (Madrid 1941); P. Vilar, *Crecimiento y desarrollo* (Barcelona 1964); Noël Salomon, *La campagne de la Nouvelle Castille a la fin du XVIᵉᵐᵉ siècle* (Paris 1964); A. Huetz de Lemps, *Vignobles et vins du nord-ouest de l'Espagne* (Bordeaux 1967); Jakob van Klaveren, *Europäische Wirtschaftsgeschicte Spaniens im XVI und XVII Jahrhundert* (Stuttgart 1960); F. Mauro, *Le Portugal et l'Atlantique au XVIIᵉᵐᵉ siècle* (Paris 1960); V. Magalhães Godinho, *L'Economie de l'empire portugais* (Paris 1969); Marjorie Grice-Hutchinson, *The School of Salamanca: Readings in Spanish Monetary Theory 1544-1605* (Oxford 1952); J. Gentil da Silva, *En Espagne. Développement économique, subsistance, déclin* (Paris 1965); M. Basas Fernández, *El Consulado de Burgos* (Madrid 1963); F. Ruiz Martín, *Lettres marchandes échangées entre Florence et Medina del Campo* (Paris 1965): an extensive prologue studies general aspects of the Castilian economy; L. Reitzer, 'Some Observations on Castilian Commerce and Finance in the Sixteenth Century', *Journal of Modern History*, Vol. XXXII (1960); R. S. Smith, *The Spanish Guild Merchant. A History of the Consulado 1250-1700* (Durham N.C., 1940); H. Lapeyre, *Simón Ruiz et les asientos de Philippe II* (Paris 1953), and the same author's *Une famille de marchands: les Ruiz* (Paris 1955); A. Rumeu de Armas, *Historia de la Previsión social en España. Gremios y Cofradías* (Madrid 1947); J. Carrera Pujal, *Historia de la economía española* (5 vols., Barcelona 1943-7). There is no good general study of the finances of the Habsburgs, but some reigns have been the object of monographs. The most important is Ramón Carande, *Carlos V y sus banqueros* 3 vols. (Madrid 1943-67). Also, Modesto Ulloa, *La Hacienda Real de Castilla en el reinado de Felipe II* (Rome 1963). On the very intricate fiscal problems of Philip iv, the present author has published a work which must be considered a first approach to a hitherto unexplored topic, *Política y Hacienda de Felipe IV* (Madrid 1960). See also J. L. Sureda Carrión, *La Hacienda castellana y los economistas del siglo XVII* (Madrid 1949).

ORTHODOXY AND HETERODOXY (CHAPTERS 14 AND 15)

For the general setting, and in view of the lack of any good history of the Spanish church, one should read Fliche and Martin, *Histoire de l'Eglise* (Paris 1934-) Vol. xvi (*La crise religieuse du XVIème siècle*), xvii (*L'Eglise a l'époque du Concile de Trente*) and xvii (*La restauration catholique*).

Among the great mass of individual studies, the following have been selected: C. Gutiérrez, *Españoles en Trento* (Valladolid 1951); R. Burgos, *España en Trento* (Madrid 1941); P. Saínz Rodríguez, *Introducción al estudio de la mística española* (Madrid 1950); F. Marquez Villanueva, *Espiritualidad y literatura en el siglo XVI* (Madrid 1968); J. Deleito, *La vida religiosa bajo el cuarto Felipe* (Madrid 1952); A. Astraín, *Historia de la Compañía de Jesús en la Asistencia de España*, 7 vols. (Madrid 1912-25); Gerald Brenan, 'St John of the Cross: His Life and Poetry', *Horizon*, Vol. xv (1947); Allison Peers, *Handbook to the Life and Times of St Teresa and St John of the Cross* (London 1954), and the same author's *The Mystics of Spain* (London 1951); M. Menéndez Pelayo, *Historia de los Heterodoxos españoles* (Madrid 1882); A. A. Parker, *Valor actual del humanismo español* (Madrid 1952); M. Bataillon, *Erasme et l'Espagne* (Paris 1937), revised and enlarged in Spanish tr., 2 vols. (Mexico 1950); H. C. Lea, *A History of the Inquisition of Spain*, 4 vols. (New York 1906); H. Kamen, *The Spanish Inquisition* (London 1965); A. S. Turberville, *The Spanish Inquisition* (London 1932); J. E. Longhurst, *Erasmus and the Spanish Inquisition* (Albuquerque 1950); also his 'Luther in Spain: 1520-40', *Proceedings of the American Philosophical Society*, Vol. ciii (1959).

CIVILISATION AND ART (CHAPTERS 16 TO 18)

See J. M. López Pinero, 'La Medecina del Barroco español', *Revista de la Universidad de Madrid*, Vol. xi. Despite their age the works of Menéndez Pelayo are still fundamental: *La Ciencia española, Historia de las ideas estéticas, Calderón y su teatro* and others. They have gone through several editions. Collected essays on Spanish science in *Estudios sobre la ciencia española del siglo XVII* (Madrid 1935), by various contributors. See also G. Brennan, *The Literature of the Spanish People* (Cambridge 1951); G. Kubler and M. Soria, *Art and Architecture in Spain and Portugal 1500–1800* (London 1959); Federico de Onis, *Ensayo sobre el sentido de la cultura española* (Madrid 1936); Carl Vossler, *Algunos carácteres de la cultura española* (1946); L. Pfandl, *Introducción a la literatura española del Siglo de Oro* (Madrid 1936); Aubrey G. Bell, *Luis de León. A Study of the Spanish Renaissance* (Oxford 1925); José A. Maravall, *Los factores de la idea del Progreso en el Renacimiento español* (Madrid 1963), and the same author's *Velázquez y el espiritu de modernidad* (Madrid 1960), and *La teoría española del estado en el siglo XVII* (Madrid 1944, French tr., Paris 1955); G. Reynier, *La vie universitaire dans l'ancienne Espagne* (Paris 1902); L. Sánchez Agesta, *El concepto de Estado en el pensamiento español del siglo XVI* (Madrid 1959); G. Lewy, *Constitutionalism and Statecraft during the Golden Age of Spain* (Geneva 1960); J. Brown Scott, *The Spanish Origin of International Law* (Washington 1928); J. Laures, *The Political Economy of Juan de Mariana* (New York 1928); B. Hamilton, *Political Thought in Sixteenth Century Spain* (Oxford 1963).

Also A. Valbuena Prat, *Historia de la literatura española* (numerous editions), and the same author's *Historia del teatro español*; Charles V. Aubrun, *La comédie espagnole 1600–1680* (Paris 1966); Marqués de Lozoya, *Historia del Arte Hispánico*, 4 vols. (Barcelona 1945); *Ars Hispaniae*, a voluminous work of collaboration; Otto Schubert, *Historia del Barroco español* (Madrid 1924); A. L. Mayer, *Historia de la pintura española* (Madrid 1942); E. Lafuente Ferrari, *Historia de la pintura española* (Madrid 1953); Karl Justi, *Velázquez* (Sp. tr. Madrid 1957); M. Gómez Moreno, *La Escultura del Renacimiento en España* (Madrid 1931); Otis H. Green, *Spain and the Western Tradition. The Castilian Mind from El Cid to Calderón*, 4 vols. (Madison 1963–6); N. D. Shergold, *A History of the Spanish Stage* (Oxford 1967); Bernard Bevan, *History of Spanish Architecture* (London 1938).

SPANISH AMERICA (CHAPTER 19)

A guide to the vast literature on America may be found in R. A. Humphreys, *Latin American History. A Guide to the Literature in English* (Oxford 1958), in periodical publications like *The Handbook of Latin American Studies*, founded in 1936 by Lewis Hanke, in the *Indice Histórico Español* mentioned above, and in the bibliographical notes and bulletins of the *Anuario de Estudios Americanos* of Seville.

All the general histories of America give a more or less generous space to the Spanish colonial period. Among them the *Historia de América y de los pueblos americanos*, a collaborative undertaking begun in 1936 under the editorship of A. Ballesteros and not yet completed. All in all it is an important work, but suffers from a lack of proportion. See also: P. Chaunu, *L'Amérique et les Amériques* (Paris 1964): a suggestive and to a large extent very novel exposition, part of the series *Destins du Monde*; F. Mauro, *L'expansion européenne* (Paris 1964), in *Nouvelle Clio*; J. H. Parry, *The Age of Reconnaissance* (London 1963), *The Spanish Seaborne Empire* (London 1966), and also *The Spanish Theory of Empire in the Sixteenth Century* (Cambridge 1940); C. H. Haring, *The Spanish Empire in America* (New York 1947); B. W. Diffie, *Latin American Civilization* (Harrisburg 1945); J. E. Fagg, *Latin America. A General History* (New York 1963); F. Esteve Barba, *Historiografía indiana* (Madrid 1964); C. Gibson, *Spain in America* (New York 1966); S. de Madariaga, *Cuadro Histórico de las Indias* (Buenos Aires 1945); R. Konetzke, *Das Spanische Weltreich. Grundlagen und Entstehung*, Sp. tr., *El imperio español. Orígenes y fundamentos* (Madrid 1946); Special mention is due to the chapters devoted to America in the *Historia social y económica de España y América*, ed. Vicens Vives, mentioned above.

EXPLORATIONS AND CONQUEST (FROM 1517)

A magnificent introduction is provided by the first part of Vol. VIII of Chaunu, *Séville et l'Atlantique*, already mentioned. See also: M. García Soriano, *El conquistador español del siglo XVI* (Tucuman 1954); F. A. Kirkpatrick, *The Spanish Conquistadors* (London 1943); Silvio Zavala, *Ensayos sobre la colonización española en América* (Buenos Aires 1944).

The classic works of Prescott on the conquest of Mexico and Peru are still useful, despite their age. They should be supplemented by more recent works like those of Raul Porras, or E. Vargas Ugarte, *Historia del Perú*.

INSTITUTIONS

E. Schaeffer, *El Consejo Real y Supremo de las Indias*, 2 vols. (Seville 1935) Silvio Zavala, *La encomienda indiana* (Madrid 1935); L. B. Simpson, *The Encomienda in New Spain: The Beginnings of Spanish Mexico* (Berkeley and L.A. 1950); G. Lohmann Villena, *El corregidor de Indios en el Perú* (Madrid 1957); J. M. Ots Capdequi, *Las instituciones de la América Española* (Barcelona 1959), and the same author's *El estado español en las Indias* (3rd ed., Mexico 1957); Juan Manzano, *Historia de las*

Recopilaciones de Indias (Madrid 1950–6); J. H. Parry, *The Sale of Public Office in the Spanish Indies under the Habsburgs* (Berkeley and Los Angeles 1953), and the same author's *The Audiencia of New Galicia in the Sixteenth Century* (Cambridge 1948); J. P. Moore, *The Cabildo in Peru under the Habsburgs* (Durham, N.C., 1954); J. C. Phelan, *The Kingdom of Quito in the Seventeenth Century* (Univ. of Wisconsin Press 1969).

ECONOMY AND SOCIETY (CHAPTER 20)

Huguette and Pierre Chaunu, *Séville et l'Atlantique*, already mentioned, is a monumental and basic work. Some of the statistical aspects have been reviewed by W. Brulez, 'Séville et l'Atlantique: quelques réflexions critiques', *Revue Belge de Philologie et d'Histoire*, Vol. XLII (1964). Pierre Chaunu is also responsible for the best work on the place of the Philippines in the Spanish financial system, *Les Philippines et le Pacifique des Ibériques* (Paris 1960). See also W. Schurz, *The Manila Galleon* (New York 1939). Another classic work is that of François Chevalier, *Land and Society in Colonial Mexico* (Berkeley and Los Angeles 1963). On Spanish-American commerce the survey of C. H. Haring, *Trade and Navigation between Spain and the Indies* (Cambridge, Mass. 1918) continues to be indispensable. See also Lewis Hanke, *The Imperial City of Potosí* (The Hague 1956); I. Sánchez Bella, *La organización financiera de las Indias: Siglo XVI* (Seville 1968); G. Céspedes del Castillo, *La avería en el comercio de Indias* (Seville 1945); G. Scelle, *La traite négrière aux Indes de Castille* (Paris 1906); W. H. Dusenberry, *The Mexican Mesta: The Administration of Ranching in Colonial Mexico* (Urbana 1963); G. Lohmann Villena, *Las minas de Huencavélica* (Seville 1949); L. B. Simpson, *Exploitation of Land in Central Mexico in the Sixteenth Century* (Berkeley and Los Angeles 1952); W. Borah, *New Spain's Century of Depression* (University of California Press 1951); S. F. Cook and W. Borah, *The Indian Population of Central Mexico 1531–1610* (Berkeley and Los Angeles 1960).

THE SPIRITUAL EMPIRE (CHAPTER 21)

J. Tudela and others, *El legado de España a América*, 2 vols. (Madrid 1954). On the American church there are two recent general works: Antonio Ibot León's two volumes in the *Historia de América* edited by A. Ballesteros, and the study of the Jesuits Lopetegui and Zubillaga, in the *Biblioteca de Autores Cristianos*. Both furnish a great wealth of information, especially as regards missionary activity, but they do not penetrate in depth the religious life of Spaniards and

Indians. Another classic work is that of Robert Ricard, *The Spiritual Conquest of Mexico* (Berkeley & Los Angeles 1966).

On the activity of the Inquisition there is the general work of H. C. Lea, *The Inquisition in the Spanish Dependencies* (New York 1908), and various very useful monographs by the Chilean Toribio Medina.

On the fight for the freedom of the Indians the fundamental works are: Lewis Hanke, *The Spanish Struggle for Justice in the Conquest of America* (Philadelphia 1949), and the same author's *Aristotle and the American Indians* (London 1959). The fundamental work of M. Giménez Fernández on *Las Casas* (Seville 1953 and 1960) was unfortunately cut short by his death. See also G. Kubler, *Mexican Architecture of the Sixteenth Century*, 2 vols. (Yale 1948).

INDEX

INDEX